Books by ROSS TERRILL

China Profile (*editor and part-author*), 1969

China and Ourselves (*editor and part-author*), 1970

Socialism as Fellowship: R. H. Tawney and His Times, 1972

800,000,000: The Real China, 1972

800,000,000

800,000,000
The Real China

by ROSS TERRILL

An Atlantic Monthly Press Book

LITTLE, BROWN AND COMPANY · BOSTON · TORONTO

LIBRARY OF CONGRESS CATALOG CARD NO. 70-185415

FIRST EDITION

T 03/72

ATLANTIC-LITTLE, BROWN BOOKS
ARE PUBLISHED BY
LITTLE, BROWN AND COMPANY
IN ASSOCIATION WITH
THE ATLANTIC MONTHLY PRESS

Published simultaneously in Canada
by Little, Brown & Company (Canada) Limited

PRINTED IN THE UNITED STATES OF AMERICA

Acknowledgments

For their kind assistance, my thanks to:

Hosts in China who did not let my impatience sap their keenness to help me see and learn; among them: Chou Nan, Liu Ju-ts'ai, Ma Yu-chen, T'ang Ming-chao, P'eng Hua, Chou P'ei-yuan, Chou I-liang.

Friends scattered abroad who lit or smoothed my path: Wilfred Burchett, who knows today's East Asia better than any of his countrymen; Paul Lin and Lee Tsung-ying, patriots in *diaspora;* Etienne Manac'h, lively mind and spirit as well as diplomat; Stephen Fitzgerald, scholar, drinker, best of traveling companions; Jack Gregory, historian of China, who first turned my gaze to the China coast; Margaret Flory and co-workers in the United Presbyterian Church; Chao Fu-san, whom I did not see in 1971 but often thought about.

Colleagues at Harvard's East Asian Research Center who make it a happy place to work in; especially the high standards, encouragement, and conversation of Ben Schwartz, John Fairbank, and Jim Thomson.

Bob Manning and Mike Janeway at the *Atlantic,* who have pulled me skillfully through the brambles of publication many times, but never before — until the China Dragon breathed upon us — squeezed eighty-three thousand words from me in three months.

R.T.

Harvard University
December 1971

SOME TERMS AND NAMES

catty	one-half kilogram
CCP	Chinese Communist party
Chi P'eng-fei	Acting Foreign Minister
Lao Tzu	Taoist philosopher-recluse of some 2,500 years ago
Liberation	Chinese term for 1949 revolution
loess	dusty yellow-red soil in parts of north and northwest China
Lu Hsun	left-wing writer and social critic (1881–1936) admired by Mao
Luxingshe	(pronounced "Loo-shing-sheh") China Travel Service
May 4 Movement	nationalistic cultural and political upsurge started by students in 1919
May 7 school	correctional school, mixing labor and study, for professionals in need of "remolding"
May 16 organization	extreme leftist network of the Cultural Revolution period, now attacked for having used violence and opposed Mao
mou	one-sixth of an acre
Pai Hsiang-kuo	Foreign Trade Minister
PLA	People's Liberation Army — the Chinese Army
Revolutionary Committee	unit of administration in China since the Cultural Revolution, from the province level to that of individual factories and communes
ta tzu pao	wall posters written in large characters
yuan (Y)	Chinese monetary unit, forty cents

Contents

800,000,000

1. To China

A heat haze sits over Hong Kong harbor on a bright June morning. The taxi draws up at Kowloon railroad station. For several years, I have looked at this building the way a discontented East German looks at the Brandenburg Gate in Berlin: an enticing, infuriating doorway to a world much desired but hard to enter. But this morning the Victorian brick station was delightfully inviting. For in my pocket was a Chinese visa and a train ticket to Canton.

In my imagination, the train was history's conveyor belt, rolling, not ninety miles to Canton, but from one universe to another. In fact, the train was its usual workaday self. It was loaded with housewives, workmen heading for the New Territories, vendors with beer and cigarettes, youths going out to Shatin for a swim. For these people the train was a "local," boring as a subway ride in Manhattan. For a few others — politicians from the Komeito (Clean Government party) of Japan, an Indian diplomat, myself — it was an international train, bound for a land which even today exudes mystery. These bored and worldly carriages also contained a certain excitement.

South China reclines green and gold beneath the hot morning sun, as we approach the border village of Lo Wu. Peasants are in lunchtime circulation, wearing broad hats, carrying bundles. Chickens scratch placidly at the foot of a banyan tree. Boys call a greeting from a railside path, appealingly unawed by proximity to this frontier, which is not only political but almost moral and philosophical. The line of demarcation is a footbridge. Walking across it, I look high into the green mountains. On the highest peak is a frontier guardhouse with glass windows. Behind me, the aggressive vendors, the gaudy clothes, the Coca-Cola. Ahead, a world which is sterner in its political imperatives, but which in human terms may be a simpler and more relaxed world.

There really *are* "two Chinas." Not "Taiwan" and the "Mainland," but rather the *image* we have of China in the United States, and the *reality* of China. Our press talks of China as power struggles and bombs and numbers. But here is China as rice and heat, glue and vaccinations, babies crying, old men playing chess. Last week, China was for me a matter of embassies and letters and magazines arriving by post. This morning, it has become a matter of trains and tea, Chinese beds, telephone numbers, weariness. There is a purging, utterly simple wonder about actually chugging mile by mile into China. The cardboard figures of a frozen scenario start to breathe and sweat and make a noise. From San Francisco to Singapore and beyond, you find pockets of Chinese society. But only in China do you see this civilization in its present power and in its ancient and beautiful cradle, and begin to sense how much the Chinese people and nation may mean in the pattern of future decades.

On the Chinese side, in the township of Shumchun, the traveler enters a building which is combined railroad station, customs house, and hotel. The color red impinges at once, as at a carnival. Political texts and admonitions light up the corridors and salons like labeled pillar-boxes. The frontier formalities are as sparse as the surrounding propaganda is luxuriant. Luggage is not examined. The questions of the border officials are not technical. The health man is first and he has been briefed. Before looking at my papers he asks with a smile, "Have you come from America or Australia this time?" The next official is a People's Liberation Army man and he has only one question: "Where did you learn *p'u-t'ung hua* [standard Chinese]?" Then I am ushered into a waiting room until lunch is served and the train for Canton is ready to depart.

The room gives onto a whitewashed balcony, covered with grapevines, and through the brilliant green leaves you see the red soil and curved hills of Kwangtung. In the foreground are two huge signboards, red and white with political exhortations, as if to stir the midday lassitude. One is about worldwide unity against imperialism. The other is about the economic tasks necessary to the building of socialism. Peasant China meanders gently by, amiable and placid in a time-honored daily round. Political China stridently addresses it from a printed board, which seems stiff and impersonal among the chickens and the children.

Mao adorns the interior of the building as Jesus adorns a church. But that morning in Shumchun, the "cult" struck me with a meaning it had never had before. I doubt I can convey it. This "image" is Mao Tse-tung, *the Chinese politician,* not some fictional device, half bogey, half god. To see these pictures in China is to be less shocked by the cult than to see them on the printed page far from China. This is not our country, or a country we can easily understand, but the country of Mao. He remarked two generations ago, "We cannot even speak of socialism if we are robbed of a country in which to practice it." He rose from obscurity and led it to dignity. He is one of these 800,-000,000 people, and his life's work has transformed their life.

I became critical of the propaganda in China, as later pages show. But this morning at the frontier, it seemed to me that the cult of Mao is not *incredible* as it seems outside China. It becomes odd when it encounters our world. On its own terms, within its own functioning political reality, it is less odd. And much of the gulf across which the cult of Mao seems odd, I felt, is not political, but cultural and linguistic. It is odd to us partly because we have no consciousness of Chinese social modes, and because we read the texts and slogans as sets of English phrases, which is like imbibing wine as frozen ice-blocks.

Behind me in another room, lunch is being noisily and aromatically prepared. A girl with braids and rosy cheeks (Miss Wang) pads in to fetch me, and we walk to the dining room past a banner which begins: "The Nixon government is beset with troubles . . ." Miss Wang is a plain girl, with kind eyes. A native of Shanghai, she finds Kwangtung too hot. She rails against Liu Shao-ch'i (purged former President of China) as she leads me to a table arrayed with chicken soup, shrimps, and boiled rice. Engagingly, she sits beside me as I eat, and, bubbling like a brook, instructs me in the concept *i-fen wei-erh*. It means "one divides into two" and is a key notion of Chairman Mao, opposed to Liu Shao-ch'i's false, liberal, harmonic concept, *ho-erh wei-i,* "two unites into one." There are contradictions in *everything,* she warns me with odd persistence as I press on with my lunch; one always divides into two. . . .

Across the room are the Komeito party politicians, and the Indian diplomat, who, like me, has his separate table. The luggage of the Komeito men is plastered with Swissair tags and labels. Diplomatically, they have avoided traveling Japan Airlines (a company then in the doghouse with Peking, for it was flying to Taipei, and thus "trading with Taiwan"). To advertise that, they have made themselves look like a PR team for Swissair. A group of Chinese officials dine at a circular table. All but one of them are from the north of China. They are tall and bony, their skins are light, and they slurp large plates of noodles. But one, whose arms are darker, is a southerner. Instead of noodles he eats boiled rice, which he replenishes constantly from a large vat on a bench near the table. Miss Wang, perhaps assured that she has made her point, leaves me to my cup of tea. The room is languid as diners sit back from their empty dishes and let the beer lull them toward somnolence. But a whistle pierces the calm; the train for Canton is ready to go. Into China at last!

I realized that day how long seven years can be. In 1964 I had ridden this train (in reverse direction). To ride it again was to recall what changes — in China, in China's relation to the world, in myself — have occurred since then. In China there has taken place the amazing upheaval of the Cultural Revolution.

In China's relation to the world there has begun a mutation of historic proportions. The walls crumble; China can no longer be called "cut off" from other peoples. But the mutual interaction that now commences is quite unlike that when China was "opened" to the West after the Opium War. The flow of power and influence was — from the Opium War at least until the 1949 revolution — largely one way. China was the *object* of

Western *impact*. But in 1971, it seemed to me, a new kind of interaction between China and the world was actively under way.

The direction of the flow of influence is no longer one way — upon China — but increasingly *from* China as well. China's actions, its ideas, its bomb, have become vital motifs of world history. To be sure, China's change from a passive to an active force in the world has been gradual, not sudden, and will yet be gradual. But Peking's new diplomacy since the Cultural Revolution, and her new ties especially with the United States and the United Nations, have greatly stressed and spurred the process. Senator Wherry, a tireless exponent of the notion that China should be the object of Western schemes, vowed in 1940, "With God's help, we will lift Shanghai up and up, ever up, until it is just like Kansas City." But the time has arrived when Kansas City is no more likely to be a model for Shanghai than is Shanghai to be a model for Kansas City (or Manila, or Bombay). This new, active importance of China I pondered as the train sped across the East River and on to Canton.

The traveler himself had also changed. I knew that I was more skeptical of the claims of any "ism" or any political system than seven years before. No longer did there seem to be a sharp and compelling choice between capitalism and communism. I liked neither. I was a *saboteur de l'absolu*. I now felt it was possible that a civilized human being ought to put certain private values above the public values of either. The day before leaving the United States for China, I delivered to its publisher a book on social democracy. Here was this traveler's creed. A socialism never frozen, but constantly tested by men's reason and values; one which holds social justice in one hand and liberty in the other; which pursues collective purposes, yet not against the opinions of ordinary people; which rejects both the political tyranny of Stalinism and the economic tyranny of unbridled capitalism.

There are four major routes into China (as well as those from Rangoon, Hanoi and Pyongyang). The Trans-Siberian railroad carries you slowly across the Eurasian landmass to Peking, from Moscow via Ulan Bator. Again from Moscow, there are flights, on both Aeroflot and China Airlines, via Irkutsk to Peking. This way I entered China in 1964. In recent years, both Air France and PIA (Pakistan) have begun service to Shanghai. The French come into China from Rangoon, the Pakistanis from Dacca. Neither is permitted to fly to Peking; only in a Chinese plane may a traveler to the capital cover the last leg of this route. The flight to Shanghai is now the most common one from Europe to China.

The fourth route was the one I followed in 1971: the three-hour train trip from Hong Kong to Canton. Like the route to Shanghai, it provides a way of traveling to Peking in stages, which is how the Chinese long required foreigners to approach their capital. The entry by train is in some ways the best. The traveler savors the landscape and peasant life of China before he is swallowed by that small part of the nation which is urban China.

The *real* vehicle for traveling into China is not a plane or a train. It is a piece of paper. Three inches by five inches, elegant in red and black ink, it is headed "Entry and Exit Visa" and stamped with the title and red flag of the People's Republic of China. In 1964 my visa had been issued in Poland. Traveling in Europe, I had applied in the summer of 1964 for a Chinese visa in London, Paris, Moscow, Budapest, and Prague. The response was not yes and not no. Disappointed, I reached Warsaw, my last port of call in Europe before returning to Melbourne. I went to the Chinese Embassy, a fawn oblong block on Bonifraterska Street, but with hardly a flicker of hope. I asked to see the ambassador, as much to complain about the discouragement offered to an (arrogant) young man who wanted to see China, as to make yet one more plea for a visa.

Surprisingly, I was seriously received. A senior Chinese diplomat sipped his tea gravely as I made my pitch. I filled in no more application forms, as I had done five times in other Chinese Embassies, but just talked about my interest in China. I was ushered out the marble lobby, a little flushed from an ardent performance. At eleven o'clock that night I was in bed at the

Hotel Bristol. A phone call came from the Chinese Embassy. A visa awaited me; would I kindly come and get it at eight the next morning?

In 1971, word of the visa also came by a telephone call. Again, there had been applications, but again the green light did not seem to come as a response to those applications. In 1967 I wished to go once more to China. After making a request through the Chinese Embassy in Warsaw, I received from Peking in May, 1967, a letter stating: "We are pleased to inform you that we agree with your visit to China." But the visit never occurred. Perhaps because of the Cultural Revolution, the actual arrangements were indefinitely delayed.

Amidst the diplomatic fluidity of the spring of 1971, I was in touch with Chinese officials on larger matters. Out of the blue on May 31 came a call from a Chinese source in Canada. Would I like to visit China? If so, I should leave within two weeks. Arrangements were to be made at the Chinese Embassy in Ottawa.

The button for number 1201 at the Juliana Apartments — a building on Bronson Avenue where the Chinese temporarily have their embassy — was so well worn that the number was now scarcely visible. Diplomats there were extremely helpful, though they had no information from Peking about the nature, timing, or duration of my visit to China. Only on the morning of receiving the visa did I fill out an application form. I asked why the visa was not stamped into the passport but provided on a separate piece of paper. "Because China and Australia do not have diplomatic relations." I pointed out that in 1964 the Chinese Embassy in Warsaw had stamped the visa in the passport. The official replied simply, "The comrades in Warsaw made a mistake."

The private citizen visiting China today will be received through one of three channels. If he is a tourist, Luxingshe, the China Travel Service, will arrange his entire journey. It may even meet him at the frontier, and escort him to the frontier when the visit is done, as the Chinese used to do with foreigners under the dynasties. Especially since the Cultural Revolution, the Chinese do not expect tourists to come merely to see the sights.

Luxingshe assumes as a matter of course that tourists will wish to examine the industrial and agricultural life of China, and the program is set up almost as a study tour.

The visitor coming on a form of cultural exchange will be dealt with by the Chinese People's Association for Friendship with Foreign Countries. This covers doctors in China at the invitation of China's medical authorities, sportsmen, personages from associations having friendly links with China. The third category is the visiting journalist. He will be handled by the Information Department of the Foreign Ministry. In all three cases the visitor follows a daily program set up by the Chinese authorities after considering the visitor's requests.

I went to China as a "journalist and scholar" and was received mainly by the Foreign Ministry. My association with the visit of the Australian Labor party delegation in July complicated this arrangement, since this delegation was received essentially by the Chinese government (acting through a semiofficial arm of the Foreign Ministry, the People's Institute for Foreign Affairs). I also had contact with the Association for Friendship with Foreign Countries.

What can the visitor learn in China? The pages of this book are my answer. They contain not what I know about China, but what I found in China in the summer of 1971. I have not set my account on a pedestal of history, or stretched it across a frame of theory; history and theory are for another occasion. What is offered is an eyewitness report. The reader can assess for himself the credibility of the report, and give it whatever wider context he chooses. As for *ways* of learning about China on a visit, I found there were five.

One may hear responsible government officials speak at first hand on Chinese policies. Instances were meetings with the Premier, Chou En-lai, and with the Vice-president of the Standing Committee of the National People's Congress, Kuo Mo-jo. Second, the visitor may obtain concrete data at particular institutions on the basic level, as in days spent at factories, communes, hospitals. Third, there can occur discussions between the visitor and Chinese of training or interests similar to his own. An example was a session with a professor of Peking University about topics in history and politics of mutual concern. Fourth, one may talk with *anyone* about his or her views and conditions of life. Though my spoken Chinese is not fluent, I learned much this way, and the reader will find many a quotation from a casual conversation in a taxi or on the street. Fifth, the visitor can simply look around him. A land of 800,000,000 people is a fantastic theater for the curious eye (and being able to read the signs and posters helps). Between political talks, I never tired of watching the grace and order and habit of Chinese social life.

To be frank, my weeks in China exceeded expectations. The 1964 visit, a brief one of only two weeks, had made sufficient impact to entice me into study of China and its language. The 1971 visit deepened my admiration for China and its people.

I happen to like the peace of the brightly colored hills and valleys of China. The concrete turn of the Chinese mind. The poise and calm, the understatement and irony, the cheerfulness and modesty, of Chinese conduct. The excellence of Chinese cuisine and the conscientious spirit of a Chinese kitchen.

I happen to admire the cultural confidence of the Chinese, which pads them against the rougher consequences of history's crimes and chaos. The long and rich past, which seems, for the Chinese, to rob the present of its tyranny and the future of total uncertainty.

I happen, too, to be moved by the social gains of the Chinese revolution. In a magnificent way, it has healed the sick, fed the hungry, and given security to the ordinary man of China. It has rolled off the weight of exploitation whose excess of evils strained patience and altruism beyond all reason. It has followed the principle of the ancient classic, *The Great Learning:* "To disperse wealth is to collect the people." It has put a flash of pride in the Chinese eye.

Yet I make serious criticisms (as the Chinese make self-criticisms). Post-1949 China is by no means a new heaven and a new earth. Wrong turns have at times been made, in economic and other policies. Disputes occur at high levels and low. The position of intellectuals, it seems to me, is especially problematic.

All this is not too surprising, given China's problems, and given the familiar flaws in the Communist view of society. The Chinese purse cannot match what the Chinese hand would like to grasp. The steamroller of exigency snuffs out ideals and spoils tidy plans in China as in other countries. Chinese spirits have unfulfilled yearnings like all others.

There is no substitute, in my view, for weighing up the Chinese revolution sector by sector, on the scale of its ongoing effect on the lives of the Chinese people. History grants no automatic victories, nor the blessing of permanence to any moment, however splendid. The Chinese have no destiny to do right what everyone has done wrong before. They are not borne upward by some preset cosmic escalator. The great social progress in China has been sweated for lap by lap. Any "blanket" faith in the Chinese way of socialism as necessarily superior to all others would be misplaced. The Chinese are unlikely to succeed in all they are attempting. They can count big achievements; they cannot deny grave problems. I *hope* China may evolve a social system that "serves the people." I cannot be sure it will.

In Canton I ran into an American clergyman friend and we talked of religion in China. He brushed off the closing of churches, temples, and mosques. "Anyway," he declared, "I am interested not in the churches but in the revolution." I saw his point, yet I felt uneasy. His remark somehow recalled the quip about De Gaulle. He loved France, but not the French. Is there such an overarching reality, the "Chinese revolution?"

I can only weigh a revolution in the lives of the people affected. I cannot condemn the Communist revolution in China, yet claim to have compassion toward the poor, the sick, the maltreated. I cannot without qualification call it a "liberation," if I think there is no reason why people should not read a Bible or pray in a temple if they wish. The revolution is food and good health; short-cropped hair and hard work; dunce caps and boarded-up churches; buses and aqueducts; educational opportunities and dignity.

In the end, it is respect for China that makes it necessary to criticize. Taking the challenge of China seriously — its power *and* its social values — I feel I must bring my own values into the picture when I report on China. This makes a visit to China a spiritual struggle. Big questions of value rise every day from the din of the factory and the dust of the commune. To write blandly about China and neglect these questions would not be to respect but to demean China, and to fail in solidarity with the people of China. The future is open and in our own hands, and the Chinese people and all other peoples are now drastically interlocked in facing it. We shall understand ourselves together, and make a livable future together, or not at all. Chairman Mao is ultimately right when he insists: "The people, and the people alone, are the motive force in the making of world history." We owe it to our common humanity, and to the children of the world, to turn a steady, critical eye on the land of the 800,000,000.

2. Perspectives

Shimmering mirage, a China is conjured in our minds by scraps of news and speculation. Devilishly well organized; neat and regimented; striding ahead to overtake Russia and America; clean, abstemious; an army of sexless puppets, their daily life an incarnation of the Thought of Mao Tse-tung. Absence from China feeds the mirage. Fear, buttressed by ignorance, hints that China is formidable, or awful, or awfully formidable. How cunning those Chinese are! Do they not constantly surprise us? Such sacrifice of indulgence today for glory tomorrow!

We can be like Voltaire, philosophic China-watcher of another age. Sitting in Paris, he spun a mental tapestry of China less from facts than from disenchantment with the Europe of his day. The picture of Confucius in his study was a totem; maybe our pictures of Mao are too. As if the Chinese millions were mere moving illustrations of a Concept. Walk-on actors in a Drama of Historical Optimism or a Drama of Historical Pessimism!

The actual world of sweat and cicadas, boiled rice and bicycles, is a bit more complex. After seven years, I was back again. Did the mirage lift for a moment? Instead of "China," here were rivers and mountains, and people getting up, working, eating, singing, arguing, planning, going to bed. Not objects for investigation, but situations, in which I seemed to be involved only a little less than the people around me.

Of course a visit has its illusions, as does absence. You feel the human simplicities of China too acutely. You get talking to Shanghai citizens about bringing up children, to a professor in

Peking about how he teaches modern history. As if you and they stood on the same ground, wrestling with the social problems of the 1970s and the human dilemmas of all time. That is illusory. For while we remain grouped in nation-states, as long as East Asia remains a place of collision between American substance and Chinese shadow, China *is* another world. Mao chairs them; Nixon presides over us. Our human solidarity is at the mercy of what they cook up between them. You leave Canton, cross the border at Shumchun, and China again becomes "China." One corner of the triangle of hope and terror, the United States, Russia, and China. Stage play of communism, before the beaming portrait of Chairman Mao. Belly of real estate at the southeast tip of Eurasia, which fifty nuclear bombs could turn into charcoal and gas within a week.

But the separateness is not forever. The strangeness of China is not objective, like that of the platypus. Separateness and strangeness both stem from the past relationship between China and ourselves. Here there are changes; will soon be more. Countries' "images" of each other can depart terribly from fact. U.S.-Chinese relations give rich illustration. Yet international politics and our human existence do play out a crazy dialectic. It means that visiting China has its bit of the future to reflect. "Being there," like waking up at 3:00 A.M., gives its own special angle on the totality of things.

Being in China in 1971 means realizing that although in the United States Vietnam looms large on our mental screens, with China a big country behind Vietnam, in Peking Vietnam fades into one of many countries down beyond the Middle Kingdom's southern provinces. It means observing that chance and distraction fleck Chinese politics no less than ours; a Foreign Ministry official remarked, when Peking in late June did a long (and favorable) commentary on the Common Market, "During the Cultural Revolution we rather neglected the Common Market; now we're catching up and getting our position straight."

Being in China means fielding queries at a university in Sian about how we dealt, at Harvard in the spring of 1970, with the question of giving or not giving grades and exams to students who went on strike because of the invasion of Cambodia. It means finding propaganda less depressing when spoken than when one reads it from afar on the printed page, because people do not always mean what they say, and when they do mean it, do not always believe it. You read a tirade about the high tide of African revolution; then next day a Chinese diplomat who has worked in Africa remarks on the immaturity of African movements and their inability to make revolution as China made it. Paraphrasing the ancient writer Sun Tzu, he smiles: "They don't know themselves and they don't know the enemy; that's the trouble." *

To be there is to recall — did I need the reminder? — that Chinese cooking is not just a "great cuisine of the world," but a daily joy to 800 million and *the* major factor in any calculation of bright and dark sides to the Chinese people's life in 1971. To hear a high official say, when speaking of Western leftists who stay away from Taiwan for reasons of conscience, "They should go, see what the place is like. When foreign leftists come to Peking, I urge them not to stay away from Moscow, but to stop over there and look around." "Being there" means boredom and humor, clashes of personality, getting up at 5:00 A.M., finding time to read the newspaper, deciding between the ballet and the cinema for tonight's entertainment.

I suppose each man has his China, as his Rousseau. A visit does not do much to replace the subjective with the objective. But the subjective has its own scale of truth and falsehood. The visitor is a human being; what hits him?

Appealing imprecision. People wander around; daydream. They will, when marketing, or in conversation, let the world go by in search of the pearl of great price. They don't mince like Japanese, but amble as men in secure possession of the earth under their feet. They will stand and stare at you, then win you with a grin if you look up in anxiety or irritation. Officials at banquets, faces pink with wine, lean head-in-hand across the

---

* Sun Tzu wrote in *The Art of War:* "Know the enemy, know yourself, and in a hundred battles you will win a hundred victories."

table, forgetting their elbows in the excitement of a line of talk. Men on duty in trains, when every passenger has been served his tea and all is calm, turn down the radio and play poker, or draw the blinds, swing two seats together, and snooze in the peace of the afternoon sun. China is comprehensively organized, but not perfectly organized — certainly not to Japanese pitch. The ragged edges, the ragamuffin element, the expansive gesture, have happily not been organized out of existence.

Asia's heart. China has a staggering cultural self-confidence, and she is beholden to no one. In the timeless haze of Peking you realize that today's Bangkok, Saigon, Taipei, are not cities of Asia's Asia but of America's Asia. Here in the "Forbidden City" is the real challenge to Western hegemony. Today but an embryonic challenge, partly of the spirit, tomorrow it will develop the sinews of a power challenge. The importance of China is being transmuted from symbol to actuality by the increasing powerlessness of the West in Asia. In China you feel a strength which comes from belief in oneself. America's Asia cannot match this kind of strength. But then America's Asia is China's periphery. And in Peking, China seems to Southeast Asia as the garment to the hem.

China's touchy pride. I went to the East Room of the Great Hall of the People on July 5 with E. Gough Whitlam, leader of the Australian Labor party, for a late-night talk with Chou En-lai. Recounting China's bitter experience with Russia, the Old Tiger warned us against trusting *our* ally, the United States. His point was a passionate assertion of each country's right to run its own affairs. Whitlam said America had not treated Australia badly, as Russia had China. The Premier threw apart his arms. "But they both want to control others." He beat his wicker chair for emphasis. "Our socialist country will not be controlled by anyone."

Chou summed up what is evident up and down China: deep sensitivity about China's dignity as an independent power. It goes back to the humiliation of the Opium War, when Britain bullied a weak China into a falling-domino torrent of concessions. You are constantly reminded that "those days are gone." The East wind prevails over the West wind. China has stood up. She will not be controlled by others.

The past is very present. Halfway between Sian and Yenan, in the orange loess-country where Chinese civilization began, lies the market town of Huang Ling. I drove there to see the tomb of the Yellow Emperor, father of the Han people. My Chinese companions (who had suggested this visit) entered with awe the gray-green gardens, lit up by the red pillars of a temple of commemorative tablets to the Yellow Emperor. It was 7:00 A.M., and the gnarled trees, one said to date from the time of the Yellow Emperor (some five thousand years ago), were ghostly in the still, clear morning air.

My Communist companions gazed at the elegant inscription: "Cradle of the Fatherland's Civilization." One of them, a diplomat called Chou Nan, who does calligraphy with a brush daily and writes poems in the traditional style, quoted suitable lines by heart from the Chinese classics. The five Chinese clustered round the hoary tablets, as Mr. Chou pointed out passages to his eager colleagues.

Not a single slogan or Mao quote is found near the mound in which the Father of China may (or may not) lie. "It would be unsuitable here," a Shensi provincial aide explained crisply. I looked around the site, well kept by the Communist government. Apart from the historical inscriptions, some in Kuo Mo-jo's rich hand, the only writing nearby was a placard on an old gray tree: "Protect the forest, fight fires."

Mental unity. Chou En-lai urged me to study the essay Peking put out to mark the fiftieth anniversary of the founding of the Chinese Communist party. "As you are a professor in America and Australia, it can be reference material for you." That essay was, in early July, a Bible in China.

Drivers read it. The girls in the elevator at the Peking Hotel read it, between passengers. The radio broadcasts it. Companions cite it. Hosts ask my reaction to it. In Shanghai it is no less omnipresent; the same in Nanking, in Wusih. Sometimes a visitor to Harvard might think students read only books by Harvard faculty. A parallel impression, magnified a thousandfold, I had in China. It is intellectual incest on a gargantuan scale. Information, opinion, comes down from the mountain of authority to the plateau of public consumption. The people all have this official information; they have no other. The whole country, from Canton to the northeast, from the east coast to Sinkiang, has at least a surface mental unity unmatched in China's history. (Just as the whole country has the chronological unity of being on Peking time.) There is a rule by phrase, a bond in headlines, a solidarity by syntax. In the beginning was the Word . . .

To the visiting writer, information is like melons in the market. If it's available, you get it. If it's not, your hands are empty. There is nothing in between. No point in trying to get light on government policy from a Chinese who has not received it from above. When you get something, however, it is reliable. The system would surely delight an eighteenth-century *philosophe;* the "Word" is sovereign. On the other hand, it is a nightmare for the diplomat who has to put something in the pouch every week. Mingling one night with foreigners in Peking, I recalled a remark of a French diplomat who served in China, then in the United States: "In Peking we had too little information. In New York we had too much. In neither case did we know what was going on."

Formidable children. Here is a French class at the Middle School attached to Peking Normal University. The faces are pictures of concentration. The class screams in unison: *"Vive le parti communiste; Vive la solidarité des peuples du monde."* I ask one pretty lass in a colored blouse why she studies French. "To further the world revolution." The answer seems ridiculous, but the ardent hunger for knowledge behind it is not.

The Chinese nation is studying as if for some cosmic examination. The bookshops are stiff with schoolchildren reading and buying textbooks, a lot published in the last year. A laundryboy is wrestling with Marx's *The Class Struggles in France.* A taxi driver has a recent pamphlet, *Philosophy for Working Men.* Tots in Shanghai sport aprons sewn with characters: "Love science, Love hygiene, Love labor."

Faces of the future; a kindergarten in Shanghai. Every fourth child in the world is Chinese. The Chinese characters in the lower photo read: "Motherland."

Nor do they stuff their minds and forget their bodies. Rise at six and you find Chinese young people exercising in parks, on the waterfront, on rooftops. They twist and spin, jerk and wheel, doing "hard" exercises (forms of karate), "soft" (forms of *t'ai-chi ch'uan,* the snakelike, rhythmic art), and countless improvisations of their own. Some do theatrical swordplay; many walk on their hands, first steadying their upturned legs against a wall.

In short, China's 300 million young schoolchildren seem a formidable prospect for tomorrow's China. True, research is in many spheres backward. True, present professional opportunities are cruelly limited. But generations of scientifically minded, intellectually hungry, fit, earnest youth will be a magnificent base for more sophisticated advances in the 1980s and 1990s.

Equality is dull. Stroll along the Whangpu River bank (the "Bund") in the evening, and you think at first the heart has gone out of Shanghai. Red neon lights up the river's ripples, but every single sign is a slogan. The row of tall British buildings, Shanghai's greeting to the Western world across the water, are shabby, and many unused. The former British Consulate, its furry lawns stretching out toward the junction of Whangpu River with Soochow Creek, is just a sailors' club. Not one prostitute, hardly a car. Some blocks beyond, "Great World," once a sparkling place of entertainment, is silent as a morgue.

Nor do the vast billboards have anything to quicken the pulse. Posters and commentaries tell the story, congress by congress, of fifty years of the Chinese Communist party. The ear cannot vary the story. "Sailing the Seas Depends upon the Helmsman" fills the air. The vast Big Ben of a clock on the Customs House strikes the hour, but instead of a chime, it booms out a rusty rendition of "The East Is Red." Is this Shanghai, or have I come upon a May 7 school (rural place of mixed labor and study for those found in the Cultural Revolution to need "remolding") set amidst a cardboard replica of the great Chinese port?

The Shanghai Bund is nothing, yet it's many things that matter. Forget the images; attend to the people. Watch them in the light of a full, bright moon, heads to the breeze off the water — a nice change, after work, from the heat of their houses. They read, lick ice creams. Lovers leave their bicycles against the rails and seek a dark spot in the park (two cents admission, full of un-lighted nooks). Listen to their talk, some on haunches in groups, young couples discussing future plans, old men at chess, preco-cious boys who ask me about my country.

Here are people in bland possession of a sector where once they were little better than things. For the Western visitor the Bund is nothing. Yet the fact that *he* is nothing as he wanders unheeded proves that what was once a preserve where he felt his authority now belongs to the Chinese people. There exists an obvious, to some people moving, egalitarianism in the social re-lationships of these streets and parks. Of course it is "dull" for the spender or the adventurer. Justice is not necessarily exciting, and it is the face of international and social justice which smiles behind the blandness of the Shanghai Bund.

3. Anatomy of a Visit

My visit, from fluttery-stomached entry to exhausted exit, spanned forty days. It took in seven major cities, as well as towns and rural pockets. When possible, I took a train or drove, in a "Shanghai" or "Volga" car: by road to Yenan, a train trip from Changsha to Canton. The long hops were generally by air, in British Viscount, large Ilyushin 18, or the grasshopper of an Ilyushin 14, in which you sit (at a giddy angle until takeoff) without seat belts, beside panoramic oblong windows. This *hsiao fei-chi* (small plane), as the Chinese call it, roars angrily but flies low, and there are splendid views.

There below is the flat, geometric somnolence of Sian, ancient capital of China and now capital of Shensi province, specked with T'ang dynasty pagodas. Its boulevards are lined with six and eight rows of trees and punctuated with four massive Ch'ing dynasty gates, sentries to a civilization. Down here now, the swelling mountains between Hunan province and Kiangsi province, which we bounce across flying from Nanchang to Changsha. At their foot, a world of rivers, canals, ponds, shimmering dusty blue in the morning heat, watering a patchwork of rice and cotton fields now alive with harvest activity and new planting.

Many of the air passengers are government officials, as often as not military men. One day on a flight to Peking I found myself next to an air force officer. He had the window seat, but when he noticed my interest in the landscape he offered to switch with me. I declined, but shifted to the window seat one row back when it proved to be vacant. The air force officer, vigilant for my convenience, saw that my view was now obstructed by the propellers. He again went to great lengths to persuade me to accept his seat, and thus get a better elevation on the rolling plains below.

The hostesses of China Airlines are cheerful and informal. On a four-and-a-half-hour flight from Canton to Peking, after eight hot hours of delay at White Cloud Airport, I fell asleep when the meal of fruit and biscuits was done. A hand banged my shoulder. *"Pu yao hsui chao le! Tao le, tao le!"* ("Stop sleeping, we're here!") But Miss Wang had a pretty smile as she handed me chewing gum with an inscription on the wrapper: "China Airlines: Safety, Speed, Comfort, Convenience." Dressed like laborers, their hair straight and short, these girls are nevertheless often pretty.

My Chinese companions — diplomats, officials of the Revolutionary Committee in each province, aides of Luxingshe, the China Travel Service — did not warm to comments on physical appearance. One night there was a dinner in Nanking given by the Foreign Affairs Section of the Revolutionary Committee. Chiang Kai-shek's old capital was living up to its reputation as one of China's "three furnaces" (Chungking and Wuhan are the others). As a sweet wine called *huang chiu* spurred the theme of "friendship between the Chinese and Australian peoples," I remarked upon the good looks of the hostess on that day's Shanghai-Nanking flight. My host looked with concentration at his "fish mandarin." "It is not the physical side but the thought which counts," he pointed out. So I rephrased my sentiment and won all-round approval: "The thought of today's hostess seemed, from whatever angle you viewed it, admirable and inspiring."

The hotels are comfortable and they have excellent service. They can be hot in summer, especially in the south, for there is no air conditioning. (In the cavernous oven called the Tung Fang Hotel at Canton, each room has a thermometer, as if to taunt the midsummer visitor with a measure of his misery.) In Peking I first stayed at the Hsin Ch'iao, a functional hotel bordering the Legation Quarter; later, when Mr. Whitlam arrived, at the luxurious Peking Hotel.

At the Hsin Ch'iao in 1964, I faced the courtyard, and early each morning could watch the hotel employees doing the rhythmic *t'ai-chi ch'uan* exercises. This time I overlook a hospital, which has written on it no nameplate but simply: "Proletariat of the World Unite!" My bathroom towels have sewn into them the characters: "Serve the People!" In Canton, the taps had the English markings for hot and cold, but here (and in all other cities) they have only Chinese characters. I mention at the service desk that I would like a radio. Within minutes there appears a set, the size of a TV, which I rent for a tiny fee. The room has a tall ceiling and a marble floor. Two large armchairs are covered with fawn linen and antimacassars. The china lamps have delicate silk shades. On the desk is a steel-nibbed pen and a bottle of ink.

The window is my TV set, and I often sit absorbed beside it. Now, a platoon of PLA (People's Liberation Army) men running by at the double early in the morning. Now, tiny tots singing political songs as they march past. Shoppers with laden baskets. Girls and youths chatting in groups. And, endlessly, the bells of a thousand bicycles. Together with the cicadas and the morning sun, they ensure early rising. Opposite my bed is a picture of the mighty Nanking Bridge. I lie — without bedclothes, like a fish upon the mattress — in the first rays of the sun, and the light is reflected brilliantly from the silken red flags atop the bridge; a rosy beam to summon me to a new day.

The Peking Hotel (normally for official or semiofficial guests) is older, with handsome, creaking wooden floors. Its staff, many of whom remember the hotel when it was under French management, are trained to a high pitch. The special delight of this hotel is the view from its vast, ornate windowsills. You see the bones of the city of Peking as Marco Polo saw them. Seven hundred years ago he noted: "The streets are so straight and wide that you can see right along them from end to end and from one gate to the other. And up and down the city there are beautiful palaces, and many and great hostelries . . . The whole city is arranged in squares just like a chessboard." It is still like that.

The great Ch'angan boulevard runs across the city, set about with rows of trees. Bicycles swarm by, ringing their bells as if in irritation. Amidst their silver tangle, like carp among the minnows, cruise red and white buses. Sometimes two are hooked together with folding canvas connections, giving a caterpillar effect.

To one side of the boulevard lies the Tien An Men square. Symmetrically, the Great Hall of the People faces two vast museums, and the Monument to the People's Heroes stands in the square's center. To the other side of the Ch'angan, there nest the purple walls and orange tiles of the former Imperial Palace (Forbidden City). The tower of the central post office rises behind the red pillars and green ridges of the compounds that flank the Palace. To the south, the Ch'ien Lung gate stands, gray and solid sentry over the heart of official Peking.

The Peace Hotel in Shanghai is one of the world's best. It no longer echoes to the sound of titillating entertainment, as it did in pre-Liberation days. But for comfort, service, and one form of the "peace" promised by its name, few hotels can match it. On my first stay, the room was so large that two elephantine white couches seemed lost within it. A separate "massage alcove" was attached, and a blackwood robing room in which the lights went out automatically, by stages, two minutes after being switched on. Fresh peaches and cakes lay about the tables.

On my second stay — after returning from a trip to Nanking and Wusih — they put me in a room completely paneled in oak squares, and pink with a fairyland of lanterns in the traditional Chinese style. The bed is turned into an arena by a rose-tinged mirror spread across the opposite wall. A bronze mirror of human height guards the entrance hall of the suite. The various closets are lined with mirrors and cunningly concealed lights. Many of the hotel staff are suave Shanghai types who speak some English or French, for whom the Peace Hotel seems almost a world in itself.

From the hotel rooms, you see the Bund (waterfront) and its row of British buildings. Next door is a former hotel that looks just like the YMCA in Great Russell Street, London. The same bleak gray concrete, the same ledges under the windows, the same railing with little pillars two floors from the top of the building, the same tower keeping watch at one corner of the roof.

I look down upon an orgasm of physical exercise along the curved public spaces of the waterfront. Girls spring up with handstands on the benches which line the Whangpu River. A boy in a tangerine-colored shirt whirls his arms at lightning speed. Old men with soft limbs do *t'ai-chi ch'uan* sequences, their eyes staring intently out into space, their breathing carefully controlled. Little boys lie on their backs, legs moving in all directions with an almost boneless suppleness. A girl in bright aqua slacks and a pink blouse has her left leg on a railing; as she twists to one side and the other her braids swirl like angry snakes. Experienced exponents of all these forms can be seen instructing beginners, and a crowd clusters around each teacher and his pupils.

Specializing on foreign-policy and education issues did not prevent visits to factories and communes; to hospitals — to see how Chinese medicine and Western medicine fit together; literary and historical spots; and the beautiful village in Hunan where Mao Tse-tung was born and raised, full of memories and mosquitoes. Impossible to miss performances of the "revolutionary operas and ballets" — eight new excellent if not very varied dramas, of universal household familiarity in China today.

Summertime makes a vast difference in visiting China. People sit languidly outside their houses, eating and even sleeping in the open air. Opportunity to observe social life, and talk informally (in winter, folk go inside to their stove or *k'ang* — combination stove-and-bed in northern peasant homes — and the air of community conviviality is gone). Scant clothing thickens the air of sensuality, which is anyway seldom absent from Chinese life. Few men wore more than shorts and singlet in Shanghai, Changsha, and Canton — different in Peking — and the brassiere, though widely available in shops, was not, it seemed, in frequent use.

I wandered into parks. Nowhere better to watch and chat with people as they lounge around, roller-skate, play chess or *wei ch'i* ("Go"), boat, and swim. Elaborate parks, such as Peihai in Peking, have been closed since the Cultural Revolution. But not ordinary ones, such as the vast People's Park around Lake Hsuan Wu in Nanking. Here I wanted to swim, and this led to over-careful preparations for my safety and comfort.

A car went on ahead to select a secluded spot. Irritated, I remarked as I got ready to dive in that it was not safe to swim alone. Alas, a casual sentence, uttered only to reinforce dissatisfaction at not being able to mingle with other swimmers, brought fresh complications. A motorboat was summoned from the far shores of the lake. While Chinese companions watched from the bank, the boat circled this poor swimmer, spitting out oil and fumes. How to protect me from my protector? I said I wanted to ride in the boat. Before anyone could say no, I sprang in and joined four young fishermen in a trip around the lake. Now I could swim where others swam, chat with people without feeling like an exhibit. A trivial incident, no doubt, yet one case of many where the line between "well cared for" and "isolated" seemed a little too fine.

In Shanghai, I came across a very different park, opposite the former British Consulate which is now the Shanghai Seamen's Club. It is a secluded garden, full of amorous couples. By night the pink glow from neon signs that dot the waterfront provides almost its only light. I stand at the gate, where you must buy a ticket to enter (two cents). A group of boys materialize around me and one of them suddenly says, "Go in, go in!"

Inside, I find an air of quiet concentration. After my eyes become accustomed to the gloom, I judge that some two-thirds of the throng on the low stone seats and along the winding gravel paths are couples. Conversation is subdued, and now and then it is drowned by a ship's foghorn from across the silky ripples of the Whangpu. Most of the couples hold hands; many have arms around each other; some are entangled in yet other ways. A girl sits beside a rockery, while four or five men try, with mixtures of shyness and aggression, to coax her from her sulky reticence. In places, you can make out the outline of human forms only by the white shirts. Close your ears to the language, and you could be in a park in any large Asian city.

Strolling to another corner of the park, I blink with discomfort at a bright light fixed above a board to which newspapers are pinned. A large crowd gathers round that day's edition of the Shanghai paper *Wen Hui Pao.* They are reading two cool and factual articles about the United States. One is a straightforward piece about Long Island. The other is an historical survey of how the original thirteen states expanded to the present fifty. Neither article contains propaganda or mentions the name of Chairman Mao.

Were there serious restraints on the visitor? Formal restrictions exist. No photos from the air, nor at certain industrial areas (such as the docks looking north from central Shanghai). Among the provinces closed to nearly all foreigners is Szechwan, whose mountains and rivers and spicy cuisine I would like to have savored. A query about a visit to Amoy brought this response: "How could you go there? It's opposite Taiwan. Your safety could not be guaranteed." Then with a smile which conveyed no great fear of Chiang Kai-shek's forces: "Why, you might be shelled by the Kuomintang!"

Generalized control stems from the practicalities of a visit. Rarely does the visitor select which factory, school, commune he will see. Taxi stands are few, so personal mobility is limited. The Peking Hotel, though a palace in its way, is also a prison, since there is no taxi rank outside; you must phone and state your destination. Somehow, my Luxingshe aide always knew when I came into a hotel (even when I did so alone). For no sooner was I in the room than he would phone to discuss the next part of my program.

Yet many things I did in perfect freedom. Two legs and some knowledge of Chinese are wings indeed in the cities. Few people closed up on a simple talk; some opened like a rose. Professional men dined alone with me in Peking restaurants. I strolled in on families at random in a Shanghai apartment block. As for officials, they allowed visits to some places which were not yet open to anyone, foreigner or Chinese: former residences in Peking and

Shanghai of the great Lu Hsun (a leading twentieth-century writer of stories and poems, much admired by Mao); an array of Han, Chou, and T'ang treasures unearthed during the Cultural Revolution. And at the Chinese border there were few formalities. I brought out unexposed film, tape recordings, and notebooks — but the border officials didn't know, because neither going in nor coming out was there any baggage examination of any kind.

One day I meandered with Stephen Fitzgerald, an Australian scholar, in Foochow Street, central Shanghai, looking for its renowned secondhand bookshops. None remain. Some are turned to other uses (the former Foreign Literature Bookshop is selling textiles); some are open only for new books on the ground floor, closed on the second floor which (I suppose) holds the secondhand books. But nearby was a *lu-kuan,* a simple Chinese hotel where foreigners never stay. We looked in, were welcomed, given fruit punch, and chatted with guests and staff. Over the inside of the doorway, in fresh red characters, there was a warning. "When leaving watch out for your purses and money." That should not be a surprise, for there is theft in China like everywhere else — though less than in most places. Bicycles are often padlocked in the street, and houses, so far as I could see, are generally locked.

Foochow Street is scarred on one side with earthworks. Air-raid shelters are being painstakingly built, often with intricate underground links between them. The finished shelter is well concealed — a small door leads down from certain shops which are well known in the neighborhood. Among the well-stocked, well-patronized food shops the pastries look good, and we go into a small place to buy some. The shopkeeper, a genial and worldly Shanghai-type of sixty-seven, tells me he graduated in commerce from a Shanghai university in 1927. Until Liberation, he owned a tea shop a few blocks away. It must be hard to adjust, I say, from being an owner to being a shop assistant. "Not really," he replies, gazing out into the street, "given all the circumstances." What are the circumstances, I wonder? "The change in society. Look outside the shop, at the people, what they wear; ask them who they work for." He turns back inside the shop and pauses. "It's a big change; exploitation has gone — my change from owning a tea shop, you have to see it in that context." My pastries are wrapped up. But anything with flour in it is rationed. "Where are your coupons?" the old man inquires, his face long in mock desolation. Of course I have none, but he lets me off as a "friend from across the seas."

Further down the street is a billboard with a vast world map in bright colors. Captions on the various countries show the "excellent situation" for revolution that seems, in the Chinese view, to prevail almost everywhere. A young man stares intently at the heading: "People of all the world unite and put down American aggressors and all their running dogs." The map is conveniently placed at a bus stop. A newsstand on the sidewalk does good business, especially in technical magazines — and that is a sign of the times in China. A new one has recently appeared, *Scientific Experimentation,* with popularized articles on the contribution science can make to society. I buy its first three issues, and some recent fiction — but am refused Shanghai newspapers (see page 41).

Turning back toward the hotel, we pass a Protestant church — its closed gates bearing the banner "Carry through the Cultural Revolution to the end" — and then come upon a municipal "cultural and scientific library and reading room." Step off the crowded street, and you find at once an air of quiet concentration. At battered wooden tables, young and old pore over books, magazines, and newspapers. Again mostly technical stuff. Although a studious man is reading *Hung Ch'i* (*Red Flag,* the monthly theory journal of the Party), and some have Marx or Lenin, no one at the tables I circle is reading Mao. At the counter I ask for the famous historical novel *Dream of the Red Chamber.* The lady seems pleased to be asked — but, no, she does not have it. Lu Hsun? "We have almost all of his works; which would you like?" But few are reading fiction.

Getting nearer to the waterfront, the streets are lined with people, and more arrive each minute in trucks, to be marched in columns of two, then spread out three-deep along the road. The bell on the old British Customs House strikes five; most of the crowd seem to have come direct from work. We draw near and find no air of excitement. But why are they here? People readily answer the question. "We are here to welcome foreign guests to Shanghai." We rack our brains and recall that a French Parliamentary Delegation is in China and that a Korean group is due in Shanghai soon. But our curiosity is not shared by the welcomers themselves. None of a dozen or so asked know who is coming or seem to care. "It's just foreign friends," one girl sums up with a trace of impatience.

Soon the fussy marshals have got everyone in line and black limousines glide into view. The crowd stiffens into ceremonial festivity, faces beam with joy, hands clap vigorously. We dash into the Peace Hotel, climb to the eighth floor, and watch the scene from the dining room. A panorama of international friendship! The limousines, looking long and flat from high up, creep slowly enough for the elated faces of the foreign guests to be visible — they seem moved indeed by the reception. It was the Koreans — we found out that night at the ballet *White-haired Girl,* which they also attended — but I suppose the afternoon throng didn't know that any more than we did.

Sometimes a change of schedule threw amusing light on the ways of Chinese hosts. With the Australian group, I was in the resort town of Wusih, to drink up the tranquillity of Lake T'ai and the hills around it (rich in mulberry trees). A visit to a peach orchard was planned, but one of the Australians had a special interest in handicrafts and wanted to see the famous clay molding of Wusih. Hastily, it was arranged that we should go to the Clay and Plaster Figures Factory.

In the reception room, brightly painted soldiers with fierce expressions stare down at us from glass cases. Some artists and cadres are here to brief us. We all sit down, and the Vice-chairman of the factory's Revolutionary Committee clears his throat to begin. But he pauses, and turns to the Foreign Ministry official who is traveling with us. I am close to both and hear his whispered query: "Who are they?" The Ministry man hisses back: "Australian Labor party." The Vice-chairman inquires

Ta tzu pao (wall posters) done by peasants at the Red Star commune near Peking

Haircut in a Peking *hu t'ung* (lane)

Pai T'a Szu (White Dagoba Temple) in western Peking

A billboard in Shanghai, depicting "Map of the Excellent World Situation." Across the top runs the exhortation: "The entire people of the world, unite and defeat American aggressors and all their running dogs."

again: "Friends?" The Ministry man returns: "Yes, you can say so." The Vice-chairman then turns back to the table, smiles broadly, and begins in a loud voice: "Friends, we are very happy . . ."

Walking around Peking brings endless fascination. I would wander in the Wang Fu Ching street, a shopping area just east of the Forbidden City. Here is the Eastern Bazaar, where you may rummage for jade and stone carvings, ivory, lacquerware, or gauze lanterns. The Wang Fu Ching department store is the biggest in Peking, though modest in size (and in its prices) by American standards. People move among the bright displays with shopping lists and bags. There is a commercial spirit in the air, but no one rushes.

Only in the fur section are there many slogans or quotations on the walls. Perhaps people who buy furs stand most in need of political exhortation! I inspect the excellent furs and am assisted by an old man with a moustache who says he has worked in Peking shops for forty-five years. You see an abacus here and there, but cash registers are more numerous in this modern store. Beside each one sits the inevitable flask of tea. The salesmen are not at all apathetic — as might be expected in a state-owned store — but eager to persuade the customer of the quality of the wares. Mr. Liu, my Luxingshe aide, and I pause to buy a fruit drink, and watch this informal, prosperous tableau of urban China.

Afterwards I go across the street to the Hsinhua bookstore, then to order the making of an ivory seal (with my name in Chinese characters) at a small old-fashioned shop where the abacus is used, the light is dim, and the service is courtly. A few blocks away, I find an air-raid shelter under construction. A double-brick tunnel leads down and sideways from one end of a literature store. Half the store is closed during the construction. When the tunnel is finished, its entrance will not be easily visible from the street.

The foreigner who feels pressured by crowds, or by the uniform "Chineseness" around him, has only to look above him. The sky is the same, man's common bond. Yet is there not something unique about the Peking sky, or the North China sky? It is a pale, high sky. By contrast, the sky of South China seems a low-hanging, deeply colored sky. Quite a different atmosphere results. The northern sky affords a sense of spaciousness and calm that you do not find in the south. Climate reinforces the feeling. The stability of the northern days makes men equable. There seems to be a compact between the people and the heavens, which puts human beings in the timeless realm of the cosmos. In the south, any moment may produce a downpour. Men must switch abruptly with nature's mood. The Cantonese temperament is more florid. Feelings are more intense, as the color of the sky is more intense; less remote, as the low-hanging sky is less remote.

Another walk took me to the Pai T'a Szu (White Dagoba Temple) in Peking's western section. This temple, which no longer functions, was originally built in 1096, and in its present form dates from 1457. Behind it is a white dagoba rising majestically above residential surroundings. Its upper part is like the tip of an auger with a series of graceful rings. Above this sits a massive plate, hung around its edge with bells, which looks like the headdress of some heavenly being (see photograph, page 31).

I had come to the dagoba after visiting the nearby former home of the writer Lu Hsun. Every *hu t'ung* (lane) is full of children at play. It is late afternoon and older folk are doing household chores or relaxing on canvas chairs. Slogans on the walls — put up during the Cultural Revolution — are now very faded. In a neighborhood tea shop, old men and boys play Chinese chess in silent concentration. The scene is relaxed, but not somnolent as a similar scene would be in much of (non-Confucian) Asia. A basic web of organization undergirds the peace of the afternoon. People have the air of being about their business, even when their business is not work.

The houses are low and old and gray. Around a group of them runs a wall, with a door from the street every few yards, leading into secluded courtyards where green foliage sprouts against the gray. The roofs are in gray tile and there are gables. Now and then a gate is ornamented with stone lions or other beasts. Pink mimosas along the streets bring to life the dull walls and gates. Often I asked Chinese — generally officials — whether they personally prefer the traditional Chinese house with its court-yard, or the modern apartment house. Always the answer was the same, always it was animated. Of *course* the courtyard house is better. You have the marvelous well of light which a courtyard gives; and you have privacy.

Later I view the area from a taller building. These traditional Chinese houses look like flocks of gray cattle standing silently to-gether. Beyond them, amidst the trees, there gathers the orange profusion, layer after layer, of the glazed tile roofs of the pavil-ions and palaces in the Forbidden City. In the sunset rays, there is an effortless peacefulness about the scene. The past is heavy and not to be ignored, but it does not seem to intimidate the Chinese of today. It only lends a historical, almost a cosmic calm.

A friendly tension existed between the authorities and myself. Some things they apparently thought I did to excess ("min-gling"). Ruses were found to limit my mingling. At intermissions of a ballet or acrobatic show, I would be whisked to the luxury of a side room, to sit in boredom with my companions. Yet they did not make mingling impossible. At a Shanghai concert, I declined to enter the side room, smoked in the foyer, and watched an amusing and vigorous struggle by a hundred people to get tickets for the next performance. And often there was ban-ter about my waywardness. "Mr. Terrill, we have to protect you; please go by car." "But Mr. Wang, China is the 'safest country on earth'; I'm going to walk." Walk I did, and no hard feelings resulted.

The overnight trip to the delightful Ts'ung Hua hot springs near Canton was typical. It is a valley of tranquillity. Also a sen-sitive place. Leaders come to take rest and the waters. Kuo Mo-jo, after a tough time during the Cultural Revolution, came here to recover. A major army base nestles in the nearby hills. Both aspects — aesthetic, military — tickle the ear at 5:30 A.M. The air is rent not by "Sailing the Seas Depends upon the Helmsman" or "The East Is Red" (China's two inescapable political songs), but — long live Chairman Mao! — by a faultless trumpet rendition of reveille! No need here for a political message to nerve the soul at dawn.

Necessarily there are restraints. The scenery lures me for a walk. Yesterday's typhoon has left things fresh and beaten. Winds still bend the fine bamboos deeply to one side. A severed tree-portion leaps crazily along the river's broad white sandbank. A stone bridge squats comfortably across the blue-yellow waters. Higher up is a towering waterfall in jostling whiteness. "Like ten thousand horses galloping," wrote a T'ang poet. But wherever I walk, there is a People's Liberation Army man with boyish grin and fixed bayonet. "Back the other way." Well, it is a sensitive area, and they did not have to bring me here. There was, in sum, an openness and a practical root to nearly all the restraints that met me in China.

4. Seven Years Later

I wondered about differences from 1964. Of course the military are more prominent. Army men in baggy green uniforms, with a red star on the cap. Navy men, the same thing in blue-gray; you could mistake it for pajamas. Air force, blue trousers with green jacket. Curiously, police uniform is the same as air force — with one variation. The policeman's cap has a red circle, not a red star like the cap of the three services.

At White Cloud Airport in Canton, during long hours of waiting for a storm to clear, most of the passengers were military men. Indeed, the delay's consolation was a chance to chat nimbly with Chinese generals. Earthy, amiable, informal men. With a Szechwanese officer, I talk as we drink tea from porcelain mugs. The face is leathery, eyes deep-set, smile disarming. Trousers rolled up to the knee — but he rolls them down as I sit beside him. His floppy uniform bears no insignia of rank — these were abolished in 1965 — but I think he may be a general. Two aides are with him (their sandals are not the usual plastic, but leather). His wristwatch is not inexpensive. I ask him why clothes in China are so loose and big. Are these shapeless garments, I muse, designed to mask the human form and keep passion at a distance? His answer is different. "Tight clothes are no good for working in; loose clothes are." Stationed in Fukien, his business in life is to keep prepared against Chiang Kai-shek. His views on Chiang are not angry, just totally scornful. Yes, he said without zeal, China is stronger since the Cultural Revolution.

More roused, he explained how Szechwan is much prettier than
Kwangtung.

But what really stirred him was an Iraqi Airlines jet which
zoomed into the tranquil haze of the afternoon. With his colleagues (and nearly everyone else in the terminal), he dashed
outside to watch it land. China has no jets on commercial service
(though it possesses Tridents, and has just bought six more). PIA
(Pakistan) is the only airline which lands passenger jets at White
Cloud; the Iraqi plane was a "special," containing ministers. To
watch a big jet is quite something to a Chinese. Even to a general. "Not bad," he grinned as he sank back on a couch and
reached for his tea.

Not only do you see many military, you meet a lot in institutions. When the Cultural Revolution reached its pitch of factionalism, People's Liberation Army men went into factories and
schools. Mostly, they are still there — as politically reliable man-
agers. The (PLA) Chairman of the Revolutionary Committee at
the Peking Petroleum Refinery had, he told me, never been to
school. He learned all he knew in the "great school" of the Army.
Yet he now administered a factory with ten thousand workers.
Another PLA officer, a tough, cheery man who confessed his
total ignorance of medicine, was head of a Peking (Chinese-Medicine) hospital. His first act on coming to the hospital, others told
me, was to spur all personnel to more devoted service by offering his own body for experimentation. Acupuncture needles were
put three to four inches into him in a test to find the root of certain nerves. It was his way of living up to Mao's idea that the
whole nation should "learn from the PLA."

A third PLA officer, the new Minister of Foreign Trade, I
met with Mr. Whitlam. (Six of the eight ministers then identified
were military men.) Pai Hsiang-kuo is a practical man, who
showed a detailed grasp of Australia's trade position. In the
business talks, the word "capitalism" was never uttered, nor
Mao's name. Gentle in manner, yet strong in argument, Pai appeared for the sessions in army uniform, without mark of rank,
and left his cap on throughout. (Even at our meeting with Chou
En-lai, which he attended but without speaking, he never took

A commercial district in central Peking. The author took this picture in 1964. Unlike such scenes in 1971 (see photos, page 63), there are no political slogans; the notices are factual labels for the streets and enterprises. Ice-cream vendors (lower right) are even commoner today than seven years ago. Chinese milk consumption, in ice cream and other products, is rising sharply.

his cap off.) None of this military presence was evident seven years ago. Indeed, I can't remember a single conversation with a military man on the 1964 visit.

I found cultural life far more politicized. In 1964, I talked with the director of the Peking Library (which has some seven million volumes) and browsed in his library. I went to church services in Canton and Peking, and interviewed Chao Fu-san, a leader of Chinese Protestantism (his barbs against Russian divines and the World Council of Churches caused reverberations in church circles of various countries). This kind of thing was, in 1971, out of the question. Public libraries, and museums too, are closed. Churches are boarded up, empty, and checkered with political slogans. National religious organizations are "suspended," while religious workers undergo an indefinite phase of "struggle, criticism, and transformation." Chao Fu-san is "not available." In 1971, you simply do not find, as you could in 1964, segments of social and intellectual life around which the tentacles of politics have not curled.

The politicization has its visual testimony. Cities are striped red and white with slogans and quotations. It is hard to locate buildings, for during the Cultural Revolution their nameplates were mostly replaced with a (more or less appropriate) slogan. The Industrial Exhibition in Canton has on it simply: "Long Live Our Great Leader Mao Tse-tung." Since it is not the only big building which displays that irreproachable sentiment, the newcomer cannot easily find his way around. On Chinese commercial airplanes, the large red characters read: "Long Life to Our Great Leader Mao Tse-tung." Less noticeable, in smaller black characters, is the airline's name: "China Airlines." Even garden plots have been ingeniously planted in the shape of characters expressing a political message; the flowers in their beds must bend and sprout to uphold Chairman Mao!

Reaching Canton, I was hit by this political gaudiness. It looked as if the left wing of the Signwriters Union had taken over China! But the impact is a double one, and the second aspect is as striking as the first. The city is plastered with banners and posters. *But they are faded.* They date from 1966 to 1968.

There has been no apparent move to refurbish them. So Canton has a face of shabby militancy. Not having been there since 1964, I was struck by the plastering. Yet an Australian scholar (Stephen Fitzgerald) who had visited in 1968 was more struck by how much it has faded. The slogans are much less obtrusive in the life of the cities, he remarked, than three years ago.

One might welcome the fading of banners, as Fitzgerald did, because of the new political moderation it signifies. Aesthetically, however, it gives Canton a shabby, run-down look — like a city after a bad flood. Parks I had enjoyed in 1964 were now scrawny and overgrown. The beautiful grounds of the Sun Yat Sen University had not recently seen a hoe or a mower. The Cultural Park, a diverting place for Cantonese, is less well cared for. So is Shameen, the shaded haven isle which in colonial days gave secluded comfort to the British and French.

The Cultural Revolution, of course, accounts for this neglect. The former political boss in Canton, T'ao Chu, was attacked in 1967 for spending too much time and energy on prettifying Canton. He wanted, said his detractors, to impress foreign businessmen arriving for the Canton Fair, and the Hong Kong folk who come to visit their families. It was, Red Guards reasoned, a wrong use of time and resources.

But the greatest change since 1964 is a heightened sense of citizenship on the part of ordinary people. I am not saying people's minds are full of Mao's Thought — who knows what is in their minds? The point is not about political orthodoxy, but about sense of involvement. The lady from whose roadside stall I buy tea in Nanking knows which four provinces still have not established new Party Committees. Shopkeepers in Shanghai venture comment on world affairs. Singers and dancers in Yenan had been to Peking during the Cultural Revolution, and now had fresh interest in the capital and what goes on there. They quoted to me an adage of their province: *"ko shan, ko ho, pu ko yin"* ("separated by mountains, by rivers, but not from the voice of Peking"). It had, they said, a new meaning for them.

Drivers and Luxingshe aides showed no timidity or subservience — in 1964 there had been some. One morning in

Canton my driver launched into a discussion of how intellectuals should behave. I don't know if he had me in mind when he spoke of the uselessness of theoretical knowledge divorced from practice. "Some intellectuals are hopeless," he observed, "electrical engineers who can't replace a fuse." A Luxingshe aide in the north was no less forthright. Often he would proffer political views. They were straight from the *People's Daily;* yet the illustrations were his own.

One afternoon at the Tomb of Sun Yat-sen in Nanking, a small argument flickered (there were several arguments in Nanking; the air seemed tense for some reason). It concerned "local" newspapers — the Chinese use the word "local" (*ti-fang*) to apply to all papers other than the *People's Daily*. The day before, in Shanghai, I had tried to buy the *Wen Hui Pao,* a Shanghai paper. Six times at six newsstands I was refused it. "Foreigners," it was explained, "may not buy local newspapers." Well, at the Tomb in Nanking, an official happened to remark, in the course of a conversation about freedom in China, that a foreigner could buy "anything he likes." I refuted him with the Shanghai example — perhaps too vigorously. My Luxingshe aide, the junior man in the group, turned to me: "Mr. Terrill, you will learn more if you are modest." In 1964 I did not find such refreshing forthrightness.

There were other differences. Service frills had been cut here and there. No beer on the planes now. In 1964, I had drunk my way across the Gobi Desert on the plane from Irkutsk to Peking, with the dusty-flavored Tsingtao beer. In Peking, you can no longer dial from your hotel room for weather forecasts, theater tickets, or subscriptions to magazines. Yet for the Chinese themselves, variety of consumer goods may be wider. Clothing seems more colorful. More household utensils are available. Supermarkets have speeded matters for big-city shoppers — as often the husband as the wife. It is only an impression, but it seemed to me, judging by the crowded state of simple restaurants, that eating out has increased in the big cities.

These neighborhood eating houses are full of interest. Here is one in Shanghai's Nanking Road. It is in the middle of a shopping district, and people come in with bags and bundles — food, textiles, and now and then a camera, radio, or watch. Noodles (boiled or fried) are the specialty of the house. They are, of course, the preferred staple in Shanghai, as boiled rice is in South China. A hearty restaurant, a carrefour of gossip, noisy with chatter and laughter.

The range of diners reflects the relative prosperity of Shanghai, with its sophisticated industry and higher wages. Here are four men, colleagues it seems, who take their noodles swimming in soup (*t'ang mien*) and already have four empty beer bottles in front of them. Beside us a quiet couple, intellectuals carrying books whose titles I can't catch, who eat fried noodles (*ch'ao mien*) and later hefty slices of the universally popular watermelon.

Decor is at the level of a public toilet. Chairs are the old wooden kitchen variety, and the wooden floorboards are hospitable to many a splash or piece of food (but no cats or dogs or flies). It is all a little different from the fancy banquets our Shanghai hosts serve at the Peace Hotel. (For a big fish dish at these feasts, a battery is put in the fish's head, so that two bright electric eyes stare out at you, as if in protest, as you hack at the fish.) But the food is excellent. It costs us under Y3 (the yuan is forty cents) for two. To remember what dishes to bring to what table, waiters fix a numbered clothespin on a bowl in the center of the table: "7" is "noodles with fish," "16" is "chicken soup." No writing down is called for, and the evidence of what you've eaten and will pay for sits there as a row of pins; "7," "7," "16," "11," "4": total, Y2.90. Stacks of small red stickers hang on the walls. A notice says: if you have an illness, put a sticker in your bowl when finished, and special care will then be taken in washing the bowl.

In 1964, there was in Peking more sense of foreboding about the international scene. And today, where there is anxiety it seems to center on Russia, whereas in 1964 it centered on the United States. Some symbols sum up the change.

In 1964, I reached Peking the week after the clashes in the

Gulf of Tonkin. One of the first sights, as the plane from Russia slid over the lovely hills into the heat haze of the capital, was a vast mass rally. It was one of many in those weeks, at which a total of twenty million Chinese raised their voices and fists against U.S. actions in and off North Vietnam. The cloud of Vietnam, and even more important, foreboding that Washington might escalate the war into China's southern provinces, hung over the entire visit.

In 1971, foreboding is replaced by buoyancy. The only American missile talked about in Peking last summer was Henry Kissinger. And when war pokes its nose in, it is not from South Asia but from North Asia. The mounds of earth in the streets of the northern cities tell the story. The air-raid shelters are insurance against "our northern neighbor" — the Prime Minister's sardonic phrase, the night we met him, for the Soviet Union.

Today, China has attained, in reasonable degree, two goals it has long held most desirable. It is more *independent* than it has been since Liberation (and well before), and it is probably more *secure* than at any point since Liberation. To put a complex process briefly, until recently China has (since 1949) always felt itself beholden to the Soviet Union, or threatened by the United States (or the Soviet Union). Today, it is not at all beholden, and much less threatened.

It is perilous to generalize about conditions in China today; a striking impression is of variations up and down the nation.

• At Tsinghua University, a briefing for the visitor sounded like a lecture on the evils of Liu Shao-ch'i (so much so that an Australian trade unionist inquired with interest, "Does Mr. Liu come from this district?"). At Sun Yat Sen University in Canton, on the other hand, no one in several hours mentioned Liu, or revisionism, until I raised the topic myself. And then the answers were formal and without passion.

• In some towns (as Nanking), military men were much to the fore, in particular institutions, and in general. In others (as Shanghai), much less so: some institutions had no PLA men at all on the Revolutionary Committee which governed them.

• In Kwangtung province, the birth rate was given as 3 percent; in neighboring Hunan province, it was only 1.5 percent.

• In Sian, the visitor was strongly discouraged from mingling with crowds. In Shanghai he was perfectly free to do so.

• At the Clay and Plaster Figures Factory in Wusih, only "revolutionary" figures were to be found. "Scholars, beauties, generals, and emperors" are no longer produced, as they were before the Cultural Revolution. Yet at a Handicrafts Factory in Peking — where an ivory-carved memorial to the visit of the American Ping-Pong players was being prepared (see page 142) — I saw being fashioned just these decadent "scholars, beauties, generals, and emperors."

• One week in Peking, "Mr. Y" praised the straightforward simplicity of the captions and displays at the buildings in Shanghai where the CCP held its first Congress. When I visited the buildings, however, I found the exhibit being dismantled, "because it contains errors."

• In some places (as the Communications University in Sian), people looked blank when asked about the effects of the "Socialist Education Campaign" (a drive, mainly in the countryside, during the early 1960s). Yet at the Arts and Crafts Factory in Peking, a lot of convincing mention was made of the effect on the factory of this campaign.

A visit can bring into relief the sharp diversities of China (which our study of documentary sources does not always do). It is not trivial to stress these variations. The Chinese do some tasks well and others less well. Temperament in this province is not the same as temperament in that province. Remote parts of China — however faithfully they may speak Peking's phrases — do not always live as Peking lives. Moreover, a certain regional differentiation — and a rapid pace of change — may itself be a major characteristic of China since the Cultural Revolution. It is only an impression, but China seemed to me less uniform in 1971 than in 1964.

5. Driving in Shensi

The name "Yenan" rings with eloquent echoes down the corridors of Chinese communism's history. In this remote town the Long March ended in 1935. The infinitely longer march of building communism began. I was happy when the Foreign Ministry agreed without hesitation to let me go there. "It is good for you to get out to Shensi province," Mr. Ma Yu-chen adjudged. "Before you talk with leading figures, you must see places where the roots of the Chinese revolution lie." I followed the same route as the first visitors to Red Yenan in the 1930s. From Peking to the flat and dusty provincial capital of Sian. Then north by car to the loess hills and caves of Yenan.

We set out from the Sian Guest House after an ample lunch of steamed mutton (a specialty of Shensi). In one car was Hanoi's Consul in Peking, with an aide and a host from the Revolutionary Committee that runs the province. In another car I traveled with Mr. Chou Nan of the Foreign Ministry, Mr. Liu Ju-ts'ai of Luxingshe, and a second Shensi host.

The two Russian "Volgas" quickly trace an unimpeded way through Sian's symmetrical avenues. It is a regal old city, where many Chinese dynasties have had their capital. The city wall, some forty feet wide in charcoal-colored brick (dating from the Ming dynasty), is still visible here and there. Beside it runs a stream in which boys fish peacefully. Along the tree-lined streets swarm hand-drawn carts, bicycles, and pedicabs bearing either a passenger or goods on a tray. The low commercial and residential buildings are gray or beige, and the dirt lanes and surrounding wheat fields lend a dusty color tone. Against these subdued hues there leap out red-painted political slogans and notice boards. The people of Sian are tall, long and craggy of face, and forthright in manner. Some sense of their city's noble past seems to lend them a sturdy, unapologetic confidence. Since Liberation, Sian has been one of the inland cities that have benefited from Peking's policy of shifting enterprises from the east coast (thus reducing the lopsidedness that the Treaty Port decades introduced into China's economy). In 1949 Sian had 500,000 people (1.2 million in the environs); today it has 1.2 million (2.8 million in the environs).

Soon we pass through vegetable districts, and then find ourselves amidst gently undulating wheat fields. Poplars line the road. For beautification? More likely, it seems, to shade the asphalt road from sun which might melt it. No cars pass us, but many trucks. The big ones have leafy branches sticking up all around — maybe to keep the heat off the peasants who recline on top of the loads. One truck veers to left and right as it comes toward us. Our driver pulls quickly to one side and stops. As the truck sways by, its driver puts his head out the window and explains gaily, "I'm a learner!" We plan to drive five hours, then stop overnight, halfway to Yenan, at the market town of Huang Ling.

The river Wei appears, broad and majestic in the crawling flow of its muddy waters. The valley of the Wei River is the heartland of Chinese civilization. Here, not on the east coast well known to foreigners, Chinese culture took on its modes. Chou Nan is a scholar of classical Chinese — especially its poetry — and an excellent traveling companion for these parts. He quotes for us poems about the region. Li Po, the great poet and great drinker of the T'ang dynasty, is among his favorites. And he gives us a couplet from another T'ang poet, Chia Tao, to express the interconnection of all things. ("When the autumn winds ruffle the Wei, leaves fall upon the whole of Ch'angan [Sian].") It is an extraordinary sight to watch farmers getting in the wheat beside a delicate aqua and orange pagoda of seven balconies, twelve hundred years old. Is it from living in the shadow of such traditions that they get their deep gaze and simple grace?

Winding north from Sian, the slogans become less grandiose and more prosaic. Around Sian, the themes were often "imperialism" and the unity of all "workers of the world." But here it is "Plant for the sake of revolution," or "In agriculture learn from Ta Chai." (Ta Chai is a successful unit of a commune in Shansi province, held up for emulation.) Others deal with the importance of fertilizers and conservation. Few are freshly painted. Many of the more informal ones, scrawled at will on any available spot during the Cultural Revolution, have now faded.

Some are on notice boards. Especially in the villages, where they are generally headed *"tsui-kao jih-shih"* ("supreme instruction"). But many are woven more naturally into the environment. The mud walls which surround houses are a good spot for a lively exhortation. Circular white stones are set into the wall at two- or three-foot intervals. On each is painted a big red character. So the mud walls are alive with high-minded suggestions.

We pass one slogan on a roadside wall: "Long Live Chairman Mao Tse-tung." But the last character of the slogan is missing. A hole has been made in the wall to make way for a path where its round white tablet previously was. It seems a symbol of the workaday spirit in China at present. A path is more useful than one more slogan, so why not give it priority? Chairman Mao can best be honored not by "formalism" but by plain hard work.

On the walls of a sprawling complex of mud buildings I notice an intriguing sign. It reads: "This kind of training is good!" Then follows a number. I point it out and ask what it refers to. There is a pregnant silence as we drive past. Maybe it is a camp of correction for "remolding" errant urban elements? The Shensi comrade says with a frown that he has no idea what it could be.

In the Sian area, cotton is the number two crop after wheat. Further north where the land is less fertile there is more millet. "Rifles and millet" were memorably coupled as the twin meager resources of the Communist army in austere Yenan days. The main animal is a rather spindly sheep. Some are white, some are black; they are raised both for meat and wool. The scene is rich in yellow and various shades of green. The golden fields are dotted with red flags. These bear the emblem of the brigade (major unit of a commune) or the team (smaller unit) which is at work in that spot. The land in north Shensi is not unfertile, but the hills make cultivation difficult and the rainfall is uncertain. Before Liberation, famine often stalked the area. In the two years to 1929, for instance, no less than 2.5 million people in Shensi (almost one third of the province population) died of starvation. Peasants wear blue and white, and in the Shensi manner some put toweling around their heads. The conical straw hat is much less common than in the south. Girls are so rosy-cheeked they look made up for a theatrical performance.

The countryside is electrified, but power machines (tractors, harvesters) are rare. You realize why Chinese become so enthusiastic about tractor-making plants when you watch the tedious hand labor in these wheat fields, and picture the enormous difference tractors would make to the work. Even in the towns of T'ung Ch'uan ("copper river") and Huang Ling ("yellow tomb") there is no indoor plumbing. Donkeys are the draft animals. But men and women can often be seen pulling hand carts, especially near T'ung Ch'uan, where there are coal mines and brick kilns. (In the T'ang and Sung dynasties this district boasted famous pottery kilns, whose exquisite products exist today in museums across the world.) This is a new China in that socialism has replaced semifeudalism. Men work for a wage and share weal and woe in communes. But it is not yet a new China in the mode and rhythm of its productive life. Slogans urging "self-reliance" are everywhere. You realize — when you see the lack of technology — that these slogans are no mere ideological affectation, but a recognition of simple necessity.

As we drive, the official from Shensi talks about overall agricultural performance in the province. Grain output was 63 billion catties at Liberation (one catty is half a kilogram). By 1965 it was 100 billion catties. In 1970 the figure was 120 billion catties. It is steady progress. But it is not spectacular, considering that the present province's population of 21 million is almost double that at Liberation. Three factors have improved agriculture in Shensi in recent years: better seeds, more waterways, leveling of land. There has also been much success with localized experimentation since the Cultural Revolution. "One brigade," my host related, "found that by planting sweet potatoes by the whole potato rather than by the shoots, yield went up by 100 percent. This improvement now spreads all over the province."

I dozed for a while, and stirred to hear the others in interesting conversation. I was in the front seat with the driver. Mr. Chou, Mr. Liu, and the Shensi host chatted in the back seat. The usual topics recurred. Provincial variations; inquiries about families; stories about the vagaries of travel by road, train, and plane. They dealt with each other in complete equality. But what struck me were the long, keen exchanges on the theme of economic development. How backward China still is. How important it is for China's national pride to modernize the economy. Each would relate problems that he knew of, success stories he had come upon. They were talking not for my benefit — I probably appeared to be asleep — but because the issues of development interested them and mattered to them. These three men, at least, are modernizers as well as patriots.

After a pause, Mr. Chou asked the man from Sian, "Where were you during the Cultural Revolution?" The mood changed abruptly. The bubbling momentum of talk about steel and cotton gave way to subdued and fragmentary remarks. The Shensi official answered: "I was in Peking." But he offered no elaboration. They made noncommittal remarks about the period of the Cultural Revolution. You sensed them brooding a little, thinking their three sets of private thoughts. The conversation was not open and shared and spontaneous as it had been on cows and computers. Were the memories of the Cultural Revolution troubling?

Further north it gets cooler and more hilly. Every inch of land must here be utilized. Boys weed and prune with handclippers right up to the edge of the road. The hills are terraced (often sown with millet) and the soil is a brighter color. There is less wheat and more maize. The skin of the peasants is browner. North Shensi is one of the worst areas in China for erosion, and you see the two weapons used against it: terracing and tree-planting. Now and then, stopping to stretch our legs and drink a bottle of *ch'i-shui* (soft drink), we get into conversation with passersby amazed to see a *wai-kuo jen* (foreigner).

While we pause in a beautiful orange valley called *Chin-suo-kuan* (Golden Key Pass), two peasant boys come up to say hello. I ask them where they are from. "We came two years ago from Kiangsu." In China today you find a lot of such movement of people across provincial lines. We also come across eleven Middle School students sent here from Peking to gain "practical experience." As with the two boys from Kiangsu, it was the Cultural Revolution which triggered their transfer to a new province and a new life. The motivation is economic only in the most indirect sense. It is for political reasons that the scrambling has occurred. To keep the youth of China realistic. To teach them about their own amazingly varied country and its many problems. Ultimately, to ensure that the whole nation is united around its fundamental tasks.

By sunset our Volga cars roll up the dusty main street of Huang Ling (named "yellow tomb" because nearby lies the Tomb of the Yellow Emperor). It seems like a cheery work camp, but it is a district headquarters of some tens of thousands of people. There is industry — mainly related to minerals, and construction of a railroad north to Yenan — which operates by laborious methods. At the brick kiln there are no trucks for transport, let alone a branch railroad track. But many donkeys. In the main street, too, donkeys shuffle by pulling squeaking carts.

Children, looking very healthy and dressed in gaudy colors, toddle by in groups. Lots of people carry cabbages they have bought from a central supply which is spread out on the roadside in the Chinese manner. There is a cinema and a Cultural Palace for Workers. Also public toilets, which smell outrageously. Many buildings are mud with thatched roofs, though there are also some modest new apartment blocks. Loudspeakers play the familiar revolutionary operas and ballets. Close your eyes and all regional difference, all gap between city and country, vanishes. These opera-ballets, by bonds of melody and lyric, make the whole nation one vast audience of 800,000,000.

We spend the night in a Guest House consisting of caves surrounding a courtyard. It is the pride of Huang Ling, and though simple (no running water, no toilets), it is extremely comfortable. Eager girls serve us the kind of feast you soon accept as routine in China. It centered on millet soup and various forms and combinations of noodles. Local hosts chuckled when Mr. Liu, who is Cantonese, declined the noodles and asked for boiled rice.

The Vietnamese Consul was cordial, though our first exchange foundered on a linguistic *faux pas.* He asked about my politics. I replied using the Chinese phrase *Kung tang* which means "Labor party." But the Consul thought I put in a middle word, *ch'ang,* between *Kung* and *tang,* which makes the phrase not "Labor party" but "Communist party." The Consul murmured nice things about the Australian Communist party and made to embrace me. His aide broke in to correct matters. The Consul transmuted an embrace into a handshake.

The caves have stone floors and are beautifully cool. To wash, you carry a basin of water from the courtyard into your cave. Trying to sleep, I hear loud chopping sounds. Why are they chopping wood in midsummer? But the sound is not of chopping. It is of chess pieces being slammed down on the board. The Vietnamese Consul and Mr. Chou are playing China's favorite game, seated on tiny chairs just outside my cave. Between the cicadas and the Chinese chess, a night in Huang Ling is not as quiet as expected.

The next thing I hear — at 6:00 A.M. — is a hearty rendition of "Sailing the Seas Depends upon the Helmsman." Loudspeakers carry it to every corner of the town. An ancient Chinese saying runs: "Rise at dawn and sweep the courtyard." This is just what the red-cheeked girls of the Guest House do. They work with discipline, yet also with a gaiety that is infectious — even at dawn. Before breakfast I wander out the gate of the Guest House, and turn into a side street. People are already at work though it is not yet seven. Mr. Chou soon appears, and we then turn around and wander straight back to the Guest House.

At breakfast the drivers join fully in the conversation. Each Chinese at the table is from a different province, and the talk is about regional quirks of food, accent, and custom. It is surprising how often conversation in China turns on these themes. I have stressed the "mental unity" in China today, and the deeply felt national pride. Yet equal stress must go on the cultural variations in this nation which is the size of the continent of Europe (and far more populous than the whole of Europe including the Soviet Union).

Before continuing toward Yenan, we go in sacred silence to salute the Yellow Emperor (Huang Ti). His Tomb is among gnarled old cypress trees on a hill above Huang Ling. One's sense of China's fantastic past is made acute by the mound opposite the Tomb. It was built by Emperor Wu of the Han dynasty, to mark a visit he made to the revered spot. Wu's dates are 141 B.C. to 87 B.C. He visited the mound where we stood that morning 2,100 years ago. Yet at least as long a stretch of time separates Han Wu Ti from Huang Ti as separates ourselves from Han Wu Ti!

On the way up to the Tomb is a temple dedicated to this legendary emperor (who is said to have reigned during the third millenium B.C.). The Communist government has restored it in careful and tasteful fashion. Many a stele (upright slab with inscription) has been put here by later emperors to honor Huang Ti and his supposed invention of pottery, the working of metal, and the wheel. It is startling to find one stele among them dated 1959. Here, in handwriting of Kuo Mo-jo done in 1958, is Communist China's own respectful glance back to antiquity. Its tone is nationalistic. Kuo's stele describes Huang Ti as "father of the Han people." I ask the Shensi official what effect the Cultural Revolution had on the way this historical site is viewed. His answer is out of no Marxist catechism. "The Cultural Revolution gave us a fresh appreciation of what a very ancient civilization China has."

As we stroll in the cobbled courtyard of the temple, the mood of contemplation is broken by a messenger. Up he dashes like a boy in ancient Sparta bearing news. He holds aloft a washcloth that someone has left in his cave at the Guest House. Nothing must be lost by the visitor to socialist China! Everyone has

turned from the steles and stares at the cloth. It was mine, and
there was no choice but to step forward meekly and claim it. I
had nowhere to put a wet facecloth at that stage of the morning,
but considerations of principle outweighed logistical detail.
Thenceforth I guarded it like a precious gem. It is embarrassing
to have one's carelessness shown up by the fantastic carefulness
of conduct in China today. The messenger brushed aside my
thanks. He got on his bicycle and pedaled back to the Guest
House as suddenly as he had come.

The road to Yenan led on through gorges of orange clay. It is
now unpaved, and deeply corrugated. There are trickling rivers,
almost lost in wide sandy beds. The water is sometimes jade-col-
ored with the reflection of gray-green trees that dot the banks. At
one river, history constrained us to stop.

The Chiehtse River is no surging torrent but it is famous.
During the war against Japan, it marked a boundary between
Mao's part of China and Chiang's part of China. It was a line
that separated China's recent past from China's emerging future.
South of the river was Chiang's faltering county of Loch'uan.
North of it was Mao's poor but vibrant Fuhsien County. Across
it many a human (and journalistic) drama unfolded. Mao wrote
of the Chiehtse at the time: "North and south of the river are
two different worlds." But today the river witnesses no drama
and forms no demarcation. A concrete tablet stands on the river-
bank. It bears the text of Mao's telegram in October, 1949,
thanking Yenan comrades for their message of congratulation on
the founding of the new regime in Peking. On one side of the
tablet, Mao himself has scrawled a handwritten exhortation:
"Bring the glorification of the revolutionary tradition to new
heights."

We pass a slogan that heralds the proximity of Yenan: "Hold
the Spirit of Yenan Forever Bright." But today "Yenan" is not
merely a town. Nor is it a special world of its own as in the heroic days when Mao, Chou, and others were molded. For today
Yenan is simply part of China, and all of China is a Yenan. We
also pass the site of one of the CCP's notable meetings in the
days of the anti-Japan war. It is a collection of long low mud

huts on a barren hillside. Here the enlarged Political Bureau met in 1937, and Mao wrote his essay "For the Mobilization of All the Nation's Forces for Victory in the War of Resistance."

We reach the town of Fuhsien — a single main street, tiled roofs in the Chinese style, *men* nursing babies — and soon the light fades and the smell of rain grows stronger than the smell of dust. Eerie shadows stretch like a tangible gray mass across the valleys. A flock of black mountain sheep shelter from the rain against a rocky hill face, tended by a wizened shepherd with a face like a copper pot. Peasants run at a trot along the road with spades and picks on their shoulders. Some straggle, unconcerned, and the drenched blue cloth of their smocks sticks to them as a second skin. The dull light now has a bronze glow, refracted from the wet red soil of the hills.

I had read of erosion in north Shensi, but now it is a living process before our eyes. The hills are alive with rushing concourses of water, as if a mass of rusty-red giant serpents writhes downwards toward the embattled valleys. The river which was just now a trickle swirls angrily. Thunder drowns out our words of gingerly speculation. In a moment we face an amber torrent, like a rich caramel custard poured across the road. The driver of the Vietnamese Consul's car is ahead. He hesitates. Then his engine roars and he goes at the water. The Volga shakes like a toy — but both cars get through. We are all silent now. The driver is the only man in the car who counts. None of the intellectuals beside and behind him have any advice to offer. Only Mr. Chou breaks the human silence. He recalls a line from the philosopher Lao Tzu to cheer us, and pronounces it with his usual confidence: "The heavier the rain, the shorter it lasts."

A few miles back a spill of rocks had protruded onto the road. On the rock nearest the passing traffic an old man was curled in peaceful sleep. But now all tranquillity has gone. Rocks tumble down upon the road regularly. The driver is fearful of landslides and rockslides. He asks himself aloud whether he ought to stop. Even the unflappable Mr. Chou has a slightly furrowed brow. The driver's question proves academic. We turn a curve and find the way barred by a jagged red hillock of rocks. The cars draw up before it, helpless like two beggars at nature's gate.

Lao Tzu's maxim is not going to help us move those rocks. We get out to start the job. Except for the Vietnamese Consul, who remains sitting in his car. I enjoyed myself; but even if I hadn't, I would not have risked looking like an unrectified intellectual inside the car. The drivers confer and decide not to try and remove the pile of rocks. They will rather level it off to a mound which the cars, by getting up speed, can drive up and over. It is an excellent idea. We remove the highest rocks and flatten the lower ones. The two drivers direct operations with resource and humor. We are soaked to the skin, and our legs are splashed red to the knee from the mud. After half an hour the heap of rocks has become an undulating curve. Two trucks which have approached from the other side will test it first, and try to flatten it a little more. It works. Like a buckjumper on a steer we negotiate our "remolded landslide." What happened to later traffic I don't know; we drove on much relieved to Yenan.

Yenan was well worth the journey. Cradle of Mao's revolution, this town evokes the austere, comradely, nonurban ambience of Chinese communism in its formative years. Its forty thousand people share a valley of intimacy and peace surrounded by steep golden mountains. The houses are simple, half-lit through windows made not of glass but of thin pale paper. The streets are rude, dusty tracks. Bicycles ply their way; a few donkey carts amble by; now and then there is a truck. The people are dark skinned, dressed in blue costumes, extremely friendly. I stroll in the lively *hu t'ung* at dusk and catch the beautiful smell of corn being cooked. A small child suddenly looks up at me; she sees I am a foreigner and screams. After a moment of embarrassment I feel pleasure. The spontaneity is refreshing after the formalism of the atmosphere in Sian.

You see the places where the CCP leaders worked and lived in the grim, heroic days of the war against Japan. Here is the meeting room of the Political Bureau. The floor is stone, the walls mud, the windows an airy void. There are wicker armchairs with blue cushions, little tables with teapots and cups. Nearby is a Ping-Pong room, where the leaders tried their hand between sessions. The hall of the Military Affairs Commission, built by the cadres themselves, is a delightful building, with a ceiling of crisscrossed bamboo beams and rows of roughly hewn benches and tables in local wood. The ballot box inside is decorated with a hammer and sickle.

We stand on the spot where Mao gave his speech "Combat Liberalism." Stroll to the hillside where he read a draft of the famous essay "Serve the People." Inspect the table where he sat with Norman Bethune. Lounge on the stone blocks where he gave an interview to Anna Louise Strong. It is moving on this still, cool morning to tread the ground where today's China was seeded; the caves where Mao added the arts of government to the arts of the guerrilla; the valley in which hope pushed through against hopelessness.

The former houses of the CCP leaders were stone-floored caves set into the hills. I visit Mao's first cave, which he had to leave after the first phase of Japanese bombing. His writing desk, his washing bowl, his *k'ang*. The second cave, where he tended a vegetable patch as a break from meetings and writing. The third, in a date orchard, where peasants came in the evening to talk to him about their farming, and he broached for them the future of China. Sometimes they would bring him steamed bread, baked in the shape of a peach, which symbolizes longevity. Sometimes they would greet him with drums and gongs. We see also his fourth house, to which he moved in the grimmest days in order to be near the Military Affairs Commission.

In this fourth place Mao made one of his great and characteristic decisions. To abandon Yenan. Many did not want to do it. Was not Yenan the symbol of the revolution? But Mao, who had himself spoken with emotion of the "caves of Yenan," showed masterly suppleness of mind. It is important to defend Yenan, he conceded. But the whole of China is more important than Yenan. Why not leave it to the enemy? It is after all only caves. When we come back we can build much better things. Mao's realism overruled sentiment. And just as well. For when the decision to abandon Yenan was taken, the Kuomintang forces in the area were some ten times as strong as CCP forces.

In Yenan, you recall that "self-reliance" is no ideal doctrine

(ABOVE) Sunday afternoon at a hot spring resort near Sian. Here Chiang Kai-shek was captured by his own forces, in the "Sian Incident" of 1936. (BELOW) At the cave-town of Yenan, where the Chinese Communist movement was based after the Long March. The author points to a plaque reading: "The former house of Premier Chou En-lai." Notice the star (representing the red star of the Chinese Communist party) at the center of the paper-filled windows.

chosen from a gallery of alternatives. It was Mao's way of using weakness as a springboard to strength. In those days the CCP had nothing. They made their own soap. Cadres built meeting rooms with their own hands before they sat in them to plan for China's future. Paper was in chronically short supply. At the Anti-Japanese University, students would sometimes have to write in the sand; cork would now and then be available as a substitute for paper. About the only industry in the town was a match factory. (I had often wondered why in Yenan, on the occasion of important Party meetings, commemorative matchboxes were produced; I suppose because it was the only manufactured item that *could* be produced.) There were so few clocks and watches that the usual method of telling the time was a primitive sundial. Yet this is the town where Mao wrote 92 of the 158 items in his *Selected Works*.

Much that Mao counts as virtue, you realize when visiting Yenan, was evolved out of sheer necessity. The Anti-Japanese University was simple and ardent. You read a book with one hand and grew cabbages with the other. Military spirit was to the fore. There was no "nonsense" about "research for its own sake." Since the Cultural Revolution, Mao seeks to make all China's universities follow this pattern. Yenan was small enough for Mao to have direct, affective contact with his people. It was a town Rousseau would have liked. It had the "natural" spirit Rousseau extolled. In the Cultural Revolution, Mao tried to bring back this ideal of direct participation. He is restive with bureaucracies that arise (unsurprisingly) to cope with organizing 800,000,000 people. He would like the Party to be the spiritual power it was in the town of Yenan. He cherishes leaders who are still tribunes of the people, and have not become desiccated organization men.

A slight illness took my mind momentarily off history, and brought great care and kindness from Yenan hosts. A doctor wearing a badge of Chairman Mao comes to see what is up. As the doctor examines me — in the usual Chinese way he puts the thermometer in the armpit — Mr. Chou, Mr. Liu, and Yenan friends gather around the bed discussing my condition in realistic detail. The doctor's pattern of training is typical of his generation (now in its forties). First he studied Western medicine (at Harbin); later he studied Chinese medicine (at Chengtu). He now blends the two styles, which is current practice. "Which medicine do you want?" he asks me gravely. "Western or Chinese?" Lying hot and weak, I have no views on this matter. "Whichever promises the quickest recovery." He gives me a final summarizing glance and announces: "I'll give you some of each." So I drink chrysanthemums soaked in a porcelain mug of hot water, and swallow Western drugs in tablet form.

A special song and dance performance was due that evening, and I decided I should not miss it. At the end of the show the doctor appeared from the crowd. He had attended especially to keep an eye on me. Back at the Guest House, he did a blood test and we talked. I had found one or two of the evening's songs tediously political. He defended them. But is *everything* political, I inquired: "Is your reason for tending me political?" He vigorously affirmed that it was. "I treat you as best I can because it is my internationalist duty to do so." He spoke softly and with sincerity. "Our whole system of medicine in China," he added, "derives from socialism. Only with socialism, is there medical care at the best level available for whoever needs it." I think the doctor was entirely right. Yet I also think his motive in treating me as kindly as he did was in part simple human compassion.

We did not return to Sian the way we came. There is no regular plane service to Yenan — nor any rail connection — but a special plane materialized to take some Japanese and myself back to the provincial capital. Throughout the morning there were consultations about the best time for departure. Chinese pilots are extremely cautious and do not fly if the weather is at all poor. Word comes that the morning rain has cleared, and as more is expected in the evening, the flight will depart after lunch. The tiny plane is an Ilyushin 14, built in China. You climb into it as into a hammock.

A young girl tells us the flight to Sian will take eighty minutes, and that photos should not be taken from the plane. No political quotations come with her remarks. As we roar up over the

Shensi hills, she brings cigarettes (what smokers the Chinese are!), orangeade, peanuts, sweets, chewing gum, and notebooks with the calligraphy of Mao on the cover. We reach the plains north of Sian, and cross the yellow and pale blue waters of the river Wei. Clusters of green dot the land as Sian approaches. Soon chimneys swing into view, and the gray-green tiles of this stately town. It seemed like cheating to swoop back to Sian as fast as this, after the laborious drive north to Yenan two days before.

6. The "Cult" and "Ultraleftism"

One morning in Peking, I talked about trends in China with an official (he once worked as a journalist in New York) senior enough to speak his mind. For three hours we sat on a vast white couch, then at a nearby table where one reckless dish after the other was relayed by wide-eyed boys. Mr. Y — I cannot use his name — suddenly asked me: "What do you think of the propaganda?" Unsure of his line of thought, I murmured an inconsequential remark. "I think it's awful," he resumed, screwing up his face. "It's boastful. And too many adjectives and adverbs. Take the exhibits at Shaoshan [Mao's birthplace]. They are overdone. And why must it end with the atom bomb — as if the point of the revolution was to make the bomb!" My own tongue was loosened by his remarks; I added criticisms. "But you know," Mr. Y continued, "it's not as bad as it was."

That is true. Giant-sized white plaster statues of Mao have come down in Peking and other cities. His photo no longer adorns the daily Hsinhua news bulletin. During the superenthusiasm of the Cultural Revolution, it was not uncommon for people to wear two, three, or even four badges of Chairman Mao. Today it is common to find people without even one badge. The *Red Book,* you might say, has given way to books. (A statistic got in Sian shows how far the glorifying of Mao went: during the Cultural Revolution, in Shensi province — whose population is about 21 million — 100 million copies of works of Mao were published!) And not only books by Mao. A driver in Canton has Engels' *Anti-Dühring.* No longer do sessions at factories and

61

communes and flights on planes begin and end with readings from Mao, as they did during the Cultural Revolution. Study has gained an edge on incantation. A workaday spirit has squeezed out rhetorical excess.

I stumbled across two startling examples of the trend. On Peking's Street of Eternal Revolution are the offices of the Municipal Revolutionary Committee. In the late-afternoon rays, as Peking sang with the bicycle bells of people riding home, I passed this building on my way to dine at Rewi Alley's house almost next door. Behold, four workmen were swiftly removing the huge Mao portrait from over the doorway! Random thoughts peppered my mind. A *coup* in the Revolutionary Committee? Making way for a *larger* portrait? Neither. Part of a general winding down of the personal display of Mao and his aphorisms.

Another afternoon, I returned to the Peking Hotel after a visit to the Peking Petroleum Refinery. On our sixth floor, the smell of fresh paint. Two quotations from Mao, in white upon red, had been painted out since lunch. I almost missed them, so cheery had they been beside the dark panels. But no replacement went up in ensuing days. Maybe the exhortation had won its incarnation in labor — the word become flesh.

Of course, slogans and quotations still abound in China, and I often puzzled over what relation the propaganda has to the worker's daily round. One Sunday afternoon I was sitting in my room at the Hsin Ch'iao Hotel, after a morning at the Ming Tombs. In the golden sunshine, the trees of the Legation Quarter made dappled pools of light and shade on the warm asphalt roads. It is 5:30 P.M. People meander home from diversions in the parks, from swimming in the splendid new pool nearby. Others are back from shopping trips in Wang Fu Ching street, with bulging shopping bags and smiles of satisfaction. Most wear blue shorts, white shirts, and plastic sandals. Out of a taxi hops a Chinese official, and disappears into the hotel. Then President Ceaucescu's car drives by. He has also been at the Ming Tombs today, and now returns to the Rumanian Embassy which is in the same street as the Hsin Ch'iao.

On the radio there suddenly bursts forth the "Red Guard Pro-

Doorway of the "Peking Chinese-Medicine Hospital" where acupuncture is practiced and medicines are generally Chinese traditional herbs. The two large billboards read: "Long live Chairman Mao" (left) and "Long live the Chinese Communist party" (right).

From the bell tower in downtown Sian, a view of a public building of the post-Liberation style, typically ornamented with pictures of Chairman Mao. The large notice reads: "Long live our great teacher, leader, commander, and helmsman Chairman Mao."

gram." For a moment it seems almost comically incongruous.
The tone is shrill, and there are constant broadsides against enemies. Sitting there in my room, two quite different ways of sum-
ming up the mood presented themselves. Listen to the radio:
here is China as "Mao Tse-tung Thought." Look out the window: here is China as a simple Sunday afternoon. Is it two
worlds? No, it is one.

I listened further to the Red Guards. It was really a civics
program. News from Ta Chai, and descriptions of this model village's achievements; debates between one group of Red Guards
and another; announcements about forthcoming community activities; uplifting messages to encourage better citizenship. It
comes in the form of Mao Tse-tung Thought, I reflected, because
*it has to be given a dramatized form if it is to reach 800,000,000
people.*

Given the size of the population (and the divisions of this far-
flung nation), myth is a necessary tool for a strong government.
Of course, it need not be this particular myth of Mao Tse-tung
Thought. But some myth is required, if the "Sunday afternoons"
of the 800,000,000 are to fit together in a workable, prosperous
organism. Especially since the Chinese government aims not only
at being a strong government, but at making an egalitarian
China. Ultimately, the point of the propaganda is to make equal
citizens of the entire 800,000,000.

Another related current trend in China is criticism of "ultraleftism." That may seem puzzling; is not Mao an . . . ? The
point is, ultraleftism had its day, when the main job was putting
down "revisionists," but that day is past. Yesterday a weapon,
today a target. The rebels have been called off, damped down.
The order of the day is noses to the grindstone of productive
work. Has the wind changed because the Cultural Revolution
succeeded, and now it's back to routine? Or because the "line"
of the Cultural Revolution was utopian, did not work, and had to
be replaced by a rebuilding of the Party along old lines, and by a
dispersal of the hot rebels to turning lathes and feeding pigs?
Here I can only describe the fresh mood.

At the Red Star commune near Peking, I saw a laundry. But

it was not a laundry. Those were not clothes pegged to a line, but *ta tzu pao,* posters newly done in black on green paper. Members of the brigade had written them willy-nilly and awaited responses from the Party Committee. I had time to read only three before companions led me elsewhere. The theme was unmistakable: "AND WHAT OF THE ULTRALEFTISTS? WHAT WERE THEY DOING DURING THE CULTURAL REVOLUTION? THEY WERE NOT AT WORK — WHAT WERE THEY DOING?" Little doubt but that they were demonstrating. Coursing up and down China lighting fires of revolution.

One of these *ta tzu pao* is worth pausing over as an instance of a widespread line of criticism of ultraleftists. It was too long to read on the spot, but I photographed it — with the permission of commune members — and read it later at leisure. In the usual way it starts with a "supreme directive" from Mao, then applies it to a concrete case. The directive urges citizens to "defeat and smash the antirevolutionary, conspiratorial organization, May 16." * The text is then headed: "A bad element has infiltrated the Red Star commune — Wang Hsu-tung." The peasant who wrote this *ta tzu pao* announces that he is going to "speak up." It is wrong, he thinks, that amidst the struggle against May 16, "our factory [one of the commune's small-scale plants] is still stagnating in silence." He says "it is an illusion to suppose that if nobody says anything, that means there is nothing to be exposed."

The writer of the *ta tzu pao* chooses to expose a student whom he suspects of extremism. Wang Hsu-tung is a "self-proclaimed student" from a technical institute who "wears glasses" and "first came to our commune toward the end of 1966." He is denigrated as a "mysterious character." He "went out early in the morning" from the high school dormitory where he slept, and "came back late at night. . . . Obviously he was engaging in some conspiratorial activities." And now the pith of the case against Wang: "He divided the people," and he was "the main cause of the vio-

* The "May 16" organization was an extreme-left network which — it is now claimed — mouthed Mao's line but actually opposed it and even planned (in 1967) a *coup.*

lent struggle that occurred in various of our factories." This rather angry literary assault, scrawled in lively prose with a black brush on green paper, was one of many against suspected "May 16" elements at the Red Star commune.

I doubt that those posters would have been written if the Party did not welcome their message. In fact, the message is omnipresent in China. In schools, you are told that ultraleftists wanted to do without teachers altogether. Some urged an end to universities, saying simply that life is the classroom. Some said you learn *only* by practice — theory is useless. These ideas are now all rejected.

At the Number 61 Middle School in Canton, it seemed that even some of Mao's own (more "leftist") ideas about education are pruned in their application. The chairman of the School's Revolutionary Committee — one of the few white-haired men I met in China — referred to "naughty" pupils. What do they do wrong? "Well, they come late to class — and they leave very early." I quoted Mao, who said if a student is bored let him leave the class; that is all right. There was laughter at the table, some of it a bit nervous. How would the jovial Hunanese chairman meet this? He spoke with a touch of intimacy, his tone an appeal to common sense. "Look, if the teacher is really bad, pupils may leave. But they must come back."

At Tsinghua University, a conversation reflected the trend of the times. Political workers who briefed our Australian group showed an ideological zeal that seemed to border on ultraleftism. One of them, responding to a question, said China had no need of intellectual exchanges with other countries; all necessary knowledge existed within China. Surprised by this, the visitors queried the answer, and some argument ensued.

The zealous cadre with gleaming eyes appeared to be out of line with Mao's view, which is that good things can and ought to be selected from abroad (and from the past). As tension rose, a Chinese Foreign Ministry official, who was accompanying the visitors to the university, intervened to contradict the Tsinghua spokesman. He referred to my interview with Kuo Mo-jo some days before (at which he had been present). "Kuo Mo-jo, President of the Academy of Sciences, said this week in an interview with Mr. Terrill that there *should* be and *will* be international exchange of scholars between China and other countries." He turned to me with a certain air of triumph: "Is that correct, Mr. Terrill?" The Tsinghua spokesman looked uncomfortable. The Ministry official had seemingly invoked Mr. Kuo to damp down an ultraleftist error.

In factories, students are often the target when ultraleftism is criticized. I found this especially so in the smaller cities. "They lacked experience." "Easily deceived." "Bad elements led them to extremes." The "bad elements" are usually identified as those in "May 16." They are to be distinguished from ultraleftists, in most explanations, but not all, by three points. They were an organized conspiracy, not merely, like the hotheads, a wind blowing where it listeth. The contradictions between them and the people are "antagonistic"; between ultraleftists and the people, the contradictions are "nonantagonistic." Third, the May 16 group took armed struggle to the point of committing criminal offenses.

At a Nanking factory I came across an example. A PLA officer, sent to meld the factions, had been kidnapped and held for three days by elements now suspected of being "May 16." In this factory, I saw a freshly written *ta tzu pao* which aggressively inquired: "Where do the May 16 elements think they can hide?" Many of the factory's workshops were plastered with the slogan *"i-ta san-fan"* ("one hit, three antis"). Counterrevolution is to be hit; corruption and graft, speculation, and waste are to be opposed. The interesting thing was that the slogan — which is susceptible of either antirightist or antileftist application — was being used overwhelmingly against ultraleftists.

Nationally, the tone was set during my visit by the trial at two public meetings of the "Red Diplomat," Yao Teng-shan. Yao had crossed the threshold into crime by burning the British Office in Peking in 1967. This was not his only crime — Yao even detained Chou En-lai during the former's giddy weeks of power as "head" of the Foreign Ministry in the summer of 1967. But the British Office affair has been made a symbol of leftist excess. No opportunity was missed in my presence to condemn it.

The French Ambassador, Etienne Manac'h, told me how Mao

himself raised the matter in conversation. Maurice Couve de Murville was in China, and Manac'h went with him to see the Chairman. "Were you in Peking when the British Office was burned?" Mao asked Manac'h. No. "Were any of your present staff?" No, a complete turnover of Embassy staff had occurred since then. Mao persisted. "Well, you must have *read* about the incident?" He wanted to speak of it. He criticized it as "indefensible." It is ultraleftism, he said; "I myself am a center-leftist."

In Canton, I found signs of retreat from leftism, in the social style with which I was received. During the Cultural Revolution, T'ao Chu, the leading political figure of Canton, was attacked for the error of spending time and money on entertainments, catering, and beautification, in order to impress visitors to South China. T'ao Chu's civic zeal was brought to mind by an exchange at a banquet in Canton the evening before I left China.

The restaurant, one of China's finest, was the famous P'an Ch'i (now Yu I, "Friendship"). Its elegant balconies, furnished in ebony and mother-of-pearl, overlook a lake bordered with willows. Some quite fantastic sweetmeats were being served. One especially took my fancy — a spiced coconut puree wrapped in a hot pancake — and I ate several. The host, himself a hearty eater, tried to broaden my approach. "Do you know, Mr. Terrill, this restaurant has more than *one hundred* varieties of sweet cakes. Recently some foreign businessmen could hardly believe this. So I ordered all one hundred kinds brought to the table!" Mr. Yang was ready to do the same for me, but my stomach was not equal to the challenge. Yet what price T'ao Chu's "errors"? Was not Cantonese chauvinism rearing its delightful head once more? I realized, again, that much backpedaling has taken place since the excessive leftism of the Cultural Revolution.

7. Kuo Mo-jo on Cultural Life

New shoots appear in intellectual life, after the winter blight of the Cultural Revolution. Some of them were spoken of in an interview — reported in *People's Daily* and other organs within China — given me by the leading intellectual of the Chinese government, Kuo Mo-jo, Vice-president of the Standing Committee of the Congress, and President of the Chinese Academy of Sciences. A rich, in some ways theatrical, personality, Kuo has trailed an astonishing array of writings and cultural activities (as well as having been Vice-premier), and is now one of the most prominent members of the regime.

He has the square, rugged Szechwan face; bright, emotional eyes — more so when he takes off his glasses. Heavy lines arch between eyes and nose, and two more curve down from nose to mouth. His hair is receding, and he relies on a hearing aid. The strongest impression of his mind is of facility, suppleness. To use favorite Chinese images, he seems a willow, not a pine. Several aides were with him, as were several officials from the Foreign Ministry with me. Kuo fascinated the whole circle. Tossing out puns and rhymes, he seemed conscious of addressing not only his interviewer, but the circle of assistants who listened to him with awe. He has been called a "cultivated leopard"; I saw mainly the cultivation, but glimpsed the leopard.

Photos were taken in the foyer, beside wrought iron wall pictures and calligraphy in the style of Anhwei province. Kuo signaled the taking off of jackets — leaving him in gray trousers and a white cotton shirt — and we sat down in the cavernous splendor of the Great Hall of the People and talked (through interpreters) for almost three hours. Nearly eighty, Kuo looked at me and said, "You are like the rising sun at eight." Since the Cultural Revolution, "young" (up to thirty-five), "medium-age" (thirty-six to fifty-five), and "old" work together in China as a "three-way combination" on many tasks. "I suggested to Chou En-lai," joked Kuo, "that we need to add a fourth category for those over seventy-five — 'superold.' But he thought it sounded too much like superpower!"

Kuo Mo-jo is considered a romantic, which seems indeed to be true. I asked him if he was still interested in any of the European writers he once devoured and translated, including Goethe and Nietzsche. "The poems of Goethe are good," he replied, "but the man I really like is Shelley." He confessed regard for another romantic work. "The *Rubaiyat of Omar Khayyám* is also wonderful. You know it is rather similar to the poetry of Li Po [a famous poet of the T'ang Dynasty]. Not in subject matter — Li Po didn't just write of wine and women — but in style." Mr. Kuo was starting to talk with some verve. But then he stopped. "We do not read any of these people nowadays . . ."

The President of the Academy of Sciences acknowledged that research had been affected by the Cultural Revolution. The scientific sections never stopped work. But the humanistic and social-science sections have been suspended for a period of "struggle, criticism, and transformation" — with the interesting exception of archaeology. Digging for national treasures went on through the turmoil. It even benefited at times, as Red Guards, coursing through the country, hit upon the edge or sign of an unearthed piece. Mr. Kuo talked with an antiquarian's enthusiasm of the finds in the Cultural Revolution period, an exhibition of which I previewed that morning in the Forbidden City. Of many of them — one superb jade "death-suit" from the Han dynasty, its tiny green pieces stitched together with wire of pure gold — he had read and written, but now could examine for the first time.

Research in all fields is poised for fresh advances. Kuo announced a new phase in the remarkable story of Chinese research on insulin. In 1966 insulin was synthesized, in work done jointly at the Academy and Peking University. Now the second stage, structural analysis of insulin, has been completed. It began in 1967, and was done in the Institutes of Organic Chemistry and Biochemistry of the Academy. Amino acids have been synthesized, surpassing even the work done by Hawkins in Britain. Important implications follow for our understanding of the origin of life. The results of the second stage, Mr. Kuo told me, were assessed at a meeting on July 15. They will soon be made public in detail.

The Chinese cultural statesman also unveiled a reorganization of the Academy. Dire rumors have circulated about the fate of the Academy. The facts are these. In accordance with a general principle of the period since the Cultural Revolution, the Academy is being drastically decentralized. Mao's idea, Kuo reminded me, is that initiative should always be a double thing: from above and from below at the same time. "China is so vast. We have found that you cannot do everything from the center." Sixty of the Academy's one hundred research institutes are being thrown down to "root levels" (under the authority of the provincial Revolutionary Committee), or shifted to "other organizations" (the Army; productive agencies). Sections outside Peking which were formerly "branches" will now be under local authority, though "overall policy" will be set by the Academy. A further twenty research institutes will henceforth be under "dual leadership," central and local together. The remaining twenty will remain with the Academy in Peking as in the past. The effect, it is hoped, will be a better integration than before of research with its application in the practical tasks facing the Chinese nation. Later in Canton, a biologist at Sun Yat Sen University confirmed that three Institutes — Microbiology, Entomology, Botany — are now under Kwangtung provincial authority, no longer under the Academy at Peking.

From Mr. Kuo (and other high sources) came news of further activity in research and publication. The *Modern History* by Fan Wen-lan, distinguished historian who died two years ago, is being revised and augmented by new chapters. The work is proceeding in the Institute of Modern History of the Academy and will appear before long. The archaeological journals, *Kao-ku* and *Wen-wu,* will shortly resume publication. A large new batch of the writings of Lu Hsun is on the way.

"Normal" intellectual contacts between China and other nations, Mr. Kuo explained — "students, lecturers, materials" — will be resumed as "struggle, criticism, and transformation" are wound up. I was not entirely reassured by the way he phrased the government's future intention: "We will give new assignments to those who have remolded themselves well." But it was interesting, and a fresh piece of information, that religious organizations have not been done away with, but only "suspended" for the duration of struggle, criticism, and transformation. Chinese delegates will soon be selected to go to international conferences of intellectuals. "We have already begun to exchange scholars again," observed Mr. Kuo. "You have come; the Japanese philosopher, Matsamura came; Japanese economists and historians also; Professors Galston and Signer from the United States came here. And many, many American scholars have *asked* to come."

Kuo Mo-jo made warm references to his contacts with Americans. He recalled Professor John Fairbank, "my old friend from days in Chungking, and later, from Shanghai." I wondered if he expected to meet Fairbank again. "I would like to see him in Peking." Then Kuo added as a kind of afterthought, "It is probably beyond me now to go to Harvard."

One of the problems in reactivating exchanges, the Chinese leader remarked, is the shortage of interpreters. You have to train them when they are young. "My Japanese is not perfect because although I have lived a lot in Japan, I was no longer a young man when I went there." He recalled how well certain sons of Western missionaries who were born in China or Japan learned to speak the languages of these countries. He spoke of Edwin Reischauer, and of James Endicott, a missionary whom he used to know in Szechwan province. "Endicott was very active in the peace movement." Kuo, who has himself been one of the leaders of the World Council of Peace and similar groups, suddenly paused. Then he added quietly, in a reference to the influence of the Soviet Union in these movements, "Of course, that was before the peace movement degenerated . . ."

Kuo Mo-jo said that an upsurge of language teaching is due. Stress will now be upon English, French, German, Arabic, and Spanish — in that order. "We are also going to give attention to the tongues of Africa, such as Swahili, and the tongues of small nations, such as Nepalese." The Peking Foreign Languages Institute will again — after a break for the Cultural Revolution — enroll regular students "this winter." Chairman Mao himself, Kuo Mo-jo informed me, is setting an example of language learning. At seventy-seven, he pursues English, and he likes to toss around newly learned phrases such as "law and order" and "anti-Mao."

Forays into bookshops confirmed the upward cultural trend, though actual stocks are still meager except on the technical side. Recently published fiction, mostly short stories written by young "workers, peasants, and soldiers," is available. Its quality is not arresting. Mr. Kuo confessed as much himself, comparing them sadly with Lu Hsun's "unshakable" work, and with the famous Chinese historical novels *Dream of the Red Chamber, All Men Are Brothers,* and *Western Pilgrimage.* These last are not in the shops, yet people of all ages manage to read them. Chairman Mao, Mr. Kuo said, not long ago read *Dream of the Red Chamber* for the fourth time.

Why, I asked Mr. Kuo, are there no writings from Chinese authors today which compare in quality with these giant works of the past? "There is a lack of life about recent writings, and a lack of vivid and direct language." Mr. Kuo argued that the Cultural Revolution has done something to rectify this situation. "Most authors come from the ranks of the intellectuals, and the intellectuals have been divorced from the masses. Their range of life was small; they did not know the language of ordinary people." The point puzzled me. How could it be that Chinese writers between Liberation and the Cultural Revolution were more divorced from the masses than were Lu Hsun and his friends before Liberation?

But Kuo Mo-jo swept on to state his high hope for the literary results of the "May 7 schools." Here the writers are being "remolded." Most members of the Writers Union, the Chinese leader observed, are in these schools, and meanwhile the activities of the Union are "suspended." "In the countryside, the intellectual learns the living language of the people. There will come new and good plays, poetry, and novels." Mr. Kuo explained to me that writers at the May 7 schools do farm work only half the day. "For half of the day they write, and many works have been produced that now await publication." I looked at this Renaissance figure of China's cultural life, and wondered just when these works will appear; he has a major say in what will or will not be published.

In one of several paradoxes, Mr. Kuo exclaimed, "So I am optimistic; yet also pessimistic." The pessimism was about himself. "I am not able now to really go among the masses, that is why I am pessimistic about myself." Looking back over the decades, he contrasted himself with Lu Hsun. While Lu Hsun was "using his pen to further the revolution," he, Kuo, went to Japan in 1928 and stayed there ten years. "I went there in the first place because of bad health." Kuo's eyes were large with nostalgia. "But to have been out of China then! All that was happening! Ching Kang Shan; the Long March; Yenan." His explanation of why his years in Japan were so rich in literary output was characteristic of the restless, ardent revolutionary that he is. "I had nothing to do, so I did research. I sat down and let my pen run."

Letting his pen run for me, Kuo wrote in flourishing Chinese characters two lines from Lu Hsun: "Fierce-browed, I coolly defy a thousand pointing fingers: Head bowed, like a willing ox I serve the children." They are from a poem, "In Mockery of Myself," of the early 1930s. The "thousand pointing fingers" are the Kuomintang enemy. Lu Hsun's message — which Mao has praised — is that the intellectual should be an "ox" for the sake of the masses. Kuo Mo-jo turned on me a sad gaze. This is the ideal. Lu Hsun is the "banner holder of culture for the new China." But he observed softly that when this poem was written, "I was in Japan and not serving as an ox for the people."

I questioned Mr. Kuo about language reform, in which he has been involved since the mid-1950s, when the government began to give the matter high priority. At one stage, it seemed that Peking intended to phoneticize the Chinese language, and (however gradually) do away with the picture-language of Chinese characters. Kuo Mo-jo's remarks to me summarized the government's present thinking. "Romanization is the ideal solution, that is true; but it is very difficult." Experience has modified earlier intentions. "We used to train children to write a romanized version, then to learn the characters later. But what did we find? When they started the characters, they forgot the romanized form."

If China were to romanize its language, Mr. Kuo summed up, standard Chinese (*p'u-t'ung hua*) must first be completely popularized. Otherwise, the loss of the characters would threaten the nation's unity. "China could even break into a number of separate states," Mr. Kuo brooded, "each with its language, crystallized by romanization." So it seems best, he continued, to concentrate on simplifying the characters, rather than planning to abolish them. "You can see for yourself that this has been a great help to ordinary people. Everyone is reading; it is a surging tide."

The literature stores do indeed seem busy. Handbooks on technical subjects pour from the press and sell briskly. I bought a new one on Chinese medicine. It is in two parts, to cope with the widely differing climate and vegetation of the country; one for North China, one for South China. There are many simpler handbooks in every branch of applied science. Books long unavailable have reappeared. In the Hsinhua bookstore in Peking, I bought Hao Ran's 1966 novel *Bright Sunny Day* (in Chinese). A week earlier I could have got the great classic, *Book of History* (ten volumes, in *pai hua,* or modernized Chinese). It had sold out almost as soon as it arrived.

I bought one of the two works by Mr. Kuo on the history shelf, essays entitled *Chung-kuo ku-tai she-hui yen-chiu (Research on Ancient Chinese Society)*. He is supposed to have said during the Cultural Revolution that it should be burned. I asked

The Chinese leader Kuo Mo-jo smiles as he autographs one of his books for the author. Entitled *Chung-kuo ku-tai she-hui yen-chiu* (*Research on Ancient Chinese Society*), it was criticized by Mr. Kuo himself during the Cultural Revolution.

him, nevertheless, to sign my copy. He was surprised that it was on sale, and had not before seen this edition. He made no effort to burn the book. Yes, he "rather regretted" having written it, he said without earnestness. That did not stop him from autographing it with a flourish.

Secondhand bookstores, where still open, are disappointing. At the Eastern Market in Peking, in 1964 a great place to rummage for old books, there is little now but engineering texts and dictionaries. In Canton I chanced upon a more promising one. From the door I could see sections on history and social studies. Young people browsed in silence. But I got no further than the door. A man sitting in the entrance barred my way with his leg. Quietly and quickly he said: "Foreigners are not allowed in here."

(From the bookstore I went to see what had happened to the old Catholic cathedral. Massive Gothic, with towers 160 feet high, visible all over Canton, it was done by a French architect in 1863. I did not expect it to be open for services. No churches in China have been since the Cultural Revolution. I found it being used as a distribution center for building materials. Stacks of bricks and timber were on the grounds. Up the "aisle" steered a girl with a wheelbarrow. The "altar" bore red-and-white quotations from Mao. As Mr. Liu — my Luxingshe aide — and I beheld the hum of activity from the gate, a man came out of a nearby doorway and said, "He can't go in there." Mr. Liu replied, "I know." We watched for another moment, and I took a photo. Back we drove, in unaccustomed silence, to the Tung Fang Hotel. It is possible that I might have felt less uneasy about these closed-up places of worship if I could have talked to Chinese believers about their experiences; but I was not able to do this.)

The interview with Kuo Mo-jo lingered on the question of "tradition" and its tension with "modernity." Mr. Kuo himself had been active in the "May 4 Movement" of half a century ago, when a (Chinese) struggle for national dignity was blended with a (universal) quest for scientific ways. He insisted that Chinese policy today is still to take the "positive elements" from outside

China. "We reject the position of Hu Shih, which favors indiscriminate westernization. We also reject the position of Ch'en Li-fu, which stands totally against anything from the West."

Mr. Kuo spoke of the new revolutionary opera-ballets, to illustrate how China meets the issue of tradition and modernity. "These works are not purely Chinese. They are not Western. They are a new thing; revolutionary works which blend both." He stressed the role of the piano, as if he thought this would especially move me. "Have you not seen our pianos? Were you impressed with that? Here we are using something from the West."

As we chatted about the opera-ballets, I remarked that the themes were rather relentlessly political. He beamed at my *faiblesse*. "You see, we live in China under the dictatorship of the proletariat." He now grew earnest. "If we do not consolidate it, in the minds of all the people, China will become social imperialist [the designation for Soviet society]."

Here was the major theme of this extraordinary octogenarian. The revolution in culture is necessary in order to consolidate what was begun at Liberation. This concern for the continuance of the revolution, said Mr. Kuo, is Mao's great contribution to communism. "Lenin died too soon to carry it through. Stalin lacked time for the research necessary to spell it out. Mao has now summed up the experience of the international Communist movement." A twinkle came into the eyes of Kuo Mo-jo. "Of course, we should be grateful to Khrushchev for his errors." He quoted Chairman Mao: "We should award Khrushchev a medal weighing one ton for the valuable lessons his mistakes have taught us."

8. Nights at the Theater

The ceremony of going into theaters was sometimes embarrassing. As a "foreign friend," I could not wander in with other patrons and find a seat. Our car drives up at the last moment. The audience is already seated. We enter from the lobby amidst tumults of applause. It is the custom to respond by clapping, as you walk the length of the theater and take a reserved place near the front. Outside Peking, audiences gape in wonder at the foreign friend. Sometimes you hear speculation in adjacent rows as to the nationality of the foreigner. "Is he French?"; "Probably Rumanian."

Though China's finest acrobats are at Wuhan, the Shensi Acrobatic Company which I saw at Sian was good enough to impress a foreigner. The keynotes were ingenuity, humor, suppleness, and striking use of colors. There are mass scenes to begin the evening. Leaning, bending, and circling in combinations, the actors turn themselves into a wobbling sea of daffodils. The girls trill at a whisper to suggest daffodils waving in the breeze. Then comes a fantastic variation on the traditional dance of the red scarf. Each dancer readies a length of flaming silk. Nimble limbs race and twirl. The scarves blend into a melting furnace of color. Suddenly the molten mass becomes set in a pattern; all movement stops. The red scarves are stretched to depict the red star of the Communist party of China.

Having saluted political reality with such a spectacle, it was as if the performers now felt free to get down to solid artistic business. The next hour was the only hour I spent in the Chinese

theater that had not a trace of politics in it. Gymnasts dash out
in long white trousers with enormously wide cuffs. Their cheeks
are like red carnations (nowhere but on the stage do you see cosmetics in China). In pairs, one stands on his head on the head of
the other. To make things difficult, they pair big with small, and
the big one is on top of the small one! Then the upturned legs of
various acrobats link up. A new batch trot onto the stage and
leap up like grasshoppers to make new levels of precarious balance twenty feet in the air. I get nervous at the risks, but looking
around I find that no one else appears to be. The audience is
keen, and earthy in its humor, but not excitable. They applaud in
a rhythmic "clap-out" manner. No performer comes forward for
an individual "hand"; only collectively do these panting youths
absorb with faint smiles the loud applause.

The gymnast of one moment is a musician the next. Ten minutes later he is back as a clown. Before the night is done he is
a hectoring propagandist. No wonder you see fatigue around the
eyes as they stand still for a bow. This jack-of-all-trades style, it
was later explained, was stimulated by the Cultural Revolution.
Specialization, on the stage as everywhere else, is frowned upon.
Communes have to strive for "overall development," growing a
variety of crops they had never thought to grow before. Stage
performers likewise are required to strive for new skills. Effi-
ciency seems at times subordinated to the impulse to dare the
impossible and the bid to become "all-round" socialist citizens.

The crowd loves the magicians. The feats themselves are not
beyond the ordinary. But superlative is the corporate rhythm of
teams of magicians working together, the gracefulness, the clever
use of suspense. It is ballet, and satire, as much as magicianship.
A favorite theme is the gap between appearance and reality. A
man who looks dumb turns out to be smart. Imminent disaster is
undercut by triumph. Another recurring theme is resourcefulness. The crowd warms up when a character seems hopelessly
disadvantaged, but manages by a cunning stratagem or by "self-
reliance" to overcome the obstacle before him.

The serried rows of perspiring patrons also hugely enjoy the
throwing of boomerangs. I wondered when and how the art of

boomerang throwing had been transmitted from Australia to China. But I found out that the performers did not even know the boomerang was an Australian weapon! It was not a proper boomerang, anyway, I pointed out to them. The boomerang is bent like a dog's leg; this Chinese boomerang was in the shape of a cross. No wonder it seldom came back to the feet of the thrower!

Despite poor acoustics — the theater is a mock opera house built in Soviet style during 1953 — the music was as good as the acting and gymnastics. A flutist, and, for dramatic moments, a trumpeter, accompany the sketches and acrobatics with virtuoso skill. Maybe they came from the Shanghai Conservatoire, which turns out first-rate solo musicians. Two boys make marvelous sounds on an instrument that is a hymn to resourceful self-reliance. It is a xylophone *à la maison*. They evoke a melody by striking not the usual row of wooden bars graduated in length, but a row of kitchen bowls of odd shapes and sizes. What a symphony of tone they get out of these humble bowls! They grimace hilariously as they play. Now in mock anguish as they strive for a perfect tone. Now in feigned surprise as a startling or amusing sound echoes from the bowls. It is characteristic of the evening: musicianship, mime, and humor mixed together.

One of the best acts was the mimicry. Three boys (who moments before were doing handsprings) gather around a microphone and make quiet sounds. Their lips and mouths twist, their eyes bulge. Amplified, the hisses and puffing and whistles turn into a civilization of noises. The audience love these concrete evocations of sounds they hear in daily life. A train seems to pass right through the middle of the theater. Birds squawk and twitter. The loudspeakers are deployed to make the sounds seem all around. You could swear the building was full of cicadas. Trucks rumble by; babies cry. The patrons shake with laughter. Then the mimics do an air raid. Planes zoom down and drop bombs. In the stalls, humor ebbs rapidly into tense concentration. The older ones in the audience are all too familiar with these awful sounds. The young ones seem unengaged. They are taught to expect these sounds to explode again one day over

China, but there is no concrete memory to produce in them a deeply felt response.

During the intermission, I am led to the comfort and seclusion of a side room. It would have been better to mingle in the lobbies, rather than sit glazed like this with my official companions. Only for a moment do I leave the VIP room — on the unanswerable pretext of going to the toilet. Outside the theater doors is a campfire atmosphere. Groups squat on their haunches chatting and smoking. Bony knees stick upwards like cranes at a construction site. In the gloom, cigarette ends light up the faces with a copper glow. The talk is not fussy, or merely polite, but quiet and earnest. You feel you are not in a theater audience but with a community. Here, for once, is not China at work or China on parade, but China at ease. When the intermission was over, I had to enter again to an ovation. It seemed ironic to be shepherded aside from the masses, then "joyously welcomed" by the masses.

The ambience of the auditorium is convivial as people chat and wait for the second half. In shirt-sleeves you feel on the formal side; singlets are the norm. The women have braids; belts keep in place the floppy trousers of the men; all wear plastic sandals. A sprinkling are half-dressed in the uniform of army, navy, or air force. Smile at someone and unfailingly he or she will smile back.

Onstage, politics reasserts itself, yet not at art's expense. A girl who looks and talks like a pillar of political orthodoxy strides on and hurls at us a quotation from Chairman Mao (Ninety percent of the superenthusiastic ideologues I came across in China were women.) I almost laugh at her pent-up stridency and piercing whine. She emits her message: China will not fight unless attacked, but if attacked the nation will fight like mad.

Two brilliant sketches with a war theme then unroll. The first is a skirmish between a girls' militia and American soldiers. Rousing music begins. Sophisticated lighting effects add to the mood of drama. The story is flashed on two oblong screens — long and narrow, for the Chinese characters on this occasion are written in the traditional top-to-bottom manner — hoisted on either side of the stage. The Americans are attacking China. The girls spearhead people's war against them. Amidst the scenes of struggle and social upheaval, one thing above all strikes me. The girls are portrayed not as outfighting but as *outwitting* the U.S. invaders. They trip Americans up. They isolate or humiliate Americans. But we are seldom shown them shooting or bayoneting an American. In the audience there is a matching sense of watching a game rather than a war. There is much laughing, little tension. Making the Americans look stupid is the artistic nerve-center of the sketch.

The second sketch caught a similar mood, but this time the invaders were Japanese. The theme was how a clever underdog can overcome a cruel but blundering invader, and make him look ridiculous. Peasants nabbed Japanese soldiers from behind bushes, set booby traps for them, even engulfed them with large vats dropped with exquisite timing from the branches of trees. The audience was delighted. But beside me were six Japanese; a delegation of the Japan-China Friendship Society. Would friendship take such barbs in its stride? The delegation was divided! Four of the Japanese still gripped the Red Book of Mao quotations (which all six — I noticed in Sian and Yenan where we were sometimes together — carried practically all day in all places). These four applauded sedately, and though they did not laugh as the rest of the audience did, a smile never left their faces. The other two — whose Red Books had somehow slipped from sight — did not laugh, applaud, or smile.

Many of the dozen shows I saw at theaters in China were opera-ballets. These standard eight works reflect the norm and the sum total of theater in the period since the Cultural Revolution swept "bourgeois relics" from the stage. The most popular of them is *White-haired Girl,* a tale of awful suffering and breathtaking heroism during the anti-Japanese war. I saw it in Sian. Like the other opera-ballets, it is heavily political. In its construction, however, the old is blended with the new, and the foreign with the Chinese. Much of its ballet is in modern Western form, which the Chinese got from Russia. Interspersed with this come sequences from classical Peking opera — like the dance of despair by the father of the imperiled white-haired girl. The orchestra is basically Western, yet the *hseng* is also used. This instrument is made of pipes tangled together like intestines, and dates from the period of the Warring States (before Christ). I noticed, too, the *p'i pa,* a stringed instrument as old as the T'ang dynasty.

Sitting in the front row, it was fascinating to watch the orchestra of Chinese musicians playing Western strings and woodwinds. All were in white shirt-sleeves with badges of Chairman Mao. It was a hot evening, and the men had rolled their trousers to the knee. Cups with tea or water sat beside the sheets of music. This is Sian's leading theater orchestra and the standards are high. Unforgettable were the faces. Shining black hair streaked across the sweating brows. Weary, patient eyes. Some of the mouths are fastidious; others have a philosophic set-ness about them. The faces are clear-boned, almost gaunt, and above all they look tired.

During the intermission I snatch a moment — returning from the toilet to the VIP room — to talk with two violinists. They are fanning themselves in the open air near the stage door. With a foreigner they are cheerful and friendly. Their tiredness is understandable. Each day they give at least one performance, and since the Cultural Revolution they spend part of each day on political work, including study of the writings of Marx, Lenin, and Mao. It must be taxing for professional violinists to start broadening their pattern of work at middle-age.

Theater reigns supreme in the world of Chinese entertainment. The cinema is important — yearly cinema attendance in China is at least 4 billion — but it relies heavily on the theater. There are films of the eight opera-ballets which are based squarely on the theater productions. Some 500 million patrons are said to have seen the film of *Red Detachment of Women.* I made it one more by attending a screening on a stifling evening in Canton.

It is my favorite among the dance-dramas, and this version is well danced and brilliantly colored. The setting is the lush island of Hainan during the ten-year civil war; the theme is struggle against landlords and Chiang Kai-shek's forces. I wondered if a

1971 audience still feels deeply about this bitter past. In front of me sit an elderly couple. When the heroine is beaten black and blue by the despotic landlord's gang, there are tears in the old lady's eyes. Later, the landlord is worsted, and his grain distributed among the poor peasants. Young people around me roar with delight. The old couple are silent but evidently moved.

A paradox attends the impact made by the performance. The theme is grim and earnest. Yet as a spectacle the drama is lavish and exciting. The costumes are gorgeous, and so is Ching-hua, the heroine. The music is stirring. Watching the faces around me, I wonder if young and old are not reacting differently. For the old, the theme outweighs the spectacle. For the young, perhaps, the spectacle holds them at least as much as the theme. The action, passion, and elegance must be quite something for the Canton worker, not to speak of the peasant in a remote pocket of China. The roars of delight — when justice caught up with Nan, the landlord — smacked of straightforward excitement rather than of intense emotion.

Some scenes of *Red Detachment of Women* — such as the sword battle in the second act — draw on classical Chinese theater. But the soaring music is Western. Old-style Chinese music does not lend itself to the new revolutionary opera-ballets. Both the piping thinness of its instruments and its sedate rhythms make it too square and intellectual. So Shanghai composers, working collectively, came up with new scores. Chinese folk songs are blended in. Old Chinese instruments are used. But the overall effect is of Tchaikovsky *à la chinoise*. Sweeping string passages match the story well. It is ardent; it sounds a tone of tragedy. It is as much like traditional Chinese music as lyric poetry is like mathematics.

I was reminded of *La Bohème*, then quickly saw dissimilarity. The deep feelings expressed in this Chinese music are tuned to collective, not individual, endeavor. *Red Detachment*, like Puccini's opera, makes an emotional tug on its audience. Yet *La Bohème* treats the heart and an artist's impulses. The Chinese work treats society and organized struggle for its improvement.

There are personal dramas, to be sure, within the collective

Rehearsing for the revolutionary dance-drama *White-haired Girl* at the studios of the Red Guard Art Troupe, in Sian. Training for the Chinese theater is often a blend of physical exercise, martial arts, and ballet steps, since recent works for the stage demand all three skills.

Swimmers saying good-bye to visitors at a Physical Training Institute in Peking. Swimming is popular in China, especially since 1966, when Mao made his famous swim in the Yangtse River.

drama of *Red Detachment,* but it is difficult for the foreigner to gauge audience involvement with these individual loves and follies. Individuals in the *audience,* however, have their loves and follies. As the film begins, I notice a girl sitting alone three rows in front of me. Minutes later a young man saunters in and sits beside her. His sauntering does not hide the prearranged nature of the rendezvous. They sidle closer; they whisper; they hold hands. For one brief moment the girl returns her gaze to the screen — while the boy takes off his shirt, folds it neatly, and resumes position in the cooler comfort of a singlet. By Act Two these determined lovers are wrapped around each other like mating crabs. When the film is over, the boy leaves first, the girl a few moments later. *Red Detachment of Women* was for this pair no more than an excuse for a tryst that was perhaps not possible elsewhere.

The final act of *Red Detachment* brings a martyr's death reminiscent of the death of Jesus Christ. A heroic Red Army cadre named Hung is captured in the very last lap of struggle. Before help can come, he is burnt on a pyre in a harrowing scene. Not a rustle could be heard in the theater as Hung was made to mount the readied logs. Was evil to prevail? The flames licked up and destroyed him. It seemed unbearable. Then began a startling transfiguration. The light from the fire turned into a noble and generalized glow. The music stirred from a double base of death's despair to swelling arpeggios of hope. Hung's embers were now the seat of a glorious new light. It was a resurrection! The Red Army arrives and liberates the area and Nan the landlord is shot. Hung is dead, but undying is the revolution. The masses join with the Red Army, and fantastic songs of battle and hope ensue. As a finale there erupts a rendition of the *Internationale,* an orgy of sound and color and movement in the name of unshakable historical optimism.

How do young people enter theatrical work in China today? In Sian, I visited the Red Guard Art Troupe, in which some two hundred actors, dancers, and musicians learn their art. I wish I could convey the lively spirit and joy in their work of these performers. In the Troupe's theater I talk with actors. They are preparing *White-haired Girl*. They train very hard. They have great opportunities before them, in a nation which values the theater as China does. A banner over the stage reads: "Art to serve workers, peasants, soldiers." In the ballet rooms I meet dancers. Vivid in pink and blue, they leap and pirouette as lilting folk songs are played on a piano. Many are strikingly good-looking. As one pair dance an heroic *pas de deux,* I notice among those at the side awaiting their turn several half-clad couples in intimate conversation. Supervising them with a critical eye is an instructor, a bohemian to his elegant fingertips, who was trained at the Peking Dancing School, 1957–1959. As the dancing pumps rustle and thump on the floorboards, I look up and there is a slogan: "Rehearse for the Revolution!"

The thirteen artists of the Red Guard Art Troupe whom I interviewed had fathers with the following jobs and backgrounds: miner, peasant, poor peasant, worker in Sian, retired cadre, servant to a landlord (before Liberation), peasant, rich peasant who was himself a singer, apprentice in a fruit marketing company, worker in Sian, peasant, worker at the Red Flag shoemaking factory in Sian, peasant. In the whole Troupe, some 10 percent had fathers who were intellectuals. The vast majority of these young enthusiasts, therefore, would have had, in China before Liberation, not a ghost of a chance of a career in the theater. To enter this well-regarded Troupe there are three requirements: sound ideology; good body; fine primary school record.

The Cultural Revolution had a marked effect on the Red Guard Art Troupe, yet not in a heavy-handed or disruptive way. A PLA Propaganda Team came to educate the Troupe in 1967, but it left in 1969. Already in February, 1968, matters were sufficiently stabilized for a Revolutionary Committee to be formed. Though these Committees in theory comprise one-third army people, the Troupe's seven-member Revolutionary Committee has no PLA personnel at all. Nor does any other military note surface amidst the trills and cries of these buoyant studios. I asked one group of three budding ballerinas in what ways they had learned from the "PLA work style" (which everyone in China these past years has been called upon to emulate). They looked utterly blank.

But the Cultural Revolution has altered the content and style of the Troupe's work. Before 1966, it specialized in national songs and dances, prepared many programs for children, and never ventured out of the city of Sian. During 1967 the artists spent eight months in the countryside "getting re-educated." In Sian itself they also joined in the war of the wall posters, in which Mao's line was pitted against Liu Shao-ch'i's line, and a profusion of "left" lines were later pitted merrily against each other.

Now there is more "revolutionary content" in their songs and dances. Programs for children are greatly cut back. With simplified costumes and properties, the artists go often to the rural areas, both to entertain the peasants and to learn the realities of Chinese life which the Chinese stage must now portray. I talked with two boys who danced for peasants in the tawny loess hills of north Shensi.

"It was not easy," said one of them shyly. "We had no stage, not even a smooth floor. We had to flatten and sweep a piece of ground to dance on." The second boy chimed in: "Peasants love revolutionary dances and songs." How can you tell? He laughs at my dullness. "By the applause!" The first boy amplifies. "We got a letter from some peasants. It said that a drama we did — which dealt with agricultural struggles — gave them new inspiration for terracing the hills, and even some practical tips on how to do it."

Since the Cultural Revolution, every artist spends one hour each day studying the writings of Chairman Mao. When performances are given, it is now two a day, rather than one a day as before 1966. Learning and rehearsal time for *White-haired Girl* now runs three months, where previously it ran five months. A small and earnest violinist tells me there is an important current slogan: "Learn as you perform." Most interestingly, the *Chineseness* of their work, in form and content alike, has intensified as a result of the Cultural Revolution. More Chinese instruments are used in the orchestra. More classical Chinese swordplay is put into the ballet. Costumes of peasants (not generals, courtiers, beauties) from Chinese history have been carefully traced and reproduced in the plays.

The Troupe has applied "self-reliance" in making its own properties. Yet I found rather mixed results in the case of ballet shoes. The chairman of the Revolutionary Committee — not an artist himself, Mr. Cheng is a Party cultural worker from Szechwan — tells me proudly the Troupe no longer purchases "expensive ballet shoes from Shanghai." They are made here at the school by the dancers themselves. It is an achievement of the Cultural Revolution. I asked to see the workroom where the shoes are made.

It turns out that theory leaves practice lagging. The Shanghai shoes used to cost $3.50 a pair to buy, Mr. Cheng explained, and now the Troupe itself can make them for $1.20 a pair. But I find that $1.20 is the cost of materials alone. Who paid for the sewing machines? "The state supplied the machines." The shoemakers pore over their scissors, threads, and brightly colored leather. They are not dancers. These two gentle old craftsmen are "veteran workers" who came in from outside to set up the shoemaking room. Where are the dancers? "Oh, the dancers help with repairs," replied one of the veteran workers cheerfully. Add together the cost of machines, the wages of the veteran workers, and the cost of setting up small-scale workshops to replace purchasing from Shanghai. It is doubtful, I conclude, that anything has been saved out of the $3.50 per pair of shoes. Nor are the dancers getting a very thoroughgoing experience in self-reliant manual toil. Fulfilling the principles of the Cultural Revolution can prove an unwieldy process.

In addition to opera-ballets, the Chinese people are offered frequent concerts. In the metropolis of Shanghai and the town of Yenan I enjoyed two quite different types. Shanghai has some Big City atmosphere; you reach automatically for a jacket and tie to go out in the evening. In the concert hall it was so warm that most patrons were in shirt-sleeves, but there was a "concertgoers" air in the foyers. Beside us in the balcony were TV cameras providing a live telecast for greater Shanghai's 10 million people. The program was a varied bill of orchestral fare. Western composers are virtually never heard in China today, even in Shanghai. If you hear Westernized music, it will be music composed by Chinese — probably a team — in a more or less West-ern manner. You may listen to something that reminds you of Tchaikovsky. You will not actually listen to Tchaikovsky, for he has now been set aside as "sentimental."

But tonight the instruments are mainly Western. An ensemble of two violins, viola, double bass, and piano play short works by local composers. Every instrument, including the first-rate piano, is made in China. There is no prejudice against the piano, or against any foreign instrument in itself. "Make foreign things serve China" is a common slogan today. It may be the most in-ternationalist cultural slogan China has ever had. Western music may be "decadent." But why not use Western instruments to make better Chinese music? The orchestra has so much brass and woodwind that it is really half-orchestra and half-band. The *p'i pa* and other ancient Chinese instruments are represented. They give piping and throbbing "Chinese" overtones to the naïve, rousing music.

Items are announced by a girl with a voice somewhere be-tween a wail and a scream. She utters a quotation ("Chairman Mao teaches us . . ."), and the name of the piece to be played, then she strides off the stage like a robot. A vast picture of Chairman Mao adorns the proscenium arch. When the solid so-prano and the austere baritone sing, the words of the song flash on screens to left and right of the stage. The chamber musicians wear blue overalls (does this make them "workers"?). Members of the orchestra and chorus wear a straight and heavy gray uni-form lit up by a Mao badge.

An astonishing scene ends the concert. The entire chorus and orchestra, together with other musicians and including the con-ductor of the orchestra, take out of their pockets the Red Book, and, waving it, sing with gusto the political song "Sailing the Seas Depends upon the Helmsman." The audience join in, first gingerly but soon with full vigor. The song is rhythmic and com-pelling. The concert hall becomes a temple of patriotic political incantation.

The handling of "foreign friends" during the intermission had none of the formalism which I experienced in Sian. A room had been prepared for our comfort (I was with Mr. Whitlam and his group). Its tables were well stocked with beer. The Australian group had made its liking for this beverage unmistakably clear on numerous occasions (after a while, the Chinese even began putting beer on the Australians' breakfast table!). I went to the guest room briefly with Mr. Whitlam, but soon wandered out to stroll in the lobby. Shanghai hosts raised no problems about this. I explained that I wished to get some air, and have a look around. Without hesitation they left me to my own devices.

In the elegant lobbies people chat with little shyness. Two boys in tight pants come up and say "hello" in English with an American accent. A sprinkling carry books (not the Red Book) in their hand. More than half are smoking, and several times a cigarette is offered. At the box office a lively scene unfolds. People line up for tickets for later performances. But the lines have turned into a surging mass. Evidently there is sharp competition, or perhaps some grievance at the procedures. Jostling occurs, a few voices are raised. A portly man shrugs his shoulders in irritation, a lady addresses firm opinions on the situation to her neighbor, a child cries at the confusion. All eloquent tribute, no doubt, to the popularity of the show.

Back in the hall I chat with a northern Chinese official about the Shanghai character. "People from Shanghai are sharp-minded and quick to learn," the dry diplomat observed as a tactful beginning. I did not treat that as his final word and waited for more. Soon he added, with a gesture of the hand to make the words seem noncommittal, "Of course, it is said that Shanghai people talk too much, and that they are not deep." I ask him how Peking people differ from those of Shanghai. The northerner in him overrides an impulse to be discreet: "Peking people are quieter and they think more."

The concert at Yenan was quite a different kettle of fish. It was a folksy offering of a ragbag collection of songs and dances. The Shanghai concert was extravagantly political in its packaging. The Yenan concert was vividly political in its every breath and note. I walk down the aisle in the usual way, with a Japanese group and the Consul of North Vietnam in Peking. The hall is small and intimate, and decorated in the favorite Chinese shades of red and green. There is nothing urban or practiced about the audience. Elbows leaning on knees, youths stare with open mouths at the foreigners. Military men sit in groups; many of the audience — judging by their rough hands — are peasants.

Bouncy songs are accompanied by whining, piping Chinese instruments, as well as violins and assorted drums. Singers strain their lungs to project the heroic and promethean lyrics. One song — which accurately reflects Peking's policy on the issue — says China hopes for foreign aid, but if it is not forthcoming, can perfectly well rely on Chinese efforts alone. Another is a haunting hymn about the conquest of nature for human purposes. "Overcome the wasteland; transform it; make it serve man."

A third song, which is combined with a ballet sequence and tickled along by a flute accompaniment, spells out a crucial theme of life in China today. Though China is backward, the Chinese people are pulling together and they will make progress. The chorus runs: "We are only ordinary workers, but we are very happy." I look into the eyes of the youths singing those lines. How many are students from Peking and Shanghai, sent to Shensi to start a new life on China's frontier, being taught to look on manual labor not as a grind but as a privilege?

A charming girl in braids and a long pink gown trips on to sing a solo entitled "Why Do I Have So Many Uncles?". She sways and chuckles her way through this interesting song. The "uncles" are her "revolutionary comrades." Before the revolution, she had many uncles because the extended family pattern was still in existence. Now it is different. *China* is today's extended family! That is why she has so many uncles. The lyric cleverly makes past Chinese tradition serve present Communist purpose.

A Foreign Ministry official pointed out to me that the concert was strong on Shensi provincial color. It was an impressive feature of the evening. Many of the songs you could hear in no other province of China. Some of these were ancient folk songs, by no means dating only from Liberation, let alone from the Cultural Revolution. Shensi costume was worn (such as toweling around the head). The most lively applause of the show greeted these local songs, and also a flute solo of great ingenuity (the only item without words).

Naturally, some of the Shensi songs are set in the "Yenan years" of the 1930s and 1940s, when the province gained glory from the presence of the CCP leadership. One song was about the receipt in Yenan of Mao's famous telegram after Liberation. It contained a marvelous line expressing the deep "sense of place" of the Chinese. "Even the mountains, even the rivers rejoiced to get the telegram from Chairman Mao!" These political odes were sung in no perfunctory, dutiful way, but with enormous zest and feeling.

One item the concert had in common with that in Shanghai. At the end came a rendition, which ebbed into a demonstration, of "Sailing the Seas Depends upon the Helmsman." Arms beat up and down with the song's martial rhythm. Voices shouted its lines of adulation to Mao. The atmosphere was not feverish, or even emotional, but it was loud and enthusiastic. Verses of the song came and went like courses at a Chinese banquet. A signal was given that the "foreign friends" should mount the stage and shake hands with the performers. The song rolled ever onwards. Up we went to greet the panting, sweating, painted singers and strike a blow for international friendship.

The six Japanese each had a Red Book which they waved as the performers waved theirs. I felt a little empty-handed but did not regret it. There was one other man without a Red Book. I looked beside me and saw the Consul of North Vietnam. His fine long fingers held no book. A weak smile broke his bland expression. The foreign friends were now in center stage, amiable targets for the popping flash bulbs. The Vietnamese and I clapped gently as the song staggered to its final verses. The Japanese waved their Red Books; the bright covers matched the red of the Mao badges pinned to their business suits.

9. Work

Here is an apartment block at a "New Workers Village," in a textile-mill district of Shanghai. We knock on doors and talk with those we find at home. It is 4:00 P.M., and those on day shift are still at work. Children play noisily under the spreading plane trees which shade the space between blocks. A group of neighbors sit fanning themselves, talking about prices, drinking tea. Mrs. Tan is at home with her son, who is back from Anhwei province for a month to see the family. He was sent there for practical work after finishing Middle School. The family of five have two rooms, plus a kitchen shared with two other families. Father earns Y72 per month, mother Y58 (a pension, three quarters of her wage before retirement). Rent is Y5 per month. Another son, graduate of Communications University at Sian, works in a mining-machine factory in remote Tsinghai province. A third is on a state farm not far away, earning only Y24 a month. Furnishings are of the simplest. But the beds, mosquito-netted and covered with tatami, are comfortable. There is a radio and a bicycle. Mrs. Tan is saving to buy a sewing machine, which will cost her Y150. Food for each person costs about Y15 per month. Meat is not cheap; Y65 for a kilo of salted pork. Only grain products are at present rationed.

The Tans' conditions of life are fairly typical. Communal provision in the Workers Village is cheap and above the standard of private provision. Medical care costs Y1 per person per year. Many go twice a week to the cinema — at tiny cost. TV is available, with two and a half hours of programs each day, only at the factory; no worker has his own set. "Pure entertainment" put on by advertisers does not exist. Drama, political commentary, documentary — these are the staple, and technically they are quite well done. TV has little hold over people, and I often found myself — perhaps in a hotel lounge — the only person watching a program. People in China *talk* — endlessly, over tea, through long meals — at times when Westerners might sit at the TV or dress up and go out to organized entertainment. Nevertheless, the government is pushing ahead with experimental development of color TV.

At the New Workers Village, the Revolutionary Committee has a special section devoted to birth control. Its chief gives me three reasons for the vigorous promotion of birth control: It makes possible better care for children, better care for mothers, and greater concentration on production. Women prefer the pill, but physical devices are still the commonest method. The least preferred method is sterilization (of either the man or the woman). Experiments proceed with acupuncture, but the official said it is "not a very popular" method. I could not find out just where they put the needles, or when.

Political meetings take a certain amount of the workers' time. Few seem either gripped or repelled by them. In hotels or factories I once or twice peered into a study meeting that reminded me, in its tight-lipped zeal, of an Evangelical Bible class. More often the ambience seemed languid; books drooping from the wrist, eyes far away — even, once at Canton's Tung Fang Hotel, a card game going on simultaneously. The issues of the Cultural Revolution did not seem to affect greatly these placid folk in the New Workers Village. But its aftermath has — especially the sending of youth to far-flung spots for experience in factory, farm, and mine.

In Canton, I talked with an interpreter (Mr. Hsieh) about his daily life. A graduate of the Canton Institute of Foreign Languages, he now works for Luxingshe, the China Travel Service. He lives in a room at the Luxingshe hostel. His wife works far away in a Hunan factory. With the two children, she lives with Mr. Hsieh's parents in Changsha. Twice a year man and wife see each other.

Each day, Mr. Hsieh and his colleagues study from 6:00 A.M. until 7:00 A.M., when they breakfast. If there is a tourist to be accompanied, they go with him until lunch at 11:30, followed by rest until midafternoon, and further interpreting after that. When they have not been assigned to a tourist, they read English texts (or favorite Chinese novels; Mr. Hsieh had just read *All Men Are Brothers*). By contrast with 1964, when I saw interpreters reading classics of English literature (Charles Dickens, Oscar Wilde, Jack London), their English texts all seemed to be translations from Chinese (*Peking Review,* works by Mao). For reference, Mr. Hsieh had *A Handbook of English Usage,* written by John Tennant and published by Longmans. In the evenings, the interpreters often have meetings to discuss questions arising from their work. When there is no meeting, many go to films or plays. Two half-days a week are consecrated to "political study." Would Mr. Hsieh (a Hunanese) prefer to live in Changsha? He answers with a broad smile, "Chairman Mao says we must serve the people. I will work where I am needed."

Mr. Hsieh was a quiet, courteous man, his Hunanese temperament milder than that of a Cantonese. Only once in a couple of days did he become ardent, and that was when I asked him about the Cultural Revolution. He was almost lyrical, and repeatedly I had to ask him to slow down to a talking speed which I could follow. He had been a Red Guard. He spoke of the evils of T'ao Chu (former Canton leader). Of traveling here and there. Of writing *ta tzu pao* (posters). What made his memories warm, it seemed to me, was that in the Cultural Revolution he had been a *participant* in activity that was freewheeling and daring.

Here are six silk-spinners in Wusih. Four women are Party members; the two men are members of the Communist Youth League. I spoke with them just after the announcement of Mr. Nixon's visit to China. On that they had little to say, and only, it seemed to me, what they had been told to (except one youth — did he· miss the briefing? — who amidst the polite nothings about "traditional friendship between the Chinese and American people" burst out, his fist to the bench: "Nixon is a bad, bad man"). But of their own lives they talked freely.

Mr. Wang earns Y41 a month, his wife (who works at another

factory) Y48, of which they save about Y200 each year. In the bank, gaining 4 percent interest, is Y1200. They have two children, and Mr. Wang's mother lives with them in their three rooms. The other four who are married earn an average husband-and-wife wage of Y109 per month. Average annual savings for each couple are Y275; bank balance, Y830. Affably, the women giggling now and then, they told me things which show the persistence of the "old" in new China. Of the six (whose ages average thirty-five), five visit the graves of ancestors not less than once a year. Of the five married ones, four used "go-betweens" to get their spouses. The go-between either introduced them (with marriage in mind), conveyed the proposal, or served as intermediary to satisfy the queries of the spouse's parents. From Y50 to Y100 was spent on the wedding dress. (For marriage, three days off work are given, for maternity, fifty-six days, all on full pay.)

These silk-spinners I found not untypical of city workers. Here are four women at a chemical-fiber factory near Nanking. The wages are a little higher (average Y124 per couple each month), houses roomier. All have two or three children and use birth control pills, available free at the factory, as a matter of course. Most have one or more grandparents living with them — taking care of the infants. The two children of one woman are living with her parents in Shanghai. She sends Y30 each month for their food and sees them three times a year. None of these mothers have ever, they said, struck one of their children. None would talk to me about sex education.

None use any cosmetics; three of the four have bicycles in the household; all have radios; three of the four have sewing machines. Between them they can name and discuss the careers of six Chinese women prominent in national affairs. The militia, to which they all belong, keeps them fit with running, shooting, swimming in the Yangtze. It also involves them in study groups on Vietnam and World Revolution.

What do these makers of chemical fibers feel about their work, and what do they like to do after work? I asked each of the four: "What has been the most exciting day in your life?" Two said

(ABOVE) A morning scene in a suburb of Peking; the strong, high cheek-boned faces show curiosity about some foreign visitors; bicycles are everywhere. (BELOW) Young and old together around a checker board, in a park of the New Workers Village, at Shanghai. Notice the fan in the left hand of the stocky man in foreground.

the day they joined the Party; two said the day they started work. Later as we strolled to the car, I tried to get one of them, a pretty mother of three, to spin out her answer. "Was having babies exciting?" I asked casually. "Was that as exciting as first coming to work?" She lit up like a torch. *"Of course* it was — but, oh, that's different, isn't it?" We reached the car, but she could hardly be stopped . . . about what grandma said . . . why the girl was rowdier than the boy. She spoke of Spring Festival, for which there is three days' holiday. "It comes next to Sunday, so we have four days for a big family reunion." Yes, they go to the cinema — "Have you seen *Red Detachment of Women?"* she asks. Of course they drink a lot of wine. . . . "Yes, babies are very exciting," she mused as I left her, "except when they're naughty."

The girls heartily praise the social amenities of the factory. Working conditions, I could see for myself, are also good. The cut in bureaucratic personnel brought by the Cultural Revolution is popular among workers. In this Nanking factory it was a cut of nearly 50 percent — elsewhere I found an average of about 40 percent. "They were not necessary," said one of the girls simply, referring to the excess administrators. On the other hand, there are no trade unions — I was told — in this factory or elsewhere. Industrial theory, if it existed, would be based on an assumed harmony — stemming from the Thought of Mao — not on conflict. And the worker cannot decide that he'd like to work in another factory, or another trade, and simply seek and get a different job. I inquired of the spokesman of the factory Revolutionary Committee, "Can a worker transfer work by his own individual decision?" I might have asked if the leopard can change his spots. *"I-ting pu-shih!"* ("Certainly not!") You must find your freedom in the collective; you cannot bid for it as an individual.

Some statistics by province, supplied to me by Revolutionary Committees, show why the worker is better off than in the recent past. Take Shensi. The value of fifteen days' industrial production in the province equals that for the whole year of 1949. The value of industrial production in 1970 was double that of 1965. (Shensi, it should be added, is one of the inland provinces particularly built up by the effort to reduce industrial concentration on the eastern seaboard. Textiles, a leading Shensi export, used to have to go to Shanghai for dyeing and other processing. Today all is done in Shensi, and finished products go direct from Sian to the foreign market.) At Liberation, there were 20,000 pupils in the Middle Schools of Shensi. Today there are 710,000 pupils (population of the province has about doubled).

In rural areas, standards are lower, and in remote counties you seem to step back in time. Many old folk are illiterate. Planting and harvesting are often done by hand. Few young people (ten a year from this commune, five from that) have gotten to a university in recent years. The shadow of the past is long. I found ex-landlords and ex-rich peasants still referred to as such, even after twenty-two years. Up to 30 percent of them are still not considered sound enough to be given the rights of ordinary commune members, and some "reactionary" ones are "under supervision."

Household income averaged Y70 at the Ma Lu commune in the Yangtze Delta (one of China's four "rice bowls" — others are the Pearl Delta, Szechwan Basin, and Hunan); Y65 at the Red Star commune near Peking. Under the work-point system, wages depend upon work done (and since the Cultural Revolution, on "attitude"). At Red Star, highest household income was 80 percent more than lowest. Education and health care are fairly good and extremely cheap. At the Ma Lu commune, each person pays Y2 per year as a medical fee, and gets free service in return. At the commune schools, Y4 each year for each child covers all fees and books.

From "private plots" (which took up 5 to 7 percent of the total land in the communes I examined) comes additional income. Frequently, commune officials accuse Liu Shao-ch'i and his associates of having "exalted" private plots. Yet I never found evidence that the percentage of commune land devoted to private plots has dropped since Liu and his revisionists were put down. Trying to explain why the figure was still 5 percent — as it had been before the Cultural Revolution — the Vice-president of the Revolutionary Committee at Red Star commune said a little lamely, "Before the Cultural Revolution, commune members paid more *attention* to their private plots."

A Ma Lu commune official estimated the products from plots to be worth only Y18 per person per year. Yet I knocked on a door and was told by the lady who answered that her family's plot brings in Y200 by raising three pigs a year, and keeps the family in vegetables as well. Again at Red Star, a family who were expecting my visit — a seven-year-old boy had rehearsed an aria for the occasion — said they earned only Y100 a year from their plot, but informal questions in the fields brought forth higher figures.

Enormous variation marks rural conditions. In ten hours' driving through the wheatlands of north Shensi, I saw only two tractors. In Hunan, by contrast, the nippy two-wheeled tractor, now made in many Chinese cities, was everywhere, and here and there four-wheelers also.

Along the unpaved roads of north Shensi you do not see much sign of "modernity." Carts inch by, with rocks for the building of the Sian-Yenan railroad — they are pulled by a man or woman. At a brick kiln near T'ung Ch'uan ("copper river"), there seem to be no power vehicles to carry the finished bricks, let alone a branch rail track; donkeys or people pull the loads. By the roadside, scores of people of both sexes and all ages squat, breaking up big rocks into smaller rocks by hand for the railroad construction. Mostly the wheat is harvested with a rude scythe — often a piece of metal tied to a handle with string.

As for threshing, I learned a new method on the rolling plains of Shensi — and promised the laughing peasants I'd transmit it back to Australia. These brown, wily types — who look quite dramatic in their headdress of toweling, a provincial feature — take the wheat, after they have cut it, and spread it out on the road. On the paved part of the journey north from Sian we drove over frequent stretches of it. The vehicle is the thresher. When enough trucks or wagons have passed over the wheat, boys take away the husks, and the grain is swept up by grateful farmers and put in bags. Of course north Shensi is not among China's richest parts. Yet the vast majority of its villages are electrified, which cannot be said of the really backward pockets of China. Birth control campaigns do not meet with equal success in all places. In Kwangtung, the birthrate figure given me was 3 percent. In Hunan, 1.5 percent (in Changsha it was down to 0.97 percent last year). Seldom did I find such earnestness as when provincial officials talked of their birth control efforts. A cloud came over a lively banquet in Canton when the 3 percent rate was announced. "It's the old problem," explained a senior editor of the *Nanfang Jih-pao* (*Southern Daily*). "Peasants have a daughter. They think, that's no good. So they keep going till they get sons."

Industry is being made to "serve agriculture." In Shensi I found a new price system in operation since the Cultural Revolution. Transport cost, to any part of the province, is included in the set price of the item at the city of Sian. Previously transport, so backward in China, was a heavy additional item of cost. Hence the purchasing power of the commune, and of the individual peasant, is enhanced. Industry grumbles, of course, but at present it grumbles in the air.

Traveling through the hills of Kwangtung, I had been impressed by the amount of terracing done since I saw the province in 1964. Of course it enlarges the cultivable area. Yet I wondered. Won't eventual mechanization be extremely difficult? Next day, a Canton official jumped at the question. He put down his chopsticks and turned to me for emphasis. "Our factories will have to adjust. This is China; this is the situation. They will have to produce machines, design new ones, which will work on terraced hillsides."

Certain basic achievements in rural life are undeniable. Simple education improves by leaps and bounds. Kuo Mo-jo disclosed a new figure on literacy in China. Just under 10 percent, he said, are now considered illiterate. This is the lowest figure ever given for illiteracy in China. It compares with perhaps 70 to 80 percent at Liberation. The terrible exploitation and inequality of pre-Liberation days has gone. (In 1949, landlords and rich peasants between them made up 7.2 percent of the population of what is now the Ma Lu commune, yet occupied *79 percent of the land,* according to commune officials.)

Five ladies weave mats. The scene is the Ma Lu commune near Shang-hai. Like a medieval community, the Chinese commune aims to be self-sufficient and self-reliant. With their savings, the ladies like to buy sewing machines and radios.

The power pump, as a boon to water control, is a thing of emotion in the Chinese countryside today. The pumps are on the banks of waterways. On the plains, wells are dug. In the hills you find reservoirs. In these ways, the ancient evil of flood and drought has been considerably throttled. In Shensi a vivid statistic is offered. Last year, 3.5 million mou of land (the mou is one-sixth of an acre) were newly irrigated in the province. From 1949 to 1965, 7.5 million mou had been irrigated. In the 2,000 years before Liberation (yet how do they know?), 3.5 million mou — the same figure as for the one year of 1970! In Hunan, waterworks done in 1970 made 900,000 mou of land newly available for cultivation.

There is still the saying in Kwangtung, "whether you get a harvest depends on water; whether you get a good harvest depends on fertilizer." But here progress is mixed. Organic fertilizer is generally relied upon. Not enough chemical fertilizer is yet made in China, nor is it always of good quality. Much has to be got from Japan. (Mr. Whitlam tried to interest the Chinese in Australian chemical fertilizers — but the price was too high.) Agricultural production figures suggest steady but not rapid advance. Grain output in Kwangtung, for instance, is now just double what it was in 1949 (population is up by more than one-third). In general, it is social advance — in health, education, security — rather than immediate economic advance which strikes the visitor to rural China today.

10. Southward by Train

After a sun-baked stay in the placid city of Changsha, I was due next in Canton. My two companions, Mr. Chou of the Foreign Ministry and Mr. Liu of Luxingshe, did not want to go by train. "We will roast," reasoned Chou, who is a prudent and measured man. "The train travels all day from Peking. At Changsha you board it at 10:00 P.M., and by then it's an oven." But I insisted, so Mr. Chou took back to China Airlines the tickets already bought for tonight's flight. We would go by train. I would see the southern countryside as I wished. Mr. Liu, who loves the technical frills of flying and hates heat — though he is Cantonese — would have to bear it. Which he did with good humor. "But you'll be sorry," he warned.

I thought the precaution of drinking a few glasses might guarantee sleep for the night hours of the trip. Opportunity came at a dinner, given as a farewell by the Foreign Affairs section of the Hunan Province Revolutionary Committee. The sickly *huang chiu* and the devastating *mao-t'ai* (rice wine) flowed freely as usual. As we left the hotel — a cavernous place, built in Russian style during the 1950s — a group of Laotians appeared in the foyer. They are delegates of the Pathet Lao. We had exchanged notes when our paths crossed — as they often did, for there are few foreigners in China. They are going also to Canton, they tell us, but by air. . . . Mr. Liu turned upon me a meaningful glance.

At Changsha railroad station a small PLA man comes forward to carry my suitcase. It is fearfully heavy with books and

Hsinhua news bulletins. But I let him take it up the long crowded platform. It's not often nor everywhere, I reflect, that I get served by an army man; savor the pleasure! As the Changsha hosts say good-bye they ask, as is current custom, for criticisms of their work on my behalf.

For once I offer them. The Guest House was comfortable, but was it not also isolated? I never got the chance to wander around the town. To which Mr. Lin (a local man) made the usual point about safety. Also, I continued, I had wanted to see a law court in action. Mr. Lin says visitors are *never* taken to courts. Perhaps it's worth making these points anyhow, for they are discussed at post-mortem sessions after the visitor has gone. Goodbyes were prolonged and amicable.

The train, labeled "Peking-Canton Express," is less hot than feared, as the day further north in Hupeh province has not been hot. But it shakes and we don't sleep much. The compartment is comfortable in an old-fashioned way. Straw mats cover the berths and each pillow is wrapped in a towel. There is a table with a lace cloth; on it a fairy-tale light with a pink silk lampshade, and an optimistic potted plant. Red carpet welcomes the feet. My berth has written on it: "Supreme Instruction: Serve the People. Number Nine — Lower."

Each passenger has a covered porcelain tea mug. The mugs are endlessly refilled by an attendant who makes cheery remarks in a broad Hunanese accent. The radio is on, with a forceful political commentary, but Mr. Chou, reading the thoughts of all, turns it off by a switch under the table. There is a Western-style toilet at the end of the corridor (as well as several of the "crouching" kind). Hot and cold water is abundant. Several travelers in the carriage — who look like officials — use streamlined cordless electric razors for their morning shave.

Fitful sleep ended and the sights of South China's rural life absorbed us. There was a tranquil and unhurried air. By 6:00 A.M. peasants are in gentle circulation, washing themselves, standing around in singlets with mugs of tea. Smoke issues from kitchens, and children in gaudy clothes run around and point at the train. By contrast with the north, the houses are generally not

mud but brick, and the donkey has given way to the water buf-
falo. The train enters the Nanling mountains and snakes through
valleys and rounded hills which are almost feminine in their
curves and undulations. Every cultivable niche is under rice or
vegetable. Now and then — to satisfy the perverse principle of
"overall development" — there is inferior wheat, just as in the
area near Peking peasants are required to raise an inferior, dry-
grown rice.

You can see the point of the Kwangtung saying, *"ko-shan
ko-su"* ("Each mountain has its own customs"), for the land is
broken constantly by mountains. And from this topography you
get a clue to the independent-minded Kwangtung mentality.
Communization is more difficult here than on the northern plains.
Not only because of the hills — cultivation is sporadic: where
can the bounds of each commune be? — but because of the hill-
people and the localism of their ways.

The terrain accounts for other features of South China life.
Fragmented settlement has made it easier for the aboriginal peoples to continue their separate ways of life. The *Yao* minority
are numerous in the valleys we traverse. Unlike North China,
where the coastline is generally flat, the coast of South China is
rocky, hilly, and indented. Life oriented to the sea is therefore
more common. Cantonese cuisine is notable for its fish special-
ties, and the seafaring motif is recurrent in the history of South
China.

The early morning sun glitters on the water of the rice pad-
dies. With shoots protruding here and there from the silver ex-
panse, the fields look like flawed mirrors. We cross the Pei Chiang
(North River), in which logs float obediently downstream to the
paper mill. On a riverside path, an old woman makes her way
with baskets on a pole. Brown as a nut, she wears the old-style
black garments of oiled silk, and the brilliant sun lights her up
like a shining ebony spider.

Long hours in the train loosen Mr. Chou's usually measured
conversation. He takes swipes at Russians as we chat about
travel. A diplomat, he has moved a lot through Russia, Europe,
Africa, and Asia. "Russian air-hostesses," he remarked as we

lolled on our berths with a mug of tea, "powder themselves instead of attending to the passengers. Every little thing you want — even a glass of water — you have to ask them for it. Otherwise they never come near you." Mr. Chou was in an interesting mood. He was not faulting the Russians this morning for being "revisionists." He was picking holes in their way of life.

He cast a cold eye on Soviet aviation standards. "My wife always gets anxious when I travel on a Russian plane. Never when I travel on Chinese planes — as with you these past weeks. She knows Chinese planes are safer." I asked him if planes ever crash in China. "Very few." But he would not let go of the Russians. "Once, our Minister of Culture was killed in an air crash in Siberia. And I could tell you of many Chinese diplomatic couriers who have lost their lives (and documents) in Russian air accidents." Chinese officials, I recalled, seldom travel to Europe via the USSR these days. They prefer the southern route using PIA (Pakistan) or Air France — both of which fly from Shanghai.

Chou Nan is convinced life is better in China than in Russia. So are other Chinese I met who know both countries. When it comes to comfort, convenience, and cooking — to things which count in daily life — Chinese officials do not envy their muttering neighbor to the north.

The train wound on through the Nanling passes. Sheer slopes faced us on one side, lush valleys lay green and gold on the other. A breakfast was prepared for us in the dining car. For the foreigner, fried eggs and bacon with huge chunks of bread. For Mr. Chou and Mr. Liu, a kind of porridge made of rice and beans, and with it pickled turnip, tomato, and slices of pork. They drink nothing, but I have one of the few cups of coffee of my weeks in China. Our entry into Kwangtung evokes some acerbic comments on the province from Mr. Chou. He comes from the province of Liaoning, and is a northerner to his fingertips. The morning advance southward seemed to give him apprehensions. As if one must gird one's loins for such nether regions.

The radio is now on again. A girl with a voice like an old violin gives a health talk. She is Cantonese but is speaking the national tongue. I remark on how clear — for a southerner — her mandarin is. "Better than usual," is Chou's grudging judgment (Mr. Liu, who is Cantonese, is safely asleep on a top berth). He goes on to wonder what weird dishes we may find ourselves eating in the days ahead. I recall in silence that in imperial China northerners would sometimes take their own food with them on trips south, rather than risk their digestion to the fertile gastronomic imagination of the Cantonese. (In fact Mr. Chou ate dog with gusto a few days later in Canton; I stuck to less domestic beasts.) We touched on the history of South China, and his main comment was unflattering. "Emperors used to send people to Kwangtung to get rid of them," he observed as an end to the topic, "much as Russian Tsars sent people to Siberia."

This trace of disdain for Kwangtung on the part of northerners may not be unconnected with Peking's detached attitude toward Hong Kong (which is part of Kwangtung province). People wonder why such an intensely patriotic country allows Britain to keep Hong Kong as a residual jewel in its imperial crown. No doubt it is in part a practical question: Hong Kong pays China in useful foreign currency for food, water, and other products sold there. Yet there may also be a touch of northern *hauteur* in Peking's casual tolerance of "barbarians" in Hong Kong.

Once we reached Canton, Mr. Chou found much to praise. He had not been there for a decade. "In those days," he recalled, "I would go into the shops and find no one could speak the national tongue. Very tiresome. But now it is quite different. I can talk with anyone." But one day we had a contrary experience. It was an afternoon with the "boat people." These are the Canton fishermen who have long lived on boats. In recent years the government has settled almost all of them (some sixty thousand) in new housing on the banks of the Pearl River.

I went to interview them because I was interested to see how they had adjusted to life on the land. (Some throw trash out the doors and windows the way they used to throw trash from the boat into the river.) Most of those we met were old. Brown and leathery, shrewd from a lifetime on the water, they were attractive people, blunt in comment and fertile in stories. But they spoke Cantonese only. Mr. Chou was not able to hide his disapproval. As one fisherman spun the story of his life, Chou turned to me and said in a loud and dignified voice, "His words are as meaningless to me as to you."

The train stations are marvelous human theaters. Young and old scurry in and out of carriages with boxes, melons, water bottles, and nameless bundles on sticks. Some carry babies; some carry chickens. Peasants are amusing when they are met by an intrusion from the technological world. The train seems to them a capricious monster, not to be relied on or trusted. They frown and rush and shout instructions to each other. Safely on with their paraphernalia, they look surprised to have made it.

You see that they are not ordinary peasants as Asia knows peasants. They pull newspapers and magazines from bags and read. Mao badges spot their garments like red taillights. Loudspeakers bring world news into the carriage and they comment on it. Some whistle arias from familiar opera-ballets. This is not the kind of countryside life Marx recoiled from as "rural idiocy." These patient faces are not lost in a backwater of history.

True, machines have hardly entered their lives. But a sense of corporate national purpose is evident. These farmers can tell you what Mao is trying to get at in his Cultural Revolution, and what China stands for in the world of nations. And the hand of organization touches them. They go to meetings, sign papers, belong to groups with economic, community, or political aims. We pass two columns of marching boys. A little cup hangs on each knapsack. Instructors lead the boys in political songs as the file wends along the ridge of a silver-colored rice paddy. In a sense these people are "moderns."

Like moderns, they enjoy a wide range of simple manufactured items. From the train you see the straw hats, hand carts, and rude scythes of time immemorial. But look closer. The people wear bright printed cottons and plastic sandals. The braids of the girls are tied with gay ribbon. Many have transistor radios and most have bicycles. All have the usual simple personal toilet articles. These are peasants with a difference.

At a small station not far from Canton, two boys catch the

eye. One is swimming with two water buffalos in a pond. Peasant houses are scattered around the yellow water. Chickens scratch idly at the foot of nearby trees. It is the searing heat of midday. The buffalos splash around, their black skin shining like a wet umbrella. The boy, jumping on and off their backs, is naked except for a straw hat in the southern, conical style. Now and then he stands still, just his head and the hat showing above the muddy sheet of water, savoring the coolness.

As he tiptoed beside the buffalos, a phrase from a writer on Chinese agriculture in the 1930s sprang to mind. The Chinese peasant, observed R. H. Tawney of the precarious position landlordism put the peasant in, is like "a man standing permanently up to the neck in water, so that even a ripple is sufficient to drown him." When Tawney wrote, desperate reality lay behind the image. As I watched the boy and his buffalos, the carefree ambience seemed to signal the fantastic improvements in China since Tawney went out to make a study for the Institute of Pacific Relations. Mao's government has not brought the Chinese peasant great prosperity, but it has given him unprecedented security. No ripple can finish him now.

Another boy is on the platform of the railroad station. I lean out the window, watching travelers buy tea and unleavened pastries. The train radio blares, but few listen. The business at hand is to get a drink and a snack. The small boy catches my attention because he carries a rifle which glints in the sun. He is not in uniform; what is he doing? I notice he is looking not around him but up at the trees. A mild sense of relief. He is shooting birds. Sparrows, by the look of the tiny corpses. His weapon is an air gun, and the basket strapped to his waist is for his feathered victims.

Such punctilious public service must amaze those who knew the fearful chaos and lethargy of China before Liberation. It springs from traits that can remind the visitor of a vast Boy Scout camp: a sense of belonging; a spirit of service; hearty use of simple methods where streamlined ones are not available; the presence of willing hands on all sides; an irrepressible buoyancy.

As we reach the Kwangtung province capital a typhoon is not

far distant. It makes the city cool and gray, refreshing after the heat and glare of Changsha. Canton is a garden city, lush with tropical vegetation. Buildings are shabby, in faded memory of the war of slogans and quotations during the Cultural Revolution. Portraits of Mao and quotations from Mao adorn almost every building. I realize Changsha (though it is Mao's home city) has far fewer of these than Canton. In Changsha, institutions have Mao trappings on display, but the whole city is not draped and placarded the way Canton, despite recent modifications, still generally is.

Mr. Yang of the provincial Revolutionary Committee's foreign affairs section is at the station to meet me. We drive together to the Tung Fang (Eastern Hotel; in 1964 it was called *Yang Ch'eng,* Goat City Hotel). I am tired from the overnight journey and unable to make much conversation. Carelessly I inquire, "Are you Cantonese?" Mr. Yang is taken aback. I look at him and realize how silly the question is. He is tall, with square, angular features. (Cantonese are smaller and rounder.) He says to me with wounded astonishment, "Do I look like a Cantonese?" He is from Shantung and proud to be so. In Canton he is doing his duty.

By now the typhoon has swept in from the coast and the city girds its loins for nature's tantrum. As we alight at the Tung Fang, trees wave and veer in a crazy fashion. Rain is whipping up and the light is eerie. Around the hotel grounds staff members scurry under sheets of pale green plastic. A few enterprising girls and men are already chopping up fallen tree-parts.

From my balcony I look out over the Pearl River delta. Silver clouds swoop down to invade the trees and taller buildings. Dull rays cast an ochre-colored light here and there. The whole scene seems to sway before the torrent of wind and rain. After the baking temperatures of Hunan province, the cool air is seductive. And the gloom broken by lightning and muffled sun rays lends an amusing psychedelic flavor. I had always wanted to see a typhoon. Yet watching the winds' occasional acts of devastation, I was glad this typhoon hit Canton only at a tangent.

Canton has none of Peking's grandeur, but all of South

China's earthy, inventive fascinations. Stroll among a late afternoon crowd in the city streets. The hot air clutches at you as in a steam bath (the Tropic of Cancer runs just north of Canton). For protection against the heavy rainfall, the sidewalks of the commercial districts have wide stone verandas. In these semienclosed corridors, every variety of ingenious Cantonese dish can be seen and smelled. Herbs and roots of Chinese medicine can also be sniffed. Their hard, piercing odor mingles with the smell of glue and paste from Chinese offices, and that of fresh rain on the luxuriant vegetation of the city's environs. Among sounds, cicadas compete with bicycle bells; underlying both there is the singsong drawl of the Cantonese dialect (which people use — rather than *p'u-t'ung hua* — for informal talk).

Off the main boulevards, commercial life gives way to a ceaseless round of community life. In a small alley, a girl in a floral blouse does homework at the door of her home. Sitting on a chair, she leans forward, legs apart, and writes against a second chair drawn up to face the first. Her braids fall down over a notebook in which she laboriously traces Chinese characters. I was transfixed for a moment watching this girl write the ideographs with which I have wrestled so pathetically as a foreigner. What is to me a challenge from over a far horizon is to her a casual chore before supper. These are *her* characters, as surely as her coal-black hair and nimble limbs and silky skin are hers, and they can never be the foreigner's.

The girl's little brother dashes by with a bowl of boiled rice, grinning broadly. A youth in striped singlet turns into the alley with a chicken carcass in each hand. An old man comes by from the other direction with bits of pork and a bunch of bamboo shoots. Inside a niche in the wall, a lady works at a sewing machine. Her children surround her, reporting their day at school, pestering her with questions. I ask if I may take her picture, and she shyly says no. Here and there people squat on a stool or a stone slab; knees high, head bent down, chopsticks fussing, bent in concentration over a succulent dinner.

As in other parts of Asia, many people (especially women) hold a fan or newspaper over their faces when exposed to direct sun. An old lady stumps by, heavily bent by a stick across her back, from which are suspended two enormous bundles of small scrap iron and nuts and bolts. Clothes hang drying on strings and poles across the alley, flags of humanity hoisted above this stoic, resilient, resourceful South China community. Later, I look down upon the same scene from a tall building, and now there is something extra. On the roofs of the lower structures, a whole realm of life comes into view: neighborhood restaurants, people asleep, gardens in boxes, little boys playing football.

These pulsating alleys are crowded and far from affluent. Yet no one is in rags; no one sits around in that state of hopeless-looking poverty all too familiar in Asia. Clothing is simple, clean, neat; food is wholesome. No one is ingratiating toward the visitor. No one badgers you to buy something, much less to beg something from you. You are a visitor and you are respected, but no special attention is paid to you, and you do not feel un-comfortable. What struck me, above all, was the equality of the life of these alleys, and because of this there is dignity even when there is poverty.

Canton can boast some fine tables. One evening I took my hosts to the Pei Yuan (Northern Garden) Restaurant, a lively place with glossy black furniture and airy windows looking out on ponds and bridges. I had left the choice of dishes in the hands of a Cantonese. When the handwritten order of dishes was pre-sented to me (as the host), my eye lit on the characters *kou-jou* (dog flesh). There was no doubting its arrival, for the smell was strong. All except me — northerners included — ate it heartily. I half closed my nostrils, and concentrated fiercely on the cham-pagne until the next dish came steaming in. The others did not like the champagne, which is made in northeast China, and chose instead the *huang chiu* (yellow wine), too sweet for many West-ern palates. Mr. Chou was soon in fine form, with culinary tales from his diplomatic experience. The cook at the Chinese Em-bassy in London, he recalled, once went to Covent Garden to buy a hen. His English being less developed than his kitchen skills, he approached a market attendant with the words: "Please, I would like a madame cock."

Another meal unfolded the night before I left China, at the Friendship Restaurant. Like the Pei Yuan, it is set in a garden bordering a large pond. The host, Mr. Yang of the Foreign Affairs Section of the Revolutionary Committee of Kwangtung, leads me to a group of ebony chairs, inlaid with pearl, on a second floor balcony. There is talk with journalists from the *Nanfang Jih-pao* (*Southern Daily*) before dinner, and we look directly down on diners in the garden. They lean noisily across large circular tables speckled with dishes and fallen pieces of food. Lit by the glow of sunset, the round tables look like an array of golden sunflowers.

In preparing a farewell banquet, they have decided to satisfy my every known whim. Having remarked the previous day that I liked shrimps, I now found shrimps on all sides, done in many cunning ways (some with honey). Since I had ordered champagne the night before — when host at the Pei Yuan — there was now a constant flow of champagne, though I knew most of the Chinese didn't like it. Here were pineapples (some fresh, some hot), bananas, and other favorite fruits. Halfway through the meal there appeared a delicate clear soup, served in an oblong hollowed-out melon! The sweetmeats I have already described (page 68).

As the relay of dishes bore us down, talk slid off Kwangtung politics to matters both smaller and larger. Mr. Chou grew philosophic about parting, and ventured some summary judgments on the state of the world (in his indirect, poetic way). Mr. Yang railed against hijacking. "We oppose that kind of thing. It's not revolutionary." I remarked — at a low temperature — that some of China's friends in the Middle East seem rather keen on it. Mr. Yang shrugged his chopsticks. "We can't be responsible for everything they do."

The food was served by the two finest waitresses I have watched. If they are relics of the past, they are relics worth preserving. In their forties, they had a concentrated earnestness but were not fussy. I watched the faces coming out of the kitchen door: there was a professional pride that seemed lodged deep within these women. The long, slim hands would make a tiny twist or flourish as they set down a new dish, or proffered a wet towel from behind. Each diner had four glasses, and no glass was permitted to get more than one-quarter empty before the relevant bottle materialized at its rim. During the endless toasts, the waitresses melted into the background and stood prim as cypresses beside an ebony pillar. How such specialized waiting skill fits in with Chinese society today I do not know. To come upon these women was like walking off a London street and finding inside a hotel two characters from the world of Charles Dickens.

Soon after reaching Canton, I went up to take the waters at the hot springs of Ts'ung Hua. Once more, like an itinerant musician, I packed my bag, and we drove by the edge of the Pearl River delta and up into tranquil hills. The typhoon has subsided, but we pass and dodge many broken tree-portions. The fields here give two crops of rice each year, as well as one crop of winter wheat. Further out from Canton, there is much jute and cassava. Trucks pass us laden with a sharp-edged mountain reed. In Canton it will be turned into a rayon-like fiber, which the Chinese are still experimenting with but so far find promising (and dirt cheap).

At the *Pin-kuan* (Guest House) we sink into simple comfort. Each visitor has his sunken bath, into which the therapeutic waters gush. The Guest House is not for tourist use, and there are no slogans on its walls. Meals are taken overlooking rustling bamboos, and the blue-yellow waters of a river rimmed by sandbanks and backed with towering hills. Waiters announce each dish as they present it. I wonder which previous guests they are using as a working model for me, since they bring beer for my breakfast!

Early in the morning, I am drawn to the window of my room by the dull silver light. Rain-sheets hurl themselves at a forty-five degree angle across the scene. They pelt into the river like a million cruel darts. The lovely hills are only intermittently visible through billowing cloud. A cluster of bamboos near the window creak and groan as they bend from side to side. Cocks crow pathetically in the distance. Opposite, a cottage nestles on the far bank of the stream, smoke curling from its chimney to meet the rain.

I go walking and find the environs well cared for. Every thirty yards on the driveways, there are handsome green-tiled lamp-posts, each one capped with two vast spherical lamps. Trash bins are made of the same green tiles. There are boating stations and basketball courts. Also military men, some with fixed bayonets, some with Bren guns, for an army base is nearby. A splendid gateway, half-hidden by waving trees, lies high above the Guest House, and here two soldiers turn me back. In the other direction, a stone bridge spanning the river is also guarded by PLA men.

Before returning to Canton, we climb skyward through the mountains to see three waterfalls, named "Galloping," "Silver Bed," and "Flying." Mr. Chou regales us with literary tidbits. As we pass bamboos, two lines from a Sung poet come to him: "Without meat to eat, a man becomes lean; without the quality of bamboo, a man becomes mean." He recalls that bamboos and pines, together with the chrysanthemum, were three species to which virtue was attached in classical Chinese literature. He gives us phrases from the poets to describe the waterfalls as we approach their rushing freshness: "long white cloud dropped from heaven"; "heavenly girl washing her long hair." The rain has gone, and sun lights up the falls like phosphorous. But underfoot it is slippery. Perching for a photo, I fall off the path. Mr. Liu cries with dismay. Happily, I hit a ledge not far below and am barely scratched. Liu's face is a study in anxiety as he peers down at me and begs, "Don't move, don't move. We will think of a way to get you up." Bright yellow butterflies hover around his head as I see it framed against the sky. Coordinating a plan with voices loud to rise above the rush of the waterfall, Mr. Liu and a Canton assistant pull me up to safety. There Mr. Chou stands grinning, hands on hips. A few moments before my fall, he and I had been discussing ideological questions. Now as I brush myself down he declares grandly, "I told you your standpoint was not firm!"

11. Education for Revolution

Education is a mirror to key values and problems in China today. I looked at six universities: Peking University, which is not often open to foreigners; Tsinghua University, a polytechnic praised by the government for its high level of political consciousness; the Communications University, formerly in Shanghai but moved in 1956 to Sian to help spread development more evenly over the whole nation; Fu Tan, a fine general university in Shanghai; Hunan Normal College for teacher training in Changsha; Sun Yat Sen University, a leading southern school at Canton. I also made visits to Middle Schools in Peking, Sian, and Canton, to a Physical Education College near Peking — where the basketball players, men and women, dwarfed my 6′1″ — and to a lively school of performing arts at Sian.

Schools, and especially universities (which I will stick to mainly), are in the grip of drastic experiments. Maoists — here I mean those who came out on top after the Cultural Revolution — said "revisionists" led by Liu Shao-ch'i sabotaged the 1958 reforms. These would have made education more egalitarian, and linked it more with the world outside the classroom. "Liuists" allegedly favored professionalism, competition, overspecialization, and individual ambition. They liked to have "professors rule the universities." Exams for them meant "ambush of the students." They exalted *san chung hsin* — "three core points" — namely, "Teachers, Classrooms, Textbooks." Ultraleftists embraced the opposite error of *san fou ting* — "three negations" — namely, total denial of the value of teachers, textbooks, and the classroom. The Cultural Revolution, claim the Maoists, fulfilled the hope of the 1958 reforms and set China on the path to a truly socialist education system. It had two principles: unity of theory and practice; education to "serve the working people." I went to see how this works.

You wonder at first if you are on a campus at all. Here at Communications University (C.U.) in Sian are people, dressed in conical hats and blue peasant jackets, threshing wheat (eighty thousand catties were produced on campus this year). In the Middle School attached to Peking Normal University, girls are making chairs. Next door are boys, helped by "veteran workers" from a nearby factory, making semiconductors. In Canton at Sun Yat Sen University (S.Y.S.U.) I found professors tending a vegetable garden, and many classrooms turned to strange uses. One is stacked high with peanuts, the next with rice — grown by the university (the campus has seventy mou under rice). When you sit inside these schools and talk, you find a sizable part of the management to be neither students nor teachers but People's Liberation Army men, manual workers, and Party cadres.

After two or three years without classes, many universities began again last fall with a small, handpicked enrollment. At Peking University (P.K.U.), where there used to be 9,000 students, the new class of September, 1970, numbered 2,667. At Fu Tan in Shanghai, formerly with 9,000, there were 1,196; at S.Y.S.U., 547 where there were previously 4,700; at Hunan Normal College (H.N.C.), 440, against 6,000 before the Cultural Revolution. Teachers outnumber students at present. Here are a few current figures for teachers, those for students in parentheses: Fu Tan, 1,263 (1,196); S.Y.S.U., 863 (547); Tsinghua, 3,000 (2,800).

These hothouse students are a new breed. None come direct from Middle School, but only after two to three years at farm or factory. They must be "politically sound" as well as bright and physically fit — much stress on health. If a would-be student is a "sturdy pine" politically, and has been strongly recommended by local units, it is not even necessary that he be a Middle School graduate. I found, however, that Peking University can and does reject applicants who have been highly recommended politically, if they are "simply not qualified" to do academic work.

An astonishing number of the new students are members of the Party or the Communist Youth League. At S.Y.S.U., for instance, 229 of the 547 students are Chinese Communist party and another 240 are CYL members. At Fu Tan, 359 of the 1,196 belong to the Chinese Communist party and another 458 to the CYL. Almost all of the new classes are offspring of "workers, peasants, or soldiers." At Fu Tan, whereas in 1956 only 25 percent were in this category, the figure is now 98 percent; at S.Y.S.U., 97 percent.

At Shanghai's Fu Tan, I drew aside one of the new students (call him Wu), a political science major. Dressed like everyone else in voluminous blue trousers, white cotton shirt, and plastic sandals, he is a peasant's son, thirty years old — the average age of the new students at Fu Tan is twenty-four. Between Middle School and coming to the university, he worked in the Bureau of Sea Transportation, and joined the Party. In the Bureau he earned Y49 each month, and following the rule for students who worked for ten years or more after Middle School, he keeps that wage while at university. (Other students get a state bursary of Y19.5.)

Wu is a canny man who knows and believes in Marxism. But he's sober as a judge — nothing at all of the panting Red Guard about him. He knows just why he's at university, and is grateful for this chance to study politics. He will probably go back to the Bureau when his course is done. Neither from Wu nor others of the 1970 batch of students I met was there any sign of student organizations of the kind that mushroomed during the Cultural Revolution. These students are handpicked, mostly from the countryside, outnumbered by teachers and cadres, and simply have their noses to the grindstone.

Life at university has changed. Courses are shorter: two or three years at Tsinghua, where it used to be six; three years at C.U., instead of five — the reduction is similar in all six universities I looked at. What has been left out, I asked repeatedly. At H.N.C. — a teacher-training college — they have dropped the courses on "methods of teaching." Not a great wrench, I gathered, partly because they'd been based on the ideas of the Russian educationist, Ivan Andreevich Kairov. At S.Y.S.U., math courses have been integrated into dynamics, physics, and electronics. The student gets his math along with one or more of these three subjects, and the math department has been dissolved and poured into these three departments. At P.K.U., ancient history is cut back and attention placed mainly on the nineteenth and twentieth centuries.

These cutbacks have brought problems — and temporary confusion. One distinguished scientist, whom I talked with on four occasions, discussed this matter of shortened courses around and around. Yet I still felt puzzled about how, as at his university, five years' scientific training could be put into two and a half. Our last meeting was at Peking Airport, and we touched the question again. He concluded on a note he had not struck before: "I was not myself opposed to keeping the five-year course. Now, well now, we just have to work out what we can realistically omit."

In the classroom, lectures are less frequent. Teachers must distribute in advance what they used to give as lectures; the class then becomes a forum. Though proportions vary a lot, often half the students' time is spent outside the classroom, on labor and "sharing experiences" with people in other walks of life. Exams have lost their terror — at least for students. Mostly, they are now open-book exams. Often there is no exam at all; the student is assessed by exercises done throughout the term. Exam questions are worked out with student participation. Not memory but analytic ability is weighed. The exam is considered a test of the teacher no less than of the student — and an educative experience for both. At the end of the course, no diploma awaits the student. Certificates may be given — practice varies widely — with written comments on the student by his teachers and some of his fellow students.

In Mao Tse-tung's home city of Changsha, I visited a place which may be considered the seedbed of these "new" educational ideas. It is the "Self-cultivation University" which Mao founded in 1921 and ran for two years. He had just returned from the first conference of the CCP in Shanghai. With his usual practical skill, he obtained a fine building for the university. Today you can still admire its spacious halls and charming courtyards. Within them, the young Mao mounted an experiment in radical education.

Since the Cultural Revolution, the visitor may peruse the university's records and documents, and copies of its bold and fiery journal *Hsin shih-tai* (*New Epoch*). In the Self-cultivation University, the purpose of study was frankly stated to be the transformation of society. Theory and practice were married; students made investigations among the peasants during vacations. There were few lectures; students read by themselves, thought for themselves, then held forums. No diplomas or exams existed. Students were not required to meet a host of regulations, and they could come or not come to "classes" as they chose. For China in 1921, it was revolutionary pedagogy (no wonder Mao found Peking University stuffy and pretentious, when he went there from Changsha in 1918). The reigning warlord, denouncing the university as a school of subversion, sent in troops to close it in 1923.

Brief as its life was, the Self-cultivation University was an early test of the ideas which have swung to the fore in Chinese education since the Cultural Revolution. "Education for revolution" was Mao's theme at Changsha in the 1920s; he would like it still to be the theme for China in the 1970s.

Mao likes to be thought of as first and foremost a teacher. It is not surprising, when you note the persistence of his early zeal for education, and his brilliant sense of pedagogy. In Shaoshan, Mao's birthplace, where exhibits of his life and work are displayed, I saw a document which is worth quoting at length for its flavor of Mao the teacher. Written in 1917, it is a notice for a new Workers' Night School which Mao founded, together with other students at the Hunan First Normal School (where Mao was training to be a teacher). Signed "Friends of School Society," its text reads:

"Gentlemen, please hear a couple of words from me.

"Gentlemen, what is the most unrewarding attribute you have? Do you know? The old saying is right: 'Can speak but cannot write, can write a few [characters] but cannot read, can count but cannot really calculate.' To be such a man is not too different from being a piece of wood or stone. So we must seek a little knowledge, learn to read and write, and do calculations, if we are to be an effective member of society. However, you gentlemen have to work in the daytime, and there is nobody to teach you. How can you learn? Well, we have come out with the best solution. We are establishing a night school at the First Normal School. It will meet two hours each night, from Monday to Friday. You can learn letter-writing, accounting and other such practical knowledge essential for everyday use. We provide the syllabus and all the course material; it is all free. For those who wish to attend these evening classes, please apply as soon as possible at the school office. Let us consider why we do this. The simple answer is that we wish all the workers well. Some might be aware of the difficulty which will be encountered when they try to go to school at night in view of the present curfew order. Well, we can guarantee safety. Each student will have an identification card issued by the night school. And if the soldiers or the policemen should ask, all you need to do is to present this identification and say that you are going to night school. If you do get into trouble with respect to the curfew, the school will act to protect you. So there is nothing to worry about. Do not hesitate; come and apply."

Some of Mao's characteristics shine from this leaflet: his drive, his practical sense, his burning desire to use knowledge for the making of a new world.

At P.K.U. I met the English class which was reading and discussing Aesop's fable "The Peasant and the Snake." They received me with clapping — though few, I found, knew where Australia is. On the walls of the airy old classroom was a picture of Mao, some quotes from him in English, and a world map. The teacher, a graduate of the University of Nanking, addressed the simply clad students by their full names. "Comrade Wu Tsetung, would you like to answer the Australian visitor's question?"

Since the teacher spoke with a BBC-British accent, so in their halting way did her enthusiastic students. This group of thirty-five had begun English only ten months before, yet could talk in simple phrases — remarkable compared with Western students after ten months of Chinese. Mostly, the students quizzed each other, in staccato English, about the fable. The courtly politeness amused me. "Who — will — answer — my — question?" Someone rises, is acknowledged, and with infinite pains stabs a reply. The questioner then says with a coast-to-coast smile: "Thankyou — very — much. Please — sit — down — now."

In a mixture of Chinese and English I questioned them (my Aesop was too rusty to go far into the fable, but I could see the moral being drawn from it: never trust appearances — that's what the peasant did, and he got bitten). Had they been out of the classroom on practical work, as the new order requires? "Well, it's not so suitable with English," explains the pink-cheeked daughter of a navy man. "The class learning Mongolian did — they went to Mongolia for several weeks. What we do is spend one day a week on a [nearby] commune." Were they sons of toil? Three of the thirty-five had military fathers; one an intellectual father; the others were sons or daughters (sexes about equal) of workers or peasants. All had, of course, spent the two or three years prior to September, 1970, in manual work — and they looked fit, even tough. I could not help concluding, after thirty minutes with this bright-eyed bunch, that P.K.U. had recruited new students who are both working-class and able.

Curriculum changes are big and complex. Let me draw their flavor by illustration. Here is Chou I-liang, Harvard-trained professor of history at P.K.U. After meeting him at the university, I invited him some days later to a quiet dinner *á deux* in the city. Middle-aged, of scholarly mien, Chou has close-cropped gray hair and large serious eyes. His specialty was once Buddhism — "but we don't do that sort of thing anymore." Now he works on Asian history.

But there has been little time for research in recent years, and his main writing work now is a modern history textbook, which will take account of "new interpretations" since the Cultural Revolution. Thus Li Hsiu-cheng and Shih Ta-k'ai, figures in the Taiping Rebellion, were previously thought admirable, but are

(ABOVE) At Fu Tan University in Shanghai, Liu Ta-chieh, professor of Chinese literature (right), with two graduate students and a PLA member of the university's Revolutionary Committee. Unusually, an English translation is supplied to the wall quotation from Mao. (BELOW) Blending practice with the theory of the classroom, pupils at a Middle School in Sian make sand wheels in the school's workshop.

now seen to have been "traitors." The team working on the text-book is a three-in-one combination of youth (Red Guards in this case), middle-aged (historians thirty-six to fifty-five), and older scholars. Until the textbook is published, many lesser colleges — who take their lead from P.K.U. — will not resume teaching modern history.

Professor Chou's own students have centered their studies this term on a nearby coal mine. One day a week for a ten-week pe-riod, they worked as laborers in the mine (Chou too). Concur-rently, they studied its history. It had been an American mine in the 1890s, then Belgian, and, later again, British. Three work groups each chose a special topic to delve into at research level. One traced the story of strikes in the mine. Another did the story of child labor; once, they found, 40 percent of the workers had been children. The third wrote a biography, based on oral data, of a veteran worker and his family. Drafts of it they read out to miners involved — a fiery baptism for the budding histori-ans. Meeting history in the flesh this way, Chou thinks, has proved an excellent pedagogical method.

At Fu Tan, I talked with Liu Ta-chieh, professor of Chinese literature. He was perhaps the only man I saw in China who looked like an old-style intellectual. The deliberate manner; the careful, almost ponderous way he would split straws; the style with which he gripped his umbrella and wielded his fan. What was the main change since the Cultural Revolution in the teach-ing of his department? "Well, my textbook has been dropped," replied Professor Liu, gravely yet with no emotion, referring to his influential three-volume work *History of the Development of Chinese Literature*. It had insufficiently stressed "class aspects" of literature. Among other changes of emphasis, *Dream of the Red Chamber* is now treated "less as a love affair — as if there's a kind of love beyond class, which comes from so-called human nature." Professor Liu had, it seemed, taken a buffeting in the Cultural Revolution. On the other hand, his salary was un-changed at Y348 a month — just under six times the lowest teacher's salary at Fu Tan (Y60).

He had assigned his new students an interesting project to

blend theory with practice. He selected a 1936 work by Hsia Yen, a leading writer of the 1930s but no longer admired. Called *"Pao shen kung"* ("Contract Work"), its setting was a mill in Shanghai, now Number 15 Cotton Mill. Hsia Yen, it is said, portrayed the workers in his story as disunited and subservient in mentality, silently accepting capitalism. "We told our students to study this work of Hsia Yen, then test the accuracy of the picture it presents. They live in Shanghai. They can go to Number 15 Cotton Mill, talk to old workers there, trace matters through. *Was* it as the author suggested?"

While Professor Liu recounted this, my Luxingshe aide whispered that when at Middle School, he himself had read this story, and it was then presented as a fine, sound piece of work. But today, Hsia Yen is known as an adversary of the great Lu Hsun. Needless to say, the students who went to the Number 15 Cotton Mill found "grievous distortions" in *"Pao shen kung."* I am not saying the "given" nature of the conclusion means the exercise had no value for the students; since I did not talk with them, I cannot tell.

These are tiny glimpses of a vast and varied educational experiment. The blend of theory and practice looks promising. There will be fewer electrical engineers, to recall the Canton driver's remark, who cannot replace a fuse. The learning process may benefit permanently. More to the point for the government, graduates will be more immediately useful to the economy, and the social gulf that always threatens China, between peasant and professional, will be minimized.

Yet problems are not lacking. In Changsha a student reasoned: "I come from the countryside. Yet no sooner had I come [to H.N.C.] than I had to go back for 'practical experience.' I don't need that again." He felt that as one of the new breed, he was "born red" and could now get straight down to study. In Canton there were grumblings from workers. This endless stream of students coming to the factory to get experience . . . It takes time to supervise them . . . Time is just not always available. Less serious, a new student at S.Y.S.U., who had been years on a commune, told me he found classroom discipline a bore. "I'm used to moving around all day, but now I have to sit like a stone at a desk."

The new order is egalitarian to a striking degree. This is true of the atmosphere of the colleges; respect based on mere status has apparently gone. And what education exists is open as never before to sons and daughters of the ordinary man. This is especially so of Middle Schools where the new order is fully operational. By cutting the years of schooling to ten, and taking pupils on a basis nearer to simple geographic proximity than to merit as tested by exam, China is making Middle School education almost universal. In Kwangtung province, these figures were given: in the past six years Middle School enrollment has leaped from 500,000 to 2.6 million (population of the province is 45 million); 95 percent of those who finish Junior Middle School now go on to Senior Middle School. Middle Schools where the children of an elite are concentrated, like the former "August 1" school for sons and daughters of military officers, seem to exist no more.

It remains to be seen whether this Middle School explosion can be matched by expansion at university level. At present, the road ends for nearly everyone after Middle School. I could get no national percentages, but clearly only a trickle of graduates from (expanded) Middle Schools can go on to (shrunken) universities. Understandably, there is a shortage of Middle School teachers. This will be made worse by the reduced college enrollment of the present period; it is hard to produce teachers when you are not sure what to teach them.

And if universities expand, what will happen to the present experiments? Can they be sustained if numbers in the universities climb back to pre-Cultural Revolution levels — some five to ten times the enrollment now? Enrollment, I was told at all six universities, is soon to be stepped up. But can special coaching for those not graduates of Middle School still be given, when there are ten times as many to coach? Can the pitch of "political soundness" be kept up — surely there cannot continue to be 80 to 90 percent of students belonging to the Party or the Communist Youth League? What about the increased burden on factories and communes which must receive students and guide their practical work? Will not troublesome student organizations reappear? Can decisions still be made by "discussion" — rather than by rule, or entrance exam, or a grading system — when there are ten times as many decisions to make?

I talked about the future with Professor P'u Chih-lung at S.Y.S.U., a biologist whose Ph.D. is from the University of Minnesota. P'u's own research has been redirected by the Cultural Revolution. No more esoteric topics that tickle his fancy, or publishing the results in learned journals. Now he heads a research project dictated by the needs of Kwangtung province. How to get rid of insect pests without using pesticides — which harm crops. He is developing new species which he calls "insects to kill insects" (as we inspected some of these monstrosities, Chou Nan dryly observed: "It's like the Nixon Doctrine — 'Asians to fight Asians'"). This way biology at S.Y.S.Y. serves the peasants of Kwangtung.

We strolled back from the laboratory to Professor P'u's two-storied home (the rent takes Y8 each month from his salary of Y360). He spread out his hands on the living room table and wrinkled his brow. "It's all experimental. We're trying to make universities more in touch with our country, its needs. We're trying to make it socialist — the door open to anyone, and doing work that will serve workers, peasants, and soldiers. But what the future holds is unclear. When you're on a new road you just don't know what is around the corner."

12. Chou En-lai

The prelude to a meeting with a Chinese leader is always the same. There is no fixed appointment time, but word is one day given "not to leave the hotel." Suddenly a phone call comes to say that the man you are to see has just left the compound where the Chinese leadership works. You leave immediately for the Great Hall of the People. The idea is to have the two parties arrive at the same time.

With Chou En-lai, Premier for twenty-two years and (last summer) number three man in China's government, the call is likely to come late at night. This war-horse of revolution, "seventy-three years young," works until 4:00 A.M. or 5:00 A.M., then sleeps until midmorning. Our group (I was with my countryman E. Gough Whitlam, leader of the Australian Labor party) was advised late on July 5 to stay about the Peking Hotel. There would be an "interesting film" that evening. The Foreign Ministry official did not explain why we were advised to put on suits and ties for the occasion. Just after 9:00 P.M. a call came: the film was off, Chou En-lai was on.

The Great Hall of the People is really the Great Hall of the Government. Only on highly formal occasions do the masses view its murals and tread its crimson carpets. A stone oblong in semi-Chinese style, it was built in a mere ten months around the time of the Great Leap Forward. Its fawn solidity stands guard over the biggest square in the world, Tien An Men; the Imperial City is to the left, the big museums opposite. The building's area of 560,000 square feet includes an auditorium for 10,000 peo-

131

ple, a room decorated in the style of each of China's provinces, and sparsely furnished halls such as the East Room, where we found the Premier.

He enters from one door, we from another. A red badge with the Chinese characters "Serve the People" lights up his tunic. He is all in gray except for black socks inside leather sandals and black hair showing strongly through silver fringes. Introduced to him by Ma Yu-chen of the Foreign Ministry (the man who attended James Reston at his hospital bed), I suddenly realized that he is a slim, short man. We talked for a moment of the background to the Whitlam visit; then he asked where I learned Chinese. Told "in America," he smiled broadly and said, "That is a fine thing, to learn Chinese in America!"

Recalling his amazing career over half a century, I marveled at his freshness. This man has been a member of the Politburo of the Chinese Communist party since 1927 (well before Mao); was forty-five years ago a close colleague of Chiang Kai-shek's in Canton; played leftist politics in Europe at the time of Lenin; covered the last miles of the Long March through north Shensi in 1935 on a stretcher, gravely ill. Now he reaches across an epoch of China's modern history to face Richard Nixon in the Ping-Pong diplomacy of the 1970s.

Though he is like David to Mr. Whitlam's Goliath (the Australian is six feet four), you quickly forget his height; it is his face and hands which rivet every eye in the room for the next two hours. The expression is tough, even forbidding, yet sometimes it melts into the disarming smile which used to flutter the hearts of foreign ladies in Chungking (Mr. Chou was the Communist representative in Chiang Kai-shek's capital during World War II). The eyes are steely, but they laugh when he wants them to. The voice, too, has double possibilities. One moment he is nearly whispering, weary and modest. The next he is soaring to contradict his visitor, and the streaky, sensual voice projects across the hall. From a side angle, a rather flat nose takes away all his fierceness. The mouth is low in the face and set forward tautly, giving a grim grandeur to the whole appearance.

The small, fine hands, moving sinuously as if direct from the shoulder, serve his rapidly varying tone and mood. Now they lie meekly on the blue-gray trousers, as he graciously compliments Mr. Whitlam on the Labor party's "struggle" to get back to power in Australia. Now they fly like an actor's in the air, as he denounces Prime Minister Sato of Japan. Now the right hand is extended, its fingers spread-eagled in professorial authority, as he instructs me to study well a recent editorial in the *People's Daily*.

Sitting back in a wicker chair, wrists flapping over the chair's arms, he seems so relaxed as to be without bones, poured into the chair, almost part of it, as persons seem part of their surroundings in old Chinese paintings. Beside this loose-limbed willow of a man, Mr. Whitlam, hunched together in concentration, seems stiff as a pine.

But the conversation is a freewheeling give-and-take. The Australian style, blunt and informal, fits in well with Mr. Chou's. The evening has a lively, argumentative note rare in talks between politicians of different countries, rarer still when the countries represent different civilizations. When he disagreed — as on how widespread militarism is in Japan — the Premier would interrupt in English: "No, no, no!" Talking of Australian affairs, he twice frankly said he hoped the Labor party would win the next election in 1972. Occasionally he struck a didactic note. "As you come to China," he said after suggesting a lesson Australia ought to draw (about the United States) from China's experience with Russia, "we ask you to take this as a matter for your reference." Both sides enjoyed themselves making barbs against John Foster Dulles's policies. The ambience was, in brief, keen and frank.

Mr. Chou's aides from the Foreign Ministry and the State Council office had prepared him well. He knew, from reports of what his visitors had said to the Chinese Foreign Minister, that on Taiwan and China's United Nations seat no great problem existed between Peking and the Labor party. Mr. Whitlam said a Labor government would switch Australia's diplomatic ties from Taipei to Peking, and vote for Peking's installation in the China seat at the UN. (Prime Minister McMahon's regime supported

Washington's unsuccessful "two Chinas" proposal in October, 1971.) So the Premier hardly touched these bilateral issues, but instead pitched a complex argument about the overall problems of Asia. (The efficient briefing continued throughout the week. At the evening's end, Mr. Whitlam happened to recall that his birthday was near. Five days later in Shanghai, the Australian found his birthday observed with a festive dinner and a large cake — tactfully adorned with a single candle.)

Mr. Chou painted a picture of China threatened by three adversaries: the United States, Russia, and Japan. In one way or another, the Chinese press has given this picture ever since November, 1969, when Japan — following the communiqué signed by Nixon and Sato — seemed to step up to the status of major enemy in Peking's eyes. Interesting in the Premier's remarks was the pattern of relationships he sketched between the three adversaries.

After preliminary talk, Mr. Chou reached for his mug of tea, sipped, swilled with deliberation, then asked a question which turned the conversation where he wanted it to go. He was going to be very direct, he warned. What was meant by saying, as the Australians had said the previous day, that the ANZUS treaty (which binds the United States, Australia, and New Zealand in mutual defense) was designed to meet any restoration of Japanese militarism? "That is a special approach to us, so I would like to ask you to inform us what articles or what points of that treaty are directed toward preventing the restoration of Japanese militarism?" Mr. Chou was fingering the apex of Peking's triangular anxiety.

The Australian background was explained. After World War II, Australia was much less anxious to sign a peace treaty with Japan than was the United States (and to this day Australians are slower to forget Japanese aggression than are Americans). The United States signed ANZUS (in 1951) in large measure to reassure an Australia (and New Zealand) still fearful of Japan. This perspective on ANZUS "down under" was shared by all shades of political opinion. The treaty was a purely defensive ar-

Just before the author was introduced to Chou En-lai, he took this close-up of the Premier. On the left is Professor Chang Hsi-jo, head of the People's Institute for Foreign Affairs; behind Mr. Chou, and obscured, are the Chinese Ministers for Foreign Affairs and Foreign Trade.

rangement, concerned not with Communist revolutions in Asia, but with Japan — the only country that has ever attacked Australia.

The Chinese leaders leaned forward attentively. The Ministers for Foreign Affairs (Chi P'eng-fei) and Foreign Trade (Pai Hsiang-kuo) were present with senior aides, but the Premier did all the talking. "You know, we too have a defensive treaty, concluded one year before the treaty you have." He recalled with a grim, ironic smile: "That treaty was called the Sino-Soviet Treaty of Friendship, Alliance, and Mutual Aid. And its first article was that the aim of the treaty is to prevent the resurgence of Japanese militarism!"

But what has happened, the Premier asked rhetorically, his eyes and hands now stirring to life. His answer, in a word, was that both Australia's ally (the United States) and China's ally (Russia) have gone back on their pledge to forestall any new danger from Japan. He charged that the Pentagon "is considering whether to give Japan tactical nuclear weapons or even something more powerful." Does not the fourth Japanese defense plan total $16 billion, one-third more than the amount spent on the three previous plans put together? The Nixon Doctrine, he noted, turns Japan into "a vanguard in the Far East." With a shrewd addition to the usual slogan ("using Asians to fight Asians"), designed to make his visitors feel their potential importance, he assailed the doctrine's motives. "It is in the spirit of using . . . 'Austro-Asians to fight Austro-Asians.' "

Then Mr. Chou weighed the actions of the Soviet Union. He never referred to it by name but by sarcastic indirection. "And what about our so-called ally? What about them? They have very warm relations with the Sato government." Unveiling China's vision of the world, the Premier wove in two further themes. The Russians, he observed, are also "engaged in warm discussions with the Nixon government on so-called nuclear disarmament." Now his point came home: "Meanwhile we, their *ally,* are being threatened by *both* [Japan, the United States] *together!*" He finished with an application to Australia's situation. "So we feel our 'ally' is not so very reliable. Is your 'ally' so very reliable?"

The Premier had a formidable case. He had put it with passion and embroidered it with detail apt for Australian listeners. It was, Whitlam conceded, a "powerful indictment," and the Australian took a few moments to marshal himself and probe its questionable parts.

• The first theme had been Japanese militarism.

• The second, the failure of Washington and Moscow to resist it.

• The third, the charge that the United States and Russia are in collusion with each other.

• The fourth, a deep skepticism that any country can really be the ally of any other, an assertion that each country is utterly alone in the world, with nothing but its own resources and its "independence" to gird it.

Throughout forty days in China, these four themes met me at high levels and low. Later there is more to say of each. But stay now with Mr. Chou, for he had a fifth theme in his analysis of the triangle of menace facing China. It was introduced by another of the curious historical analogies he is fond of deploying.

During the talk Mr. Chou showed a kind of fascination with John Foster Dulles. I remembered with a certain shame what had reportedly happened between these two men at the Geneva Conference in 1954. After lunch one day Dulles walked into the chamber and found only one man there — Chou En-lai. An embarrassing turn of events! Chou held out his hand. Dulles declined it (one account says he murmured "I cannot"), gripped his hands behind his back, and strode out. But this evening Mr. Chou displayed no bitterness, just amusement, at Dulles; and a hearty contempt for his policies. Recalling the circle of defense pacts, multilateral and bilateral, which Dulles made with nations on China's southeastern borders — and showing accurate knowledge of Dulles's role as an adviser to the Truman Administration before he became Secretary of State — the Premier mused that it seemed to be an imperative of the "soul" of Dulles to throw a military harness around China. He spoke, I felt, as a man gazing down the corridor of history rather than as one faced with burglars at the door.

Suddenly it became clear that this historical excursion was for the purpose of analogy. He switched to the present. "Now Dulles has a successor," said Mr. Chou with a laugh that was not a laugh of amusement, "in our northern neighbor." The Premier was launched in earnest on his fifth theme. *Today's military encirclement of China is by Russia.*

This emphasis — that the Dulleses of the 1970s sit in Moscow — was confirmed when discussion turned to present trends within the United States. Mr. Whitlam said that the "soul of Dulles does not go marching on" in America. American public opinion, he judged, would not again permit its government to practice the interventionism in Asia that resulted from the "destructive zeal" of Dulles. Mr. Chou responded: "I have similar sentiments to you on such a positive appraisal of the American people." By implication he agreed that Dullesism was now eclipsed in the United States.

Later he spoke admiringly of the strength of antiwar feeling from coast to coast in the United States ("Even military men on active service and veterans have gone to Washington to demonstrate"). He frankly revealed the source of his confidence about the future course of U.S. policy: "The American people will *force* the American government to change its policies." Casting around the room, Mr. Chou asked if his visitors had "in the past two years or so" been in the United States. They had. He then summed up with heavy stress: "So you realize from your own experience that in these past years the American people have been in the process of change."

Of course, the Chinese Premier disapproves of particular current U.S. actions in Asia; his words on Indo-China made that quite plain. But when he mapped *trends,* the United States did not seem to loom largest among his concerns. And when he analyzed the dynamics within the triangle of threat, the United States was evidently not the ultimate focus of opposition. He lashed Washington less for its own activities than for its support of Japanese activities and for its collusion with Russian activities.

Caution would be wise in construing what Mr. Chou said. Maybe the three threats to China are so diverse in character that comparing their magnitude is invalid. The Japanese threat is "rising." The Russian threat is "immediate" in a crude military sense. The U.S. threat may yet be the "biggest" if the three were to be measured objectively against each other at the present moment. A conversation cannot give systematic finality to this caldron of slippery variables. Nevertheless, it was all very different from what Peking was saying in 1964 or even two years ago. Here was a picture of the world that featured power more than ideology, fluid forces more than rigid blocs, emerging problems more than well-worn problems.

Recall that the Premier was talking to Australians, and with an Australian political leader whose views on Taiwan were not opposed to his own. So the two chief bones of bilateral contention between Peking and Washington — the UN seat, the U.S. military presence in Taiwan — did not even come into the conversation. Maybe Mr. Chou calculated that of the three threats to Chinese security, Japan was the one to stress to these visitors. The Russians are far from Australia. The American tie is intimate, and no Australian leader is about to break it. Japan, however, is both important to Australia *and* a country about which Australians have ambivalent feelings. Yet it was remarkable that Mr. Chou did not raise — nor did his Foreign Minister the previous day — queries about the substantial and sensitive American bases (some related to nuclear weaponry) that dot Australia. Mr. Whitlam told me he had expected — as I had — that the Chinese would harp upon these bases.

It was easy to see that Japan was in the forefront of the Premier's mind. Whichever country came up, he linked it somehow with Japan. He quoted the Japan Socialist party to buttress his point of view. Broaching the subject of nuclear weapons, he seemed more worried by potential Japanese weapons than by existing massive American and Russian stockpiles. Discussing the Australian Labor party's international connections, he wondered in particular if it was close to the Japanese socialists. Should not Mr. Whitlam, when he left China for Japan — Mr. Chou had somehow unearthed this unpublicized fact of Mr. Whitlam's itinerary — make a point of having serious talks with the Japanese socialist leaders as well as with Mr. Sato? The Komeito (Clean Government party) especially kept popping up. Mr. Chou had met with its leaders the previous week (I had traveled into China in their compartment and watched them photograph each other, the train, and the countryside all the way from Hong Kong to Canton). Was it not "quite something for a Japanese, Buddhist, pacifist party" to make the shift it has this year (to a rather pro-Peking position)? Musing on the Labor party's prospects of winning power in Australia next year, Mr. Chou again brought in the Komeito party, and made a comparison with it. But seeing its inaptness, he diplomatically qualified himself: "Of course it's different; your party is very near to power." A few days later, Mr. Whitlam was surprised that the Chinese put on his program a Japanese movie. Entitled *Our Navy,* it dealt with World War II and its background. The film was not out of the ordinary. But it seemed remarkable that the Chinese chose to show a foreign (military-political) film to a delegation visiting China; and no accident that it was Japanese.

13. Why Did Peking Receive Nixon?

Let us leave Chou En-lai there, broaden the canvas a little, and consider more of his remarks as they come into the story. As to diplomacy, I found Peking in a springtime mood of growth and hope. Some Western ambassadors, glazed by long years of boredom in Peking, flexed their muscles like invalids just out of bed. New ambassadors were arriving every few weeks, as the list of countries newly recognizing the People's Republic of China lengthened: Canada, Equatorial Guinea, Belgium, Italy, Nigeria, Chile, Kuwait, Ethiopia, Iran, Cameroon, Austria, Sierra Leone, Togo, Turkey, Rwanda, Iceland. The Chinese Foreign Ministry, severely short of personnel since the time of the Cultural Revolution, resembled a marketplace bursting with products but short of salesmen.

A bevy of ambassadors accredited to Peking had just returned from a "diplomatic tour" of South China. Nothing like this had occurred for years — for some it was their first sight of a Chinese city other than Peking — and they were accompanied in cordial fashion on the trip by a Vice Foreign Minister. Contacts between foreign diplomats and Chinese officials have this year increased manyfold. The French Ambassador remarked over dinner that his last guest had been Ch'iao Kuan-hua, Vice Foreign Minister and perhaps the leading craftsman of China's policy toward the West. (Ch'iao arrived in New York in November, 1971, to head China's UN delegation.) The Indian and British chargés, so long in the doghouse, still glowed from getting a warm smile and pleasant words from Chairman Mao at the last May 1 festivity. It was all like rain after a long drought.

But the most poignant element was the contrasting stance of the Russians and the Americans. The whole situation had put the men from Moscow in a foul mood. In Peking, where men will measure time less in weeks than in decades, foreigners were reminded of China's phase of diplomatic openness in the early 1960s — but now Russia was the odd man out in China's diplomatic thaw, instead of America.

The pinnacle of the summer's excitement — it was salt in Russia's wounds — was the Sino-American meeting in Peking in the second week of July and the announcement that Nixon himself had arranged to visit the Middle Kingdom. During my first week in China, I spent a morning at the Peking Arts and Crafts Factory, where delicate work is done in jade and ivory carving, lacquer, and the incredible *nei-hua* (painting a picture on a tiny bottle from the *inside*). Here were superb things — one piece just done was going on the market at 100,000 yuan ($40,000) — and several craftsmen, exponents of *nei-hua* and designers of gaudy birds, were ripe with fifty years' experience. But the factory's star project, now in the design stage, was an intricate ivory-carved memorial — paddles, balls, Glenn Cowan's long hair and all — of the visit to China by the American Ping-Pong players! No wonder the Russians gnash their teeth.

In the Chinese capital, during June, there were occasions to glimpse the unfolding of an apparently new America policy. It is a story of caution, uncertainty, yet basic consistency from the Chinese side. On Saturday morning, June 19, two Chinese diplomats received me in a faded lounge of the International Club. Beer and cakes were served — ambitious fare for nine-thirty on a Peking summer morning. I expected a *tour d'horizon* of Chinese foreign policy, and some exchange on Chinese/Australian relations.

But these two officials had other fish to fry. America was their interest, and I was hard put to get questions in on other matters. We discussed the various positions on China policy within the U.S. Administration and among Democratic senators and academics. We considered how McGovern differed from Kennedy on "one China" and "two Chinas." Why the Pentagon seemed tougher over Taiwan than certain elements in the White House. What the nuances of Harvard Professor John Fairbank's "culturalistic" approach to the Taiwan issue were, in contrast to his colleague Professor Jerome Cohen's "legalistic" approach. The center of gravity of their interest was entirely concrete and practical. Impossible to miss the difference from talking on equivalent topics to Americans. In America the thrust of the questioning of a foreigner is often "What do you think of us?" But these Chinese officials, caring little what the foreigner thought of China, were concerned instead with the question "How can China get what it wants?"

The second issue was the 1972 election. It was a thing of wonder to hear these officials of the most secretive foreign policy establishment on earth discuss the foreign policy angles of an American election. The cast of mind was like a blend of Jeane Dixon and the most ambitious kind of social science. They expected a statement, free of any ifs or buts, of who was going to win. It dawned on me that Peking might prefer to deal with a monolithic, dictatorial Washington rather than with the cacophonic pluralism of voices which democratic America is.

Like terriers to a favorite bone, they seemed to come back always to one issue. It boiled down to this. Which was the better prospect: the reasonable China policy of certain Democratic senators — with the uncertain chance of its becoming U.S. policy; or the less reasonable but evolving China policy of Nixon — with the certainty that here was a real live government you could do business with? I later learned that this was perhaps the crucial question on America policy facing Peking in the late spring and early summer.

The third issue was Henry Kissinger. How much power does he have over U.S. policy? Is it true that he is more "open-minded" toward China than key officials in the Pentagon and the State Department who also advise Mr. Nixon? Kissinger's alleged hostility to the Soviet Union strikes Chinese as one of his most positive attributes. I remarked that Kissinger finds Moscow's methods baffling: he sees decisions suddenly reversed, as if there were a "government A" and a "government B" tugging away in different directions. One of the Chinese said that that was exactly Peking's impression of Moscow. It reminded him of a saying dating from the fluid Warring States period (fourth century B.C.): *"ch'ao Ch'in mu Ch'u"* ("In the morning for Ch'in, in the evening for Ch'u"). "The Russians are just like that," he said; "you never know where you stand with them."

Struck by the interest in Kissinger's mind and writings, I did not yet know how immediate these matters were for Peking officials. But two features of the conversation at the International Club stuck in my mind: the apparent pragmatism of the analysis of American trends, and the isolation of two policies — Taiwan and the UN seat — to a degree that they seemed erected into absolute goals in themselves, not to be qualified by other goals.

Many people asked themselves, during these days in Peking, why the Chinese Ambassador to Canada, Huang Hua, still had not left for Ottawa. He had been named to the post months before, and his counterpart in Peking, Ralph Collins, was already installed. Late in June, I met a friend and colleague of Huang Hua, and asked him why Huang had not left for Canada. This Chinese diplomat said to me: "In April I talked to Huang Hua and said, 'When are you leaving for Canada?' He replied, 'Any day now.' Two weeks ago I saw him again and asked the same question, and he replied, 'Any day now.' " In fact, Huang Hua was being held back in Peking to prepare for the visit by Kissinger in early July.

Over the next few days I went to talk with more Chinese officials and with five European ambassadors (or chargés, in the case of countries which do not have full-fledged embassies in Peking) about Peking's America policy. Three points of note emerged concerning the genesis of the Sino-American flirtation.

A basis was laid in 1969, when Nixon saw De Gaulle and De Gaulle reported the talk to the Chinese, for an American move toward China which made it a little less difficult, two years later, for Peking to bring itself to believe that the U.S. President meant business. It is no secret that Nixon admired De Gaulle (this at least he has in common with Mr. Mao). He seemed moved to talk to the French President about some of his long-term goals. The man whom De Gaulle chose to relay Nixon's views to Peking told me of them, and of how they were received by the Chinese. Nixon declared to De Gaulle — in his third month in office — that he was going to withdraw from Vietnam come what may, and that he was going, step by step, to normalize relations with China. Peking was impressed with the first aim, and as events unrolled and U.S. troops came back from Saigon, began to realize that Nixon had meant what he told De Gaulle.

On the second aim — normalizing relations with China — Peking was more cautious. Could this traveling salesman in the lurid merchandise of anticommunism really bury the past on China policy? But at least an intriguing seed had been planted in the back of Peking's mind. Subsequent events — including Nixon's zigzag steps along the path of Vietnam withdrawal — suggested to the Chinese that the gap between words and deeds might be less in Nixon's case than it had been with Johnson. If he was doing what he said he would on Vietnam, perhaps he would on China also? This background — as European go-betweens testify — steadied Peking's hand during the Sino-American flirtation that swelled in the spring of 1971.

The second point is a double one about Laos. The "incursion" into southern Laos in February deeply alarmed China. One of the highest officials in the State Department cynically styled the attack a "widening down" of the war. Peking was more struck by the "widening" aspect than the "down" aspect. I had known in January — through friends of China's whom Peking consulted on the matter — that China was concerned at the possible use of tactical nuclear weapons in conjunction with the buildup on the southern Laos border (and the evacuation of South Vietnam's northern provinces). When the "incursion" began, Peking was anxious lest the government of Souvanna Phouma cave in under the pressure and fall to a rightist coup. Concerned also about northern Laos — Hanoi's chief concern, of course, was the Ho Chi Minh Trail in *southern* Laos — China had substantial forces put on alert in its bordering province of Yunnan.

But did Washington not assure Peking that the aims in Laos

were "limited"? A Northern European ambassador discussed this with Ch'iao Kuan-hua, Vice Foreign Minister of China. "We can never be sure," observed Dr. Ch'iao. He recalled the self-unleashing of General MacArthur on the Chinese-Korean border while Truman protested the "limited" nature of the United States's Korean operation. "We were fairly confident of Nixon's limited intentions in Laos, but not sure some general wouldn't take it into his head to provoke China, or cover failure with a drastic escalation." This Chinese view of events, said Dr. Ch'iao, can be discerned between the lines of the speech that Chou En-lai made during his March visit to Hanoi.

When the U.S.-backed incursion by Saigon into Laos failed, bringing none of the military and political complications that Peking earlier thought possible, Peking was buoyed. If anything, Chinese optimism about Indo-China was now higher than it had been before the Laos operation began. Saigon had (as a Chinese saying goes) "picked up a stone to throw against the people's forces only to drop it on its own feet." It had merely given fresh evidence of its military and political weakness. Peking's conviction that effective U.S. force in Asia is in a large and long decline also deepened. For Washington did nothing drastic to salvage the Laos incursion. In fact, the flirtation with the United States would not have unfolded if the U.S.-Saigon thrust into Laos had gone well (or greatly widened the war). Yet its lack of success provided all the more reason — given the logic which underlies Peking's whole America policy — to put aside doubts and press on with the flirtation.

The third point concerned tactics, and hinged on Peking's reading of the American domestic political scene. In the early spring, Peking had reached the point of being ready to permit one or more leading Democratic senators to visit China. It was part of the Ping-Pong package: there would be opposition politicians, as well as sportsmen, journalists, and scholars. But before the decision could be implemented, the mutual coaxing between the Nixon government and Peking accelerated. Hesitations about the Democratic senators occurred. The option was the one that we had discussed at the International Club: to coax Nixon further, or to cultivate the Democratic opposition. The Chinese were not sure they could do both. For the time being, at least, they (evidently) resolved to keep the line open with Nixon and see where it would lead. Exchanges continued between Washington and Peking. Neither McGovern nor Kennedy came to China in June, though at one stage it had seemed certain that one of them would.

To understand China's actions, it should be pointed out that in important respects the Republicans are less unacceptable to Peking than the Democrats. This is because of their greater hostility to the Soviet Union. Democrats, one Chinese official pointed out, "have been very keen on collusion with Moscow." He cited Averell Harriman, and the East Coast foreign policy establishment generally, to support his point. During the meeting with Chou En-lai, I noticed that in his indictment of Dulles, he stressed that Dulles worked out and began implementing his evil schemes while advising Truman, *before* he became Secretary of State in the Republican Administration. One may go further back — to Dean Acheson, whom the Chinese did not like — and the point is reinforced: Peking has no love for Democrats. Especially, today, because of the Democrats' alleged greater warmth toward the Soviet Union.

On July 2, I spent four hours with an eloquent spokesman of the Chinese government in a suite at the Peking Hotel. "Mr. Y" I called him in chapter six, in quoting his criticisms of Chinese propaganda; he, too, came to New York in November as a member of China's UN delegation. Though we planned to talk mainly of social developments and political thought, America was also much on Mr. Y's mind.

One small measure of his interest in the U.S. press — it turned upon an interesting detail — was that in speaking of what Chou En-lai said to the American Ping-Pong team, he unwittingly quoted not from the Chinese text but from the U.S. press. The Premier had said, recalled Mr. Y, that the event meant "a new page" in friendly exchange between Chinese and American people. I pointed out that the Chinese text said merely that the event "opened the door" to friendly exchange. Mr. Y explained he had got "new page" from the *New York Times*. His aide, who had been present at the meeting of the Premier with the U.S. Ping-Pong players, broke in to confirm that "new page" had indeed *not* been Chou En-lai's original phrase. Mr. Y (whose English is faultless) laughed when it was suggested that in recent months he seemed to be an even more assiduous reader of the American than of the Chinese papers.

This strategist and "ideas man" has for many years dealt with international matters. He was like a ship in full sail when explaining the new phase in China's foreign outlook. It clearly pleased him. He had argued for it; he knew its rationale. He made several points which are crucial to understanding why Peking is going down the path of détente with Nixon.

"The opening up is going to go far," he told me; "it's a big thing." He added sharply: "And it's about time we did it, too." But why has it now become possible? We spoke of the Taiwan problem, on which he gave the long-standing Chinese position and said that "everything" in Sino-American relations depends upon the removal of this bone in the national throat of China. But why, I asked, had China started people-to-people diplomacy with the United States at a time when Washington's policy on Taiwan was just as it had always been? Nothing on the Taiwan question, it seemed, could account for the genesis of the Ping-Pong diplomacy. Mr. Y had quite a different reason to give. "Yes, you are right. The U.S. government made no change on Taiwan. We did it because of the new attitudes among the American people."

This is not to say Peking was unimpressed by the gestures — in trade and other matters — which Nixon made toward China. Early in the summer of 1971, Chou En-lai inquired of a European ambassador in Peking: "What was the impact of the Ping-Pong trip, within the United States?" Said the ambassador: "It has helped the Democratic opposition to Nixon, yet it has also helped Nixon." The Chinese Premier came back: "I don't mind that. I am happy that China should take some steps in response to Nixon's."

But if certain of Peking's specific gestures are a response to certain of Nixon's gestures, the reason for China's new readiness to deal with America lies deeper. Mr. Y spelled it out in various ways. Essentially it amounted to this: China thinks *America no longer has the capacity to work its will in Asia.* Now Mr. Y warmed up to broach broad themes of history and theory. The gist lay in a distinction between military power and political goals. Washington has the first, but is muddled about the second. Hardly new to those who have lived through the "Vietnam years" in America.

But to hear it in Peking is to hear it in quite a fresh tone. Mr. Y is not bent on a theoretical discussion of options. This is not a "dissenting" quibble from within the camp. The hour is long past when Washington missed its chance to grasp the fact that military power from outside Asia is unlikely to attain political goals within Asia. Now I was listening to a Chinese official coolly describe the consequences in Asia of Lyndon Johnson's failure to grasp the point. An abstract truth at home had become concrete truth here in Peking. At home one debates the point dialectically — still hoping that wisdom may prevail. From a Chinese in 1971, the point somehow strikes home with a more final logic, if only because it comes from outside you, and with the weight behind it of Asia's most influential government.

There was therefore a curious authority to Mr. Y's analysis. A point I had made in the wilderness of theory and dissent since 1965 now stared me in the face as a cold, hard fact of international politics. The Far East is now the way it is because Asians like Mr. Y saw, and Johnson did not, the political limits of alien military force. I realized, as Mr. Y discoursed, to what effect the Chinese, with their long memories and their patience, had waited and watched through the "Vietnam years" while America bloodied its head against a wall largely of its own making.

"The United States put a million men around China." Mr. Y did not say "in Vietnam," "off Japan," "in Thailand," and so on, but "around China." And to what avail? "It simply has not worked." There was not a trace of moralism; he was like history's physician. "You can't do that for long. First, you have to *pay* for them while they are out there, far from home. You have to feed them, supply them, and this takes taxes which the American people will not sustain."

Some of his remarks came in Marxist dress, and the reasons he gave for the subsidence of U.S. power in Asia could be questioned. But he summed up well the nature of America's failure to prevail in Vietnam *and* the reasons why China is now ready to sit down and talk with the United States.

He came to a second problem that Washington has faced. "You have the troops there; you start a war, fought with no clear aims; but how do you end it? It is so easy to start these kinds of wars, but not so easy to wind them up." Finally he spoke of the various forms of power. "The third problem was that spreading all those troops around China did not even increase the bargaining power of the United States."

Do nuclear weapons increase a country's bargaining power? "Only if the other country fears them," he replied. "If the other country does not fear them, then nuclear weapons are not a deterrent, much less a decisive force in international struggles." Mr. Y was making an assumption that seemed basic to his view of the United States — that the United States almost certainly would not *use* nuclear weapons. Here was one more sign of its flagging will. He is less confident that the Russians lack the will to use nuclear weapons.

But Mr. Y did not merely mean that nuclear weapons are without power because they are unlikely to be used. He meant that they are literally without any power to change the world! For a country cannot be "captured" — occupied and ruled — by the use of nuclear weapons; only physically laid waste. And the importance of nuclear weapons short of their actual use — their deterrent effect — exists only if the potential victim fears them.

Mr. Y gave a picture of a China less pressured than in the past. More buoyant about its options. Possessing more room to maneuver. I sensed a link between enhanced international confidence and a readiness to be self-critical. Mr. Y spoke of the overselling of national historical monuments. "We have had so much escalating rhetoric here," he confessed. "Once I even went to two tombs in different places, each of which claimed to contain the same Han dynasty emperor!" The next moment he rather confidently dissects the troubles within the United States. It seemed that America's troubles were a kind of encouragement to this Chinese official (who does not hide from himself China's own troubles).

And America's troubles, Mr. Y felt, meant that America would now give China less trouble. Having lived for so long in a world they never made, encircled by those one million Americans under arms, the Chinese are starting to think that they may take a share in shaping at least Asia's future patterns. Like the two diplomats at the International Club, Mr. Y put greatest policy emphasis on Taiwan and the UN seat. He believed — and events so far have not shown him wrong — that there was a better chance now than in the past of China's getting an acceptable arrangement with the United States on these two long-standing goals.

He was candidly aware that some of America's "troubles" arise from its democratic institutions. Mr. Y is familiar with these institutions, and knows that "the people" means something totally different in U.S. foreign policy than "the people" means in Chinese foreign policy. In fact, it is not just or mainly that U.S. *power* to trouble China has declined. U.S. *will* to trouble China with energetic military activity far from America's own shores has sagged, because many Americans have lost confidence in the *morality* as well as the efficacy of that activity. Peking, of course, is not "troubled" by the complication of an influential public opinion on foreign policy.

Mr. Y was not blind to the sweetness, from China's point of view, of the displeasure caused in Moscow by the Sino-American flirtation. With his eagle-eyed watch on the U.S. scene, he had noticed things I had written. I recalled to him that in 1968 I had published (in *Motive* magazine) the prediction: "There will come eventually one small sign that Washington has accepted the Chinese present as a chapter in world history: the readiness of officials . . . to refer to 'Communist China' by its name, the

'People's Republic of China,' the way they brought themselves to refer to 'Communist Russia' by its name, the 'Soviet Union.' " Mr. Y had heard about the first occasion on which Mr. Nixon had publicly used the phrase "People's Republic of China" — when the Rumanian President visited Washington. He had also heard that the Soviet Ambassador in Washington, Anatoly Dobrynin, phoned Henry Kissinger in agitation the same evening to find out the meaning of this outrageous verbal accuracy. The incident made him chuckle. Pleasant that China, which Mr. Y was old enough to remember as the hopelessly "sick man of Asia," could without lifting a finger cause a ruffle between the "superpowers." It seemed to me, however, that he saw the frustration of Moscow as a by-product of the Chinese-American détente, not as a major Chinese goal in the pursuit of that détente.

That week in Peking, Kissinger's name cropped up with a frequency that puzzled me at the time. On the morning that Mr. Y mused on Kissinger's readiness to disregard Russian sensibilities if the science of power required it, Hsinhua, the Chinese news agency, reported Kissinger's arrival in Saigon. I did not know — no foreigner in Peking did, and precious few Chinese, since the Politburo kept the Chinese Foreign Ministry even more in the dark about the trip than Mr. Nixon kept the American State Department — that a later stop on the same journey would be Peking. But three days later, on July 6, the professor was again brought into the conversation, by Kuo Mo-jo, Vice-president of the Congress. During an interview about intellectual life in China, he interpolated musings about Kissinger's trip to Asia. Not again, I thought with a sinking feeling, for I wanted to draw the Chinese leader out more on cultural matters. But Mr. Kuo would make statements about Kissinger that sat in the air inviting response. "We don't know enough about the thinking of this man . . ."

There were others in Peking who would have liked to know more about the "thinking of this man." On July 10, Kissinger's main day of talks with Chinese leaders, I found myself at the North Vietnamese Embassy. The Hanoi official didn't know of

Kissinger's presence — he would not have talked to me at length that day if he had — but he smelled a rat in Sino-American relations. His informality — putting a hand on my knee, drinking despite the morning hour — did not hide but rather underlined his anxiety at some of the developments that had unfolded in the spring and summer of 1971.

Of course, Hanoi was pleased that Peking stressed so much, and so unusually, the seven-point peace proposal that Madame Binh of the Viet Cong made in Paris on July 1. But Nixon had launched "sinister schemes," said the Vietnamese diplomat. He grew more explicit. "We know that the ending of the U.S. trade embargo against China was designed to produce a response from China which might pose problems for our struggle." Hanoi's nightmare, I gathered from other sources, was that a "linking" might somehow be effected between Indo-China issues and the Taiwan issue. Knowing that some people in Washington have toyed with this idea, I now asked directly if North Vietnam had any fear that Peking might under some circumstances agree to such a linking. The answer was nonexistent but eloquent. The man from Hanoi alternately smiled and furrowed his brow. He leaned forward and put his hand on my knee. "What have the Chinese comrades indicated to you about this?"

14. Issues between China and America

Six days later I arrived by train from Nanking at the lakeside resort of Wusih (the town's name means "no tin." In the Han dynasty, two thousand years ago, the district exhausted its tin mines). Driving to a hotel in the midday heat, I heard the radio announcement of Kissinger's visit and Nixon's impending visit to China. Unadorned by commentary, it was identical with the seven-line story in the next day's *People's Daily*. There was no follow-up coverage, much less an orgy of speculation, as in the American press. The Chinese government closed up like a clam on informal talk with visitors about foreign affairs. Rich conversations of previous weeks were not repeated after July 16. Nor was I able, despite earnest requests, to go back immediately to Peking.

My hosts in Wusih, like workers in the city's factories, showed interest in the announcement, but were reticent about commenting on it. The Foreign Ministry official traveling with me, however, did not hide his satisfaction. The U.S. President was coming *to* China; this he stressed. Nixon said he wanted to come; Peking graciously agreed; the meetings would take place on Chinese soil.

Into policy matters the official did not venture. This was not merely because the phone call he had just received from Peking briefed him only in outline. He seemed totally confident that China's policies (touching Sino-American relations) had not changed and would not need to change. He spoke as if China were a fixed point in a fluid world. The United States was re-thinking matters. That is interesting, and can only be for the better. China is always ready to talk should America drop its hostility toward China.

Such blandness lay also, it seems to me, behind the lack of public attention in China to the turn of events. Of course, foreign policy options are not debated out loud in China as in the United States. Still, you cannot overlook the almost offhand confidence of Peking's approach to the flirtation with Washington. The Chinese want certain things from the United States. But they have waited a long time for them. They can wait longer. Especially since they see American opinion stirring unilaterally in rejection of rigid and expansionist policies of the past.

It is Nixon who is committing himself most. It is he who is under pressure to deliver the goods. So the Chinese attitude is, in a certain measure, to sit back and see what Nixon brings to Peking. Peking has formulated an eight-point agenda of items to discuss with the U.S. President. On these items the Chinese position has not noticeably softened. But the Chinese think that Nixon will have to soften *his* positions on some items, if his requested trip to Peking and subsequent diplomatic dealings are to prove a boon to him and not a liability.

It is not surprising, then, that the Chinese were rather tough with Kissinger in the July sessions. The last of the three talks began (according to the distinguished French reporter, Jean Lacouture) with Chou En-Lai dramatically declaring to Kissinger: "I am charged by Chairman Mao Tse-tung to tell you that miracles should not be expected from Nixon's visit here. It is not an end in itself. Its success depends on real steps accomplished beforehand by the one who will visit."

At the same time, the Chinese feel that they gain more than they risk from détente with the United States. They have been seated in the UN. Equally important, the international status of the government of Taiwan slides quickly downward. A wedge, too, is inserted between Taipei and Washington. As a result of these developments, Peking's desired solution to the Taiwan issue becomes more likely. Russia gets stung. Not least, Peking obtains a dose of generalized prestige from the fact that President Nixon visits China, at his own request, before he visits

Moscow or Tokyo. (Indeed, Peking will be ahead of Moscow and Tokyo in having *any* U.S. President visit it.) On the side of cost, there is a possible loss of credibility with various anti-imperialists. But Hanoi's anxiety — now less deep than last summer — is the only serious problem here.

A barometer of the atmosphere at the Kissinger-Chou talks is the UN issue (though it has never been the most important issue in Sino-American relations). I do not believe that Kissinger and Chou set the UN issue "aside" when they met last July — as was often said in the press. Nor that Peking was ready to go ahead with détente regardless of what happened in the UN. I believe the issue was set aside, after July, because the two sides knew what was going to happen in the UN. Fragments of information available to me about the July parleys add up to a picture of delicate diplomacy-at-a-tangent. During the many hours of rather tough talks, the two sides gave each other a statement of intention on the UN issue. Since the talk dealt with votes and agendas in an international organization, each side could state what it would *seek,* but not guarantee what it would *attain.*

The distinction was crucial. It permitted two statements of intention to seem — to a beholder who wanted to see it that way — like an agreement on what would result. The Chinese were satisfied with what they concluded from this diplomacy by indirection. No sign exists that the United States was deeply dissatisfied.

First, it seems, the Americans indicated that they would support the seating of Peking in the China seat at the UN this year — which means a Security Council seat, as one of the permanent five members wielding a veto. Second, the visitors served notice that, should Taipei fight to keep some sort of UN place for itself, the United States must support this attempt. This place would be, at most, membership in the General Assembly. Third — here we enter the twilight land of signals — the U.S. side said it "did not know" whether the attempt to keep Taipei in the UN would succeed or not.

The Chinese responded also in three parts. They took note with undemonstrative approval of Washington's decision to back the installation of the People's Republic of China in the China seat. Second, they warned that should the effort to retain the Kuomintang regime in some UN role be mounted, Peking would vigorously fight against it. Finally, the Chinese gave their own signal with all its overtones: the government of China was confident that the effort to salvage a role for Taipei would fail.

Given the context — that the mutual coaxing during the spring had gone well enough to bring Kissinger over the Himalayas to Peking, and that Nixon wanted to come to China within a year — the U.S. position in these talks could be interpreted as having an element of shadowboxing about it. Secretary of State William Rogers' subsequent statement of August 2 did not mean quite what it said on the printed page. Yes, the United States will fight to keep a UN place for Chiang Kai-shek. But if the United States "does not know" whether this will succeed, and China is sure it won't, the two sides are not as far apart as they seem. Peking was not as outraged by Rogers' statement as its press made out. Though enticed to do so by journalists, no Peking official said Rogers' statement meant Washington had gone back on anything Kissinger conveyed to Chou. Yes, the Chinese called the Rogers formulation "absurd." But they did not say that the United States had deceived China or broken a promise.

In Washington a certain backpedaling began. Mr. Rogers confessed, with more sorrow than anger, that the United States had found through international consultations that "there is a good deal of support" for assigning the China seat in the Security Council to Peking rather than Taipei. He added, "We haven't made a decision about our own policy." Two weeks later, Mr. Nixon decided — in Peking's favor. Washington then came out with a double proposal for the UN debate: Peking to have the China seat; a separate, lower place to be salvaged for Taipei in the Assembly.

Meanwhile, U.S. spokesmen underlined that though every effort was being made, success for this position could not be guaranteed. By the time Foreign Minister Fukuda of Japan came to Washington in early September, it smelled as if Mr. Rogers were foreshadowing failure and looking around for others to share whatever blame failure might trigger. If Japan did not cosponsor the U.S. resolution, he warned, this would have "a detrimental effect" on the resolution's chance of success. Japan did cosponsor, but the resolution failed.

The grief in Washington was not searing. Mr. Nixon seemed more upset by the "manners" of the voters than by the vote itself. Mr. Rogers cried out "We tried hard" more relentlessly than sincerity would seem to have required. George Bush, American Ambassador to the UN, was not unhappy with his image as a mighty arm-twister. Given Nixon's fear of a right-wing rampage if U.S. fortunes in Asia should plummet, it is no surprise that Bush was told to make an elaborate effort to hold an Assembly seat for Taiwan. Yet the photographs of Kissinger conferring in Peking in the days before the UN voted were more eloquent than anything Bush did in New York.

Interestingly, Washington wished Kissinger's second visit to China to take place a little earlier than did Peking. According to the joint announcement of October 5, the trip was to be in "the latter part of October," but on the same day Kissinger spoke of going to China "shortly after the middle of the month." In fact, Kissinger reached Peking only on October 20, by which time the UN drama was building to its climax. Moreover, the White House had said on October 14 that the visit would last "about four days," but it actually lasted six days, even though business was not so pressing as to prevent Kissinger from going sight-seeing and to the theater. So it turned out that Kissinger was still in Peking when the vital UN votes were taken, and signs are that Peking wanted it this way. Maybe the Chinese had in mind a slightly different course of events, should a slipup have occurred at Turtle Bay on October 24 and 25.

The gap between "seek" and "attain" had richly served Sino-American relations. Nixon lost a battle at the UN on October 25, but salvaged a campaign (perhaps *two* campaigns). The Pakistani delegate at the UN aptly said just after the vote that one big reason for the outcome was Nixon's new China policy. (Chou En-lai himself said the same thing one month later.) Nixon's new China policy, in turn, will ultimately benefit from the

UN vote, as may Nixon's prospects for reelection. Meanwhile, Peking took it all so calmly that not a single Chinese newspaperman was sent to the UN to cover a drama climaxing twenty-two years of struggle in which China was the key party involved.

Within China, the UN issue seems a bagatelle compared with the Taiwan issue. At the Museum of the Peasant Institute in Canton, a vast wall map gives details of the Revolutionary Committee of each province. When you press a button, a light flashes on with the date on which the Committee was established. I pressed Taiwan (Taiwan is invariably included on any map of China within China). A red light flashed with the characters: "We shall certainly liberate Taiwan!" The phrase is a theme song all over China.

In the beautiful hills near Sian lies the craggy cliff where Chiang Kai-shek was captured in 1936 by one of his own disgruntled generals — the famous Sian Incident. The place is now a lush and tranquil hot-spring resort. Emperors of the Han and Sui dynasties had summer palaces here, and the Communist government has built superb pavilions in traditional style to fit the history-laden ambience. My companions laughed and joked as we inspected the room from which Chiang fled — leaving his dentures behind — when shots pierced his windows.

We climbed the hill where Chiang had clambered in his nightdress. At the place of his capture stands a handsome portico. But it was built not by the Communists, to mark this spot of Chiang Kai-shek's personal tribulation, but by Chiang's own government, in 1946, apparently to try and blot out with glory an ugly memory! After 1949 the new government left the portico intact. Beside it, in red paint on the cliff face, they have simply added: "We shall certainly liberate Taiwan!" As if to suggest that, just as Chiang was nabbed here, so in the fullness of time he will be nabbed in Taiwan.

No issue seems more important than Taiwan when you talk with Chinese, official or nonofficial, about international affairs. It is pointed out that in 1950 the U.S. government reversed itself on Taiwan. Until that time, Washington considered Taiwan part of China, and planned no support for Chiang Kai-shek's bid to set up an alternative China. Came the Korean War. As part of its military encirclement of China, the United States, it is recalled, then backtracked and began the long, increasingly ludicrous sponsorship of Chiang and his dreams. Ignoring that Chiang had lost out to a stronger and more popular force, the United States from then to this day has (officially) considered his group the government of China.

But now the movement at the UN has unfrozen the Taiwan issue. As Peking envisaged, the displacement of Taipei from a UN seat begins a "softening up" of the Taipei regime's front of bravado. Practical talk on modalities will now become possible between Peking and Taipei. A Chinese official said to me in July that China would not go into the UN if the arrangements left Taiwan some kind of "international label or status." That statement implies that Peking expected resolution of the UN issue to go a long way toward resolving the "international" aspect of the Taiwan issue.

So it is proving. A long-overdue downgrading of the Taiwan issue is taking place. In Washington, as in other capitals, Taiwan's importance in the whole landscape of China policy increasingly shrinks. U.S. officials seem now to think, for instance, that the effect of Nixon's new China-policy on Japan is far more important than its effect on Taiwan.

Visiting China in the summer of 1971, I considered the key question over Taiwan to be *how* Peking's sovereignty over the island is to be reasserted. Of course there are people who argue fiercely against this. Some cry out — at this very late hour — for the lofty cause of self-determination. Others, forgetting that Chiang's brilliant future is entirely behind him, would back him to the hilt and even "unleash" him against the "mainland." But the real question now is *how* an end will be put to the present false status of Taiwan, and its relationship to the rest of China modulated. Diplomacy must henceforth focus, it seemed to me, on encouraging Peking to reassert its sovereignty over Taiwan gradually, peacefully, and partially (granting the island a certain autonomy); rather than suddenly, violently, and without regard to the fact that the island is not just a province like any other province.

So I probed in Peking the possibility that China might give clarifications on three points. What method would it consider appropriate for taking over Taiwan? Would the province of Taiwan, after its liberation, have any military role, and if so, what? (Will there be major air bases such as the United States now maintains — the Ching Chuan Kang base and the Shulinko base — or nuclear weapons as the United States probably now has on the island?) What will Peking's economic policies in Taiwan be, and will there be reprisals against those who have opposed communism? Every side would gain, including Peking, if undertakings could be given on these questions which trouble anyone concerned that justice be done to the people in Taiwan.

On June 18 I learned, when dining with them, that Seymour Topping of the *New York Times* and William Attwood of *Newsday* would soon talk with the Premier on U.S.-China relations. The next morning was my session at the International Club with the two Chinese foreign affairs officials. If the Premier, as rumored, was going to say something notable on Chinese attitudes toward the United States, could he clarify one or more of these three questions about Taiwan? Appreciation for China's position within the U.S., it seemed to me, might increase if Peking would speak at least in general terms about the future of Taiwan. It would be harder for extreme anti-Peking elements, such as the "China Lobby" remnants, to claim that a smile at Peking today will mean a bloodbath for the people in Taiwan tomorrow.

Two days later, the Chinese Premier talked about Taiwan with Topping, Attwood, and Robert Keatley of the *Wall Street Journal*. In the past, Chinese leaders have refused to discuss how they would deal with Taiwan if they re-took it (as well as how they would re-take it). It has always been claimed that this is purely an internal Chinese matter. But on June 21 Chou En-lai departed from this practice.

First, he stressed that the island would benefit economically by returning to mainland rule. Income tax would be abolished, existing wage scales would be kept, living standards would be "gradually improved." Second, far from there being reprisals, Peking will "reward" Taiwan for the contribution it will begin to make to the motherland. In particular, the Premier said any unemployed residents of Taiwan who left the mainland in 1949 "could go back to their home provinces and they will not be discriminated against." Hinting at Peking's probable attitude toward Kuomintang leaders, Mr. Chou recalled that those leaders who have already gone over to the mainland — many did in 1949, a few did later — are being "well looked after."

Third, the Premier acknowledged that such clarifications do have a link with the prospects for Sino-U.S. relations (a marked departure from the old insistence that Taiwan's affairs are absolutely no one else's business). Observing that Taiwan will "benefit and not be harmed" by its return to mainland rule, he added, "If this is done, then relations between China and the United States will be all the better." In other words, Chou recognized the reality, if not the right, of American concern with the fate of Taiwan.

On June 23 I met at the Foreign Ministry one of the two officials who had talked with me at the International Club on June 19. Accounts of the Premier's talk with the three American newspapermen had been published. He smiled as he held one report in his hand. "Well, here is the clarification about Taiwan. The Premier has now spoken of what will happen to Taiwan after its liberation." I remarked that Mr. Chou had indeed clarified one of the three questions — what will happen to the island economically, and will there be reprisals. But not the other two.

In fact Chou En-lai had specifically confronted one of the other questions — by what method would Taiwan be liberated — and flatly refused to clarify it. "How Taiwan will be liberated is our internal affair," he had said to Topping, Attwood, and Keatley. The official in front of me on the steps of the Foreign Ministry said, "Look, you will never get 'clarifications' on these two military points."

Nevertheless, when Mr. Whitlam arrived, the Chinese were again asked for clarifications on the remaining two points. (On China policy in Australia, Mr. Whitlam's position rather matches Senator Kennedy's in the United States. He accepts none of Chiang Kai-shek's claims. But he cannot shrug off all concern for what happens on Taiwan if and after Peking takes it.)

On July 4, Whitlam broached the topic with Foreign Minister Chi P'eng-fei. By what means does Peking envisage "liberating" the island? And will the island have any significant military role after its liberation? (This latter point is a matter of concern to countries close by to Taiwan, and directly affects the desirable possibility of creating a zone free of nuclear weapons in northeast Asia — whereby South Korea, Japan, and neighboring waters would be kept free of such weapons if China kept her eastern provinces free of them.)

Mr. Chi did not much like the question, yet it is noteworthy that he did give an answer. In the past it has been explained that China has no obligation to answer such "domestic" questions. Mr. Chi said two things with some deliberation. "China believes in political, not military, solutions for such problems," and then: "The process will not be too difficult."

All this is far from a full picture of Peking's intentions toward Taiwan. Yet it does offer clarifications and it does convey a mood of flexibility. Mr. Chou's and Mr. Chi's remarks indicate that China is unlikely to disregard world opinion as the moment of opportunity comes for it to reach out for Taiwan. Peking is unlikely to deal as harshly with Taiwan as it dealt with Tibet. All signs are that they expect a political bargaining process to eventually take place, in which Peking will make — at least for a transitional period — certain concessions to whatever elements in Taiwan are able to demonstrate political strength.

But this political bargaining cannot begin in earnest until Taiwan is fully defused as an international issue. The UN developments have done this to a degree; the big next step will be military withdrawal by the United States from Taiwan. I understand that in July, 1971, Kissinger talked to the Chinese about this matter. Before the Chinese agreed to invite Nixon, the United States side intimated that by the time Nixon reached Peking, further reductions in the United States military presence on Taiwan would have taken place.

In the Chinese view, there are two parts to the Taiwan problem. One is the United States military presence on the island. The other is the political gulf between Peking and Taipei, and the methods of bridging it. Only the first part, say the Chinese, concerns the United States (or any other nation). Washington is not being asked to "hand over" Taiwan to Peking — only to stop regarding its government as the government of China, and to takes its bases away. This leaves the door open to give-and-take between the two sets of Chinese, and to a process of reabsorption that could stretch out over decades.

In his talk with me, the nimble-minded Mr. Y observed, "There's an easy way out for the United States on Taiwan. Simply announce a return to the position Truman stated in 1949–1950 — that the U.S. is not going to interfere in the destiny of Taiwan." We do not know, because it has not been put to the test, how reasonable Peking would be about the second part of the problem (Taiwan's political reintegration into the mainland) if the U.S. were, as Mr. Y suggests, to solve the first part (U.S. disengagement from the problem) by returning to the Truman formula. It may well be in American interests to do this. To gradually phase out Taiwan as a base, and concentrate American bargaining power with Peking on trying to ensure that China will reassert its sovereignty over Taiwan gradually, peacefully, and with provisions for the island to enjoy a certain "autonomy" in the Chinese tradition.

What overall impressions does the visitor to China get about Peking's view of America? Toward the United States, China has a mainly negative aim: to be free of the military harness that the U.S. has thrown around East Asia since the Korean War. China wants to consolidate its revolution. The only way America can help, in China's view, is by not interfering. The Chinese know they are still weak by the standards of the superpowers, yet they know also that they are rising. They consider that time is on their side.

There are strong lines of continuity with the past in these attitudes. Not so much with the Confucian past of the dynasties, but rather with the anticolonial experience of the last century. Americans may be shocked by the suggestion, but the Chinese see *post-1945* America as a direct successor to the colonial powers which bullied Asia. The period from the Opium War until the present is a seamless stretch of history to Peking. First, because throughout it, China has faced superior material force on its doorstep. Second, because the Chinese mind has felt frustration, and often humiliation, when looking during this period at the West. The West has threatened China; yet the West is more advanced than China. It is a painful mixture for the patriotic Chinese mind. To *keep the West at bay* and to *catch up with the West* have both been among China's concerns.

One reason that communism wins wide allegiance in China is that it helps China achieve both these aims. It gives China the unity and the ideology to be anti-Western. And it is a vehicle of modernization. But Mr. Nixon has also made a contribution to easing the first concern. He called a halt to American expansion in East Asia, and now actually reverses the process. This is what Peking has always wanted. The Democratic Administrations saw the Chinese question too much as a mere problem of communication. They offered Peking exchanges of doctors, seeds, journalists, and other good things of life. But at the same time they kept on building up the military harness around China's throat. Peking scoffed at Johnson's honeyed offers, and deeply feared his imperialistic actions. But Nixon is delivering the goods. Month by month, he draws back more and more ground troops from China's doorstep.

With their long view of history, the Chinese sit back and talk about this historic shift with a philosopher's detachment. It was inevitable, they say, that the U.S. should have found its East Asian adventures counterproductive. China did not have to wait all that long to see it happen. America's burst of global imperialism was, by Chinese standards, an affair of a single evening. It only ran from the quivering sense of power of 1945, until the lesson of the powerlessness of power in Vietnam.

When the Australians met Chou En-lai, Mr. Whitlam started to rake over the embers of Vietnam, saying how misguided the United States had been, what a tragedy the war was. But the seventy-three-year-old Premier cut him off. With a large gesture, he said grandly, "What is past is past," and went on to chew at the bone of Japanese militarism. Mr. Chou feels able now to look beyond the twenty-five-year spasm of American expansionism in Asia. Dozens of talks that I had in China ran along the same lines.

Some Chinese dwell much on internal upheavals in the United States. "We notice the obsession with sex," one official remarked. "It is the sign of a crumbling order. The late Ming period was the same. Sex was everywhere. Soon the dynasty collapsed." But what occurs within the U.S. is minor to the Chinese. It is what the U.S. does in Asia that concerns them.

Of course, as China grows in power, its ambitions will increase. It will go, when it is able to, from "strategic defense" to "counteroffensive." China may not always be in a condition of relative weakness. It will not forever be in the mental situation of coping with a painful past. Positive goals will be asserted. Having "stood up" (Mao's phrase), China is likely to "stretch out."

The Nixon visit to Peking begins a dialogue that results from a shift in the balance of forces in East Asia. The United States is adjusting its role; Peking welcomes the adjustment. The tough bilateral issue is Taiwan (it is interesting — and not unpleasant in Peking's ears — that Henry Kissinger considers Vietnam essentially a problem of the past, and Taiwan the next East Asian problem). If Taiwan gets settled, the way is wide open for Washington and Peking to cooperate in whatever ways the flux of world power may at any point intimate. The conflict of interest between the United States and China is not extensive. (That between Japan and China is greater, and so is that between Russia and China.) Nixon and Mao are not rigid men, and they look out today on a strikingly fluid world.

One day in Peking I met a jade carver at a handicrafts factory. He was a shrewd, humorous old man who has practiced his art for forty years. I watched his nimble fingers and darting eyes. He was carving fruit and vegetables. Struck by the range of colors, I asked if they were natural. "Yes, the jade has many different colors," the craftsman replied. Then he explained to me an uncertainty about carving vegetables in jade. "I cannot tell, when I start, what color the jade is inside." He showed me a jade piece, cut at an angle; the edge was green and the middle red. "So I am not sure, at the start, what vegetable I will end up carving from the piece of jade. Take the piece I am working on now. If the inside is red, I will make tomatoes. If it is green, I will make cucumbers."

So it may be with the relationship Nixon and Mao are carving out. The lump of jade is the international context of the Sino-American dialogue. Who knows whether it will turn out "red" or "green"; whether Nixon and Mao will make "tomatoes" or "cucumbers"? The Chinese leaders may be as uncertain as the jade carver about what product (beyond a Taiwan settlement) will appear. They are so worried about Russia and Japan that they may want to go far down the road of détente with the United States. But how far does the inscrutable Mr. Nixon want to go?

15. *Chez* Sihanouk

One of Peking's finest residences is the former French Embassy in the old Legation Quarter. Its oak panels, stone balconies, and central location are no longer enjoyed by the French — who occupy a bare and functional villa in the new diplomatic section — but by the Royal Government of National Union of Cambodia. The leafy compound bounded by a big red gate and two lions contains Prince Norodom Sihanouk and ten of his ministers who operate from China. It also contains the Chinese Ambassador to Cambodia, K'ang Mao-chao. Mr. K'ang was too busy to see me (What does he do?), but the Prince himself passed a morning talking about the Cambodian tragedy, and offering impressions of the senior Chinese leadership.

Beyond the top of a spiral staircase the furnishings are mostly Chinese. Near my chair hangs a glinting mother-of-pearl montage of the Nanking Bridge. But when the Prince bounces in it is easy to forget you are in China. He is Latin-like and passionate. He tries to convince you of his opinions with frank and very personal argument. In all respects he presents a total contrast to Chinese style. The hands are small like the whole body, but the eyes are tremendous as he warms up. He has a most expressive way of turning his mouth down, now in candor, now in disgust. At times he edges almost off his chair, as when he describes the Vietnamese, with an expansive gesture of face and limbs together, as *"Très forts! Très, très forts!"*

At the conversation's end a photographer came in to take a picture. But was he really a photographer? He pointed the camera almost at our feet. When the picture was developed, the Prince let out a cry of dismay to find just our two pairs of legs — and those at a thirty-degree angle. The second effort was little better. Only under Sihanouk's detailed supervision — it was like the old days in Phnom Penh, when Sihanouk directed films and dramatic performances — did the beaming Cambodian assistant manage to get both the Prince and myself into a photo. Glossing the picture, Sihanouk jerked his head toward the photographer and asked me, "Do you know who he is?" I knew only that he wasn't a professional photographer. "It's Sisowath Sirik Matak's brother [Sisowath Metheavei]," Sihanouk casually remarked. "He used to be my Ambassador in East Germany before the *coup.*"

The Prince referred back to an early part of our talk. "You remember I told you Lon Nol, Sirik Matak, and the others listen to my broadcasts from Peking? How do I know? Well he [pointing to the former Ambassador] gets letters from Sirik Matak and others in the family. They describe the scene. On the evenings when my broadcast in Khmer comes — about 7:00 P.M. in Phnom Penh — they gather round the radio. They listen in silence." Sihanouk's establishment in Peking is that sort of place — an ambassador takes the pictures. The Cambodian situation is that sort of situation — one brother runs one government, another works for the rival government, and the two of them exchange letters. Sihanouk is that sort of man — even his successors and would-be murderers are not immune to the emotional appeal of his patriotic commentaries.

The Prince had kept me waiting a moment at the start. He was sending a cable of thanks to President Kaunda. Zambia had just become the latest country to recognize his government. Sihanouk thinks the National United Front (N.U.F., the movement on which his government is based) will take Cambodia back by the end of 1972. "By then Nixon will be forced to withdraw just about all his troops. And we can cope with Lon Nol and Thieu." He felt good about the military situation. Two-thirds of Cambodia and 4 million of its 7 to 8 million people, he claimed, are controlled by the N.U.F. "Lon Nol has to import rice but we

Prince Norodom Sihanouk with the author, in the headquarters of the Royal Government of National Union of Cambodia (formerly the French Embassy). This is the picture taken by the brother of Sirik Matak.

The author snaps his two constant companions in China, atop the Great Wall: Mr. Chou Nan of the Chinese Foreign Ministry (now at the UN) and Mr. Liu Ju-ts'ai of Luxingshe. Military men are much in evidence; an army group relaxes further down the Wall. Like a piece of twine tossed by the gods across the mighty hills of North China, the Wall ran some 2,500 miles.

have enough rice in our liberated areas. We also supply food — rice and fish — to the Vietnamese and Laotian forces operating in Cambodia." He has no doubts about his own continued popularity within Cambodia. And it is hard not to be convinced of his argument that the people of Cambodia are far worse off now than when he ruled them.

Toward the United States, Sihanouk showed little emotion, but insisted that Washington stop "interfering" in Indo-Chinese affairs. On the one hand, he demanded American withdrawal; not only of ground forces, but of air and naval forces. "The U.S. may give weapons to Lon Nol, if it likes, but must not participate in the war itself. China gives weapons to one side; America has the right to do that also." On the other hand, the Prince found something to praise in Mr. Nixon. "I am happy to see his statement that after the United States withdraws, if the fighting still continues, that is a purely Indo-Chinese affair. This is a reasonable position."

The Prince has grave problems within his own camp. They stem from the fact that he, a Buddhist socialist whose career has been the very definition of nonalignment, now works in harness with Communists. The N.U.F. includes the Khmer Rouge, which has "pro-Vietminh" elements, "pro-Chinese" elements (younger men), and "pro-Russian elements." These last, oddly enough, are substantially represented among the ten ministers in Peking. "They are discreet, knowing the realities in China," Sihanouk observed, "but they like Russia." The crucial line of division within the N.U.F., however, is not within the Khmer Rouge but between the Khmer Rouge and the "Sihanoukists."

The Prince willingly entered this alliance with the Communists. The Lon Nol *coup,* he says, forced an unwelcome choice between the "Free World" (his phrase) and the "Socialist Camp." But he knows he will not necessarily like the ultimate outcome. Even now his control is slipping. He calls the Communists "my red Khmers" and there is evidently a strong nationalistic bond between Khmer Rouge and "Sihanoukist." Yet the Prince sees that the Cambodian Communists will draw further away from him so long as the tragic polarization in Indo-China continues.

I knew Chou En-lai had discouraged Sihanouk from traveling outside the triangle of China, North Vietnam, and North Korea. But the Prince put a new complexion on the matter. "My own Prime Minister [Penn Nouth] does not want me to travel outside these three countries." Sihanouk did not hide the trend of things within the N.U.F. "After Liberation perhaps there will be a Marxist Cambodia. Frankly, the ministers who are leading the struggle are all extreme leftists. My Sihanoukists are administered by the extremists." He had been mixing English with bits of French, but now he went on in his preferred French. "My red Khmers don't want me to go back to Cambodia. So in the long run the Sihanoukists may also become leftists. I don't criticize them for it . . ."

His exposition I found moving. He does not like the idea of a Communist Cambodia ("Cambodians have no vocation to be Spartan"). But seeing no alternative other than U.S.-sponsored endless war, he has nodded in this direction. At the same time he retains his beliefs and dignity as a Buddhist socialist. He will not become a red Khmer just because that is the trend of events. And he is able to detach — how painful it must be for this ball of patriotism! — his own future from that of Cambodia. He is serving as midwife of a new Marxist alignment for tomorrow's Cambodia. But he himself will go back to France as Cambodia enters the Communist camp.

On the question of Vietnamese in Cambodia, Sihanouk showed his regret, but coped with it in a philosophic way. The problem, he pointed out, is that as the Saigon armies pushed toward Phnom Penh, Cambodian peasants fled to the capital and were largely replaced by Vietnamese. Said Sihanouk, "We'll have to let them stay. We can't treat the Vietnamese worse than Lon Nol has treated them." He paused and sighed, and one hand stretched out to adjust a daffodil in the bowl before him. "So we will have Vietnamese living in our country. It is an insoluble problem."

What are Norodom Sihanouk's impressions from his rich contacts with the Peking leadership? He reviewed his fall off the tightrope of nonalignment in March, 1970. When word reached

him in Russia of the *coup* by Lon Nol, he did not return immediately to Cambodia because he would have been killed. He
learned in Moscow, from two colonels loyal to himself, of a plan
hatched by the Lon Nol group. Should he arrive at Pochentong
airport, he was to be driven not into Phnom Penh but along
Route 4 to Kirirom and there shot like a dog. So he did not return. Kosygin promised support. Sihanouk said he must go to
China and get support there also. On the plane to Peking he
drafted his appeal to the Cambodian people. Moscow went back
on its promise. But Sihanouk found himself taken seriously by
the Chinese leaders. Several days in a row he talked with Chou
En-lai.

What was China to do in this situation pregnant with implications for both the war and relations within the Communist camp?
At first Chou did not commit himself. He mainly quizzed Sihanouk on his views and plans. The Prince — he told me — said to
Chou that there was no choice but to mount immediate struggle
against Lon Nol. The Chinese Premier noted this but struck a
note of caution. "We must warn you. We have experience. Wars
like this are not easy; they are hard and long. Reflect upon it."
Sihanouk in his emotional state wanted no delay. It seemed that
the reflection was more on the Chinese side.

Between this session and the next, Chou consulted (then)
Vice-president Lin Piao. This was not the last time the number
three man referred to the (then) number two man during that
week of Sihanouk's destiny. On "all important questions," the
Prince recalled, "Chou En-lai went to talk with Lin Piao." On
some of these important questions Chairman Mao himself adju-
dicated. Sihanouk did not himself deal directly with Lin Piao.
Apart from Chou, the Chinese leader he saw most frequently
(through the summer of 1971) was Huang Yung-sheng, Chief
of the General Staff. Of Lin Piao's position at that time the Prince
remarked, "Lin is kept free from most day-to-day responsibility
in order to prevent him becoming vulnerable to criticism. It is
Chou who takes the responsibility."

The Chinese decided to ask Hanoi's Premier, Pham Van
Dong, to come straightway to Peking. Sihanouk was a little wary

of the Vietnamese leader — Cambodians generally are of Vietnamese. The two of them did not meet immediately. Chou met
with Pham Van Dong, then Chou and Sihanouk met again. At
these meetings the outlines of a bargain crystallized. By now
Mao had laid down that Sihanouk was a crucial figure and must
be backed to the hilt at all cost. Indeed, the Chinese now urged
upon Sihanouk that he personally must head any struggle that
was to unfold. The Prince had opted for struggle. But not necessarily with himself at its head, for he may have had in mind to
go very soon to France. The Chinese opted for the Prince, for a
kind of struggle in which the Prince would be indispensable.

Whether Pham Van Dong was as keen as Mao to put all eggs
in the Prince's basket is unclear. At any rate, Chou En-lai
brought Sihanouk and Pham Van Dong together in a compact of
which China was the initiator and guarantor. This was reflected
in the pattern of meetings. Once the Chinese position was firm,
and Chou had held separate sessions with Sihanouk and Pham
Van Dong, the latter two met with each other. Chou had paved
the way to this agreement.

The Prince was to join the "front of the three Indo-Chinese
peoples in full solidarity against imperialism." Pham Van Dong
said to Sihanouk, "We are happy to have you as comrade-in-
arms." Hanoi promised that after the war Cambodia would be
"independent, neutral, and free of any Vietnamese military presence." Sihanouk was highly satisfied to have Pham Van Dong de-
clare, "After Liberation, we'll go together to the Vietnam-Cam-
bodia border and plant frontier marks, at the existing borders,
with the international press present, to indicate the complete in-
tegrity and independence of each country."

Apparently the Chinese as well as Sihanouk were eager to get
it clear that Vietnamese forces would not stay in Cambodia any
longer than was necessary. Chou said to Sihanouk, "We do not
support the so-called Maoists in Cambodia. China is one country, Cambodia is quite another — you should remain neutral."
Such a statement, given the angled complexities of Chinese foreign policy, can be construed different ways. But Peking certainly backed Sihanouk handsomely, despite all the odds against
exile governments doing anything but wither on the vine. Enor-

mous and open-ended sums of money were promised him, to cover all military and political expenses. "To respect our dignity," Sihanouk explained, "they called it a loan." But the question of paying it back will not be opened until thirty years after the war has ended.

I asked him if China may under any circumstances send troops into Cambodia or other parts of Indo-China. "They have told me," the Prince replied, "that they will send volunteers to Cambodia if I request it, but that in their opinion, it is better not to have any Chinese soldiers in Cambodia."

Sihanouk eventually had a "long and cordial" session with Chairman Mao. China, Mao made clear, was going to take Cambodia seriously on its own terms, not just as ideological potential for international communism. Said the Chairman to the Prince, "You know, I like princes when they're not reactionary, but with their people, and against imperialism as you are. I'm not only in favor of the people, I'm in favor of princes too, if they're good." It was vintage Mao, if unconventional by Leninist norms. Sihanouk was convinced the backing from China was a personal enthusiasm of the old rebel who "liked princes." Mao said to him at the end, "You can have anything you want from China."

But how to account for the difficulties — beyond the normal frustrations of being in exile — Sihanouk has had since that spring of 1970? Are they due only to developments within the N.U.F., and to the difference of interests between Hanoi and the Sihanoukists? Or has Peking edged back from its support for Sihanouk's nationalist and neutral position? The Prince's hand seems to have weakened on certain issues. The Khmer Rouge (Communist) influence within the N.U.F. rises while the Sihanoukist (neutralist) influence wanes. The Prince did not say how strong the tie-up now is between Hanoi and the Khmer Rouge (through its pro-Vietminh elements). But he does not believe the Chinese are actively trying to undermine the Sihanoukists within the N.U.F.

On the matter of the Prince's travels, however, the Chinese do seem to be clipping his presently folded wings of neutralism. He has said to Chou En-lai, "You should help me travel outside the triangle of China, North Vietnam, and North Korea. Some people say I'm a prisoner. Its not good to have this believed." The Chinese Premier said he feared for Sihanouk's safety if he should venture to additional countries. "The CIA may kidnap you," he warned. Sihanouk not long ago asked Chou straight out to put a plane at his disposal for wider travels. According to the Prince the answer was furry. "The Premier says he is preparing a plane. But he does not seem keen, I don't know why . . ."

Toward the end of our morning together I asked Sihanouk about the future. What ground can there be to hope Cambodia will regain the independence he so ardently believes in? "Marxist or not," the Prince said with some feeling, "Cambodia will always be independent-minded. Hanoi is independent-minded — that is the important thing. Cambodia has no borders with China. So long as Hanoi is independent-minded, Cambodia will not be dominated." He presented a second line of argument. "It is not in China's *interests* to make Cambodia a satellite. First, because it is a poor country, and would be a burden. Second, because if China subjected Cambodia, it would no longer be able to convince Afro-Asians that China respects small nations."

Prince Sihanouk left me with a summary of China's present strategic outlook as he understands it. "In their view," he said, *"Russia is China's biggest problem,* and *Japan is Asia's biggest problem."* On July 15, I later learned, Chou En-lai visited Sihanouk late at night to brief him personally on the announcement (due ten hours thence) of Kissinger's trip to Peking and Nixon's impending trip. (China's allies got a little more advance notice than America's allies!) The Chinese Premier assured the Cambodian of "total solidarity." An anti-Russian theme quickly entered. "We are not like the leaders in Moscow; we will not sacrifice our friendships and principles for the sake of détente."

Then Chou added, "Even if we get the necessary concessions out of the Americans, we will not be finished with imperialism in our region. *For the Japanese are ready to take over."* For his part, Sihanouk welcomed the news of the impending Mao-Nixon meeting. He thought it a "stroke of genius" by the Chinese leaders. It would, he judged, "isolate and disconcert" America's allies in Asia — above all Lon Nol.

16. Barbarians in the Middle Kingdom

I found myself wearing two hats in China. That of an Australian accompanying Mr. Whitlam; and that of a scholar from the United States. Peking was aware that I work at Harvard. But 1971 political developments — especially in China-Australia relations — explain the timing of my China visa. By the time the phone rang on Memorial Day with word from Peking of a visa, much had happened in the political sphere which gave my visit its context (every visit to China has its context in Peking's eyes).

Australia has no diplomatic relations with Peking. But China is a major buyer of Australian products, especially wheat, on which over the past decade she has spent a yearly average of $110 million (sometimes 25 percent or more of the entire Australian wheat crop). The China trade is vital to many Australian farmers, and important to the political party — named without embellishment "Country party" — based on their support. A blind eye is turned by the Country party to matters of ideology, for trade's sake. It has also suited Peking, Canberra's embassy in Taipei notwithstanding, to buy heavily in Australia. (One reason is hardly flattering. Australian wheat, a trade official explained to me in Peking, suits China more than some other foreign wheat because its "quality is not so high." This makes it suitable to mix with the even lower quality Chinese wheat!)

Last year the wheat order from Peking had been especially large (2.2 million metric tons). But in 1971 no order was placed. Consternation among the farmers "down under." Political rumblings, too, because the large opposition Labor party charged the

177

government with having lost business for farmers due to rigid political hostility to China. The Country party sat on the horns of a dilemma. Many of its members and leaders have wanted to recognize Peking for some time. But the party is in coalition with the right-wing Liberal party, which insults Peking at every opportunity and embraces Taipei with a zealot's persistence. The Labor party has long had a policy of recognizing Peking, dropping Taipei, and voting for Peking's seating in the China seat of the UN. It stood to gain in the situation which developed in the spring of 1971. And gain it did.

It is interesting to see how Peking proceeded. It blew no trumpets, spoke in whispers. At a Peking dinner in mid-March, a Director of the Chinese Ministry of Foreign Trade casually remarked to the British chargé that China didn't want Australian wheat this year. When it needed wheat, purred the official, it would turn to countries more friendly than Australia. China, after all, had "friends all over the world." Canberra officials, it had to be remembered, have said "foolish things" about China. Specific scorn was heaped by the Chinese trade official on a statement of a former Australian Foreign Minister. This self-righteous fellow had spoken of "serious questionings of conscience in Australia about how far we're justified in trading with China."

Of course the British passed on this offhand bombshell to Canberra. In late March, the Chinese Natural Resources authorities in Hong Kong did agree to meet with Australian wheat men. But the message was the same. In the first week of April, Canberra got a report of this meeting that confirmed what the British had heard in Peking. Meanwhile, Chinese officials told an influential Australian-born journalist that China would transfer whatever imports it conveniently could from Australia to West Germany. The reasons given were, first, that West Germany was not involved in Indo-China; second, that West Germany was less involved than Australia with Taiwan.

Of this bleak news the Australian government dared say nothing in public. Friends of Mr. Whitlam, however, got hold of it. The Labor party went onto the offensive. The complacent moguls of the government said politics had nothing to do with China's failure to order Australian wheat. The Chinese are just "carpetbaggers," explained Prime Minister McMahon. Another minister dismissed as "cocktail party gossip in Hong Kong" the alleged message from Peking. Mr. Whitlam, now privy to the message, was able to shoot down the prevarications about cocktail party gossip. The Labor party decided to publicly put to the test the government's argument that politics had nothing to do with Australia-China trade. It took a spectacular step. On April 14 it cabled Chou En-lai. Would China receive a delegation from the Labor party to talk things over?

The Prime Minister exploded, in a speech on April 15, about this political delegation "going to China, to Peking China." His majestic scorn for a hopeless venture was strangely mixed with a troubled fury at it. He reaffirmed his support for Taipei. Before Peking could ever become a "member" of the UN, he declared, "there must be some kind of assurances that they will live up to their international obligations." It was vintage Liberal party myopia, emitted with a rare smugness that only conservatism and insularity joined together can produce.

Meanwhile Peking was considering the Labor party's request. Friends of Mr. Whitlam were interceding with the Chinese to interpret it and urge a favorable response. Within Australian politics, the issue blew up to one of the biggest foreign policy issues Australia has had. Was Mr. Whitlam out on a limb? Or was he positioned for a big *coup?* It was easier to be pessimistic than optimistic. Especially since the Labor party needed an *early* reply. Also, it was known that the Australian "Maoists" were vigorously urging Peking *not* to invite Labor party people. Would Peking see eye to eye with their left arm in Australia?

No. On May 10 came a cable from the People's Institute for Foreign Affairs in Peking. A delegation from the Labor party was invited "for discussions on questions concerning relations between the two countries." Mr. Whitlam was elated. The Prime Minister did a somersault — letting his policies, it seemed, be determined by Peking's actions — and on May 11 and May 13 came out for détente with China. He put aside his rich collection of veiled titles for China: "Continental China," "Mainland China," "Peking China," "Communist China." Panic lent him boldness. He now said he sought "normal bilateral relations with the People's Republic of China." He now felt "contacts" with China were highly desirable. His government quickly moved to make its own diplomatic contacts. At Australian request, the Chinese and Australian Ambassadors at Paris soon held two (unfruitful) meetings. Meanwhile, Mr. Whitlam reached China on July 2 for a twelve-day visit.

The Whitlam mission was the most important Australian visit to China ever, and one of the few visits made to China by the leader of a social democratic party. E. Gough Whitlam reveled in the opportunity. A tall man of boundless energy, he took a grueling schedule in his stride. Up and down China, his intellectual curiosity never flagged. Peering at machines; sitting at a child's school desk reading the Red Book; making humorous and well-informed after-banquet speeches; downing the explosive rice wine, *mao-t'ai*.

On a flight from Peking to Shanghai, an Australian journalist asked Whitlam what the previous evening's film show had been about. The Labor party leader explained that it dealt with the unearthing of cultural treasures during the Cultural Revolution, "some of them Han bronzes." The reporter inquired, "How old are these treasures?" Whitlam instructed him patiently: "Well, as you know, the Han dynasty ran from 206 B.C. to A.D. 220 . . ." Typically, Whitlam was better informed than the journalist. Typically, too, he had attended the film, which was a special screening for the Australian group; most of the press corps had skipped it out of fatigue.

What did the Chinese have in mind with these initiatives toward Australia? Was this a typical example of the new foreign policy line which has followed the distractions of the Cultural Revolution? A pattern behind the invitation was borne out by events during the visit itself. The starting points were two. China was trying to get the UN and Taiwan issues fixed up to its satisfaction. Australia could help here. But not, it seemed, the present Australian government, given its present approach. Second,

China's need for imported wheat had shrunk. The Foreign Trade Minister explained, "China has had several good seasons and this year's has been reasonable." Grain reserves above the commune level stood at 40 million tons late in 1970. (True, China bought in 1971 from Canada 10 percent more wheat than she had bought in 1970. But this was a gesture in response to Canada's recognition of China, and Peking has already conveyed to Canada that there will be no similar increase in 1972.) China could therefore be choosy about Australian wheat. It could tie economic issues to political issues.

So last spring there unfolded a sequence of events not without its logic. The wheat order was omitted. Word passed that political attitudes played a part in this omission. Then the invitation to Whitlam (whose party has the "correct" position on Taiwan and the UN). At the same time a few mild slaps in the face were administered by Peking to Australian Maoists.

The Chinese by early summer were actually relating to Australia on three political levels. Contact at Paris with the McMahon government; the Labor party mission; continuing fraternal ties with the Maoists. But the Labor party was getting most of the smiles, for, given Peking's current aims, its role was crucial. This is not to say Peking was certain Mr. Whitlam will soon be Prime Minister. He may well be. But in any event the way to prod McMahon, as events so eloquently proved, was to smile upon Whitlam. And if this tactic involved a little bitterness for the Maoists? Well, any Maoist should know that tactics (flexible, short-term) are not to be confused with strategy (unwavering, long-term). To satisfy immediate needs is not, for Peking any more than for Rome, to prejudice ultimate visions.

Within China, it was absorbing to compare Chinese attitudes toward Australia and toward America. While Mr. Whitlam was there, Peking saw me as an Australian, accredited correspondent for a Sydney publication. Before and after the Whitlam mission I was a "scholar and writer" from the United States, who was going to write for American readers. The Chinese liked to keep the two aspects distinct. (One day a Scandinavian head of mission, pondering this Chinese insistence on keeping national categories crystal clear, told me this story. Sweden is planning the biggest trade exhibition it has ever held outside Sweden for April, 1972, in Peking. Air France, with an eye to filling acres of empty seats on its Europe to Shanghai service, sent an employee who is a Swedish citizen to Peking to get a foot in the door for some of the air traffic. This Air France official was told that nothing is known about the planning for the exhibition. In fact, the Chinese had already been dealing with SAS (Scandinavian Airlines) about flights to and from the exhibition. An SAS official had visited Peking and made preliminary arrangements. The Chinese considered it a matter of principle: a Swedish exhibition should be serviced by SAS, not Air France or any other airline.)

I found that the U.S. liberal approaches China more idealistically than the Australian laborite (the same is true of journalists from the two countries). The American tends to be very well informed, excited to be in China, and concerned with large questions of value about Chinese society. U.S.-China relations are something of personal importance to him. He carries himself — even if he's a newspaperman — like an unofficial ambassador for America. What his President does or doesn't do about China matters to him, and seems tied intimately to what he feels he ought to do in China. He is acutely conscious of the ambiguity of past U.S.-China relations, but optimistic that if the two peoples' leaders can sit down with each other, intimacies can quickly start afresh.

The Australian is casual, detached, and pragmatic. He goes without awe to China. Australia, of course, has never been in passionate embrace with China, as the U.S. government and public once were. Nor does anything of moment for the world hang on China-Australia relations. A steady if small traffic of Australian visitors has been going to China ever since Liberation. There is less excitement for the Antipodean than for the U.S. visitor, because the fruit of the Middle Kingdom has never been absolutely forbidden to Australians. If the Australian journalist is pragmatic about China, it only reflects the ties between the two nations. Say "China" in Australia and (until recently) you have said little more than "wheat."

In the factories, on the farms, the Aussie's comparative lack of idealism is marked. His questions betray no overriding awareness that this society is Communist. He thinks not of systems but looks for performance. If a thing seems to work — as it sometimes but not always does — he waves aside the categories. The typical question of the U.S. liberal in a factory concerns freedom of choice in work and living patterns. The Australian laborite typically asks where are the trade unions, and why on earth do workers put up with military men on the factory floor.

The Australian does not take the Chinese leaders with any more seriousness than he takes his own leaders. That means he treats them bluntly, yet with a touch of naïveté that bluntness sometimes masks. All in all it is quite a contrast. The Chinese try to accommodate these differences which they hardly expect. They cannot always hide their shock at Australian insular pragmatism. Nor their discomfort when American moralism exceeds their own. When it comes to language, the Chinese much prefer Americans. Radio and, in the case of older people, pre-Liberation encounters, make them familiar with the American accent. But the Australian accent is a thing of terror to any Chinese who thinks he knows the English language.

To watch the Chinese dealing with Mr. Whitlam was to glimpse their hand on several issues. On diplomatic ties, Whitlam sought and obtained Chinese assurance that Peking and Canberra could exchange ambassadors on the "Canadian formula"; that is, recognizing the Peking government of China, and taking note of, without necessarily endorsing, Peking's claim to Taiwan. However, Canada had no embassy in Taipei, as Australia has had since 1966. What, asked Chi P'eng-fei, wreathed in his enigmatic smile, will you do about that? "I will not send an ambassador to Taipei," replied Whitlam.

It seemed a crab-like approach, since an Australian envoy is already there, warmly nesting with the government of the "Republic of China." To further Chinese questions, Whitlam said a Labor government would, as recognition arrangements proceed, "withdraw" the embassy from Taipei. In private remarks, Whitlam restated this intention vigorously. He does not bother to hide his nonregard for Chiang's regime (which he has taken pains never to visit — other than one airport stop). In Shanghai on July 11, he publicly put the matter beyond doubt: "When we propose to establish diplomatic relations with Peking as the sole legal government of China, we will close the embassy in Taipei. . ."

The Labor leader wondered about Peking's attitude toward Australian Maoists, tightly grouped under Comrade Ted Hill in the Australian Communist party (Marxist-Leninist). What kind of backing would Hill enjoy from China when a Labor government got the reins of power in Canberra? The Chinese Foreign Minister said "noninterference" was the policy. "We do not know what is best for Australia."

The answer remained general, but light shines on the matter from other sources. There is in Sweden a group similar to Hill's in Australia. A man in a position to know says the only aid Peking gives these Swedish Maoists is mass purchase of their publications — a form of subsidy — for distribution in China's airports and hotels. After Mr. Whitlam had left China, Peking made a gesture which signified not only "noninterference" in Australian affairs, but a quiet effort to clip Comrade Hill's wings.

Richard Hughes of the London *Sunday Times* wrote from Hong Kong that Australian Maoists had urged Peking not to receive Mr. Whitlam (also not to give me a visa). This had been suspected in Australia. The startling thing was that "official Communist sources," according to Hughes, made a "deliberate disclosure" to him of these fruitless interventions. These sources added for Hughes's information the fact that Comrade Hill had cabled Peking with his Party's recommendations. Maybe Peking is irritated that Hill should claim a "monopoly" on channels between China and Australia, and a veto power on China's behalf over who from Australia may visit China. Frankly, I believed the Chinese when they said they have little possibility and less interest in making revolution in Australia.

Foreign Minister Chi was generally practical and to the point. The only time Chairman Mao's name came up, through a morning of talk between him and the Australians, was when Mr. Whitlam asked to have his respects passed on to Mr. Mao. For some

Australians in the Great Hall of the People. From the right of Chou En-lai are: Mr. Whitlam, Tom Burns (President of the Labor party), Chi P'eng-fei (Foreign Minister). To Chou's left is Rex Patterson (Labor party parliamentarian) and, behind Patterson, the author. At the right-hand end of the front row is Pai Hsiang-kuo (Minister of Foreign Trade) and on his right, the white-haired professor Chang Hsi-jo (President, Chinese People's Institute for Foreign Affairs).

Mr. Whitlam with the author at the Ma Lu commune near Shanghai

The author and Dr. Stephen Fitzgerald, advisor to Mr. Whitlam, at Petrochemical plant near Peking

reason, Mr. Chi during this private talk was less harsh on the present Australian government than was Chou En-lai in a semi-public dialogue the next day. Chi did not burn his bridges, as Mr. Chou seemed to do, for any serious dealings with Mr. McMahon. On one issue, Mr. Whitlam got essentially no more satisfaction than the Australian government (through intermediaries) has gotten: the fate of the eccentric Australian journalist and adventurer, Francis James, who is held by the Chinese for having used forged travel papers in China. Despite careful and persistent efforts, Mr. Whitlam found out no more than that Mr. James is alive and well.

When the topic of U.S.-China relations came up, Mr. Chi said frankly that "Taiwan is the crux." On Japan he was tough as everyone in Peking is tough. He hammered at three outrages on Tokyo's part. The "illegal peace treaty between Japan and the so-called Republic of China"; the plans to acquire nuclear weapons; the Japan-Taiwan–South Korea liaison committee for exploiting resources on the continental shelf near China. It seemed from what Chi and other Chinese said to Whitlam that Peking's hostility toward Japan nearly always boils down to Japan's involvement with two specific areas vital to China: Taiwan and Korea.

Broaching the UN, the Foreign Minister put unexpected stress on its Specialized Agencies. He accepted that an Australian Labor government would vote for Peking's seating in the China seat. But he wanted to be clear that Whitlam would vote the right way to ensure the "removal of the Chiang group from every part of the specialized agencies of the UN." He was after a "UN solution" which not only gets Peking to New York, but shoots down every vestige of Taipei's claim to be a separate state.

The trade talks with the Australians showed that Chinese interest in foreign trade — now aimed far more toward the non-Communist world than toward China's fellow Communist states — is expanding in a number of directions. Politics, we came to believe, is brought into trade when Peking has wide options open to it, but kept out when such options do not exist.

This resembles the relation in old China between the "tribute system" and trade. The tribute system expressed the Chinese view of the world. The Chinese emperor was not just ruler of China but Son of Heaven. He reigned over all known civilization and all activities theoretically fell within his preserve. But Peking did not always have the capacity to make its authority operative. Sometimes theory and practice did not mesh. Thus in the first half of the eighteenth century, Russia traded much with China but only once made the respectful mission of tribute. It is this way with trade today. China cannot always maintain the politics-trade connection. But it does so when it is able to.

Peking could put pressure on Australia this year because of China's favorable overall grain situation. Pai Hsiang-kuo, the Chinese Minister for Foreign Trade, told Whitlam that China-Australia trade "cannot but be affected" by political ties or the lack of them. He and his aides laid down principles for such trade with Australia as involved Japanese and American companies. With any company in Australia that is 100 percent owned by Americans, China will have nothing to do. The door was not specifically closed, however, to dealings with companies *almost* totally American owned.

Regarding Australian-Japanese companies, the Foreign Trade Minister applied in an extended way the "four principles" which Chou En-lai gave for China-Japan trade in April, 1970. China will not trade with any company in Australia linked with a Japanese company which is disqualified by the Four Principles from trading with China. Curiously, the Chinese showed no great concern about the lopsided character (in Australia's favor) of China-Australia trade. In 1970, for example, China bought from Australia (U.S.) $146 million worth of goods, and sold to Australia only $41 million worth of goods. Yet Pai Hsiang-kuo talked with Whitlam far more about what extra goods China might *buy* than about what extra goods it might *sell*.

The Chinese did not say, as some had expected, that Peking would balk at Australian companies continuing to trade with Taiwan. It was understood that Australia (under Whitlam) would not trade with Taiwan *through governmental agencies*. But private companies may trade with the island. The Australians had

wheat uppermost in their minds when they entered the Hall on
Number 42 Anti-Imperialist Road for trade talks. But the
Chinese indicated that the major prospects for Chinese purchases
in Australia were iron, steel, and bauxite. Wheat will still be
needed, though in smaller quantities. Dairy products (powdered)
and wool will also be sought.

As important as wheat, Chinese officials said, will be sugar.
China's increased desire for sugar reflects a stress on consumer
needs; it goes into cakes and ice cream. China produces 2.8
million tons of sugar and imports some as well (notably 500,000
tons each year from Cuba). When "prices are favorable," China
re-exports sugar to Hong Kong, Malaysia, and other places. "As
living standards rise," the Australians were told, "and given our
annual population increase of 15 million," more extra sugar will
be needed than China can produce from land available for additional cultivation. So Peking will consider Australia if Canberra
mends its political fences with China. The trade official summed
up: "When normal relations between China and Australia have
been established, China will be very interested to buy Australian
sugar, within the framework of the International Sugar Agreement."

17. How China Makes Its Foreign Policy

Lights burn late in the new cream-brick block which houses China's Ministry of Foreign Affairs. After the Cultural Revolution, the number of personnel at the Ministry was slashed by almost one-half. Those who remain must work fantastic hours to cope with a swelling volume of business. Some work who are too tired and ill to work, like Vice Minister Ch'iao Kuan-hua this past summer. Some who speak a Western tongue fluently must punctuate policy work with translating tasks. "Peking wives" — it occurred to me — must have even more to put up with than "Washington wives." (I say "wife," but in fact the Chinese no longer use the established word for wife, *"t'ai-t'ai";* they use *"ai-jen,"* "lover," for spouse or amorous friend alike.)

Yet morale is high. Officials are naturally encouraged that their Ministry has become as much a focus of attention as any foreign ministry in the world. The more so because it firmly relegates to an unlamented past the period of 1966–1967 when the Chinese foreign policy establishment was very nearly derailed by a hot avalanche of ultraleftism. Ch'en Yi, the Foreign Minister at that time, was harassed and "supervised" so unrelentingly by Red Guards that Mao eventually declared: "How can Ch'en be struck down? He has been with us forty years and has so many achievements. He has lost twenty-seven pounds in weight. I cannot show him to foreign guests in this condition."

Ch'en Yi no longer works on foreign policy, but it does not seem that he has been purged. A senior Chinese military man, when it was remarked to him by a European ambassador that Ch'en's going was a "loss," replied with a broad smile: "Your loss is our gain." One of China's true military experts, Ch'en Yi, though seriously ill, has probably been working on high military matters. He resurfaced last summer as a vice chairman of the top Military Affairs Committee.* Of other high officials in the Ministry, it is remarkable how few were blown away by the storms of the Cultural Revolution. In 1967, the two Vice Ministers most assailed by the zealots were Chi P'eng-fei and Ch'iao Kuan-hua. Yet how little the huffing and puffing availed. Today, Chi is Acting Foreign Minister, and Ch'iao is the Vice Minister in charge of Western affairs and top man at the UN for the 1971 session.

At one point in the struggle of the Cultural Revolution, ninety-one senior men in the Ministry put up a manifesto backing Ch'en Yi against those who reviled him as "poison" and classified him as "bourgeois." Almost every responsible man one meets in the Ministry today is one of the ninety-one, as are most of the ambassadors who have been flying out to occupy new posts and dust down old ones. I often talked with one official, of middle age, as much a scholar as a diplomat. Like his wife, he is a graduate of Yenching University. His home is as well furnished with books as his mind is with ideas. I asked if the zealots (in conversation they were always called *"chi-tso fen-tzu,"* "ultraleftists") had tried to get at his books. For there was a bit of "book burning" in 1967. Self-appointed maestros passed the wand of ideology over certain works, and pronounced even gold to be dross. "No," he answered with an expression that gave nothing away. And if they had come? "If they had quoted Chairman Mao to me, I would have quoted other parts of Chairman Mao to them — and I would have won." (Remarkable was the diplomat's belief in the power of persuasion, in the importance of the correct Word. But you find it everywhere in China. The Chinese apparently have not, like many in the West, from the greatest philosophers to the hippie at the corner, lost confidence that reason and conduct are related.)

We find continuities in the history of new China's foreign pol-

---

* Ch'en Yi died of cancer in early January, 1972.

icy community that rival Andrei Gromyko and J. Edgar Hoover. There have been only two regular Foreign Ministers in the regime's twenty-two years. Most of China's senior diplomats come from a small circle of negotiators and propagandists who cut their teeth on four diplomatic operations prior to Liberation. First, a liaison group headed by Chou En-lai at the Nationalist capital of Hankow (and after Hankow fell to the Japanese, at Chungking); second, a branch outfit at Kweilin which put out a news service. A third knot worked out of Hong Kong; Ch'iao Kuan-hua distinguished himself there. Fourth, the Chinese Communist party was represented on the "truce teams" which the Marshall Mission operated in North China and Manchuria. Huang Hua, the present ambassador to the UN, was an active part of the Marshall Mission machinery. He ran the information work at the Mission's Executive Headquarters in Peking. Many of China's senior diplomats are Averell Harrimans of the East, their resilient careers interlaced with decades of their country's (or Party's) foreign policy.

What does the Chinese foreign policy machine consist of? It is small by U.S. standards — the Foreign Ministry has no more than a thousand people — but not simple. Chou En-lai as Premier heads the State Council. It is a kind of cabinet at the pinnacle of the state administration. Its well-staffed corridors include a Staff Office for Foreign Affairs. The Foreign Minister feeds to this office — for the benefit of Chou and his staff — papers from his Ministry. Into the Staff Office also goes material from the "international liaison" section of the Party Secretariat of the Chinese Communist party. This section may well be extremely important, especially for relations with Communist countries, but the visitor learns nothing about it.

The Ministry itself seems in some ways a very conventional place. You cannot altogether wonder that the zealots of 1966–1967 considered it a "bourgeois" island cut adrift from the seething Maoist mainland. Diplomatic procedures are much as in a European foreign ministry. There are ambassadors, and there are third secretaries; commercial counselors and military attachés. Very few become ambassadors who have not been career diplomats for many years. Secret files exist. Zealots briefly challenged this practice in 1967, one crying out as he rifled the files on May 13, "What's so terrific about secrets? To hell with them." Yet the attempt in the middle of the Cultural Revolution to transform the style of Chinese foreign policy in the end went little further than frills like what clothes to wear and how many courses to serve at diplomatic dinners.

One important change in organization did occur (beyond the cutting down in size). A Revolutionary Committee now runs the Ministry, and several sources style it a quite effective example of this new kind of organ. It is chaired by Chi P'eng-fei, top man among the Vice Ministers, and Acting Foreign Minister. But the second and third figures in the Revolutionary Committee are not Vice Ministers. They are People's Liberation Army men (Li Yao-wen, Ma Wen-po). At a banquet given late in June by the diplomatic corps, to thank the Ministry for the recent diplomatic tour of various provinces, it was made clear in the ways the Chinese make these things clear that Mr. Li and Mr. Ma ranked above Ch'iao Kuan-hua and other Vice Ministers. So the Army has found its way to the highest levels of the Foreign Ministry. What looks like genuine collective leadership has been set up in the Revolutionary Committee. It is quite different from the days when Ch'en Yi ran the Ministry with brusque authority. PLA men and Vice Ministers work things out together. The amiable and somewhat reticent Chi is no strong man. Having set this new pattern and found it good, China may not appoint a really strong successor to Ch'en Yi for some time.

Geographic groupings within the Ministry have altered interestingly over the years. The original tendency in 1949 to divide the world into "socialist countries" and "the rest" has totally gone. In those days one Vice Minister, Wang Chia-hsiang, looked after the Communist bloc and another, Chang Han-fu, spanned everything else. Gone, too, is the inclusion of the Asian Communist states in the same department as the European Communist states. Later they formed a separate and important department of their own. Preferring to salute the future rather than reflect the present, Peking included the affairs of Laos and Cambodia with "Asian Communist states."

Since the Cultural Revolution brought a severe pruning of the Ministry, there is now a single department for "Asia," Communist and non-Communist states together. The other geographic departments are West Asia and Africa (this starts west of Afghanistan); East Europe (including the USSR); the West. This last department takes in not only the United States, but West Europe and Australia and New Zealand. But it has a quite powerful Deputy Director heading an America-Australasia subdepartment (Mr. Ling Ching) and another (Mr. T'ang Hai-kuang) heading a West Europe subdepartment. In addition to these geographic departments, the Foreign Ministry contains five functional departments: Information, Protocol, Personnel, Treaty and Legal, and General Affairs.

Outside Peking are officials who work in the "foreign affairs section" of each province's Revolutionary Committee. These people, twenty or thirty strong in the provinces I visited, deferred on all nonlocal points to the Foreign Ministry people who traveled with me from Peking. They have no policy role, and concentrate on receiving foreign visitors with charm and informed conversation. One in Canton had dug up a fact about Australia that few Australians know. "Oh, you are from Melbourne," he remarked the morning he met me at the Canton train station. "It is, of course, the former capital, in the days before Canberra was built." There is little point in talking about foreign affairs to most of these provincial foreign affairs officials. They seem to specialize in what might be called the "kangaroo" or "fauna and flora" aspects of foreign lands. ("China has never had a Prime Minister drown in the sea, as your Prime Minister did in 1967.") But they can give the visitor data about their province.

Officially separate from the Foreign Ministry are a number of "people's organizations" essential to the conduct of Chinese foreign policy. Their personnel circulate like satellites in the outer orbit of the Ministry. One of these bodies is the People's Institute for Foreign Affairs. It was for years a mysterious body until it surfaced last summer. It receives ex-statesmen, such as Clement Attlee in 1954 or the ex-President of Mexico some years later, and it receives people "who are not governmental but too distinguished to come to China in an ordinary way." Its former research function has in recent years been "neglected." Only a dozen people work full time at its offices now. Its directors are mostly former ambassadors or distinguished professors, many of them extremely able, most of them fairly old.

The Chairman of the Institute, Chang Hsi-jo, is a former Minister of Education and one of China's most prominent non-Party intellectuals. Chatting with him at banquets and receptions, I found myself in yesterday's spacious, languid world. The patrician head of well-groomed white hair, the silk clothes, the polished walking stick which he wields with authority, suggest an Oriental aristocrat from the pages of Somerset Maugham. Here is a man who participated in the 1911 revolution and went soon after to study in London, yet who is part of Mao's foreign policy establishment in the post-Red Guard era. The elegance and cultivation are matched by a certain strength reserved for occasions of need. During the Hundred Flowers period in the spring of 1957, Professor Chang assailed the Chinese Communist party for having "contempt for the past" and a "blind belief in the future." He is still capable of caustic comment on bureaucrats, and gentle irony about ideologists who talk as if they had history's agenda tucked in an inside pocket.

We discussed political science, which he studied at Columbia University and the London School of Economics, and taught for many years at Tsinghua and other leading Chinese universities. This meant neither the Thought of Mao nor computerized social science. In the warm Peking afternoon, banners of Mao's quotations above us, we talked about the ideas of Harold Laski, Graham Wallas, and A. L. Lowell! Required by the occasion one evening to allude to Australia, Professor Chang managed to recall two famous Australian tennis players he had once watched play in New York. It was "people's diplomacy" of a casual and catholic kind. You could mistake Chang for a retired professor presiding over a lawn tennis association, rather than a retired professor presiding over Chinese Communist semiofficial diplomacy.

Another finger on the hand of Chinese diplomacy is the Association for Friendship with Foreign Countries. It deals with notable foreigners who seem well-disposed toward China. I never found out where its offices are. Its leaders are like a heavenly host making appearances but having no known abode. You can sometimes get from them illuminating, informal explanations of Peking's foreign policy line. Edgar Snow had given me a letter of introduction to an Association figure. One morning I got into a taxi at the Hsin Ch'iao Hotel to deliver it. The driver said he did not know where the offices of this body were. He went into the staff booth to inquire. Sitting in the taxi, I watched a series of consultations in the staff booth. Twenty minutes later a Luxingshe aide came out of the hotel and said I was wanted on the phone. It was the Foreign Ministry. Could I come immediately? Postponing the delivery of the letter, I drove instead to the Ministry. We had a "business meeting" about my program, none of it of an immediate character. Eventually the subject of Snow's letter of introduction to a leader of the Association was broached. Just what was this letter? I explained its harmless nature. "We will deliver it for you." So I handed it over. Three days later when the Association figure gave a lunch for me at the Peking Hotel, a Foreign Ministry official was present throughout our four hours of conversation. Liaison between the Ministry and the Association is clearly close. Maybe the Ministry would like it to be even closer.

These semiofficial agencies of the Chinese foreign policy establishment — others include the Overseas Chinese Commission, the Friendship Associations between China and various nations, the Council for the Promotion of International Trade — are led by a fascinating array of able and experienced diplomats. You find they are finely tuned to the Foreign Ministry. Yet they have a flexibility which makes them better gatherers of information on the world, and better defenders of the Chinese position, than many diplomats in the formal structure of the Ministry.

Wang Kuo-chuan, ambassador to Poland in the mid-1960s, now does important work on Japan questions from a base in the China-Japan Friendship Association. Li Shu-teh, an economist on the Council for the Promotion of International Trade, played a key role in talks with Mr. Whitlam about trade between China and Australia. When the Trade Minister had a session with Whit-lam, he was accompanied by a deputy director of his ministry, and by Mr. Li. Similarly, in the session with the Foreign Minister there was present one senior Ministry aide and also one aide from the world of semiofficial diplomacy: Ling Ching, head of American-Australian affairs in the Ministry, together with Chou Chiu-yeh, a former ambassador now prominent in the People's Institute of Foreign Affairs.

In short, the Chinese foreign policy machine is like an orchestra of diverse instruments. Now a drum is used; now a violin for a mellow effect; now a flute to achieve a delicate and modest melody line; now a trumpet such as Radio Peking to sound the major theme in unmistakable fashion. The musicians are highly professional even when they are packaged as amateurs, and most of them have been at the job, with a change of instruments, for many years.

Of the training of new diplomats the visitor discovers little except that it is done not by a single method but by many. A few have a background in the Institute of International Relations of the Academy of Sciences. But this has been suspended since the Cultural Revolution. Its members have gone off to communes to exchange the care of nations for the care of pigs. The Foreign Language Institutes are an important source. They began the path back to regular work late in 1971 (with even more emphasis than before on Western tongues). There used to be an Institute of International Relations in Peking, which taught at the graduate-student level. But some of its former students (who include foreigners) told me that it no longer functions.

In the next few years, diplomats with an Army training will emerge in China's embassies. Just how they are being trained is not known, but two interesting points surround the Army's role in the foreign policy corps. One is that a number of able men were sent into the Army, some at Chou En-lai's own instigation, to "hide" from the furies of the Cultural Revolution which might otherwise have cut them down. This is one more case of the Premier running the Cultural Revolution with his left hand while limiting its destructiveness with his right. It is also one more case of the Army extending its role beyond military tasks. The result is that there are many diplomats (and other professionals) in the Army who are not ordinary Army men, but whose career patterns are now bound up with the Army.

The second point can be put simply. Watch out for the Navy and the Air Force. After Lin Piao took over Defense from the less "Maoist" P'eng Teh-huai, the Army swelled up with prestige as a "model" and a "school" for the whole nation. A little resentment stirs in the other two services. They feel that the colossal stress upon politics has left the more professional and more technical aspects of military work enfeebled. The Navy and the Air Force are the natural repositories of these neglected aspects. In recent months there has been pressure to give more prominence than Lin Piao's policies did to air and naval work and weapons. This may well affect defense and foreign policy by the end of 1972. Already in the fall of 1971, it became one of several issues surrounding the eclipse of Lin Piao, and accompanying changes in the relation of the Army to politics.

In the leading universities, teaching of international relations resumed in the fall of 1970. One place I glimpsed it was Peking University. The seven subjects taught in the Department of International Politics are not designed to tease an idle imagination: Philosophy of Marxism; History of the CCP; History of the International Communist Movement (starting with the First International); Anti-Imperialism (starting in 1945); Anti-Revisionism (from the Third International or "Comintern"); National Liberation; Foreign Languages. Yet into these austere categories some teachers manage to fit interesting material.

Liu Shao-ch'i seems more famous since his fall than before it. Three of the courses (Anti-Imperialism and National Liberation as well as Anti-Revisionism) make him a prime target. The slogan for him is *san-ho i-shao* ("three reconciliations, one reduction"). He was, it is now said, on good terms with three enemies: reactionaries, revisionists, imperialists. He reduced support for glorious national liberation struggles. Some of the students from this department were doing their practical work on map-making at a Peking publishing house. Others were laboring on the construction of a new harbor near Tientsin.

I will not soon forget the teaching of the Korean War in Chinese schools. Few events are better known to Chinese students of society than this one. There is a double stress (beyond the themes of patriotism and Chinese-Korean solidarity). It was one episode in the long story of the United States trying to "get at" China. Three paths to China's heartland, it is said, were mapped out by Washington: via Taiwan, Korea, and Vietnam. And over twenty-three years the U.S. has trodden each path. The second stress is upon Russian selfishness. It is not asserted, though it is hinted, that Moscow cooked the whole adventure up. At any rate, China had to bear the burden. Every gun and bullet China got from Russia she paid for at "the highest prices."

It is odd to hear the Korean War taught this way. You have heard American students taught that Russia and China, composing a "monolithic Communist conspiracy," together hatched the whole thing. You have been told that the United States could never have wished to "get at" China. Actually, the version I heard in Chinese schools is nearer the truth than that taught in the United States. China did *not* push North Korea into war. General MacArthur *did* get at China — by the time Peking entered the war, he had bombed bridges touching Chinese territory.

But beyond the soundness of what was being taught, the seriousness of the tone in these classes on Korea was haunting. In Western classes, students take up this political topic or that, but how few topics really grip them. Fewer still if we think only of international politics. But these Chinese students talked about the Korean War with a clear and immediate sense of its connection to their own lives. A threat to China stirred in them deep personal feelings. If some will tomorrow be diplomats, the Chinese Foreign Ministry — whatever it may lack in experience of the world — will not lack conviction and purpose.

18. Foreign Residents in Peking

The diplomatic community in Peking is marked by irony and by a sense of brotherhood rare in the bitchy world of diplomacy. Irony because of a gap between repute and reality. The image: diplomats in Peking are intimate monitors of Chinese foreign policy, agog at each fresh twist of Middle Kingdom intrigue. The reality: diplomats in Peking often sit around and drink, and some are so cut off from the Chinese that they wonder if they mightn't be better off in Hong Kong. Brotherhood because this state of affairs binds the diplomats together in the furtive secret of their shared dilemma, and because Peking has few distractions, and diplomats are thrown relentlessly into each other's company.

I have caricatured, yet no one could deny a leisured manner and signs of boredom within the embassies of the Chinese capital. It is a delightful world for the scholar-diplomat, and ideal for those who like to bring up their children by paying much attention to them. There is no superfluity of paper to read. Much of what there is cannot be read by most ambassadors, for it is written in Chinese. In the summer, few chancelleries work after lunch. Parties begin early and end late. They are lavish because there is time to make them so. It comes as a shock to find Chinese servants of an older breed, schooled in deference and discretion before Liberation, when you walk off the street into certain European legations. A silver-haired, impassive butler clips cigars in the Dutch residence as he has been doing for decades. A waiter at the French Embassy walks with Gallic light-

ness (no resemblance to the Chinese shamble). He handles a ca-
pacious wine cellar with informed calm and the French language
without disaster.

At embassy functions, there is a tendency for stories and rumors to bounce back repeatedly like Ping-Pong balls in a very
small room. Yet the absence of "news" has a good side. Long-
range reflection germinates in those with a taste for it. Some ambassadors will stroll on their verandas, and talk very well about
the larger trends concerning China and the world. If Peking is
seldom a good place for an ambassador to report from, it is not a
bad place for him to think in.

There is little travel outside Peking, for the Chinese government seldom permits it. This is one reason why diplomats envy
the visitor. The only place they can go to automatically is the
holiday town of Peitaiho. Well known to Old China Hands, it is
on the seacoast east of Peking. Many ambassadors were lolling
there in sun-baked peace when Kissinger came in and out of Peking in July. Diplomats do not go to and from their nation's consulates in other cities. For the only operating consulates I know
of in this country of 800,000,000 people are a Polish and a Vietnamese consulate in Canton and a Nepalese consulate in Lhasa
(Tibet). If a diplomat leaves Peking, he is likely bound either for
Hong Kong or for his home capital.

Almost daily the Chinese Foreign Ministry issues a bulletin in
English of "News from Foreign Agencies and Press." It is com-
prehensive, unbiased, unedited. Most of its material comes from
wire services and newspapers of the West. The bulletin was unavailable during most of the Cultural Revolution. Only last June
did it appear again for its select audience of diplomats and
journalists (there is a Chinese version, similar but not identical,
sent to high officials, and to lower officials who work with foreigners). Though the bulletin did not appear during the Cultural
Revolution, it is clear from its numbering sequence that it never
stopped production for any length of time. Moreover, inquiries
revealed that at least the Albanians and Rumanians continued to
receive it. The Chinese version also kept coming out. This bulletin is extremely valuable to the foreigner in Peking. Of interna-

tional news and commentary it has as much as any daily newspaper in the world.

There are really two diplomatic quarters in Peking. The old
Legation Quarter lies just east of the Tien An Men square. Ar-
chitecturally it is a hodgepodge of nineteenth-century European
turrets and gargoyles and pillars. But it is picturesque and not
without charm, and some of Peking's most splendid villas sit
among its trees. In this area, only nations which are (or recently
were) friendly toward China remain. The Burmese are in the former Belgian mission. Prince Sihanouk has the old French Embassy. The Rumanians are busily here. The Hungarians occupy
the superb mansion built in the days of colonial largesse by the
Empire of Austria-Hungary.

The other diplomatic quarter is bland and remote. Northeast
of the city, it accommodates all the countries which recognized
China substantially later than 1950, and all those which wished
to put up new buildings. Not far away is a forest of new apartment blocks for Chinese workers. This section is almost like
Manhattan, with its soaring heights and geometric regularity. On
a summer evening you catch the smell of cooking, and the shouts
of children playing. Older people sit and smoke, on chairs or tatami under carefully planted trees that line the streets.

But the new diplomatic area itself is flat and placid. Pink mimosas line the dusty yellow streets. A pale blue sky above fits
the delicate and understated color tones of the scene. Noise, too,
is muted, and with virtually no traffic the cicadas have the air-
waves all to themselves. PLA soldiers guard each embassy gate
without martial fuss. They will chat and laugh freely with a pas-
serby. The tensions of 1967 — when these streets rang with the
sounds of demonstration and sometimes of battle — have totally
gone.

Arriving a little early one evening for a British dinner, I stroll
from gate to gate. The Pakistanis are out in the grounds of their
vast brown monolith, playing badminton. They are in crisp white
shirts hanging long outside dark trousers, and they talk at each
other loudly and rapidly. In front of the Egyptian Embassy,
Arabs clamber out of cars with bundles. The Finnish Embassy

looks like a country cottage that has not been lived in with any vigor for some time.

At the British office the man on duty is a cockney for whom Peking seems to offer too few listeners. He keeps himself and others amused by offering commentaries on the BBC news bulletin which is transcribed each afternoon. "Laurie Constantine is dead," he begins with a long face. A whole bag of anecdotes tumble out about this West Indian cricket champion. As I leave him he does not stop: "A great fast bowler, Constantine, one of the very greatest . . . ."

Many embassies contain one or two younger China specialists poring over documents. The Russian, French, and East German offices have quite a lot of them. These Sinologues do not often see responsible Chinese officials. Yet they pick things up from living in Peking with a knowledge of Chinese. They can sift the bookshops; they chat with people in the street. Ambassadors vary enormously from the brilliant to the bovine. Effectiveness depends on how Peking at any point of time regards their country, and what background and interest they have for the job. Peking is a post that can make a poor diplomat worse and a good one very good. If he is cut off from the country and the leadership, and cannot overcome this, he withers into a clerk. If he can get an angle on events in this vast nation, and a foot in the door with officials, the challenges to mind and spirit (and digestion) are limitless.

Observing the foreign policies of China from a Peking chancellery is quite different from reading Chinese foreign policy documents in Washington or Paris or Hong Kong. First, you realize that China's political language loses point and freshness on the printed English page. Breathing the air of China, where the cryptic, earthy Chinese language has constant spoken life, and where you hear political language as debate and exchange as well as read it as pontification, the whole effect seems more serious and lively.

Second, you are better placed to see that the practice of Chinese foreign policy is not a mechanical reflection of its theory. In Hong Kong you have the ideological documents, and you have the reports of what Peking actually does. Relating the two is not always easy. In Peking you may discern the "middle ground" — those sinews of reason and judgment which link ideology with day-to-day decision. Third, the diplomat in the Chinese capital can supplement public statements with private talks. This is the crucial superiority of Peking as a vantage point. For it is in these talks that the thought processes of the Chinese reach the non-Chinese world.

The printed page cannot ask a question, yet the questions Chinese officials ask tell as much as the answers they give. I found this true in the weeks preceding Kissinger's July visit to China. One ambassador furnished me with a recent instance of his own.

He had just been talking with a department deputy director at the Foreign Ministry. Persistently the Chinese official questioned him about the office of Secretary-General at the UN. Who were the candidates to replace U Thant? What of the so-called troika system? Meanwhile, it became quite clear not only that the Chinese are interested in all current details about the office, but that they scorn any "troika" arrangement and favor a "strong" office with power to act quickly and effectively.

Ambassadors at Peking generally praise the competence of the Chinese Foreign Ministry. A Scandinavian ambassador about to return after four and a half years in his post looked back: "Going to the Foreign Ministry here has been just the same as going to the Quai d'Orsay. The level of knowledge is similar. You have the same kind of free, frank exchange about world affairs. Of course, it's not as close as when we talk to Washington or London — for with these two my country has a special tie. But it's about like talking with the French."

Sometimes — I am not referring to the Scandinavian — there is effusive praise that rings a little oddly. It is streaked with condescension, as if the foreigner did not expect anything but a sub-European level of competence from the Chinese, and overreacts when he is surprised.

In the areas I could observe, the Chinese seem as well-informed as the foreign ministries of medium-rank nations. But their political shrewdness, their sense of the volatile nature of power, is outstanding. Often they get hold of angles quite absent in Western thinking. You could not find cooler practitioners of the science of power anywhere. This does not mean they have shrunk back from revolutionary aims and values. It is just that they are clear-headed about the distinction between means and ends. And — an even more important point — they have relatively few illusions about themselves.

How the mountain looks, of course, depends on what path you approach it by. Some ambassadors have excellent access to the Chinese leadership. Others are like fish upon the sand. Here are three cases:

France. Etienne Manac'h is perhaps the outstanding ambassador in Peking today. This stems both from the cordial Paris-Peking relationship and from Manac'h's acuteness and long background in Asian affairs. A precise, modest man, he has long been a socialist. Enjoying a good relationship with De Gaulle, he was chosen personally by the General for the Peking Embassy. Trade between France and China did not leap after diplomatic ties were set up in 1964, though many Frenchmen expected it would. Indeed, it is smaller than Chinese trade with West Germany, which has no diplomatic relations with Peking. In 1970, for instance, total French-Chinese trade turnover was $151 million. Total West German–Chinese trade turnover was $253 million.

But there is a similar way of thinking about "independence" and "superpowers" in Peking and Paris. Both are sticklers for "national sovereignty." Both suspect that Russia and America would like to divide and order the world on their own terms. Both lack a little bit in power what they think they have in status. Both berate superpowers. Yet this prevents neither from thinking of itself as a *supercivilization*. These modes France and China share.

France is busy as intermediary between Peking and certain hesitant nations. Thus during 1971, China and Thailand nibbled at each other through the grille of French diplomacy. Paris has been China's major diplomatic base in Europe and a site for wider activities. New agreements to establish relations — such as that with Turkey last summer — have been hammered out in Paris.

Manac'h sees the Chinese leadership regularly. More than once Chou En-lai, inveterate night owl that he is, has drawn Manac'h aside after a reception and started (at midnight) a two- or three-hour chat in a side room in the Great Hall of the People. The Frenchman sees Chairman Mao from time to time. He has found Mao an eager student of French history: fascinated by Napoleon and the Paris Commune, avid for details on the Siege of Toulouse, impressed by De Gaulle.

The Chinese statesman, it seems, admired both De Gaulle's realism about the world of nations and his poised style and tendency to take a lofty view of politics. (The visitor to China often hears praise of De Gaulle. Chou En-lai invoked him — in scorn of SEATO — when debating with Mr. Whitlam. Officials more than once drew to my attention the fact that Mao took the unusual step of sending a message on the death of a foreign leader when De Gaulle died in 1970.)

Laos is an opposite case. Not because Laos is unimportant to China. But China supports the Pathet Lao, which is in rebellion against the Vientiane government that is represented in Peking. So Kienthong Keorajvongsay, the polite and stoic Laotian chargé, in his neat villa on a quiet street of the new diplomatic quarter, is truly a fish upon the sand. He might as well be on the planet Mars. It is a minor miracle, of course, that Vientiane has a diplomat in Peking at all. Mr. Kienthong watches the Pathet Lao leaders trip to Peking for talks with Chou and Huang Yung-sheng (Chief of the General Staff). Yet he himself from one year's end to the next sees no one higher than a desk officer at the Foreign Ministry. No one in his tranquil little embassy speaks or reads Chinese.

This charming man knows in full measure what Chinese aloofness can be like. All he can do is talk with other foreigners and make detached social observations. "How hard the Chinese work," he said with a certain awe as we sipped a morning cognac. "Not like Laotians." He gestured outside to the street where PLA men were on duty. "You don't see them drinking as they work. They eat frugally. They come home from a meeting, and you ask them what happened. They tell you not a word. In Laos people will chat about it: this man was criticized, that man was amusing. But here the discipline is so strong. Oh, no, not like Laos at all . . ." He took more cognac, and said I really ought to visit Laos sometime.

Britain. John Bull is something else again. He is not stranded like the Laotian, but he does not enjoy Manac'h's entrée. Britain was one of the first countries to recognize the Chinese Communist government (January, 1950). But in their usual manner, the British did not make a clean sweep of things; they tried to have a shilling each way. They kept a consulate on Taiwan (accredited not to the Republic of China but to the provincial government of Taiwan, which Chiang Kai-shek pretends has a separate life of its own). London also supported (until 1971) America's "important question" resolution in the UN, a procedural device to make it more difficult than it would otherwise have been for Peking to take its seat.

These two points China has held against Britain. For twenty-one years Peking has declined to exchange ambassadors with London. Each country has in the other only a chargé d'affaires office, not an embassy. In Peking, the Chinese maintain the distinction fastidiously. Even the taximen are schooled. If in haste you ask to go to "the British Embassy," they correct you and say they are prepared to take you to "the British chargé's office."

The British have an able staff of a dozen or so in Peking — a lot smaller than the French. Face red and suit white, the chargé, John Denson, looks a colonial type but is not. He purrs with pleasure that relations between the two countries have been improving ever since he crossed the bridge at Lo Wu in 1969. The dark days of 1967, when the British office was burned and its staff imperiled, are altogether gone. London abandoned the "important question" device at the UN in 1971. It has overcome Conservative Party hesitations and made the decision in principle — nothing is yet announced — to remove the offending consulate from Taiwan. Even if trade with Taiwan suffers, the loss cannot be great. Britain's trade with China is worth some ten times its trade with Taiwan. A Chinese order for six Trident aircraft nicely boosted the late 1971 trading lists.

Meanwhile, sweetness and light prevail in Hong Kong. Dealings between the Hong Kong government and Chinese Communists in the colony and in Canton have been smooth, at least since the attempted hijacking to China of a Philippines plane in March, 1971. A senior British official in Hong Kong recalled: "The Chinese hate hijacking. They're totally against it. When the Filipino incident occurred, an official at our Hong Kong airport just picked up the phone and called White Cloud Airport in Canton. Immediately, matters were fixed up. The Canton people gave the details: how much fuel, how many passengers, what time the plane would take off. Very businesslike; no problems; no politics."

The British in Peking do not enjoy easy access to the Chinese leadership. Until Denson saw Chou En-lai during 1971, there had been very little access at all. But they feel the trend is upward. With the modulated optimism the British have always shown in China, they are slowly erecting a new residence to house the ambassador-to-be. With a new ambassador to China arriving every couple of weeks, the British frankly confess that they do not want to be left paddling in the shallows as the new diplomatic wave surges upward. However, the Chinese are not giving the British an easy road, and since the summer of 1971 a new obstacle has loomed large: London's insistence that the status of Taiwan remain "undetermined." Peking says the British wish to retain this formula as a basis — should future developments make it convenient — to recognize an independent Taiwan. So the feud still simmers, despite the resolution of the UN issue and London's readiness to remove its consulate from Taiwan.

A few score foreigners other than diplomats live in Peking. Of various nationalities — including American — they have thrown in their lot with China. Some work on China's foreign language publications (scattering idioms like "jackals of the same lair" through the pages of *Peking Review*). Others who are especially well regarded, such as the American Saul Adler, work in the "international liaison" section of the CCP. A few, of whom the New Zealander Rewi Alley is the most notable, work as independent writers and publicists. They have been called "300-percenters" because of their fulsome support for Peking's policies.

These ardent exiles are often marvelously well informed about China. They are helped by wider travel possibilities than are open to visitors not committed to the Chinese government or the Chinese line. Rewi Alley made my mouth water with details of his visits to Sinkiang, Hainan Island, and Tibet. These are three of China's most sensitive spots. Sinkiang because of problems on the border with the USSR, Hainan Island because it is so close to the Vietnam war, Tibet because of smoldering social and political tensions.

At the same time there can be a stiffness about these "300-percenters." A poignant paradox attends their "pro-Chinese" stance. Their eager orthodoxy sometimes hides an alienation from the sheer "Chineseness" of the life they have chosen to share. The result is occasionally a brittleness from which disillusionment is not far removed.

In the Cultural Revolution a number of "300-percenters" fell from grace with a bang. Sidney Rittenberg and his wife (an American couple) were among several who backed "ultraleftism" with a vigor that betrayed a touch of insecurity. The Rittenbergs worked zealously in the May 16 organization which is now so much under attack. They sought to be as Maoist as the Maoists. In the process they misjudged the nuances of the situation. They became more Maoist than the Maoists, and got into trouble. Many others did the same and have now left China. At the border, the luggage of "300-percenters" was often closely searched by Chinese officials. This proved disastrous for one man who was not only taking *ta tzu pao* (wall posters) out of China illegally, but had actually secreted them behind a framed portrait of Mao! He was detained for more than a year before finally being allowed to leave China.

Among those who remain, the Cultural Revolution has cast a

shadow hard to dodge. I went to see Rewi Alley in his apartment in the Peace Committee Compound. The enormous high-ceilinged rooms are shabby but comfortable in the nineteenth-century manner. Vast couches, embroidered cushions, bits of old China, and a silent old Manchu servant recall an earlier era. Shelves are stuffed with books in Chinese and English. Manuscripts are piled here and there (Alley has written far more than he has published). He shows me a photo of his friend Lu Hsun. It is the last photo ever taken of the writer, at an exhibition from which he went home and died. Downstairs used to be the apartment of Anna Louise Strong, the American journalist who died in 1970. Alley used to eat dinner with her and misses her bubbling talk. Now she is gone he is in a way the dean of the "300-percenters."

Alley has lived in China for the past forty-five years. He knows physical China like the palm of his hand. But his craggy looks and dry voice and the gentle irony of his style place him as a New Zealander. His Chinese is perfect and he loves China. Yet he seems to feel his separateness from the Chinese more than before. He is sharp on ultraleftism. I mentioned I was going next day to Peking University. "I haven't been out there for quite a while," he said quietly, "not since they were killing each other with spears." Of recent creative writing in China he was critical. "They have just sent me some poems to translate." He screwed up his face. "But they are untranslatable — just a string of slogans." One more disappointing fruit of ultraleftism. A boy comes in with the mail which includes *Time, Newsweek,* and the *Economist.* "I have a secretary now," Alley remarks with a very faint smile. "During the fiery years [the Cultural Revolution] I had a guard instead."

Rewi Alley had an explanation for ultraleftism. "You notice they were mostly from middle-class families. Yao Teng-shan (the 'Red Diplomat') was a product of a mission school. ['X' and 'Y'] who were so mixed up with May 16, are from a New Zealand family with big financial connections." He also saw an element of the generation gap in the Cultural Revolution. "Many cadres were summarily pushed out by inexperienced youth who didn't know what the revolution was about." Then he added, not without a trace of satisfaction, "Now it seems the old cadres are coming back from the correctional schools, and young ultraleftists are going in their place."

The New Zealander saw things in the cities during 1966–1968 which he did not like. But he said — and he knows the countryside well — that work on the communes was not interrupted by the goings on. "The Chinese peasant got used to working through flood and famine and war. He worked through the Cultural Revolution too." For his part, Alley goes on reporting the life and struggles and achievements of the Chinese. "I do not try to pontificate anymore." He is gazing into the distance. "I just write what I see. There are others to pontificate." If he is still an alien in an unfathomable land, Alley is also one of the very few true China Hands.

19. How Do the Chinese See the World?

What in the world does China want? How do the Chinese see the rest of the nations with which their own destiny is now intertwined? With China more than with most countries, what she *is* and how she *understands herself* weigh as much as what she explicitly *seeks*. A visit puts a light on some territory in back of China's approach to the world. It is four shades of this subsoil of Peking's foreign policy that I sift in the following pages.

1. Sense of place

Stray from Peking and the gateway cities of Canton and Shanghai, and it is easy to forget that the world beyond China exists. You meet no foreigners, see no foreign products, hear little foreign news. You observe in the Chinese mentality such a strong "sense of place" that China seems by nature isolationist. A Chinese word for landscape is made up of two characters meaning "mountains" and "waters." One day in Yenan, I recalled with amusement a phrase used to me at the U.S. State Department in 1966: "the China that exists on the mainland"! (And where are the others?) Of no country on earth could it be more absurd to separate the *location* from the *essence of the nation*. There is nothing abstract about China's view of itself (as perhaps there is of Gaullist France's view of itself).

It is not only that the Chinese have dwelt for four thousand years amidst these incomparable mountains and rivers. The rounded mountains and yellow rivers *are* China, the soil and the

A tale of two cities. (ABOVE) Sian, typical Chinese city, with low, tiled buildings, and gates standing sentry at all four points of the compass. (BELOW) Shanghai (Soochow Creek, with the Post Office tower just beyond the second bridge), the only "Westernized" city in China, which sprang up as a Treaty Port after the Opium War.

nation are almost one. In Chinese literature you find natural features given personalities. So it is said that, when Mao sent his telegram to Yenan in 1949, "even the mountains and rivers rejoiced" to receive it. Chinese towns and provinces are often geographically named. Hunan, Mao's province, means "south of the lake." Yunnan, the hilly province near Vietnam, means "south of the clouds." Peking translates as "northern capital," Shanghai as "on the sea." China seldom names towns after a great man (as Washington, San Francisco). Or after a place in another country (as New York).

In China's heartland, the cliché of China as "Middle Kingdom" (which is the literal translation of the Chinese word for "China") does not seem absurd. Here is a superior people, you reflect, but whose sense of their superiority is rooted in contentment with their own mountains and rivers. Not an active sense of superiority which pants to convert the world to its excellence. A passive sense of superiority, which basks, inward-turned, within its own possessed excellence.

At a banquet given for Mr. Whitlam, the head of the Institute for Foreign Affairs, Chang Hsi-jo, spoke about relations between China and Australia. Despite the "vast oceans that separate us," Chang pointed out, there is a "tradition of rich contacts." He illustrated the tradition, mentioning sportsmen, scientists, writers, and others. But he spoke only of Australians who have gone to China. Not a single example did he give of a Chinese visiting Australia. I don't think this lopsidedness was mere chance. Professor Chang was expressing a widespread Chinese attitude when he spoke of relations between China and another country in terms only of the foreigners coming *to* China. The Middle Kingdom receives; less often does it stir itself to send. And when it does send, it is not often with any high sense of mission or expectation, but with entirely practical goals in mind.

Of course, a nation's foreign policy is a stew of many morsels. It refracts much more than cultural attitudes. Yet this "sense of place" deeply affects every Chinese's view of the world. It underlies China's lack of interest in conquering, subverting, or even understanding other countries. True, Marxism has brought to one level of the Chinese official mind a global sense and global concerns. Communism has "internationalized" China to a degree. No less true, there is in China today an impulse to "catch up" with advanced countries. Many factories display a poignant quotation from Mao: "The Chinese people have will and ability. In the not-too-distant future they will certainly catch up to and surpass advanced world levels." Yet my abiding impression is of cultural self-confidence, outweighing national insecurity.

The Chinese are a rooted and a continental people (they have emigrated only when their own country was in chaos). Their cultural memories run the length of the dynasties. They possess effortless assurance of their own cultural identity. This does not negate the fact that Peking sees the world through the spectacles of Communist ideology. But something in the Chinese way damps down the lust and swagger of Marxism. The Chinese frequently take a long view of things. Dwelling amidst the mountains and waters of ancestors ten times as ancient as the Pilgrim Fathers has given the Chinese a patience of the ages. They do not, in fact, go around the world lighting fires of revolution, for they are genuinely skeptical that one nation can ignite another. And they believe in their hearts that few others, if any, can follow the epic Chinese way to revolution and socialism.

Most Americans would be surprised, I believe, by the tranquil confidence of China today. It is not a restless nation keen to prove itself in ambitious worldwide schemes. A fundamental contentment springs from cultural security. China seems less dismayed than amused that the chief of superpowers should fear them. Most Chinese do not *care* enough about the world to want to uplift others. Nor did they fret terribly when other nations kept China from its seat at the UN. They are secure and content in their habitation.

I watch lovers strolling around the Monument to the People's Heroes in Peking at sunset. Little boys pissing peacefully under a tree of the Tien An Men Square, then mounting the solemn stone lions beside the Forbidden City to play at riding and hunting. PLA men during a lunchtime break at Sian, talking with nostalgia and absorption of their home counties: what they eat there, how the accent varies, who the local folk heroes from antiquity are. Students in Canton, reading *Dream of the Red Chamber* under a tree, asking me not about Australia but about the way of life of Chinese in Australia. These people, it seemed to me, are not missionaries to the world but gardeners of their own heritage.

2. Independence

Five roots sit under China's insistence on complete independence (and associated principles such as "self-reliance").

• First, the cultural particularity which I have illustrated by the deep Chinese "sense of place."

• Second, the simple geographic fact that China is a continental nation cut off by sea or mountains from other major world centers. Except for receiving Buddhism from India, China drew little on other cultures. It had no experience of allying with a second nation in order to counter a third nation. China's isolation was its independence.

• Third, China's buffeting by foreign powers since the Opium War has made it acutely sensitive to any pressures which qualify its total independence. Having known dependence so recently, China is daily conscious of the quality of the air of independence it now breathes.

• Fourth, the Chinese Communist party did not win power in China by following Soviet models or by virtue of Soviet help but by turning inward to tap China's own resources of sinew, mind, and will. In the Chinese Communist party's experience, the evening cup of alliance turned sour by morning. The Chinese made their revolution by self-reliance. The experience has convinced them that no one — not even China — can make another nation's revolution for it.

• Fifth, the aggravating presence of two superpowers makes it natural for Peking to stand up for the principle of independence. Superpower hegemony threatens independence, whether it is the Russians in Eastern Europe or the Americans in Central America. China is incommoded by the "blocs" orchestrated by each superpower. It is the card of independence that it can best play amidst the power realities of today's world. Independence is the logical banner for a self-respecting major power which has no bloc of its own and could only be "number two" in another bloc.

Always I found the principle of independence echoing in foreign policy talks with Chinese. It accounts for their sensitivity to the pretensions of superpowers. It is the basis of their intimacy with Rumania and France. It justifies (to themselves) support for Pakistan. They were against any sympathy for Bangladesh which implied questioning of the Pakistan government's right to run its own affairs. Chou En-lai gave the principle of independence extraordinary stress. "Why is it," he asked, "that there is a lack of any ability in the Eastern part of Europe?" Politicians rarely say such astonishing things in public. For his gasping listeners, the Premier supplied an answer. "Because the biggest country there [in Eastern Europe] wants to control the others." It was a lavish assertion of the fruits of independence (and the costs of dependence) in the husbandry of nations.

During the same conversation, Mr. Chou underlined that China likes to pay debts promptly and owes nothing to anybody. He referred to the painful period in 1960 when the USSR suddenly took back all its aid and its experts. "But in those years of our greatest difficulty we paid back all our debts to the Soviet Union." The Premier was not finished with the theme. He recalled how China has always paid quickly and in cash for Australian wheat. He inquired with a broad smile and a gesture of both hands, "Do we still owe you anything?" Mr. Whitlam shot back with an allusion to the lack of a wheat order from China, "I wish you did." Mr. Chou laughed. The Foreign Trade Minister smiled faintly. Chou En-lai wanted us to understand that China is beholden to nobody.

Chinese military strategy likewise enshrines the principle of independence. "People's war" — one of Mao's central notions — is a formula for a nation standing alone. Not allies but "the people" play the decisive role. The enemy is lured in deep. He is invited to overextend himself. Then he is met by a people's struggle. By definition, it can be mounted only by the inhabitants of the territory which is resisting.

Perhaps if China had had allies in the 1930s, "people's war" would never have entered Chinese Communist party military theory. But China did not. Neither Britain, the United States, Russia, nor yet the League of Nations was prepared to help China stop Japan at a time when Japan could have been stopped. So the Chinese Communist party — which did the bulk of the fighting in China's Anti-Japanese War — had no choice but to turn inward to the resourcefulness of the Chinese people. Mao said the soldiers of the Red Armies were "fish" depending entirely on the peasant masses of China, who were "water."

The same ideas prevailed in the military controversies of the 1960s. This time the threat came not from Japan but from the United States. How to resist a possible attack? Some military professionals took a conventional view. Rely on Russia and its advanced weapons. Go outside China if necessary (perhaps into Vietnam) to stop the enemy before he gets to China.

Mao and Lin Piao took a different view. Rely on nothing else but the Chinese people. Prepare them politically. That is more important than lining up allies and fancy weapons. Wait for the enemy. Lure him in. Go onto the "strategic defensive" at first; then when the enemy gets bogged down, seize the moment to go over to the "counteroffensive." Get your arms the way the PLA has always got its arms: from the enemy. Mao and Lin won this debate over how to fight a war. Their theories are complex and I have done them no justice. But the heart of them is "people's war" based on *self-reliance* in order to preserve *independence*.

Mao supports his military ideas by citing ancient Chinese strategists, including Sun Tzu who wrote a treatise, *The Art of War,* some twenty-five hundred years ago. To the lay eye, "flexibility" is the keynote of Chinese military tradition. To maintain flexibility, to keep the initiative in your own hands, you must hold onto your independence. In 1928, Mao set down a formula which is close to Sun Tzu: "The enemy advances, we retreat; the enemy camps, we harass; the enemy tires, we attack; the enemy retreats, we pursue." It is the motto of an army that puts "mind" over "mechanization." Of an army which knows itself weaker than the enemy at the start of the struggle. An army patient and steady-nerved enough to turn aside at times from confrontation, wait for a mistake by the enemy, then spring back selectively at a moment of its own choosing.

Above all, it is the motto of an army which can switch and turn because it keeps in its hands full independence of action. The Chinese *think* this way about war and diplomacy because they have always had to *act* this way. It is a method of coping with weakness. Independence, and the stratagems that fit with it, have often been the only strength the Chinese Communist party had in the face of a superior foe.

3. Unlike the Russians, the Chinese reject "bloc thinking"

The point touches both Chinese insistence on independence and the Chinese view of power's fluidity. One terrible error about China from the 1930s through the 1960s was the view of the CCP as a mere appendage of Bolshevism. Shrewd men (George Kennan; numerous U.S. diplomats in China) saw from the start that the Sino-Soviet tie was not tight or enduring. Among many reasons for this are the divergent ways of thinking in Moscow and Peking about the relation between communism and the nation-state. Through the 1960s, the divergence grew. In the two Communist giants' attitudes toward Prince Sihanouk of Cambodia after his fall in March, 1970, it is displayed in a pure form.

Moscow thinks — Stalin taught it how to — in terms of a Communist bloc. The land of the October Revolution naturally heads the bloc. National sovereignty within the bloc is not total (as Prague recalls). Should one lamb in the flock stray from the proper path of socialism, the shepherd has the right to reach into his life and set him right. It is all-important to Moscow whether a nation is inside or outside the bloc. In Indo-China, to choose an instance, only Hanoi really counts to the Russians. Hanoi is (Moscow hopes) part of the bloc. Everything in Soviet-Vietnamese relations follows from that. The rest of Indo-China seems to be viewed from the Kremlin mainly by the yardstick of its "Leninist potential."

While I was in Peking, President Ceaucescu of Rumania visited China, and the fury of the Russians at his flirting with the Chinese was richly evident. Moscow reproaches Ceaucescu with not being a loyal member of the "socialist camp." The Rumanians actually stand between the Russians and the Chinese in their attitude to the socialist camp. They accept a notion of a "bloc" (which China no longer does), but they insist on the complete independence and sovereignty of each country within the bloc (which Russia no longer permits).

The Chinese are altogether more flexible. They reject "bloc thinking." First, it does not fit in with independence. Second, it tends to go against China's experience that socialism can only be won from within a nation. Third, Mao has a view of power too volatile to be accommodated by "bloc thinking."

Mao scandalizes the Russians by asserting that even a bloc has "contradictions." The Leninist fold may be divided against itself. One of its members may be "chauvinist" and seek "hegemony" over the rest. It comes as no surprise that Peking tosses around the term "superpower." In no sense is it a Marxist term. It describes not a class reality but a power reality. The Chinese have started no Comintern of their own. It is by no means only Communist parties which interest them. So we confront a paradox. The Chinese are more rigid about national sovereignty than bloc-thinking allows. Yet they have a more flexible notion of power than bloc-thinking permits.

On this visit to China, I heard several echoes of how the experience of the Korean War soured China's view of the "bloc" (and the Sino-Soviet tie generally). It seems that the Chinese group at the Twenty-second Congress of the Communist party of the USSR, in 1961, had some disagreement within it about how far China should commit itself in Vietnam. Under Russian pressure — Moscow derided the idea of any socialist country "going it alone" — certain Chinese (maybe P'eng Chen among them) were ready to commit China further than Mao Tse-tung wished. (Chou En-lai flew back to Peking early, leaving P'eng Chen in charge at the Congress.) Mao stated: "We don't want another Korean

War!" He feared that he might again be led into a war situation created by Moscow, and then have to do the fighting himself. He apparently suspected that Moscow might "do another Korea" on China, in the case of Vietnam and adjacent areas. According to my sources, the phrase "We don't want another Korean War" surfaced again in 1965. Mao used it against Liu Shao-ch'i and Lo Jui-ch'ing, who were both ready for bolder action in support of Vietnam than Mao was. The Korean War, it seems, may have taught Mao a bitter lesson about the open-ended commitments which entanglement in a "bloc" can entail.

Today, the key unit of Chinese thinking about strategy in the world is not the *bloc* but the *united front*. What is the difference? The bloc is a phalanx of the faithful. The united front is a loose partnership set up for a specific task. The partners do not come together out of agreement on socialism. Partners change as circumstances change. A new target calls for new partners. So in the 1930s when Japan became the chief target, the Chinese Communist party linked arms with the Kuomintang, which had in recent years been steadily murdering CCP forces. No less suddenly, a power shift may render today's partner unnecessary for tomorrow's struggle. He is tossed aside like a used Kleenex. This is the Chinese way of politics. They can be tough as a pine or as bending as a willow. But they simply do not think in terms of blocs.

Why has Peking embraced Sihanouk while Moscow continues to recognize the Lon Nol regime? Here the difference between the two capitals over bloc thinking is illustrated. Chou En-lai spoke a lot of this "extraordinary man" Sihanouk. "A Prince, a Buddhist, a pacifist," he remarked to us, "has now become a fighter against American imperialism." It seemed less than vital to the Premier that Sihanouk is not Marxist. Crucial was the Cambodian's membership in the united front against the United States.

One of Mao's maxims runs: "Learn to play the piano." In playing the piano, all ten fingers should be used to get maximum effect. But not all at once. The art is to use the right finger for the right task: to have a wide range; to be flexible in utilizing the range. Sihanouk is one of those ten fingers. He is not suitable for all purposes, but for some purposes he is ideal.

The Russians are more rigid. They do not trust Sihanouk, and have given him no support (though Kosygin remarked to the Prince when he [Sihanouk] reached Moscow Airport from Paris just after the coup against him: "We will support you to the end"). Sihanouk explained the Soviet attitude to me. "Their chief concern is their particular brand of communism. One reason they stay in Phnom Penh is to propagandize among young Cambodians for anti-Maoist communism. The same with the East Germans. They have mounted a vast effort to educate Cambodians in revisionism." Sihanouk was not Moscow's kind of socialist, so they dropped him.

The Chinese were more supple. Their view of the flux of power in Indo-China is not bound in a straitjacket of ideology. The Chinese never use the term "Maoism." They never refer — except in embarrassed caricature — to "Maoists" outside China. Sihanouk made this point at length. It is plain to any visitor to China or reader of China's press. Peking refers a lot to foreign "friends of China," but never to foreign "Maoists."

Here they have stepped out of Communist tradition. Moscow is proud to point to "Leninists" in foreign lands. But the Chinese — I feel — do not really believe in "international ideology." Sihanouk is weighed on another scale entirely. He is part of the united front against Washington. He is a welcome barrier to any ambitions Hanoi may cherish for a Cambodia made in Vietnam's image. (Chou En-lai remarked to a European ambassador while I was in Peking, "We do not want to see any one country of Indo-China dominate the others.") These are notions within reach of Lenin but within even closer reach of the ancient strategist Sun Tzu.

James Reston wondered why Chou En-lai, when speaking of Soviet policies toward China, used the word "lasso." A story around Peking during July gives an answer. Mr. Chou himself recounted the story to a French visitor. In a herd of Mongolian horses, when the leader bolts, the herdsman has but one recourse. He must lasso the leading horse. Otherwise he will lose his herd forever. The Premier likened the herdsman to the Soviet Union. It fears for its herd. China has bolted away, and many "horses" go with her. Moscow sees only one recourse. *It tries to lasso China.* Chou En-lai laughed for his French visitor and quipped: "But the Chinese horse is still bolting!" China will not be lassoed. And she continues to disrupt the tidy "herd," which is Russia's best vision of the world of nations.

4. *The Chinese have not abandoned their Communist theory, but Realpolitik is built into the very heart of Chinese Communist theory*

Am I trying to suggest the Chinese leaders are Bismarckian pragmatists? No, they are Communists. They believe capitalism is in decline, that the world will one day be Communist. They take their theory of the world as seriously as any government does. Cadres in China believe as much in the Thought of Mao as lawyers in the United States believe in the American Constitution. But what is often missed is that Mao's theory is no armchair speculation. It is distilled from practice. "If you want to know the taste of a pear," wrote Mao in *On Practice,* "you must change the pear by eating it yourself. . . . All genuine knowledge originates in direct experience."

And what has the Chinese experience been? It consists among other things of two broad yet vital ingredients: Chinese cultural history, and China's collapse before the impact of the West after 1840. From both sources an apparent pragmatism has entered Chinese communism. Fifty years in the land of Confucius has stripped Marxism in China of the vaporous clouds of German metaphysics. As for one hundred years of pressure from superior outside forces, it has mercilessly confronted China with the fact of her own weakness. She has had to learn how to "pit one against ten" and still win. This has led her to stitch many a practical patch on the splendid but unserviceable garment of Marxism.

Consider the two basic Maoist ideas of "contradiction" and "united front." Mao's method of analysis is, first, to identify the principal contradiction in a situation. After 1937 it was between

China and Japan. Today it is between the revolutionary peoples of the world and U.S. imperialism. Then Mao builds a united front against the target. You "unite with all whom you can unite with." We see that pure power considerations are intrinsic to united-front thinking. Get with you whomever you can get! After 1937 Mao was even prepared to go into a united front with Chiang Kai-shek.

But there comes a fresh stage. You go over to the offensive. Press for your goals in sharper form. Mao has a theory for this transition. Each contradiction, he submits, has a principal aspect (the stronger side) and a nonprincipal aspect (the weaker side). When do the scales tip? When does the nonprincipal aspect of a contradiction turn into the principal aspect? Mao puts it simply. When the "overall balance of forces" alters. *When we become stronger than the enemy.* Then one can be more choosy about allies, no longer having to link up with just anyone.

Again, power factors are found at the heart of Chinese strategy. "Contradiction" and "united front" are sacred vessels in the church of Chinese Communist theory. But the way they work is prosaic. The oil in the vessels is no holier than that in any other vessels of political theory. It is power. Considerations of power are not exactly in *tension* with considerations of ideology. They are the operative means of getting to the ideology's goals.

So it is not "un-Maoist" (whatever else it may be) for China to ally with Pakistan. Pakistan is an ideal member of the united front that Peking maintains against several adversaries. It is neither "un-Maoist" nor inconsistent to let Britain keep Hong Kong while loudly protesting U.S. occupation of Taiwan. The United States, not Britain, is China's main target. Certainly Peking wants Hong Kong back. But there is no hurry. Toothless Britain presents small challenge to the emerging future Mao sees over history's horizon. Meanwhile, letting Hong Kong stay in British hands brings Peking some $600 million a year in foreign currency.

Taiwan is another kettle of fish. Peking makes it a number-one issue, not just because it wants Taiwan back, but because the issue of Taiwan has involved a U.S. military challenge to China.

To be sure, national emotions stir over Taiwan. But that does not explain Peking's stress upon it. The Chinese are always patient when there is no reason to be impatient. It was as the United States step by step installed itself on the island that Peking step by step elevated the Taiwan issue to top priority.

So China's policies toward these two lost bits of her territory — Hong Kong and Taiwan — are not a case of random ad hoc pragmatism. The methods bend like a bamboo. Transcending methods, however, fixed and firm as a pine, is the Chinese Communist vision of tomorrow's world and China's role in it.

I am not discounting ideology or Peking's belief in its ideology. The issue is more oblique. How does ideology sway day-to-day practice? And here one more point arises. *Realpolitik* is not a science like physics. Its practice rests on how you first see the conditions around you. The perceptions of the crudest pragmatist are filtered through a honeycomb of prejudices. It is *as Marxists* that the Chinese leaders weigh and reason about international affairs.

They study a situation. What they see is not separable from the Marxist spectacles through which they peer. Take the Ceylon rebellion of 1971. Mr. Y told me why Peking did not support the rebels. "You see, there were two things wrong with them." He sounded like a mechanic accounting for a stalled motor. "They put the gun above the Party. And they did not practice the mass line." Mr. Y summed them up as "Guevarist."

Now, is this really why Peking would not back the Ceylonese rebels? China's position has two inseparable roots. Peking felt the rebels would lose. Here were grounds for keeping clear of them. But the *reasons* which convinced Peking the rebels would lose were ideological. As Mr. Y detailed, the youthful Ceylonese had fallen into two errors which Peking believes fundamental.

The "reality" which the exponent of *Realpolitik* reveres cannot be measured by thermometer or scale. What you see is not unaffected by what you believe. Mao thought the Ceylon rebels were wrong — and calculated accordingly. Che Guevara might have thought them correct — and calculated accordingly.

To sum up. The Chinese are certainly among the Realists of

history, not the Zealots or the Romantics. Yet their realism is at once an aspect and an application of their (China-tested) Communist convictions. The Chinese are not Communists with the left hand and Bismarckians with the right. To an extent remarkable for men of ideology, they see the world with a single eye.

While watching a Ping-Pong exhibition at a Physical Training Institute near Peking, it occurred to me that the game of Ping-Pong illustrates Chinese foreign policy. Ping-Pong is almost *premised on adversity*. Light as a feather, the ball is incredibly wayward. Now it hangs in the air on a tiny gust; now it sulkily falls short of its expected destination. One recalls the chances and trials of the CCP. Seldom could it make common-sense projections; often it was blown off course.

The bat is modest. A frail wand hardly larger than the muscular hand which grips it. Yet it must guard thirty feet of space. I thought of the CCP pitted against Japan. Sometimes its weapons were poor enough to make a peasant blush. Always it had to make up for with timing what it lacked in brute force.

The table is frustratingly small. Can that floating ball be delivered from twenty feet to such suburban confinement? The groping athletes in blue shorts and red shirts turn into PLA guerrillas before the eyes. Mao's rule of guerrilla war comes to mind: "Our strategy is 'pit one against ten' and our tactics are 'pit ten against one.'" What did he mean? Dare the impossible in the long run (one against ten). But calculate to the last detail in the short run (ten against one). The Ping-Pong player has feeble tools at his command. His task — to work his will on that feather of a ball — seems more than you can expect him to fulfill. Even now a cross-breeze wafts by to upset all calculation.

But what is long odds *strategically* he makes short odds *tactically*. He divides the job into its several aspects. Is the ball far to the left? He leaps like a tiger to get near it. Then he abandons vigor and goes limp. The fingers twitch imperceptibly and he caresses the celluloid in a mini-lob. It grazes the net from the sharpest of angles. His rushing opponent is confounded by the surprise of it. He has met the challenge of one against ten by finding the moment to pit ten against one. Mao wrote of the uphill fight against Chiang in the early 1930s: "We generally spend more time in moving than in fighting." So with the sharp-eyed player and his mini-lob. Position was vital, the blow itself almost incidental.

The plotting minds of the players are an almost tangible force in the stadium. You see that the human beings are everything, the "weapons" nothing. Did not Mao say of the struggle for China's destiny that ultimately men always count more than weapons? It is in Ping-Pong as in guerrilla war. *Human resourcefulness in adversity* is the theme. The name of China's game has been to turn weakness into strength. To transform defense into offense. To snatch mastery from the jaws of necessity.

20. The Myth of Mao

Leaving China by train through the technicolor lushness of Kwangtung's rounded hills, I felt a complex emotion. Fazed by South China's beauty on a summer morning, I could not yet untangle its two conflicting strands. First there was a feeling that rubs off from the buoyancy of corporate aspiration in China. The people seemed like Rousseau's "Spartan mother," putting country before self, living as lambs of Shepherd Mao — and that is ennobling. But — here was the second current — also a feeling of painful separation from the high pitch of collective spirit. I could not live like that — how can others do so?

Behind the pain and separation lies anxiety at the "mental unity." Mao rules them, Nixon rules us, I said before; yet the systems of government have almost nothing in common. We have no mental unity, we have "freedom," and of our kind of freedom China has none. Peking has a parliament, but it has no more power in China than Queen Elizabeth has in England. The individual in China, insofar as he reaches beyond the practicalities of life — I don't know how many do — is enveloped by an Idea, the Thought of Mao Tse-tung. The myth of Mao Thought has reached into homes and even spirits (which Leninism or Stalinism hardly did in Russia).

This near-total control is not by police terror. The techniques of Stalinist terror — armed police everywhere, mass killings, murder of political opponents, knocks on the door at 3:00 A.M., then a shot — are not evident in China today. Though force remains the ultimate basis of any state, control of the people in

227

China is more nearly psychological than by physical coercion. Its extent would be hard to overstate. As this book records, politics reaches into almost every corner. Yet the method of control is amazingly light-handed by Communist standards. The informal way PLA men mingle and work with the population is remarkable to see. Peking trusts its citizens in their millions with rifles at home (members of the militia). What it does not trust them with — for the Dictatorship is by Idea — is their own minds.

There is paradox in the impression, got especially in rural parts, that people proceed with their daily lives in a relatively unpressured way. On one hand, Mao Thought pervades. On the other, the family (for instance) is extremely important to Chinese I met on this trip. The bridge is the age-old social discipline of the Chinese. The CCP has *used* the traditional bonds. An instance is reverence for ancestors. The Party does not stop the girls at the Nanking factory from visiting ancestors' graves, but it tries through propaganda to turn ancestor-reverence as much as possible toward *revolutionary martyrs*. In the environs of Nanking, I saw roadside ancestral altars turned into little shrines of Mao Tse-tung Thought; the central tablet was redone in red, featuring the star of the CCP, and quotations from the Chairman ran in strips from top to bottom down each side.

It is no longer simply "Communists" on one hand and "Chinese society" on the other. A merger has occurred at many points — a new kind of *tao* (way) emerges. This makes possible a Dictatorship by Idea (rather than by force). It is not like Poland or Hungary, where the Communists are a blanket spread over the body social. This may be what gave me an impression in China of pervasive yet light-handed control.

Is it not worse in China than Poland or Hungary, in that the people seem to cooperate in their own un-freedom? No, because the Idea fits the experience of most Chinese. At the Peking Chinese-Medicine Hospital, I met a railway worker who'd been hit by a train, and the resulting spine disorder paralyzed him from the waist down. His legs had shrunk, his hope had dwindled, and he had lain in bed like a vegetable for eighteen years. In the Cultural Revolution, when doctors were urged to tackle "even the impossible," a team at the hospital began acupuncture

The village of Shaoshan, where Mao Tse-tung was born and raised. It lies in a peaceful valley, three hours drive from Changsha, capital of Hunan province.

A hymn in concrete to self-reliance: The Nanking Bridge, built entirely by Chinese work and materials, after Russia had ceased aiding China. Finished in 1968, the bridge is 1,577 meters long and carries 90 trains a day as well as road traffic.

treatment on 151 such half-paralyzed people. Most had lain in bed so long that the marks of bedsores were on them like burns. One hundred and twenty-four can now walk with a stick; fifteen can walk without a stick, and eight of these are at work again.

The railway worker hobbled across the room on crutches to greet me, and said: "I am out of bed because of Chairman Mao's Thought. Soon I will go back to work for the sake of the revolution." At that moment the remark seemed embarrassing, yet the Myth of Mao is functional to medicine and to much endeavor in China. Was the schoolgirl really studying French to "further world revolution"? No, but the myth of revolution gives her the zeal to study French well. "Myth" is not falsehood but dramatization with a kernel of truth. The Myth of Mao sums up bitter Chinese experience and lends hope. It seemed to give the railway worker a mental picture of a world he could rejoin, and his doctors a vital extra ounce of resourcefulness.

For the nation, it gives a recognizable (if distorted) summation of past struggles against landlords and foreigners, and an impulse to keep going further in the collective drama of China "standing up."

When Professor P'u at Sun Yat Sen University said his new research was aimed to serve "workers, peasants, and soldiers," he invoked a myth. This "Blessed Trinity" suffuses China today. Everything is weighed against its service to these three groups. I sometimes found that what this Trinity put out the front door it let slip in the back (a violinist in the Red Guard Art Troupe in Sian said his father had been a "peasant," but he'd been a landlord who later corrected his ideas; a cadre's daughter at Peking University contrived to call her father a "worker"). But though not a full portrayal of reality, the "Blessed Trinity" has meaning as an alchemy of fact and hope which suggests what the collective drama of China's revolution is about.

Workers stands for industrialization. They come first, since according to Marx, workers make the revolution. Workers didn't in China, but modernizing China is a good part of the revolution's aims. Mao has not made an idol of industrialization as some

Marxists have in Russia. But ever since the impact of the materially superior West shattered the Ch'ing dynasty, China's opinion leaders have defined the national power they seek partly in terms of large-scale production. Here Marxist theory and national aspiration and the instinct of the "modern" Chinese mind all coincide.

Peasants stands for the reality of a China still 80 percent rural. The revolution came from the villages. It had to; there was no other adequate source. Mao became its leader by grasping this, and he still resists notions of development (perhaps Liu Shao-ch'i's) which would leave rural China lagging behind the industrial sector. Producing enough food for 800,000,000 people is *the* great daily task of the Chinese nation; three-quarters of Chinese spend their time growing their own food; the industrial and service sectors are tiny beside the food-producing sector. To keep the country ticking over and hold it together, peasants are the key. To pursue equality, as Mao is doing, the peasants are also, of course, the key.

Soldiers stands for the international defense of the revolution, and also for a crucial fact about the politics of the revolution. Peking's leaders won power by the gun. They have always felt threatened by U.S. encirclement. At any moment it might have been necessary once more, as against Japan, to mount "people's war." Soldiers are in this way central to China's revolutionary drama.

But the People's Liberation Army is also the linchpin of China's politics today. For it is the *bridge between the peasant reality of China and the modernizing tasks*. It is a peasant army. As such it is the national institution which best represents the political reality of China. Better than the Party, better than the state administration. That is why Mao used it in the Cultural Revolution for a political task — as he had used it before. It is his weapon against "revisionists" (but perhaps they are China's most orthodox Marxists!) who put their socialist faith in historical process propelled by transformation of the material base, and would leave the peasants behind. It is his weapon against "ultraleftists" (but perhaps they are China's purest Maoists!) who took

Mao's idea of uninterrupted revolution all too seriously, and spi-raled into the factionalism of 1967.

Workers, peasants, soldiers. Like so many slogans in China, it has a practical kernel. It ties together aims, methods, and resources. It is a myth with roots in reality.

I cannot say in blanket fashion whether this Mao Myth is "good or bad." For the ordinary Chinese it seems to give mean-ing to things. He can see such spectacular benefits from this pres-ent government that the collective drama — which the Mao Myth expresses — seems an acceptable way to try and get the further improvements in his life that he would like. It also stirs his national pride.

Recall, too, that the individualistic or "privatistic" alternative, in a country with per capita income perhaps one-twentieth of America's, is not a glittering one for the ordinary Chinese. And China simply could not afford to encourage the privatistic alter-native. At today's economic levels, Peking could hardly permit its 800,000,000 people to build their separate individual worlds, to carve out separate career patterns and philosophies, to sur-round themselves with their separate sets of possessions.

It is the intellectual who pays the big price. A scholar in a Chinese city, at the end of an evening's conversation, said three big things have happened since Liberation. China has "stood up." Class exploitation has gone. The nation is being "proletar-ianized." The first two he elaborated effectively, but he didn't convey much of the third. Either the idea seemed forced, elusive to him, or he had regrets about the way it has worked out.

Was he thinking of how the Mao Myth had "proletarianized" his field of study, twisting it to fit the needs of the collective drama? I thought of his daughter, a bright graduate of a major university now working as a farm laborer. He had said of her in a rather flat way: "We hope that later she may be given a job that will make use of her abilities." For this man, the Mao Myth leaves high and dry his own concerns (and those of his children, and many of his colleagues). Whether the spoiling of these "ca-reers" is worthwhile for the sake of the Chinese millions whose interests are put first — it is a question of values, in Peking as in

Boston. In a new way, each man still has his China, as he has his Rousseau.

Remembering what I saw in China — and the feeling of painful separation on the train from Canton — I venture to say that it must be terribly hard for Chinese intellectuals to accept the Mao Myth. Of course they can and do support the revolution's nationalism. That China has "stood up" puts a flash of pride in any Chinese eye. Yet they can hardly approve — especially since the Cultural Revolution, which several seemed embarrassed to talk about — of Dictatorship by Idea.

People ask, "Is China free?," but there is no objective measure of the freedom of a whole society. Observation in China, as study of China, suggests that the revolution has been good for workers and peasants but problematic for intellectuals. It is hard to go on from there and make overall value judgments that are honest.

First, there are so many gaps in our knowledge of China that it can be like judging America on the basis of the Kent State and Attica events (I know this because I used, before I came here, to judge the United States mainly by its spectacular lapses). Second, our experience has been so different from China's. Not having plumbed the depths of brokenness and humiliation that China did in the century following the Opium War, we cannot know the corporate emotion that comes with the recovery. Third — a related point — the relatively powerful should judge the less powerful with caution. It is easy for the rich man to scorn the loose morals of the poor man who steals his dinner. Easy for pluralist America, which has 6 percent of world population and about 35 percent of its wealth, to attack the regimentation of China, which has about 25 percent of world population and 4 percent of its wealth. Easy, too, for tired America to shake its head at the psychological simplicities of China's nation-building mood, and forget that America was itself once in a proud, naïve stage of nation-building, bristling with a sense of innocence and mission.

Yet at one point we and China face the same value judgment. Which gets priority: the individual's freedom or the relationships of the whole society? Which *unit* is to be taken for policy and moral judgment alike: the nation, trade union, our class, my cronies, me? This is the hinge on which the whole issue turns. Professor P'u at S.Y.S.U. did not make his own decision to take up the problem of insect pests — it was handed him. Is that wrong? The writer, Kuo Mo-jo recalled, cannot now do books for three thousand or at most eight thousand readers, as Kuo used to in Shanghai in the 1930s, but must write for the mass millions — and he's judged by whether he can do that well or not. Is that wrong?

I am not a good guide here. I felt the double emotion on the train from Canton because I am both moved by the collective priorities of China's new order *and* sad at the lack of individuality and choice. As a democratic socialist (Australian variety) I am — to use caricatures — against both the "jungle" of capitalism and the "prison" of communism. This is not a popular position today, when revolution and reaction snarl a *pas de deux*. I criticize the Dictatorship by Idea in China, but not with capitalism's yardstick. To put a big matter in three sentences, I criticize China not for lacking capitalism's freedom, but for distrusting the creative personality. The yardstick used — the dignity of each person, the fellowship of all persons — is the same one I use against capitalism. Capitalism opens the door to tyranny of wealth; Chinese communism opens the door to the tyranny of a corporate design.

After leaving China, I met in Hong Kong a young man caught between "jungle" and "prison." Chu — as I shall call him — swam from Kwangtung province to Hong Kong, ten hours by night in the water, mainly to get better educational opportunities. (In 1971 some twenty thousand left China for Hong Kong, many of them young people who wanted to go to college and got sent to a village instead.) But his father, a teacher of Japanese in Hong Kong, would not or could not pay the big sum of money needed to educate him, so Chu went to work in a factory. Now he is disillusioned with Hong Kong. "I work hard — and for nothing. To work hard for my country, that's all right. But here, it's not for China; it's not for anything. All you can do in Hong Kong is spend." Chu is capable, and left China because he wasn't using his abilities there. Now the lack of social purpose and the jumbled priorities of Hong Kong weigh on him. As we parted he asked my advice — should he go back?

I am not going to end with moral judgments, because history is just now scrambling up our moral categories rather drastically, not least those used between Americans and Chinese. A symbol catches the change. In Taiwan today you watch Chinese boys play baseball — America's game. In Hong Kong you watch Chinese boys play cricket — Britain's game. In 1971 Peking launched its new America policy with table tennis — China's game.*

The point is that China, so long the object of our policies and our judgments, is no longer a passive but an active factor in the world. Moral judgments are inescapable, but the formulation of the issues is often at history's mercy. The flux of 1971 may turn out to have been a watershed in the way people look at China. What we think of China will matter a little less. What China thinks of us will matter a little more.

This happens by delicate nuance; yet it adds up to a major historical mutation. The Chinese are going to start asking some questions of us. No doubt they will be just as odd as some of our questions about China. A Chinese official who follows American affairs, unable even to conceive that Daniel Ellsberg may have acted alone in divulging the Pentagon Papers, inquired of me one day in a confidential tone, "Is it the Morgans, or the Rockefellers, who are behind him?"

* Not in point of origin — it came from Britain — but in the sense that Chinese are especially skillful at it.

Sanderson

When the Stars Lead to You

RONNI DAVIS

LB

LITTLE, BROWN YOUNG READERS
New York Boston

Copyright © 2019 by Ronica Davis
Cover photo © Guille Faingold/Stocksy.com. Cover design by Marcie Lawrence.
Cover copyright © 2019 by Hachette Book Group, Inc.

Little, Brown and Company
Hachette Book Group
1290 Avenue of the Americas, New York, NY 10104
Visit us at LBYR.com

First Edition: November 2019

Little, Brown and Company is a division of Hachette Book Group, Inc.
The Little, Brown name and logo are trademarks of Hachette Book Group, Inc.
The publisher is not responsible for websites (or their content) that are not owned by the publisher.

Library of Congress Cataloging-in-Publication Data
Names: Davis, Ronni, author.
Title: When the stars lead to you / Ronni Davis.
Description: First edition. | New York ; Boston : Little, Brown Young Readers, 2019. |
Summary: After Ashton broke Devon's heart, she focused on preparing for her future as an astrophysicist but Ashton's appearance on the first day of her senior year forces her to revisit their magical summer together.
Identifiers: LCCN 2018057312 | ISBN 9780316490702 (hardcover) | ISBN 9780316490696 (pbk.) | ISBN 9780316490689 (ebk.)
Subjects: | CYAC: Love—Fiction. | High schools—Fiction. | Schools—Fiction. | Depression, Mental—Fiction. | Racially mixed people—Fiction.
Classification: LCC PZ7.1.D3837 Whe 2019 | DDC [Fic]—dc23
LC record available at https://lccn.loc.gov/2018057312

ISBNs: 978-0-316-49070-2 (hardcover), 978-0-316-49068-9 (ebook)

Printed in the United States of America

LSC-C

10 9 8 7 6 5 4 3 2 1

To Mommy
for teaching me to love books
and
to Ms. Wheeler
for encouraging me to write them

BEFORE

-Then-

You'd think someone who wanted to study the stars would know better than to wish on them. There was no logical reason for me to put so much hope in exploding balls of hydrogen and helium, especially since they were millions of light-years away. But it didn't matter. Every single night, I turned my head toward the sky, closed my eyes, and dreamed.

Like right now, sitting on the beach during the summer solstice, watching Arcturus rise. The red giant, twenty-five times bigger than the sun, burning brighter than every star in the northern hemisphere, both awed and terrified me. But it also somehow comforted me. Made me feel safe. So I gave him one simple wish: that I'd have the best summer ever.

My cousin Stephanie and her family lived at the beach year-round. Her parents owned one of the souvenir shops and

a restaurant here. It was just a few hours' drive north from my hometown, so I visited every year while my parents did non-church-affiliated (they really wanted everyone to know that part) missionary work in Honduras. If they knew the things Stephanie and I got up to (boys! parties! kissing!), they probably wouldn't have been so quick to let me go every summer.

I loved these quiet nights before the tourists took over. The tide rolling in, the cool Atlantic waves splashing over my ankles and making me shiver. Pretty soon, they'd be splashing over my knees, then my thighs. I buried my toes in the sand. I liked the way it tickled when the surf carried the grains from under my feet. And I loved the stars scattering all over the sky like diamonds against blue velvet.

This was the dream life.

"Yo, Devon," Stephanie called. "Come here. I want you to meet someone."

And then there was reality.

My cousin fancied herself a matchmaker, but she had no clue about the type of guys I liked. *I* barely had a clue about the type of guys I liked, because I got attracted to so many different kinds. Tall and skinny with pale skin, dark hair, and hazel eyes. Dark-brown skin, deep brown eyes, and locs. Tan skin, dimples, blue eyes, and blond hair.

Two things I did know: He had to be kind, and he had to be a gentleman.

Because honestly? I was sick of kissing a guy only to have him dragging my hand to his pants ten seconds later.

The firelight threw shadows over Stephanie's silvery-blond

hair, making her look almost unearthly. Two boys stood with her, both in silhouette, both holding plastic red cups.

"Devon! Get your booty over here," she commanded.

I groaned, but I trudged over anyway. "Hey, Steph."

"About time." She thrust a red cup into my hand, then threw her arm around me and grinned. Her cheeks were already flushed, her breath warm and boozy. "This is Todd and his cousin Ashton."

"Nice to meet you," Todd said. Polite, but clearly way more interested in Stephanie. I couldn't even blame him. She was adorable; short and curvy with dark-green eyes and a tiny button nose. Completely opposite of Todd, the epitome of tall, dark, and handsome, with piercing blue eyes and jet-black hair. They looked good standing together.

Then I turned to Ashton.

Sweet six-pound, five-ounce baby Jesus.

It's so clichéd, but there was a reason those clichés existed.

Ashton.

Was.

Gorgeous. With a capital *G*.

I had never, ever seen anyone like him. Straight nose, wide mouth, full lips that were slightly pouty. Impossibly clear skin with the tiniest hint of sunburn coloring his cheeks. His short bronze-colored hair was wavy and thick, and my fingers tingled with longing to get tangled up in it. Everything on his face was in proportion, and yet he wasn't shiny-perfect. His ears stuck out a little too much and he was a little too skinny. But that was okay. I didn't mind thin guys. Plus, there was something different about Ashton. A stillness—major contrast to the whooping and hollering around us. And his eyes. So intense. So mysterious. A deep, deep brown that invited me to dive in and get lost.

So I got lost.

Falling, falling, spinning somewhere I'd never been before, but a place I knew I wanted to be. I tried not to stare, but he was staring at me. The world melted away, leaving only me and him and the crashing waves.

"Hey," he said with a gentle smile. His teeth were perfectly white and straight, the result of either amazing genetics or thousands of dollars of orthodontia. With his track record so far, I was betting on the former.

"Hi," I said breathlessly. *Breathlessly.* I was breathless. What was going on?

"So...Devon?"

"Yes," I managed to get out. Seriously? His voice was smooth with a touch of gravel, like how velvet would sound if you rubbed it against the grain. Oh my God. Chills. Everywhere.

"I'm Ashton. Nice to meet you."

I had a weakness for perfect handshakes, and Ashton's was just right. Not so hard it crushed my hand, but not one of those limp noodle ones, either.

"Todd and I are going to get refills," Stephanie said, finally breaking Ashton's hold on me. Yeah...forgot she was even there. "You guys want?"

"I'm good." Ashton raised his cup, which was almost full.

He was still looking at me.

"So am I," I said.

I was still looking at him.

"We'll leave you to it," Stephanie said, then she and Todd were gone.

I raised my eyebrow when Ashton poured his beer into the sand. He blinked at me and blushed.

"I don't drink," he explained. "Your cousin poured it for me, and I didn't want to be rude."

"No worries." I shrugged and poured my own beer into the sand. "I don't drink much, either. She never remembers that."

His eyes scanned the entire length of my body, then met mine head-on. This boy was *so* checking me out...and I could tell by the way his lips parted that he liked what he saw. I'm sure I was looking at him the same way. Because oh yes, I definitely liked what I saw. He must have had terrible-smelling feet or something because there was no way this guy was this perfect.

"So, Devon," he said again. "Hi."

I grinned. "Hi."

He covered his eyes and scrunched up his nose. "Oh my God. We did this already." He peeked at me through his fingers. "Sorry."

Adorable. "Your first time here?"

He shook his head. "My family first brought me when I was five, but I barely remember it. So I have no idea what people do around here. Besides the obvious stuff, I mean."

I shrugged. "Not much, to be honest. I like to walk on the boardwalk or go swimming. Lots of parties, if you're into that sort of thing."

"More into video games or taking pictures," he said. "Sometimes I go horseback riding."

"You have a horse?"

"His name's Leander. I've had him since I was eleven. So, five years."

Ashton was sixteen. Like me.

He pulled out his phone and started scrolling. *Really?* Minus ten points for that. I hated when people couldn't stay off their phones for five stinking minutes. Weren't we having a conversation?

But then he said, "This is him," and held his phone out to me. Immediate guilt for going off in my head.

"He's incredible. Is he an Arabian?"

Ashton smiled at his phone. "Yeah. He's great. Do you have a horse?"

"I like them. But no."

"Oh. That's too bad." He dropped the phone into one of the pockets on his cargo shorts.

"Plus, my cousin says I keep to myself too much," I said. "I have a best friend...but if I had a horse I'd never hang out with people." I buried my pink toenails in the sand. "She likes to tease me."

He looked perplexed. "Why?"

"Why do I keep to myself or why does Steph tease me?"

"Both."

"I'm a big nerd. It's why she's always introducing me to people."

His gaze was steady. "I'm glad she introduced us."

I shivered all over. "Me too."

He looked down at the sand, then caught my eye again. "Do you wanna come with me to get some ice cream?"

A warm, fuzzy feeling spread through my entire being. "I'd love to."

His face broke into a slow grin that made me want to melt right into the sand. Then *I* grinned. We stood there grinning at each other like goofballs until my stomach growled.

Laughing, he held out his hand. "Come on, let's go handle that monster."

I let my fingers intertwine with his.

My summer was already looking promising.

-Then-

THE FIRST WEEKEND OF THE SUMMER SEASON—ONCE THE tourists were good and ingratiated—was always epic. You couldn't walk two feet without bumping into a rip-roaring party. But pick the wrong one and it could ruin your entire summer. Too much beer, people vomiting at your feet, hooking up with the wrong person, STDs. Terrible decisions all around.

Lucky for us, Stephanie always managed to find the right parties. The ones on private beaches with a full bar instead of just a keg. The ones with actual DJs instead of someone's random playlist that always had a Chicago song on it for some reason. The ones where the hosts actually served food like hamburgers and crudités instead of just chips...or nothing at all.

Tonight, we strolled—fashionably late—into an enormous beach house blasting music so loudly the wicker furniture jumped to the beat. There were people everywhere, not that we could see them very well. The only lighting came from the twinkle lights and LED candles and a fancy show from the DJ booth.

"You made it!" Tall, Dark, and Handsome was back, pulling Stephanie and me into a group hug. He was damp, smelling like chlorine. Cold droplets from his hair dripped onto my back, making me shiver.

"We made it," Stephanie said, then turned to me. "You remember Todd?"

"Of course I remember," I said. But I remembered his cousin more. Had it just been last night that we met?

"This is my buddy Justin's place, but I'm the official host. Because Justin's a bitch-ass bitch who doesn't even have a fake ID." Todd turned to me. "Make yourself at home, help yourself to anything." To Stephanie, he said, "*You* come with me."

And great. Now I was alone.

The best and worst part about tourist season was that the faces changed constantly. Meeting new people was always cool. And if a hookup was disappointing, chances were high I'd never see the dude again. Bad because if you did find someone you liked hanging out with, they'd likely be gone in a week. Then you'd have to start all over.

But I loved the possibilities. Anything that happened could be life changing. And tonight, everyone was new.

I grabbed a soda and wandered around, letting the beats soak into my bones and make my body sway. Sweat dripped down my neck as the house heated up from the warm bodies getting caught up in the music.

I made my way out to the pool, where the air was only slightly cooler. A heat wave had kicked off this morning, and the humidity soaked my hair and made the curls shrink into tight spirals. I pulled my hair up into a big pouf, letting the slight sea breeze cool my back.

I was watching a game of beer pong gear up when a voice came from behind me. "You *are* here." My heart sped up at the sound of the low, gravelly rumble that had played nonstop in my brain for the last twenty-four hours.

I whirled around and there he was. An oasis in the midst of noise, sweat, and cigarettes. "Hi."

Ashton smiled, the corners of his eyes crinkling. "I thought Todd was bullshitting me. So when you said you were busy tonight…it was this?"

"*I* never said anything. Steph hijacked my phone, telling me something about making you wait three days." Even though she hadn't made Todd wait three days. But whatever. No way was I going to admit to Ashton that I kinda hoped I'd run into him here.

He frowned and shook his head. "I don't get those rules. Seems like if you want to see someone, just see them."

My knees weakened. "You wanted to see me again?"

His gaze was solemn. "Wasn't it obvious?"

"Ashton!" A girl popped up beside him and shook out her long blond hair. "I can't believe you're actually here!"

He gave her a closemouthed smile. "Here I am."

"You should come sit with me." She licked her pink glossy lips. "Over there."

She didn't even acknowledge my presence.

"I'm good." Ashton stroked my thumb, sending flutters clear up my arm.

With hard eyes, the blonde gave me a once-over that almost canceled the goose bumps from Ashton's touch. Then she turned back to him, all warmth and smiles. "Next time."

My skin prickled as she sauntered off. Then I glanced at Ashton. "Who's she?"

"I met her yesterday. I think she's staying a couple houses down from us."

"Do girls always act like that around you?"

"*You* were going to make me wait three days."

I tilted my head. "Would you have waited?"

He looked me up and down, then his gaze met mine head-on. "Without question."

Holy shit.

We sat on a patio love seat and watched guys toss girls into the pool. People stumbled in and out of the hot tub, holding red cups full of God knows what.

"The people-watching." Ashton shook his head.

"I know."

He leaned back and stretched, slipping his arm around my shoulders. I laughed so hard I almost dropped my soda. "Seriously?"

His broad smile made his entire being light up. "You're not pulling away."

I snuggled into his shoulder. *Mmm*, he smelled so good—cool and clean, like a fresh waterfall. "I guess not."

We watched a group of girls take selfies in front of the pool. A guy to the left of us offered a hit off his bong, which Ashton refused. Then he squirmed. "I always feel so out of place at these things."

I nodded. "I used to love parties. But now? Give me Netflix and junk food, please."

"Exactly! Okay. If we were watching Netflix right now, what would be on the screen?"

"Hold on. Is this a Netflix-and-chill situation, or are we actually watching something?"

"It's a legit binge session."

"Hmm." I twirled a stray curl, thinking. "What do you watch with your friends?"

"My best friend and I like totally different things," he said. "He likes to watch people eating weird shit. I watch sitcoms. What about you? What do you watch with your friends?"

"Romantic comedies," I said without missing a beat. "But what would I watch with you?" I tapped my lip. "Since we don't know each other that well yet, I'll say something funny, like stand-up. But not raunchy stand-up. Because that could get awkward."

"Makes sense. I like it. And we'd have popcorn and M&M's and chocolate chip cookies."

"Yes! Perfect!" I snuggled closer and intertwined my hand with his. "I wish..."

I could smell the mint on his breath. Could practically taste the saltiness of his skin. "What do you wish?" he whispered.

I never got to finish that thought. A loud crash came from just inside the door, followed by a lot of yelling. Then the beer pong game got louder, the splashing in the pool got rowdier...

"...and someone just puked in the hot tub." Ashton frowned, his face a slight green.

"I think that's our cue."

He squeezed my hand. "Let's get out of here."

We left the party and headed down to the public beach. It was empty and dark, except for a few red lights bobbing farther down the shore. We found a quiet spot right in front of the dunes. I kicked off my sandals and stretched my legs. Arcturus had long set by now, but there were still so many other stars.

The cool sea breeze felt good on my warm skin. My entire body flushed because Ashton and I were alone. Even if nothing else came out of tonight, I wanted to kiss him. So much.

"I have to know all about you," he said to me.

"Ask me anything."

"I'll start small. What's your favorite color?"

"Purple. But not any purple. More like a mix between lilac and lavender silk with sunlight shining through it."

He scrunched his nose. "That is oddly specific."

"What's yours?"

"Changes with my mood, I guess. Green or blue when I'm calm, red when I'm pissed."

"So if I see you wearing red, I should steer clear?"

He laughed, showing off those perfect teeth. "I don't know if it's that deep. What music do you listen to?"

I traced swirls in the sand with my toes. "My best friend turned me on to classical, but I also like R & B and pop. And sometimes I listen to show tunes."

His face lit up. "Like Broadway?"

"My dad plays the cast albums all the time. *Rent* is my favorite."

"*Hamilton* for me. It's so good. But I like *Rent*, too." He started humming the melody to "One Song Glory."

"You have a good humming voice," I said. "Do you sing?"

"All the time." He gave me a pointed look. "When I'm alone."

"One day you're going to sing for me," I said, "and you're going to like it."

He bopped my nose. "We'll see about that."

"What other music do you like?" I asked.

"Hip-hop."

"What is it with white boys loving hip-hop? You don't rap, do you?"

"God, no. Rapping is not my lane. I just listen and learn."

I nodded in appreciation. "Okay."

He grew serious, his eyes still on mine. "Tell me more."

This time the words came easier. I told him about how I visited my cousin here at the beach every year. I told him my favorite foods (sushi and sub sandwiches), that I loved burning incense, and that I hated the sound of people chewing. That I earned the money for my first telescope by doing odd jobs for my neighbors, and that I loved being an only child. I told him how I cried every morning my first week of kindergarten, and about the time I wet myself in second grade because mean old Miss Bradley refused to give me the hall pass.

"I've never told anyone half this stuff," I admitted.

He brushed a curl behind my ear. "I'm glad I was the first."

It was silly and weird and a bit scary how the words flew out of me like butterflies, even when I was recounting my most embarrassing moments. How he seemed interested in getting to know me instead of only interested in getting off.

"I want to ask you one more thing," he said.

"Go for it."

"Say we're watching Netflix, but now we know each other way better. What would you binge with me?"

"Documentaries."

He paused. "Seriously?"

"The ones about the universe and space."

He nodded slowly. "I get it. That stuff's cool."

I picked up some sand and let it fall through my fingers. "You think so? Because I want to tell you something else about me."

Ashton leaned back on his elbows. Totally relaxed. "Go for it."

I took a deep breath. "I love the stars."

He sat up again and fully fixed his attention on me. So I kept going. "I *live* for the stars. And one day, I'm going to be an astrophysicist."

He smiled in wonder. "Wow. You're beaming. I love it. So is astrophysics like astronomy?"

"It's a part of it. It deals more with the nature of heavenly bodies. Things like what galaxies, red giants, and black holes are made of. How long they've been out there, and what they mean for us, as humans. Or I can go all theoretical and focus on things like time travel." I wrapped my arms around myself. "I want to solve the mysteries of deep space. And I want to discover new worlds."

His mouth shaped into an O. "This has got to be the coolest thing I've ever heard."

"I can go on and on," I warned him. "You might not think it's so cool then."

"Try me."

So I did. I talked about the stars and physics and deep space. I talked about all the things I'd have to study, like geometry, calculus, and physics. "I want to get my doctorate," I said.

Ashton's expression was steady. As if he actually gave a damn about what I dreamed about. Most people glazed over when I got too into it. But *he listened*.

He nodded, his eyes still on me. "Dr. Devon."

"Kearney. Dr. Devon Kearney," I said.

"Devon Kearney, PhD," he said, smiling. "Has the perfect ring to it. I can't wait till you get there."

"If I get there."

"You will. I believe in you."

That's when my physical attraction shifted into something more: I wanted to be his friend, too.

I lightly poked his shoulder. "If I'm spilling all my secrets, it's only fair you tell me all yours."

"But you know that means we'll have to spend more time together," he said. Then he got really quiet. "I'd like that. A lot. Would you?"

I didn't even hesitate. "I would."

-Then-

MOST PEOPLE PROBABLY THINK WAKING UP AT THE CRACK of dawn during summer vacation is plain nonsense, but I wouldn't have had it any other way. Every morning, I let the lightening sky kiss my eyelids until they fluttered open, then I bounced out of bed, ready to embrace the day.

The kitchen was quiet while I poured hot tea into a to-go cup. Then I grabbed my beach bag and headed down. The sea breeze blew curls around my face, and the rising sun warmed my skin while showing me a sky full of pastel swirls.

Morning yoga, in my opinion, was the very best yoga, and I loved doing Sun Salutations while dawn bloomed.

Every day, once my practice was over, my stomach would announce itself in the most obnoxious way, so I'd head back for breakfast. By now, the household would be up. Uncle Steven already off to the restaurant to fire things up for the morning rush. Aunt Susan hopping onto her bike to start her day at the souvenir shop. Stephanie frying bacon and scrambling eggs, grumbling about having to be up so early (to help in her mom's souvenir shop) even though by now it was already 8:00 AM.

Except today, she was smirking when I walked in the door. "Someone's here for you."

"What? Oh!"

"Hi," Ashton said. He was sitting at the kitchen table, flipping a fork through his fingers. "Sorry for randomly showing up like this. I couldn't sleep, so I took a walk, and..."

"You just *happened* to end up here?" Stephanie's eyes flashed with mirth.

"Something like that," he murmured, then turned to me. "Do you wanna hang out?"

My breath quickened and I tingled all over.

Because, um. Hell yes.

"I need to grab a shower, if you don't mind waiting a bit," I said.

Stephanie set a plate of food in front of him. "This should keep him busy."

Quick shower. Brush teeth. Hair in ponytail. Throw on bathing suit with sundress on top. Comfortable sandals. And... go.

Ashton had just put his clean dish in the rack when I came back out. I grabbed a muffin, then turned to him. "Ready?"

He took my hand. "Let's go."

"It just occurred to me," I said as we strolled along the board-walk, "the only things I know about you are your favorite color, you have a horse, and you like *Hamilton*."

Ashton frowned thoughtfully. "Honestly, you're not missing much. I'm not that fascinating."

"I don't believe that. Plus, turnabout is fair play."

He stopped walking. "Turna-who what now?"

"You had a turn to learn about me. It's my turn to learn about you."

A slow nod. "What do you want to know?"

We sat on a bench. I pulled out my muffin and inhaled deeply. *Mmm*, strawberry. "Tell me the weird things," I said. "Do you have terrible handwriting? Do you pick your nose and eat it? That sort of thing."

His forehead wrinkled. "What the hell?"

"It's important."

"It's gross."

I raised my eyebrows. "Are you going to answer the question, though?"

"I don't pick my nose and eat it, Devon. Where did you even come up with that?"

"I always wonder random things about people. For instance." I pointed to a blond woman bouncing a chubby blond baby. "Do you think she snores? Or eats onions?"

He tilted his head sideways. "I'm going to say she snores when she's got a cold, and she only eats Vidalia onions."

I turned to him, eyebrows raised. "Wow. You're better at this than I expected."

"I mean, it's kind of fun," he said. "What about that guy over there? Do you think he's ever slipped on a banana peel?"

"Totally. And he's the type to fart and blame the dog. But. We are getting off topic. Do *you* snore? Or eat onions?"

"I'll pretty much eat whatever you put in front of me, and I don't snore. I've tripped over shoelaces, but never a banana peel."

"How do you know you don't snore?"

"It's just a feeling I have," he said with a cocky grin.

Here is something else I learned about Ashton that day: He was kind of musical. There was always change or keys jangling in his pocket as he walked. He constantly bopped his head to some tune only he could hear. He drummed his fingers on his thighs when he was concentrating. Sometimes he drummed his fingers on me—my arm when he wanted to show me something. Or just while he was looking at me, before breaking into a slow smile.

He couldn't keep his hands still. Either it was the drumming or he was flipping a pen or a toothpick or a straw between his fingers. Almost like a meditation.

Because he drifted away. Often. His eyes focused on something I couldn't see. Like now, at dinner. I watched him as he sat, myriad pensive expressions dancing across his face.

"Dollar for your thoughts," I said.

Those brown eyes swung toward me. "A dollar? You know the phrase is 'penny,' right? They aren't even worth that much."

I reached over and touched his hand. "I don't believe that."

He looked at me, his expression curious, but I didn't get a chance to read too much into it before the waiter brought us our food.

"Okay. Here's something weird about me," Ashton said while we were eating. Sitting on the same side of the table in a diner booth because we were already somehow becoming *that couple.* "I like the sound of paper crumpling. Right by my ear. It relaxes me."

Without thinking, I reached up and stroked his earlobe. "What else do you do to relax?"

He sighed and leaned into my hand. "I play video games. A super-violent one when I'm mad. Sometimes I play one where I control virtual people, but that one's a total time suck." He paused, then let out a deep breath. "Right now, my favorite is one I don't tell anyone about because it's a cute game, and my friends and I don't *do* cute games."

"What? That's ridiculous. You like what you like."

"Yeah, doesn't quite work that way."

Then he got really quiet.

The minutes ticked by as he picked at his chicken strips.

"Where do you go?" I asked him.

"What do you mean?"

"When you get quiet like that."

"Oh." He stole one of my tater tots and popped it into his mouth. "I'm right here with you. The only place I want to be."

-Then-

AFTER FOUR WEEKS, OUR ROUTINE HAD BECOME FAMILIAR, and I wondered how I'd ever filled my summer days before Ashton came along. Most mornings, he'd show up for breakfast, and then, hand in hand, we'd stroll down the boardwalk. Or we'd run down to the beach and swim in the ocean for hours. By now, his hair had lightened from all the sun, and my skin had darkened to a deep tawny.

Some days, Ashton was animated, and he went on a mile a minute about anything and everything. His favorite video game, which he now played on his phone in front of me with zero shame. The latest dumpster fire on Twitter. Some messed-up thing Todd had said to him or tried to rope him into. On our best days, we sang lyrics from *Rent* to each other.

Other times, he was quiet. Subdued. Content to listen to

the surf crashing as the tide rose, to take deep breaths of the crisp salty air. I'd reach over and tweak his nose, and he'd turn to me with the gentlest smile before lightly planting a kiss on my temple.

He'd been busy today, doing something with his family that he didn't seem to want to share much about. By the time he picked me up, he was reflective, but he didn't seem too far away as he held out his hand. "Let's walk."

Right before sunset, we made our way down to a quiet part of the beach. "Be careful where you step," he said. "There might be jellyfish."

We found a safe spot far away from the surf. I pulled a beach blanket from my bag, and then Ashton and I cuddled close, watching the fiery dusk descend and a full moon rise. The temperature had dropped, and I shivered as the sea breeze cut through my shawl.

He slid his arms around me, and with a happy sigh, I settled against him. I loved this. His fingertips stroking my shoulder. The rise and fall of his chest with his breath. Being so close to him.

Pure heaven.

It had been four weeks since we'd first laid eyes on each other, and I was falling for him.

I should've been cautious. But I didn't want to be. Because *I was falling for him*.

"Hey, Dev?"

I smiled. Weirdly enough, no one had ever shortened my name like that, and I loved the way he sounded when he did it. There was a tenderness in his voice that made me shiver all over.

"What do you think we'd be watching on Netflix now?" he asked.

"Baking shows."

He stared at me in disbelief. "What?"

I nodded. "Yes. We'd be watching people make fancy cakes and try not to drop them. Or we'd be watching that show about all the people trying to make stuff and epically failing. Or *House Hunters*. Why? What would you choose?"

He blinked several times. "You'd pick *House Hunters*?"

"Without hesitation."

"But that's not even *on* Netflix."

I pointed to him. "Aha! Only someone looking for it would know that!"

"Look, I'm not ashamed to say I enjoy watching people get all bent out of shape over stupid shit like pedestal sinks and space for entertaining."

And out of nowhere, my brain decided to pop in an image of Ashton and me, looking for our own place. What silly things would we squabble over? What would be the one dramatic hard line one or both of us would have to take, just so there'd be drama?

What the *hell* was I thinking about this for?

To cover my thoughts, I snatched his phone. "How do you even play this game you love so much?"

"You meet neighbors, stock materials, grow things. Do cute little quests."

I squinted at the screen. "Is this *FarmVille?*"

He stared at me as if I'd grown two heads. "It's *Harvest Dreams.*"

"Oh," I said. "It *is* cute."

"Let me set up a profile for you."

While he did that, I stared up at the sky. Clouds were rolling in and the sea was getting choppy. A storm was coming.

Two failed quests later, I was done for the night. I handed him back his phone, which he dropped into the pocket of his shorts. "You're new," he said. "We can try again tomorrow."

"No thanks. My special talent is being defeated by every single video game ever created."

"That's because you have better things to focus on. Like becoming Dr. Devon Kearney."

"God. It seems so far off."

"Will you be sitting on a beach like this, studying your stars?"

"Yes. Or maybe a lab. Hopefully in Paris."

He raised his eyebrows. "Why Paris?"

"They have one of the best observatories in the world."

"When you're there I'll have to call you *Docteur* Devon Kearney."

I loved how he talked like he was still going to be in my life all those years from now. I poked his shoulder. "Tell me *your* dreams."

"*My* dreams." He thought while the wind whipped our hair. Then he gazed at me in his soft, special way. "Feels like I'm living them right now."

"Yeah?"

"It's summer. I'm on the beach." He paused. "I'm here with you."

"Me?" I looked down. "Never thought I'd be part of someone's dreams."

"Well, I don't know if *you* noticed, but we've been spending a lot of time together." His voice was light, but the way my heart sped up showed me there was something serious under his joking tone.

Thunder rumbled in the distance. "Yeah. We have."

"I don't want to spend time with anyone but you," he said.

I sat up and stared at him. "So you mean..."

His gaze was fully focused on me. Steady. Sure. "I want to make this a thing. Me and you."

"Us." *Breathless.* This boy was constantly taking my breath away.

"Yeah." His lips curved slightly. "Us. I want to officially watch Netflix with you."

The laughter burst out of me. "What?"

He brushed a golden spiral from my forehead. "I want you to be my girlfriend."

The storm was coming. And I should have been cautious.

But that went out the window a long time ago.

"I'm in."

—Then—

"I HAVE SOMETHING FOR YOU."

"Really?" I grinned at Ashton and clapped my hands. I loved getting presents.

"Close your eyes."

I let my eyelids flutter shut, the impression of the night sky still swirling in my mind. Some nights, the stars were shy, hiding behind fluffy clouds. Tonight, they'd put on a show. There were so many of them, some so densely packed together they looked like blobs of smoke.

Absolutely breathtaking.

I felt Ashton move behind me, then lift my hair.

I shivered all over. "That tickles."

He laughed softly in my ear. "Stand still. I'll be done in a second."

A deep breath. "Okay."

His fingers trembled as he fixed a clasp at the back of my neck. At the same time, I felt the weight of a pendant settle on my chest. "Now you can open them."

I gasped as I lifted the silver key. Smooth and shiny. The top a hollow heart, the shaft a thin cylinder, with a T perpendicular to the tip. "Oh my God, Ashton."

"I know we only became official yesterday," he said. "But I wanted to get you something to show you how much I like you. I guess it's like a key to my heart."

A pause. Then we burst out laughing. "I'm sorry—that was so cheesy," he said.

"*So* cheesy."

"But true," he said, growing serious. "It's yours, Dev. I'm yours."

"You are a romantic."

"Only with you. And I don't care if it is cheesy."

"I love it, Ash." I stroked his cheek. "I won't ever take it off."

-Then-

THE LAST DAYS OF SUMMER ALWAYS CHURNED MY EMOtions. I loved playing in the ocean, burying my feet in the sand, gazing at the sky every night. But the long lazy days eventually got to me, and I became eager to get back into my routine of school and hanging with my best friend and sleeping in my own bed.

Still. I was going to miss my morning yoga routine on the beach, inhaling the sea's briny scent with every deep breath. I was going to miss the oceanfront view out my bedroom window. I'd miss Stephanie and her schemes to draw me out of my shell.

Most of all, I was going to miss the adorable boy who'd managed to sneak away with my heart this summer. Thank God for this one last day with him.

The sun wasn't up yet, but the heat was already heavy and thick. I sat on the porch in my light, pink sundress and straw sun hat, staring at the walkway to Stephanie's house. Listening for the jingle of keys or coins that signaled Ashton's appearance. He should've been here fifteen minutes ago. It wasn't like him to be late. The sun was coming up soon, and I didn't want to watch it without him. We'd been talking all summer about catching the sunrise together, but with us both leaving tomorrow, this was our last chance.

Our plans were literally from dawn until dusk, and then beyond. I couldn't wait for our day to start, even though I'd hate when it ended.

Where was he?

-Then-

THE SUN ROSE IN A SWIRL OF PINK AND YELLOW COTTON
candy clouds.

I watched it alone.

-Then-

I TEXTED HIM.
    I called him.
    I left messages.
    Then I started all over again.

-Then-

My skin turned hot and red. Gnats hovered around my forehead, but I couldn't find the strength to brush them away.

He and I should've been sitting down for lunch now. Instead, I was staring at my phone. Where my texts remained unread.

-Then-

Every time my phone buzzed, I jumped. But it was always something else. An email from my school. A reminder to drink water. A text from my mom, finalizing details for my trip home tomorrow.

It was never him.

-Then-

I LEFT VOICE MAILS UNTIL THE BOX WAS FULL.

I sent more texts.

They stayed unread.

What the hell?

-Then-

MOSQUITOES FEASTED ON MY ANKLES, AND STILL, I couldn't...wouldn't move from the porch. I just sat there. Even as the moon rose and the stars began to shine, twinkling at me like so much laughter.

We were supposed to be kissing under those stars. Right now. Letting the night take us wherever. Giving in to doing... whatever.

"Oh my God, Devon. Are you okay?" Stephanie asked.

I blinked cobwebs from my eyes. "I'm fine. Go have fun with your friends."

"Devon—"

I hid my face so she couldn't see I was about to lose it. "No. Really!"

Still, she hesitated. "Should I stay with you?"

"Your friends are waiting. Get out of here."

I must have sounded convincing enough, because eventually, she did leave.

Why was *I* still here?

I needed to go. *Now.*

I grabbed a bike and headed to his beach house.

-Then-

THERE WERE NO CARS IN THE DRIVEWAY.

There were no lights in the enormous dining room.

There was no sign of life anywhere.

He was gone.

And he'd never said good-bye.

SUPERNOVA

Chapter 1

I took a deep breath, inhaling the rich leather scent of Blair's cherry-red Mercedes. I clutched my pendant as Bishop Hall—Preston Academy's main building—loomed ahead. Ready or not, there was no turning back once I stepped through those tall wooden doors.

I couldn't see the stars right now, but I still made a wish: to have the perfect senior year.

Then I turned to my best friend. "It's bittersweet, isn't it?"

"Sure." Blair switched off the ignition. "Just take away the bitter part."

The sudden absence of Léo Delibes's "Sylvia, Act III: Cortege de Bacchus" made my ears ring. Something about blasting those violins and flutes usually fortified me for the day better than caffeine ever could. But today, the music only made me shaky and anxious.

Blair's forehead wrinkled. "Are you okay?"

I wiped my palms on my green plaid skirt. "I'm nervous. Why am I so nervous?"

"Girl," she said, wrinkles gone, sapphire eyes dancing. "It's the first day of senior year. And you, in all your nerdilicious glory, are already freaking out about getting into your dream college. Aren't you?"

The corner of my mouth lifted in a small smile. "Pretty much."

"Devon," she said, turning serious. "You got this. You know that, right?"

I didn't, really. But she looked so hopeful, I didn't want to let her down. We hooked pinkies. "Let's do this."

I climbed out of the car and stared at what had been my second home for the past three years. People gathered on the stairs, scrolling through their phones or embracing one another, squealing choruses of "How was your summer?" and "Oh my God, you look great!" People called to us, and I waved back, feeling more and more at home with every step. A light breeze rustled oak and maple leaves as Blair and I crossed the courtyard, but it didn't do anything to break up the humidity in the air.

Bishop Hall looked like a medieval cathedral, with sweeping arches and twisting chimeras, its focal point an impressive clock tower of gray stone rising to the sky. As the bells struck eight, the sound resonated throughout the grounds, echoing off classroom buildings and dormitories. Three years ago, this place had been intimidating. Now it felt majestic. Powerful. Blair and I were silent, almost reverent, until the last *bong*.

That never got old.

"We need to go in," I said. "Don't want to be late for Assembly."

"Only"—she tilted her head—"thirty-three more left."

My mouth fell open. "You actually counted how many Assemblies we have left?"

"Sure did. Because now the end to this oppressive high school regime is in sight. And we only have to sing that dreadful school song thirty-three more times."

Only she would consider a cushy private school oppressive. But then, she'd been at Preston since kindergarten, while I didn't start until my freshman year. I loved it here. The uniforms. The way our teachers were called professors. The way everyone took their studies seriously. I even liked the food in the dining hall.

Preston Academy: a school nestled in the midst of golf courses and polo fields. A school where I got graded for things like properly riding a horse. A school full of kids whose parents were Fortune 500 CEOs, international luminaries, Broadway actors. I've heard more than my fair share of talk about inner-city kids being thugs, but I'd seen a politician's kid start a fight on the third day of sophomore year. And who would give a sixteen-year-old a Lamborghini (that he crashed a week later)? A movie star would, that was who.

Every single day I wondered how the hell I'd gotten here.

I mean, I *knew* how it came to be. My grades were extraordinarily good, and it was no secret that the private schools in the area had been recruiting for diversity. Apparently, I was the perfect match: diversity points for being both Black and white, academic points for being hardworking and smart. The application fees had been waived. I got accepted to four schools, but Preston was the only one that offered a full scholarship.

So here I was.

I pulled open the heavy auditorium door and a blast of cold air whipped my hair, tossing coppery-blond spirals all over. I shivered and drew my dark-green blazer tight.

"Let's sit in the back," Blair said. As we got comfortable, I scanned the rows, taking in my fellow students for the year. Most of the freshmen looked terrified, but some of the girls gaped at Blair in awe. I bit back a smile. I'd looked at her the exact same way my first day. Who wouldn't? With her cool ivory skin and sleek mahogany locks, Blair Montgomery was a glamorous and preppy Snow White come to life.

My own first day was still clear in my head. I'd been scared out of my mind, surrounded by all those pretty people with their designer bags, expensive shoes, and sparkling jewelry that winked and gleamed. A sea of creamy white faces and straight, shiny hair.

What would they think of my wild curls, light golden-brown skin, and silvery-gray eyes? Did my Fjällräven bag or Aldo shoes scream "scholarship student"? And would anyone think less of me because they did?

It wasn't so scary now that I was a senior and everyone

knew who I was: Devon Kearney, top student and aspiring astrophysicist. And if they'd figured out that I was a scholarship student? So what? I was proud of that, too.

The seniors spread throughout the auditorium, some of them acting too cool to be here, not even sparing their classmates a glance.

Auden Cooper was not one of them. She stared right at me, flipping her Pantene-shiny strawberry-blond hair and sending me her smug grin. Like she knew she was going to knock me from the top of the class and nab Preston's college scholarship, awarded to every valedictorian. Like she was going to take everything and rock it better than I ever could. My skin burned when she looked at me like that, and she *always* looked at me like that.

"Ignore her," Blair said.

"Can't. Remember that saying about keeping your enemies close?"

"But she's annoying, like a bug. Someone needs to squish her." Blair's eyes narrowed. "Maybe that someone is me."

I lifted my shoulder, then let it fall. "Eh, competition's good for the soul."

She sat back and crossed her legs. "You know what else is good for the soul?"

I sighed. I knew that tone, and I was not in the mood. "Not this again."

"Oh yes," she said with a devilish grin, "this again."

"Do we have to talk about this now?"

"If we're going to make this year the best ever, it's time for you to let go." She started singing. "Let it go, let it *goooooo*..."

"What makes you so sure I haven't?" I stopped her before she embarrassed us both. Or worse, before people started singing along.

"The fact that you're still single despite going on how many dates?"

I tapped my Preston Academy notebook. "Boys can wait."

She fixed her blue eyes on me, steady and determined. "Look, I get that you're super focused, but you were a ball of stress last year, and we both know it was because of that boy."

I squirmed. "I'll have you know that I hadn't thought about him all morning, until you brought it up."

Her eyebrows shot up in disbelief. "All I'm saying is that it's time you toss your hat back in the ring. My bubbe says the best way to get over a guy is by getting under another."

I gaped at her. "Your grandmother said that? To you."

She shrugged and nodded.

"That explains so much."

"Good morning!" Our headmistress began Assembly with a big smile. "Welcome, everyone. I'm glad you're all here. This morning marks the beginning of Preston Academy's two hundred thirty-fifth year!"

A cheer rose from the crowd and I flushed with pride. My school's legacy was unparalleled. Preston had a long waitlist, and every single day I was grateful to be here. Even while freezing during Assembly.

I pulled my blazer even tighter while Dr. Steelwood gave her speech about the upcoming school year. There was so much to look forward to, like competitions, activities, and the Harvest

Ball. She pretty much gave the same speech every year, but there was something about starting a new school year that made me so optimistic. A clean slate, shiny and new, just like my fresh school uniforms and supplies.

Blair was wrong. I didn't need a boyfriend. My life was full enough: school, family, Blair. And right now, that was all I wanted.

The creak of the door behind me barely registered; I was so focused on Dr. Steelwood's speech. Then there was a presence beside me, one that came with a slight tinkling sound. One that filled the last empty seat in the auditorium, and filled my nose with the most familiar, amazing scent.

Strange. Being late to Assembly = at least one demerit. A demerit went on your permanent record. I glanced over at this brave soul and

Oh.

My.

God.

My breath stopped. My mouth went dry. Dr. Steelwood's speech ceased to exist. The auditorium ceased to exist. Everything ceased to exist, except the boy sitting next to me, frowning up at the lectern.

Because now I knew why I recognized that scent, like waterfalls cascading over the side of a mountain. I knew that golden-brown hair with its slight curl—I'd buried my fingers in it more times than I could count. I knew the heart shape of those lips because I'd kissed them a million times. And when he turned to me, no doubt sensing my stunned stare, there was no denying that face. Because despite what I'd told Blair, this face had been on my mind all morning. And haunting my dreams every night.

It was right next to me and I couldn't breathe. I could not breathe.

Breathe, Devon.

His eyes widened. His cheeks tensed. His gaze seared into me, his deep-set brown eyes mirroring my shock.

He was here. He was here.

He was here.

Yes, I wish on stars. And my biggest and most secret wish was that this boy, who I'd loved one summer, would come back to me. But wishes on stars didn't really come true, so how could he be here? After disappearing that summer without a trace? After leaving without a good-bye? How could he be here, sitting right next to me?

How *dare* he be here? After all this time?

"Devon!" Blair's voice sounded as if it were in a space vacuum. "Assembly's over. Let's go." She paused. "Devon?"

I yanked my eyes away from his and turned to Blair. But she was looking past me, her forehead wrinkled in confusion and rank suspicion. Then her glance flicked to me. Whatever my face showed her must have freaked her out, because her eyes widened as she grabbed my arm. "Let's go. Now."

Chapter 2

In Campbell Hall, the student center, I fell onto a squashy sofa and stared ahead without seeing a thing. How had I even gotten here? I didn't remember leaving Bishop Hall or walking across the courtyard. All I knew was that Ashton Edwards, the one person I never expected to see again, was probably crossing that same courtyard this very minute.

A deep breath, and the scent of Murphy Oil Soap coaxed me out of my trance. I looked around to ground myself. Yes, this was familiar. Steady. Students milling around the cubbies, pulling out notes or candy bars. Gamers hanging out in the computer lab. Flyers, sign-up sheets, and posters already decorating wood-paneled walls. Vending machines offering fruit and bottled water, and people lining up to get their caffeine fix at the hot beverage bar.

Blair stared at her compact and touched up her makeup. She was the only person I knew who got away with wearing red lipstick *and* red nail polish. I'd look like a clown if I tried to pull that off.

She really didn't need to touch up anything. She was giving me time to gather myself.

"Ready to talk about it?" she asked once she'd shoved the compact into her bag.

"I think so."

"Are you okay?"

"I am the furthest thing from okay." There was a slight hysterical twinge in my voice. "I'm the exact opposite of okay." I buried my head in shaking hands.

"Devon." She squeezed my arm. "Was that the Rat Bastard?"

"That was the Rat Bastard."

Her mouth dropped. "How the hell did he end up here?"

"I don't know." My voice shook.

Inhale two ... three ... four.

Exhale two ... three ... four.

It was all I could do to keep breathing.

To keep from crying.

Blair stared in disbelief. "Holy shit."

She had that right. Crap. Definitely not how I expected to start off the best year ever.

Her expression softened. "Are you going to be okay?"

No. "I don't know."

She glanced over my shoulder, and her voice dropped. "He's here."

I closed my eyes and let out a deep breath. Shook out my trembling hands. "I can't deal with this."

"Too bad he's such a good-looking son of a bitch," she muttered.

I tried to resist looking at him, but I couldn't help it. My stomach flipped as I turned. He pulled open his locker, then ignored it as he frowned at his phone. "He's perfectly engineered to make girls lose their minds."

And losing their minds they were. Blair and I certainly weren't the only ones looking at Ashton. Almost every girl who walked past him did a double take, and some of them weren't even trying to act cool about it.

"He seems so familiar to me, but I can't place him," Blair said. "A guy like him should not be forgettable. Look at that face. A perfect mix of masculinity and vulnerability. He's exquisite."

I sighed. Even she was falling under his spell. *Exquisite.* Like she was describing a valuable work of art, or a fine jewel.

"I never should've let my guard down with him," I said, turning away. "A guy like that? He can't do anything but hurt you."

"I don't know if I believe that," Blair said, tilting her head. "Not all beautiful people are evil."

Heh. Spoken like a Beautiful Person herself.

She leaned in. "He's staring at you."

A jolt zinged down my spine. "He is?"

"He's not even trying to hide it, Devon."

I turned again. She was right. His gaze was fixed on me,

strong and unwavering. The searing look was gone, replaced with a softness that made my heart skip. Was he...*happy* to see me?

God. How could I even think about calming down when he looked at me like I was the only person in the world?

"He needs to come with a warning," Blair said.

I let out a slow breath. "No kidding."

Someone stepped into my line of sight, blocking my view. I gripped the arm of the sofa and tried to center myself. To breathe. Blair watched me, her head still tilted, the gears clicking away. I turned from the scrutiny, letting my eyes skip to the different flyers on the walls. Intramural volleyball. Tea Tasting Club. The Harvest Ball.

"Is that your poster?" I asked.

Blair grinned, her cheeks flushing pink. "All mine."

"It looks great." And it did, with its golden background, script lettering, and simple graphics arranged to mimic an old-fashioned poster from the 1940s.

"I worked on it all summer." Her voice lowered. "Do you really like it?"

"I love it. It's elegant without being stuffy."

"I know, right?" She grinned. "Wait till you see the invitations."

"I can't wait."

"You're coming, right?" she asked, her eyebrows raised.

"Of course," I said. "Gotta support my girl."

Almost against my will, I glanced over at Ashton. Would he go to the Harvest Ball?

Then I mentally slapped myself. Just because he'd appeared at *my freaking school* was no reason for me to lose focus.

The first bell rang.

I pulled out my schedule. "Oh good. Everything I wanted."

"Let me see." Blair snatched the slip of paper from my hand. "Although I can probably guess. Advanced Geometric Calculus, Scientific Trigonomic Physics for College-bound Seniors..."

"Shut up." But I was grinning. She loved to tease me about my science-heavy schedules.

"No, seriously. Multivariable Calculus. Advanced Physics." Then she paused. "*Astronomy Methods?* What in the world is that? And why would they even offer it?"

"It's interesting."

"It's weird."

I snatched my schedule back. "You know what I want to study. It makes sense."

She looked thoughtful. "You're going to be a scientist. That's really badass, to be honest."

I nibbled my bottom lip. "First I have to get into college."

"Stop it. You're a shoo-in."

Maybe, but I wanted McCafferty University. Their astrophysics program was world renowned and highly competitive. I needed top grades so I could get accepted. And get scholarship money—McCafferty was also expensive.

Blair wrinkled her nose at her schedule. "Meanwhile, I get to suffer in Home Management."

I screwed up my face. "Home Management?"

"I *know.*"

The warning bell rang.

Despite myself, I glanced toward Ashton's locker again. The person who had been blocking my view had gone. Ashton was still there. Still looking at me. Then he gave me the slightest of nods. My breath caught in my throat, then I returned the acknowledgment.

Blair glanced over my shoulder. "You're going to be okay. You know that, right?"

I took a deep breath. "I know. I will survive this. I'm strong and smart and capable."

"Damn right."

It was cute how she believed me so readily. Preston was a small school, and ready or not, I was going to have to talk to Ashton sooner or later.

God help me.

Chapter 3

THE FIRST DAY OF SCHOOL = A CHAOTIC MESS. THE MORNING classes were abbreviated because of Assembly, but the teachers still tried to cram forty minutes of material into classes that were half the length. And because I preferred writing my notes instead of typing or recording them, my wrists were on fire by the time the last bell rang.

But my schedule looked promising. Astronomy Methods, yay! Multicultural Literature. African American History. Advanced Physics. Advanced Conversational French, because I was definitely going for an internship at the Paris Observatory, one of the largest astronomical research centers in the world. How awesome would that be?

And then there was Calculus. I did really well at math, so

the subject didn't scare me. It was Auden Cooper's smug smile that made me groan.

"Hey there, Ninety-Nine!"

One test. She got a higher score than me one time, and refused to let me live it down.

"How was your summer?" she chirped. "What'd you do?"

I forced a smile and turned to her. "It was good. I spent most of it with Blair in the Hamptons, and then a week at astronomy camp." I swallowed the pang that came with remembering how I'd skipped my usual summer with Stephanie. The Hamptons had been great, but I'd missed my favorite beach.

"Astronomy camp?" She raised her eyebrow. "Seriously?"

Grr. I turned my smile up until my cheeks burned. "How about your summer?"

"The best. I went to Paris and Jamaica." She held out her arm. "Look at my tan! I'm darker than you! If I keep this up, I'll practically be Black."

And there it was. One of the many reasons she irritated me so much. Things like this slipped out of her mouth constantly. *Practically Black.* Ha! Not even close, girlfriend.

I turned my attention to the professor and his lecture.

But she wasn't done. After class, she eased up to me and murmured, "You're going down." Then she whipped around, her strawberry-scented hair hitting me in the face, and slipped into the hall.

Oh hell no. This bitch was not about to yank away my valedictorian spot, and I definitely wasn't letting her nab the

Preston senior scholarship. Ten thousand dollars per year toward the college of the winner's choice. Auden drove a freaking BMW. I needed that scholarship way more than she did.

I made it through the day without seeing Ashton, which was a miracle, considering how small our senior class was, and without having a nervous breakdown, which was another miracle, considering how rattled I was. Too bad I'd skipped lunch. Terrible decision, but I hadn't wanted to risk running into him in the dining hall. Now I was borderline hangry on top of everything else.

Blair stood at my locker, scrolling through something on her phone. "I figured out why your guy looked so familiar."

I was in such a funk that I almost didn't care.

"Wait. Eat this." She handed me a granola bar and waited until I took a huge bite. "And next time, don't skip lunch to avoid him."

Busted.

"What did you find out?"

"It just so happens that I attended lower school with the honorable Ashton Edwards."

"Honorable?"

"Ashton Bishop Carter Preston Edwards."

I froze with the granola bar halfway to my mouth. "Should that mean something to me?"

"His father is Tristan Carter Preston Edwards."

I sighed. People here were obsessed with what everyone's

parents did. Who had what job, and who could affect the economy of entire cities or the livelihood of working-class families. Blair's father worked in the entertainment industry, and when I say worked, I mean he had the final say in what shows got aired on a certain cable network each season. How did people even get that powerful? Or that rich? Hard work? My dad worked seventy hours a week, and while we weren't poor, we certainly weren't rich. Definitely not powerful.

I was so tired of hearing about everyone's fathers and how freaking important they were.

"Should this mean something to me?" I asked again.

"It should mean everything to you. Tristan Carter *Preston Edwards*," she repeated when I stared at her blankly.

Then it dawned on me. "What?"

"They founded this school. They are faculty chairs. And they're the reason Preston's endowment is so big."

Oh.

Oh no.

"Great. I hooked up with the guy who's bankrolling my education."

"You really had no idea?" Blair asked, eyebrows sky-high.

"It says *Preston Endowment Fund* on my statements. Nothing about Edwards. Are you laughing at me?"

She let the laughter bubble out. "This would only happen to you."

Appetite gone, I groaned and leaned my forehead against the cool metal locker. "How did you even figure this out?"

"I googled. Learned his last name in Photography class."

Photography? This shouldn't have surprised me. That summer, Ashton was constantly pulling out his phone and snapping pictures. He also had a really nice camera—he'd taken a bunch of photos of me at one of the beaches.

The memory crashed through me. Driftwood scattered in the sand, all smooth logs and wiry branches. The tide pools swimming with tiny silver fish. The sun sliding its way to the horizon.

Magic hour.

Ashton had stared at me, his lips slightly parted. "God, Dev. You're breathtaking."

He hurriedly raised the camera and the shutter clicked away. Ashton's smile peeked from under the camera body. "My sunset girl," he murmured.

His girl. I'd felt such a thrill over that.

Wait. No. Focus. "Why are *you* taking Photography?"

"I'm broadening my horizons. Also, I can learn how to take better pictures of the dresses I design and make."

Which made sense. Besides her Mercedes, Blair's sewing machine was her favorite possession. The clothes she made were gorgeous. Still…something else nagged at me. "How did he live here all along and we never knew?"

"Except I did know. I just forgot. But it's weird that you guys never talked about your hometowns. Didn't he know what school you went to?"

"We didn't really talk about school."

"What the hell *did* you talk about?"

"Oh my God. Our feelings. Our dreams. Stuff we liked.

Politics. Religion. Can I just say I never expected a rich white male to be so liberal? He's a total bleeding heart."

"Just like you."

"Sometimes we sang show tunes."

"You *sang* to him?"

"He said I had a good voice."

"Wow. That's disgusting. Cute, but disgusting." She shook her hair back. "Anyway, if you'd told me his last name, this mystery could have been solved last year."

I yanked open my locker. "Blair, he destroyed me. I wasn't about to google-stalk him."

"First of all, you weren't *destroyed*, just definitely not okay. Second of all, I'm trying to figure out what was so special about him that you were such a mess when you came back. Therefore, I totally google-stalked him." With a flourish, she held out her phone. "Behold."

My Calculus book hit the floor. "He has a Wikipedia page?"

"Well, his ancestors started the very educational institution we're standing in right now. He's kind of a big deal," she pointed out.

Except when you attended a school like Preston where *everyone* was a big deal, it became the norm. Unless, apparently, you were descended from the founders.

I sighed again. "Okay."

"He used to go to boarding school overseas. Which is weird, seeing as his family pretty much invented *this* school."

"Really weird." I picked up my book and shoved it into

my bag. "Why pay all that money when he could go here for free?"

"It's a rich-people thing," Blair said. "Like my dad. He'll take out a calculator at a restaurant so he doesn't overtip, but he'll spend three thousand dollars for the perfect desk chair."

"Wait, what?"

"I mean, it *is* a nice chair. Pisses him off when I twirl around in it. Anyway. Back to Ashton. His family travels every summer, but so do you. Maybe it was serendipity that you both ended up on that beach."

"It was something."

She shoved her phone into her bag. "Your boy is mysterious. Like I said, I went to lower school with him, but after fifth grade, he disappeared."

"He's good at that."

"So it's not like you'd have seen him around town. I wasn't friends with him or anything, so I didn't give him much thought when he didn't show up for sixth grade. When you told me your boyfriend's name was Ashton, it didn't even register. He completely fell off my radar. Until now."

I slammed my locker. "So now what?"

"Well, that's up to you, isn't it?"

Sometimes when Blair drove me home, we talked until our throats went dry. Today, we were quiet for the half-hour ride. The sky was a brilliant blue and Blair had the top down on her convertible. Classical music ("The Sleeping Beauty,

Op. 66: Introduction") floated from the speakers while she smoked cigarette after cigarette and the wind blew our hair everywhere.

The golf course gave way to gated communities. Then the gated communities faded away. The houses grew smaller and closer together until we were in my subdivision: Villa Park. The houses were definitely not villas, but we did have a park.

"You want to come in?" I asked when she pulled up to my driveway. "My mom's ordering sushi for dinner."

She looked tempted. *Really* tempted. Blair constantly told me that she liked my family's cozy ranch house a lot more than her family's McMansion.

"I want to," she said, looking regretful. Then she rolled her eyes. "My esteemed mother insisted I be home tonight for a formal dinner. Apparently she and Daddy are having important guests, and it's vital that Theo and I are there."

"Isn't your brother away at school?"

"That's how important this dinner is. They called him home."

"Yikes." Her family's formal dinners were the opposite of fun. And her brother—yuck. A cocky, self-important jerk who always looked at me with his lip curled.

"Whatever. I'll survive. I always do." She kissed my cheek. "See you in the morning."

I grabbed the mail and went inside. A stack of college brochures for me. Some boring trade magazines for my father, not that he had time to read them. Nothing for Mom, who was sitting on the couch, pecking away at her laptop. Her smooth brown skin glowed in the sun's rays that streamed through the window, and a mop of springy curls twirled all over her head. She worked in real estate, so her hours were flexible. She was almost always home after school.

I kissed the top of her head and inhaled her coconut scent. "Hi, Mom."

She took off her glasses and focused on me. "Hey, Bun. How was it?"

"Don't ask," I muttered.

She raised an eyebrow. But Mom knew when to back off. "Dad's gonna be late," she said. "New client's being a pain in the you-know-what."

I hung my blazer on the coatrack. "And that's different from when, exactly?"

She chuckled. Dad worked as an art director at an advertising agency and constantly got into it with one client or another. He thrived on fighting, at least while negotiating contracts.

"I'll order the sushi in about an hour," Mom said. "You want your usual?"

My stomach grumbled at the thought of salmon nigiri and a dragon roll. "Yeah, that sounds good."

"Give me a hug, baby doll," she said. I wrapped my arms around her and squeezed. When I went to pull away, she stopped me and looked closely at my face. "You okay?"

A brisk nod. "I'm fine."

"I don't believe you, but I hope you'll talk to me when you're ready."

"I'm going to start on my homework."

"Homework already? On the first day?"

"That's how you make valedictorian."

She was already back to her computer. I went into my room and closed the door. Lit an incense stick, hoping the sandalwood scent would calm my racing heart. Changed into yoga shorts and a tank top. Then I flipped open my laptop. While I waited for the Wi-Fi to connect, I dug deep into my documents folder, clicking through layers and layers until I got to a folder labeled *X*. I let the pointer hover, then double-clicked.

There we were, the stars of photo after photo. Huddled together in the sand, me in my bikini, him in swim trunks. Kissing on his parents' yacht on July Fourth while fireworks bloomed above us. Holding sparklers on Stephanie's birthday, laughing as if we'd had no cares in the world.

And then my favorite picture. *Used* to be my favorite picture. Ashton and me on the beach, the sky a tapestry of pinks and purples behind us. We'd been kissing when Stephanie called our names and pointed her phone at us. The way he and I were turned toward each other, the way his arm draped over my shoulders...it was obvious we were a couple. I'd felt so close to him. I'd felt like we'd had all the time in the world. Except that hadn't been the case at all. I closed my eyes as the sadness washed over me.

No! I wasn't about to start feeling sorry for myself.

Not again. Never again.

I slammed my laptop shut and grabbed my running shoes.

Time to refocus.

Chapter 4

I WAS GREETED THE NEXT MORNING BY A POUNDING HEAD and heart. I'd been having a delicious dream, and I wanted at least another hour of sleep. But my internal alarm clock went off at five forty-five every morning. And once I'm up, I'm up.

Wait.

That dream.

Ashton.

Oh my God.

I needed my subconscious to explain itself. Immediately. Because I certainly did not go to sleep wishing for freaky-deaky XXX dreams about me and my ex-boyfriend.

I rubbed my eyes and stared at my phone—5:46. Hours until I had to leave for school. Time for a vigorous, sweaty yoga flow to clear my head and set me straight. I hopped out of bed, twisted my hair into a bun, and stepped onto my mat. Then I took a deep breath, closed my eyes, and began. Inhale, arms reaching up. Exhale, folding forward, head to knee. Connect. Center. Balance. *Om.*

It didn't work. The images refused to leave my brain. I pushed until my heart was racing and sweat was dripping onto my mat, and Ashton *was still there.* Every stretch reminded me of being wrapped around him, getting lost with him. Every breath reminded me of the passionate nights when we'd kiss for hours. Touching each other everywhere, pushing each other to the brink.

I collapsed an hour later, more frustrated and confused than ever.

The frustration and confusion didn't end in the car ride to school while Blair babbled on and on about Louboutin shoes and Vuitton bags. Girlfriend was obsessed with all things fashion. Meanwhile, my mind played *what the fuck* on a constant loop. Because seriously, who has a sex dream about the boy who abandoned them?

The frustration and confusion expanded triple-fold when I got to my locker and spotted Ashton at his. Unfair. Why did he have to be here, and why did he have to be so yummy? The freaking school uniform made him look like he'd walked straight out of a Ralph Lauren ad.

Rat Bastard.

He deliberately picked through his books, slowly placing them into his bag. I was mesmerized by the way he chewed his bottom lip while he concentrated. By the way he blinked. The way he took a deep breath before closing his locker.

Longing and

anger and

desire and—

He turned, totally catching me.

My face grew hot, hot, hot. I tried to look away. I tried so hard. No luck. I was stuck. In. Place.

And now he was coming over. I promptly dropped my Astronomy book because apparently my hands forgot how to work properly.

He picked up the book and handed it to me. His fingers brushed mine, sending sparks all through me. "I don't think you want to lose this."

"Thanks," I managed to get out.

Ashton was at my locker.

Breathe.

"Devon," he said, that soft look on his face again. "I can't believe it's you. You look beautiful."

His voice had deepened slightly since that summer. I hated that it still gave me chills.

"Thanks," I said again.

"So, we should—" He froze then, his eyes focused on my neck. "You're still wearing it."

I touched the key-shaped pendant. "Yeah. I guess I am."

"Dev..." His voice shook.

The bell rang, making us both jump. "I–I have to go," I

stammered. And without another word, I turned and all but ran to my Astronomy class.

My lunch tray hit the table with a loud *smack*.

Blair, the unshakable bombshell, kept scrolling through her phone. "Rough morning?"

I sank into a chair and rubbed at the headache forming behind my eyes. "You could say that."

She leaned back in her chair and crossed her legs. "Does it have anything to do with your blast from the past over there?"

"Everything to do with it."

She raised her eyebrows, waiting not-so-patiently for me to elaborate.

"I talked to him this morning."

She dropped her phone. "Holy crap, Devon. Are you okay?"

"I'm fine."

"You're lying. You're so not okay."

I bit my thumbnail. "So?"

She tilted her head in his direction. "He's sitting by himself, like yesterday. He stared at his phone all period."

"Did he?" I kept my voice flat and disinterested.

But Blair didn't fall for it. "He's not very social, is he?"

"He likes to keep to himself."

"You guys are alike in that way." She picked up her phone, swiped at some things on the screen, then put it back down. "So, listen. I did some more research."

"Why?"

She picked up her fork. "Because I'm worried about you. I see how you look at him."

I squeezed mustard onto my sandwich. I didn't want to think about how I looked at him. It probably involved a blank stare and drooling.

"He's switched schools a ton of times. Switzerland. Germany. The UK. That's not normal unless you have military parents. Which he doesn't." She frowned and shook her head. "There's something there, but I can't figure it out. Did he get expelled? Did he leave on his own? It's like you said. He's good at disappearing. But...why? What's he running from?"

"How do you even find this stuff?"

She held up her hand. "If I told you, I'd have to kill you."

I had a feeling she wasn't joking.

Chapter 5

ONE OF THE BEST THINGS ABOUT BEING A SENIOR AT PRESton was that we got a free period right after lunch, two days a week. They called it Enrichment, the implication being that the time was to be used wisely, maybe for studying or an extracurricular. Blair joined an art club, one that focused on sketching.

After years of working on the staff, I'd been appointed coeditor of the Yearbook Club.

Along with Auden Cooper.

Professor Wilcox, the adviser, had said we were both too good, that she couldn't just choose one.

Fun.

Auden handed me a printout of a spreadsheet. "We don't have a lot of people on our staff. So I divided the duties like this."

Business manager, in addition to Clubs & Organizations Editor. "Auden, we should have decided on this together."

"I know, but I got all antsy and couldn't wait!"

"It wasn't even one day."

Whenever Auden got in her "take charge" mode, she pulled her massive amounts of hair into a ball on top of her head. She stuck a pencil in that ball now. "Do you want to handle the money or not? I mean, you know what you're doing with budgets and all that. I figured you'd be perfect."

How dare she appeal to my ego? "I'll do it. But next time, don't make any big decisions without me."

Tyrell Jenkins and Colton Myers, two boys who couldn't have been more different but were somehow the best of friends, strutted into the room like they owned the place.

Tyrell, tall with beautiful brown skin, deep dimples, and locs that hung down his back. Lover of jazz, anime, and painting. Blair's object of obsessive desire. Too bad he was loud and proud about his dating preferences, which did not include white girls.

Colton, also tall, with beige skin, blond hair, steely blue eyes. Football bro, whose dating preferences pretty much included anyone who was breathing.

"Tech Director! Photo Editor!" Tyrell pumped his fist. "Yes!"

"Auden, you lovely creature you." Colton wrapped his arms around her. "Assigning me to Sports & People."

"I had a feeling you'd be okay with that," she said, then glanced sideways at me. "I considered everyone's interests and strengths when sorting all this out."

Just then, Professor Wilcox swept into the room. "Sorry I'm late!"

"It's okay, professor," Auden said sweetly. "I've got it all under control."

Suck-up.

Wilcox handed a stack of papers to Auden for her to pass to the rest of us. "Agenda. We've got a lot to cover today. Main thing being: What will be our theme for this year?"

Auden and I looked at each other. The official motto of Preston was *Unity, Respect, Growth*. But that would not do for the yearbook.

"If you haven't been brainstorming yet, it's time to think about getting on that." Wilcox turned on the projector, and an image of her laptop screen appeared on the whiteboard. "But first you need to go over how to use the software."

Colton's voice piped up from beside me. "But—"

"I know what you're going to say, Mr. Myers: You know the software already. But it's been an entire season since you last worked on the yearbook. This is a refresher. It's actually pretty straightforward, but I'm a lousy teacher. I've cued up a couple YouTube videos for you to watch while I go get a cup of coffee." She hit PLAY. "I'll be back."

With a swish of brown hair, she was out the door.

"Hold up," Tyrell said. "How is she a teacher if she can't teach?"

While the video played, I jotted down ideas for this year's theme. It had to be a good one.

Chapter 6

"DEVON! MY FAVORITE BUDDING ASTROPHYSICIST." PROFESsor Trask beamed, his denim-blue eyes twinkling. With his round belly and rosy cheeks, my astronomy teacher/adviser could have been related to Santa Claus. As usual, Professor Trask had accessorized to the nines with Mickey Mouse. His tie. His watch. His suspenders. I'd never known anyone so obsessed with a Disney character. "Have a seat. I have your transcripts right here."

I plopped into a chair and watched as Professor Trask picked up my file. "How was your summer?" I asked him.

"Really good. I worked a part-time gig at Disney World, selling pins."

I chuckled. "Of course you did."

"You laugh now, but wait until you get to go."

"I've been! My parents took me when I was five."

He nodded appreciatively. "Then you should understand the magic. I'd love to talk your ear off about how you should go back as soon as possible, but we only have thirty minutes to discuss your college plans."

"Okay."

"You're already here on the second day of school. Very impressive." He flipped through the papers and then pulled one out. "McCafferty, huh?"

"It's what I've been working toward."

"I can see that. Your transcripts look wonderful. Straight As, top of the class three years running. Well-rounded extra-curricular activities, great recommendations." He peered at me over his glasses. "On paper, you're a shoo-in."

I grinned. It was good to know that my hard work might actually pay off.

"But."

The grin slid off my face. "But what?"

"But so are a lot of other students, many of them right here at Preston."

I knew this. Of course I knew this. I couldn't eat/sleep/breathe this dream without this knowledge constantly pounding around in my head. Competition to get into McCafferty was fierce, and my classmates were some of my biggest competitors.

"One of the largest obstacles for you, Devon, is that you are not a legacy. The other is that you indicated you will need financial aid to attend. The legacy part can be overcome with your academic history," Professor Trask said, stroking his beard. "But the finances might be tricky."

I clutched my pen. Tight. "Would they deny me admission because I'm not rich? Can they do that?"

"Unfortunately, some universities factor finances into their selection process."

I took several deep breaths and tried to fight the dejection clawing up my spine. I hated how this process made me feel. As if I weren't good enough because I wasn't wealthy. So many of my classmates could write a check and attend school anywhere in the world. Money was no object at all for them, and I had to admit I was super envious of that.

I tried to ignore my sweaty hands. "Should I even bother applying?"

He took off his glasses and looked me in the eye. "Definitely. Don't give up hope. McCafferty has been known to generously reward those who show a tremendous amount of potential, and I believe you do. In fact, I'm going to suggest you apply early action. That way, if you get an acceptance in December, you can start making concrete plans for financing your tuition. But I want you to consider some other less expensive, yet still high-quality, options."

I *had* to go to McCafferty. Even the undergraduate students got to travel to the biggest telescopes in the world for research. Getting an assistantship during graduate school guaranteed placement at one of the top air and space associations in the country. There really was no other option for me. I'd apply to the safety schools, but I couldn't see myself at any of them.

Professor Trask gave me a bunch of scholarship applications.

"But I'm not Swedish," I said, reading over the top one.

"Look closer. It says preference given to students of Swedish descent, but what if no Swedish students apply? That money could go to you," he said. "What have you got to lose?"

I nodded. "Fair enough. And maybe they have scholarships for Black students. Or Irish ones. Or biracial ones. I could qualify for all of them."

"You never know. One thing I do know, though, is that if you don't apply, the answer is already no. That's why we're doing this." He nodded briskly. "Listen, deadlines will be here in a flash. I want you to have your Common App account completely set up, and at least three other college choices ready to go, by the end of the month. I'll look them over, and we'll move forward from there."

I gave him a nod back. "You got it."

Chapter 7

GRADES, SCHOLARSHIPS, McCAFFERTY. GRADES, SCHOLARSHIPS, McCafferty. Grades, scholarships, McCaff—

"Hi," Ashton said, slamming my mantra to a halt. "I was wondering if we could talk." He sounded confident, but the slight pink in his cheeks betrayed his nerves.

"Okay." I didn't sound confident at all. I cleared my throat and slammed my locker door.

Ashton stared at me with those damn eyes that were full of galaxies, hypnotizing me, making my knees shake. "Hi," he said again.

My mouth opened slightly, then I closed it and shook my head. "I don't even know what to say to you."

He nodded, glanced at the floor, then looked at me again. "I don't blame you."

All I could feel was my longing to stroke his face. Even despite my anger, my embarrassment, my confusion.

He caught his lip between his teeth. "I need to apologize to you. Big-time. What I did... it was messed up. Inexcusable."

I was instantly transported back to that awful day. Sitting on the porch, my heart shattering. Humiliation suffocating me so I couldn't even breathe. The great horned owl hooting on the bird clock. Because it was midnight, and Ashton never came.

"Devon?"

Except now it was over a year later and he was here.

"Devon?" he said again.

I gripped my bag to keep from shoving him into a locker. "I thought you were dead."

He had a way of looking at me that haunted me all day and night. It was the way his face softened, the way his eyelids lowered slightly. As if he were trying to bare his very soul to me without saying a word. He stared at me with that look now, making my anger dissipate, but only a little bit.

"It was a shitty thing for me to do, and you never, ever deserved it," Ashton said, stroking the strap of his bag with trembling fingers. "And I'm sorry, Devon. I'm so, so sorry. I don't expect you to believe me, but I never meant for our summer to end that way."

Damn. The look in his eyes punched me right in the gut. Contrite. Nervous. Vulnerable.

I swallowed. Hard. "So why did it?"

He stood there, mouth opening and closing, face flushed. How sad was it that a tiny part of me felt sorry for him?

"I have so much to tell you," he finally said.

"There you are." Blair popped up beside me. "It's mani-pedi time. Are you ready?"

I blinked while the world came back into focus. "Huh?"

She threw Ashton a hard glance, then turned back to me. "We need to go."

"Oh, right."

She looked Ashton up and down like he was vermin.

"I'm Ashton Edwards," he said, his expression now neutral. He reached his hand out to her. "You're in my Photography class."

She reluctantly shook his hand. "That's right. Blair Montgomery."

"Nice to officially meet you."

"We used to go to the lower school together," she said.

He raised his eyebrows. "Sorry. I feel terrible that I don't remember."

"I don't expect you to. It was a long time ago." She turned back to me. "We have fifteen minutes to make our appointment."

"Dev?" Ashton's voice shook slightly. "Can we talk soon? Please?"

I stiffened, then nodded slightly.

To give Blair credit, she kept her mouth shut until we got to her car. But once the doors slammed, all bets were off. "Are you effing kidding me?"

"What are you talking about?"

"You should see your face. You're all...pink and glowy," she said, her own face flushed. "This is bad, Devon."

"I'm not glowy. I'm mad."

"Good. You should be." Blair's voice softened. "Remember how screwed up you were last year?"

Last year. It took everything in me to hold back a snort. There was no past tense about this. My feelings were happening *now* and I didn't even know what the hell my feelings *were* and seriously *screw him* for coming back here and—

Blair huffed. "I swear, I'm going to throat punch him. Twice. Once for hurting you. Once for getting you all flustered. Once for being so damned gorgeous."

"That's three times."

Her eyes flashed. "You're missing my point, Devvy. There was obviously something way deeper than a fling between you two."

"He was my best friend that summer." I looked down at my shaking hands. "He was amazing."

"Not that amazing, if he just up and left you. What did he want, anyway?"

"To apologize."

"Good," she said again. "You should make him grovel. Beg, even. I want him on his fucking knees."

"Blair. This morning. He freaked out about my necklace."

She froze mid-cussword. "Necklace?"

I pulled out my key pendant. "This."

She yanked the pendant closer to her. "Why would he freak out over your necklace?"

"He gave it to me."

She stared at me. "He gave you a Tiffany necklace after dating you for what? Two months? Are you serious right now?"

"One. He gave it to me on the anniversary of our first date. Monthversary. Whatever. And how did you know it was Tiffany?"

She stared harder. "Devon. Did you forget who I am? I know jewelry. He spent at least two hundred dollars on that thing. After being with you for a month. No guy does that. It's not normal. It's almost kind of creepy."

"It wasn't creepy. It was sweet."

"Except for the part where he abandoned you." She frowned. "I thought your parents gave you that necklace."

"Nope."

"You need to get an explanation out of him, and it better be good or he's going to be sorry he even showed his face here."

Blair started the car. Eerie violins and haunting brass filled my ears and made me squirm. Beethoven: Symphony no. 7 in A Major, Op. 92: II. Allegretto. This composition always felt like a chastisement.

"This is bad news," she said. "I don't know how I feel about him weaseling his way back into your life. I saw how you were looking at him. Like you wanted to slap him and then throw him down and have your way with him. Devvy, you need to be careful."

But *would* I be careful? That was the million-dollar question.

At the red light, she studied me closely. "Do you think he still wants you?"

I stared at the light, willing it to turn green. I knew what I wanted the answer to be.

"Devon? Do you want him to still want you?"

I didn't hesitate. "Yes."

"You're kind of a train wreck."

"You think?"

She tilted her head in that thoughtful way. "Here's the thing. You're going to do what you want. But I sure as hell don't trust him."

I nibbled my nails, which I only did in supreme hot-mess mode.

This was not good.

Ashton was distracting me way too much. Look how quickly he'd managed to make me forget about scholarships and McCafferty and school. Look how I was *sitting here right now* trying to analyze him when I needed to just stop. But I couldn't stop. Memories from that summer rushed back like comets. Him and me, walking along the boardwalk, holding hands and sharing our hopes and dreams and fears. Sitting in the surf together, laughing while the waves knocked us around. Kissing deeply under the stars. I'd known his every heartbeat, his every breath, and I'd wanted it all. I'd wanted all of *him* ... and I'd wanted him forever.

"I know," I said. "But—"

"The heart wants what it wants."

"Exactly."

"And judging by the way you were looking at him, other body parts, too," she muttered.

And now we were back to that dream.

That dream.

It wasn't even based in reality. Ashton and I came close, but we never "sealed the deal." I'd flip-flopped between being glad about it and regretting that I didn't take the chance, but now I knew it was for the best we hadn't. Because it was a summer fling, right? But silly me had thought this was different. I'd thought *we* were different. But nope. And ever since, I'd been stuck with an emptiness in my heart that I hadn't been able to fill.

Sleeping with him now would not fix it.

Telling myself that was one thing. Believing it was quite another.

"Devon?"

"Yeah?"

"Promise me you'll be careful. Okay?"

How could I promise that to her when I couldn't even promise it to myself?

Chapter 8

"Hours for your community service projects need to be turned in by October 2," Professor Trask reminded us in Advisory. "That's three weeks. Some of you," he said, glancing around the classroom, "have your work cut out."

Cue the moaning and groaning. Most of my classmates would rather write a check than set foot in a disadvantaged neighborhood or spend time with sick kids or old people. But that didn't matter. If you wanted to graduate from Preston Academy, you had to clock forty hours of actual community service.

"Sign-up sheets are on my desk," Professor Trask continued, "but you need to hurry. Top choices are going fast."

I'd already done most of my hours, so my mind was a

million miles away, at Ashton's locker, which had stayed shut all morning. It was only the third day of school, during a short week, and he was already skipping?

Blair's tormented groan ripped me out of my reverie. Alarmed, I whipped around and stared at her. How had I missed how pinched her forehead was? "What's wrong?"

"I really don't have time for this," she groaned. "The Harvest Ball is in three weeks. *Three.* I need to be focusing on that, not community service. Devon, if this dance isn't the best that Preston's ever had, I'll die." She buried her head in her hands and whimpered. Then her head snapped up. "I need copious amounts of caffeine, and I need uppers."

My mouth dropped. "Uppers? What the hell, Blair?"

"I'm kidding, Devon."

But the thing is, I wasn't sure she actually *was* kidding.

She flipped open her bullet journal. The page was completely black, a million to-dos checked off and a million more that weren't. "This sucks big hairy banana balls. What are you doing tonight? I need to buy an espresso machine. Wanna come with me?"

"I've got a field trip to the planetarium with my Astronomy class. We're going to study Cassiopeia."

She stared at me. "Who?"

"It's an asterism."

"A *what*?"

"So, okay. I know you've heard of constellations?"

She shrugged. "Sure. Big Dipper, Orion's belt. All that jazz."

"Except not. Most people think the stars are what make up the constellation, but a constellation is a specific area of the celestial sphere. An asterism is a shape of stars that make up the patterns you're used to seeing. So the Big Dipper asterism is part of the constellation Ursa Major, which means Big Bear."

"You're making my eyes glaze over, Devvy," she said with affection. Then she stared at her planner again, her face crumpling.

I grabbed her hands. "Blair. You got this. I promise."

"If you two are done with your lovefest," Professor Trask's voice floated over to us, "the bell rang two minutes ago. You should get a move on."

I gave Blair's hand one more squeeze before heading to Multicultural Literature.

Happy Paws was the only no-kill animal shelter in town. Since it was funded entirely by grants and donations, volunteers were essential. I was excited to finish my community service requirement here.

I stepped into the bright, airy lobby with its picture windows, dark bookcases filled with white binders, and large reception desk. A couple sat on a sleek black couch and filled out paperwork on a square coffee table. The animals were separated by glass doors, Doggie Town to my left and Kitty City to my right.

"Good morning!" A petite, goth-looking girl bounced up to me. "Are you one of our Preston helpers?"

"Yes. I'm Devon."

"Angelica, volunteer coordinator. I'm so glad you're here." She pumped my hand aggressively. Holy cow. Way too perky for a Saturday morning.

She gestured to the reception desk. "You can sign in over there. I was thinking I'd put you in with the dogs."

"Whatever you need." I printed my name, then scribbled my signature on the sheet.

Angelica checked her clipboard. "Looks like there's only one more student volunteer coming in today. He's been here before, so we won't wait for him." She led me into a small office and thrust a stack of papers at me. "Go ahead and fill these out, then I'll show you around."

"Thanks." I looked over the forms. Official Preston letterheads. A medical release. A sheet for filling out my hours. An evaluation form. By far the most intense onboarding of any volunteer hours I'd done.

"Hey, Angelica."

I dropped my pen. Oh God, no. Not him.

"Good morning, Ashton! I'm glad you're here! There's one other volunteer, and I was thinking I'd pair you up. You might already know her."

I wasn't ready for this. An entire day with him?

Deep breaths. I had this. By the time Angelica brought Ashton into the room, I'd managed to compose myself. Calm, cool, and collected! That was me!

"Dev!" His face lit up. "I didn't know you were volunteering here."

"Service requirement," I reminded him.

"This is a great place to do it," he said. "I'm going to keep volunteering when my forty hours are done." He hung up his jacket. "Be right back. I need to wash my hands."

I stared at him as he left the room. He looked gorgeous in his dark jeans and light-blue T-shirt.

Damned gorgeous.

My heart fluttered like hummingbird wings. A billion beats per minute.

Inhale...two...three...four.

Exhale...two...three...four.

Get a grip, Devon.

Now.

Angelica tossed me a peach-colored apron and walked me to Doggie Town. Seven dogs charged, barking and jumping, until Angelica whistled, making them stop in their tracks. I shrieked when a tiny brown Chihuahua skidded into my leg. He sat there, stunned, then sniffed my shoes and ran off again.

Ashton was already in the room, nuzzling a medium-size black-and-white mutt. "You're such a good boy," he cooed, stroking the dog's broad head. Then he looked up at me. "This is Buddy. Isn't he incredible?"

Cautiously, I knelt down beside the dog. "He's what they call special needs," Ashton continued. "See how he doesn't have a right eye?"

I touched Buddy's nose and a pink tongue came out to lick my fingertips.

"No one knows what happened to him. They say he's been here forever." Ashton scratched Buddy's ears. "He's awesome."

Why is he talking to me like everything is good between us?

The tips of Ashton's ears were bright red. They only did that whenever he was nervous and uneasy. Maybe I'm a terrible person, but seeing him a bit aflutter made me feel a lot better.

And Buddy really was awesome.

Ashton was nuzzling Buddy again, and Buddy seemed as if he were in heaven, his tail thumping against the floor.

Lucky, lucky Buddy.

Yeah...this wasn't going to work. I jumped up and started gathering squeaky toys and slobbery plush animals.

"Time for breakfast!" Angelica called. "Ashton, can you handle? I've got to submit this paperwork now or the director will have my head."

"I got this. Come on, Dev. Let me show you how to feed these rascals."

Dev. He kept calling me by that nickname. I could even hear the affection in his voice, the same lilt from that summer. It made me want to melt.

Or smack him. I wasn't sure yet.

Once the pooches were happily munching, Ashton and I finished picking up dog toys and cleaning. There was a lot of work to do, but that was a good thing. I could focus on tasks instead of my emotional turmoil.

After lunch we had cleaning duty again. Washing toys and shaking out bedding. Sweeping up kibble and mopping up pee. Keeping myself busy so I could avoid Ashton and those deep brown eyes.

He did the exact opposite. He'd look right at me, almost as if he were daring me to keep staying away from him. Then he'd look off into the distance, his face troubled. He'd freeze in place, only moving when one of the dogs jumped onto his lap, snapping him out of his reverie. Then he'd brighten, burying his face in fluffy canine fur.

His mood swings were super confusing.

Every bone in my body ached by the time the dogs went for their afternoon walk. I wanted tea, I needed a nap, and instead I got Ashton poking his head around the corner and grinning at me.

"You look like you could use a break," he announced. "Come with me."

I took one step, then hesitated. "Where?"

"Trust me."

"Why?"

He blinked those eyes, turning on the charm full blast. "Please?"

Dammit.

"Lie down and close your eyes," he said once we came to a bright room in the far corner of Doggie Town.

"Excuse me?"

"Trust me," he said again.

I actually lay down on the floor. But because I was very tired, of course.

As long as I kept telling myself that, it would eventually come true.

"The key is to give in." Ashton's voice came from above me. "Surrender to what's about to happen."

What the hell had I gotten myself into? "Which is what, exactly?"

"*Shh.*" And suddenly I was buried in a whirlwind of little paws and wet noses and puppy breath. I shrieked and opened my eyes, and there was Ashton on the floor beside me, a look of utter happiness on his face as the puppies jumped from me to him, their tiny barks echoing all over Doggie Town.

"Oh my God," I said, not even trying to hold back my laughter. "Where'd they come from?"

"Their foster just dropped them off. This is the intake room."

I scratched the tiny black puppy nipping at my nose. "Best energy boost ever."

Ashton gave me a heart-melting grin. My hands trembled with the effort of trying to resist it. To resist *him*. But damn, if this boy wasn't an abyss.

I turned away and focused on the puppy, who had settled onto my stomach with a plop and a sigh.

But I was still so aware of Ashton lying there. What was he thinking? Feeling?

I turned to face him, and he was looking at me, a gentle smile playing around his lips. One that mirrored the pure joy in his eyes. Was he so happy because being buried in puppies was the best thing ever, or was it because he was here with me? Did it even matter?

God, this was so hard.

"These little cuties are all cleared for adoption." Angelica's perky voice broke the spell. "I need you to bring them to Puppy Palace. Everything's all set for them, but I want you two to get them settled in their new home."

"How do we do that?" I asked.

She grinned. "Easy. Play with them!"

Ashton saluted her, hopped up, and started gathering the squirming, yapping puppies. "Best day ever."

Angelica shook her head and left the room.

"Duty calls," Ashton said to me.

And it kept calling for the next three hours. Puppy Palace was huge, with floor-to-ceiling windows that let in streaming sunlight. There were fluffy doggie beds and rubbery balls and bowls of food and water. And toys. So many toys for them to absolutely destroy.

I couldn't keep ahead of them. I'd pick up all the toys, and the puppies would immediately have them all over the place. Rubber strips and ripped-up stuffed animals and random squeakers covered the floor. On top of that, not all the puppies were potty trained, so the mopping was never-ending. There was no way I could take control, and I was *this close* to full-on give-me-*all*-the-junk-food meltdown mode.

But then the biggest puppy, a golden cutie named Darby, totally obliterated a stuffed mouse and left the carnage in a puddle of pee.

"I'm gonna cry," I whimpered, letting the mop clatter to the floor.

Ashton glanced over, saw what I was gaping at, stared at me in disbelief, then collapsed to the floor in laughter. He laughed so hard his cheeks turned red and he snorted. He actually snorted. That set me off, and we both started howling. Which made some of the dogs howl. Which made us laugh even more. Every time Ashton and I caught each other's eyes, the snorts bubbled up again and again.

"I'm sorry I suck," I said between gasps.

And there was that tender look of his. "You don't suck. This place falls apart every single day. Believe me, it's not you."

"It's you?"

A devilish smirk. "You caught me."

Dammit, Ashton, stop with all the nice stuff. I'm furious at you, and I'm determined to stay that way. I crossed my arms. "Now what?"

"We wait for the dogs to settle down. Then we clean again."

That wasn't what I'd meant. At all.

Another deep stare, and no Angelica to interrupt this time. Just a cold, wet nose burrowing into my ear. I squealed and jumped up. Happy for an excuse to get away from Ashton. To center myself. To breathe. This up-and-down was taking its toll and I needed to sort myself out. Now. "Hand me some more paper towels."

By four o'clock, I was exhausted and covered in fur, but happy. Because honestly, it was impossible to stay sad after playing with dogs all day. And now I could go home, take a bubble bath, and be Ashton-free until Monday. Tuesday if I was really lucky.

I've never been really lucky.

"Did you have a good day?" His voice came from behind me as I was washing my hands.

Why couldn't he be a straight-up asshole? Then it would be easier to hate him. But no, he had to be nice. He'd always been nice. Maybe that was part of the problem.

Sometimes "nice" wasn't enough.

I stood up straighter. "It was okay."

He nodded and moved in to wash his own hands. The silence stretched out the awkwardness. I shook droplets off my hands and stopped dead when my stomach decided to break the tension with a loud growl. Ashton's mouth dropped open, then his face relaxed into a slow grin.

Embarrassed, I concentrated on drying my hands. But I could feel his eyes on me. Imploring me. Pulling me in. Almost against my will, I glanced at him. He watched me with a thoughtful expression, then: "You wanna . . . grab a bite?"

I did. "I should get home."

He nodded. "Okay."

My stomach betrayed me with another loud growl. He raised his eyebrow, but didn't let any other emotion cross his face.

"We can't just . . ." I shook my head.

"I know." He tugged the zipper on his jacket. "But I'd like to start by getting you dinner."

"You don't have to do that."

"I want to."

I counted to five in my head. Told myself I was making a huge mistake. But then I said, "Okay."

Chapter 9

IN THE PARKING LOT, THERE WAS A DEFINITE BITE IN THE air, a crispness that showed the time for apple picking and hayrides wasn't too far off. The scent of burning leaves tickled my nose, reminding me of jack-o'-lanterns and hot cider and cozy nights in front of the fireplace.

"This is your ride?" We'd stopped at a black Porsche Panamera.

He gave me a bewildered look. "You've never seen my car?"

"We only walked or rode bikes at the beach. Remember?"

He opened the door for me, and a blast of heat nearly seared my eyebrows off. Someone had apparently parked in the sun all day. "You're right. We took a million walks that summer."

That summer.

Normally I would have been geeking out over this luxury car with its leather seats and wooden panels and clean car smell. But I was too nervous, nibbling my nails and not really seeing our small downtown blurring past. I took deep breaths, trying to calm my racing heart and cool my flushing skin.

"Is fast food okay?" Ashton asked. "I'm craving fries."

Quick and easy. Great. "Sounds good to me."

We pulled up to a burger joint. "I don't even care that I smell like dog hair," he said. "I want to eat inside. That okay?"

"That's fine. I hate the drive-through."

We ordered burgers, fries, and apple pies. My stomach grumbled again, earning me a teasing grin. "Your stomach means business," he said, eyes twinkling.

"It doesn't like missing meals. Or snacks. Or candy."

"Too bad I didn't know that. I'd have given you some of my M&M's earlier."

"You should have given me M&M's anyway, selfish."

"Sorry. They're my favorite."

Of course. His massive sweet tooth. How could I have forgotten? It was one of the main things he and I had in common. We'd spent so many nights on the beach scarfing down ice cream or funnel cakes or cotton candy, then making out in a whirl of sugary bliss.

Focus.

"I'll grab ketchup and napkins," I murmured.

By the time I'd filled my drink and gathered the condiments, Ashton had made his way over to me with a tray of steaming food. We had our pick of tables, and I slid into a booth across from him.

We focused on unwrapping our burgers. Salting our fries. Checking for rogue onions.

Maybe that last part was just me.

"Dev, it was fun working with you today."

I'd had fun with him, too. But he didn't need to know that. He didn't need to know my heart and my brain were engaging in a whirlwind of confusing, conflicting feelings. Anger. Desire. Fury. Lust. I gripped my fruit punch and tried not to squeeze.

"Same," I finally said.

He gave me a small smile. "You're so formal sometimes."

My grip on the drink relaxed. "I'm not sure how to act around you."

"Is that why you've been avoiding me?"

"Yeah." I fiddled with my straw. "You're bad for my sanity."

The smile faded.

"I'm kidding," I said.

But not really.

We were quiet for a while.

"Is this weird?" he asked.

"Definitely weird."

We got quiet again.

These silences were killing me. So I blurted out the first thing that popped into my head. "You weren't at school yesterday."

Great. Why did I have to say that? Now he probably thought I was a stalker.

He looked down at his food. "I have a lot on my mind."

I should have let it go. Instead, I dragged a fry through my ketchup and took a deep breath. "Want to talk about it?"

He hesitated before meeting my eyes. "I don't want to dump on you."

"Is everything okay?"

"I don't know." Then he was quiet for a long time. Sliding his fingers back and forth across the table. His expression telling me his mind was light-years away, and that it wasn't nice, wherever that was.

My heart ached, desperate to comfort him. To bring back that annoying heart-melting grin from earlier.

My skin ached, desperate to feel him warm and smooth against me.

My brain ached, because God, what was I doing here?

"Ashton," I said quietly. "Where are you?"

The raw vulnerability in his eyes almost knocked me over. "Do you ever get overwhelmed? By everything?"

I thought about the emotional roller coaster I currently had unlimited tickets for. "Constantly."

"So you get it, then." His fingers stilled as he gave me another small smile. "You always have. More than anyone."

You are angry at him, Devon. Furious. Stay strong! This boy had flaked on me big-time, so why was I trying to make him open up to me? It made no logical sense. But something would not let me be that flippant to another person.

Sometimes I hated that about myself.

"Tell me," I said.

He buried his head in his hands, then mumbled something under his breath.

I leaned across the table. "I didn't hear you."

He shook his head. "It's so messed up."

I could've sworn he'd said *I'm so messed up.*

He crumpled his burger wrapper and squeezed it in his fist. "My father says he's at his 'wit's end' with me. That I need to toughen up. Apparently, I have one more chance to mess up before I get shipped to military school."

"Military school?"

"I'm not down on military school or anything. But I know myself. It would kill me." His expression turned from pained to thoughtful. "Maybe I *should* go there."

"To get killed?"

He shrugged. "Probably easier than doing it myself."

I dropped what was left of my burger. "What?"

He shook his head. "Nothing. I'm being stupid. Don't pay me any attention."

Yeah, okay. Fat chance of that happening now.

"Ashton, do I need to be worried about you?"

"No. Like I said, I was being stupid."

I frowned. Here was the thing: Memories of that summer were still constantly flowing into my brain. Times when he'd say things that seemed a bit off. Like one time when he'd gotten into it with his dad and said, "He'd probably be happier if I wasn't around." And the time he'd said, "I need to just be done with everything." I'd taken it as Ashton needing to get away from his family for a while. That he'd be fine once he cooled off. But now that he was still talking like this...maybe it had been more.

I wanted to pry it all out of him, but it wasn't my place to push. *Was it?*

"I wish you wouldn't say those things about yourself," I said softly.

"I wish I didn't think these things about myself, but there you go." He made a fist and pressed it into the table. "We should talk about something else. How's your food?"

The abrupt subject change threw me off. "Um, what?"

"Your food. Is it good?"

I picked up my burger again. "What do you want me to say? It's fast food."

His hand relaxed. "We had fast food in France, but it wasn't as delightfully crappy as it is here."

"You lived in France?"

He broke his apple pie in half and nodded. "Went to school there this past year. It was nice because I could see my grandma during my breaks instead of coming home. She lives in Monaco."

I smirked. "You probably got into all kinds of trouble."

A real smile this time. "Surprisingly little. When I was really young, I hated going there. Which didn't make any sense, because she spoiled me rotten. But I guess it felt too much like my parents sent me there because they didn't want me around, and that's a shitty feeling. But then I realized how awesome Grandma is. I love hanging with her. I talk to her about everything."

Then the smile turned into a frown. "How are we talking about me again? God, I'm the biggest asshole."

"You're kind of fascinating," I admitted.

He let out a snort. "I'm really not. Not even a little bit. You're the fascinating one. Are you still studying your stars?"

"Absolutely."

"Awesome. I love how you see pictures *and* stories in the sky. Like that night you told me about that one star. Arc—?"

"Arcturus."

His face relaxed into a wistful smile. "I remember it."

I remembered, too. It had been such a magical night. A banana moon. The scent of saltwater filling the air. The cool ocean waves crashing over our toes as the tide rolled in. He'd asked me a million questions about the moon and the tide, and he'd asked me to point out my favorite stars to him. I'd taken his hand and pointed to Arcturus—but he wasn't looking at the sky.

He was looking at me.

He was looking at me as if he would rather look at nothing else. As if I were the only thing that existed and he still couldn't get enough. Then he'd gently tugged me so that

I tumbled against him. I could feel his heart pounding. His warm breath against my lips. Then his lips against my lips.

Our first kiss.

"That was a good night," Ashton said quietly.

Blinking slowly, I reluctantly came back to the restaurant. To right now. "Yeah. It was."

He was gazing at my mouth with the kind of stare that could unsettle the most stoic of stoics. The kind of look that sent fire to my stomach and made my fingers tremble.

He shook his head slightly, as if he were coming out of a trance, and said, "I love that you know this stuff. About the stars. It's one of my favorite things about you."

And when he said stuff like this...it was hard to stay so infuriated with him.

"But don't quiz me or anything. I'm not going to remember. It's been a long time," he said. And all the hurt came crashing back.

"That's not my fault," I said quietly.

"I know." He looked down at the table. "Our summer shouldn't have ended that way."

"But it did."

"And I hate myself for it," he said, his expression so miserable.

Coming here had definitely been a mistake. I didn't even know what I'd been trying to accomplish, but feeling bad for him? Concerned? Not even. He should be feeling bad for *me*. I'm the one who floundered for a year, wondering where the hell he'd been all this time when I'd been here. *Right here.*

"Why did you leave me?" My eyes and throat burned, but I needed to know.

"I didn't want to."

"That's not what I asked."

He looked at the crumpled wrappers. "This isn't a conversation I want to have here."

"Then let's go somewhere and have it."

He nodded and picked up the tray. "Let's go."

Chapter 10

"Thanks for dinner," I said in the Porsche.

"Of course." He started the car. "I like spending time with you."

"Me too."

Our gazes locked. And despite every warning going off in my brain, I didn't look away. I let myself study the contours of his face. The deepness in his eyes. The light flush in his cheeks.

I wanted to kiss him so, so much.

I gripped my key pendant. "We've got to talk."

"I know," he said, his expression serious. "Let's go to my house. We'll have privacy there."

I should have made him take me home right then. Actually, it would probably be better to text my mom for a ride so I could get the hell away from him. He'd changed. I was sure deep down was my incredible boyfriend who'd surprised me with picnics on the beach and won me stuffed animals at silly boardwalk games. But now his happy-go-lucky nature was tempered by darkness. Now he was a hurricane, with pain behind his eyes and scary words escaping his lips.

Like about military school. All the talk about him losing it. I didn't know what to think.

The tension made the fifteen-minute ride seem way longer. After what felt like ages, we pulled up to a gated property that stood alone rather than as part of a community of McMansions.

The Founder's Mansion. A landmark in our quaint, scenic town. The brick Georgian-style house was mammoth and intimidating, with shuttered dormer windows and a neatly manicured lawn. Perfectly round juniper bushes stood on each side of the portico while pink chrysanthemums bloomed in uniform flower beds. A circular drive wound around a white three-tiered fountain. Ashton bypassed that and drove straight back, behind the house.

The Founder's Mansion. Because of course I had to have fallen for one of the most important people in town.

Ashton parked in a garage filled with a bunch of luxury cars and then we made our way into the kitchen, which looked like a set from a Food Network show. Gleaming stainless steel appliances. Loads of counter space. A bowl of fresh fruit on the island. I didn't like to cook, but if I had a kitchen like this, I'd be willing to start.

"My humble abode," he said as I tried not to gape.

"Humble," I repeated. "Did I see a Maserati out there?"

"You sure did. And I know this place is ridiculous. There's only the three of us living here, too." He looked at me, a thoughtful expression on his face. "You're into cars, aren't you?"

"I like foreign ones that are pretty and go fast."

He nodded. "So does my father. You should see our other garage."

Other garage. Holy Christ.

He opened the Sub-Zero fridge and peered inside. "Can I get you something to drink?"

"Water, please," I said. My mouth was suddenly so dry.

"Coming right up." He pulled out two Smartwaters and handed one to me.

"Thanks. Where are your parents?"

He screwed up his face. "My father's traveling for business, and my mother is at some D-O-R function."

"D-O-R?"

"It might be D-*A*-R. Daughters of the Revolution or something like that."

I screwed up *my* face.

He gave a slight smile. "Yep, that about sums it up. Let's go sit in the garden."

"No tour?"

He threw his jacket on the counter. "I can take you on one if you really want, but I'm a lousy guide."

"I was kidding." Although I kind of wasn't. I really did want to check out the rest of this house.

I immediately loved Ashton's garden. It was like one of

those conservatories by the zoo, complete with statues and benches and birdbaths and butterflies. Fat bumblebees hovered around daisies, and the scent of roses hung in the air. My throat was already itching, but I was too enamored by their beauty to care.

Then I remembered why I was here. My nerves turned up to one hundred, and suddenly I wasn't so sure I wanted answers about that summer at all.

"Ashton. Are those swans?"

He grimaced. "My mother's idea. Don't go near them. They're mean as hell."

I gave him a sideways glance. "Sounds like you're speaking from experience."

"They don't like it when people try to pet them. They really hate it if you try to pick them up."

I couldn't help smirking. "You tried to pick up a swan?"

"Oh sure, laugh at my pain." He clutched at his heart.

"I'm sorry, but the thought of you wrestling with one of those things is too much."

"It was messed up. That's what it was."

I looked at the pond again. The swans—all-white, except for their black bills—floated peacefully. Trumpeter swans. How rich did you have to be to own trumpeter swans? "What are their names?"

"Freddie and Flossie."

"After the Bobbsey Twins?"

He nodded. "Yep."

"Did you name the swans?"

"I did. Maybe that's why they hate me so much," he said thoughtfully. "I should've named them Edgar and Agnes."

"Why those names?"

"'Cause they sound cranky, like the swans."

I shook my head. "I can't believe this is your house. What does your family even do with all this space?"

"Fill it up with useless crap." He shrugged. "My mother loves antiques. The house has been in my family for generations."

If Preston Academy was founded 235 years ago, then Ashton's family had to have been here well before then. Wow. Talk about a legacy.

"My ancestors felt that they should have an impressive and imposing place," he added.

"It's both of those, all right."

"It's a lot to live up to," he said quietly, all smiles gone. "Come sit down."

We settled on a gray stone bench that was halfway hidden behind a giant sugar maple. Far enough from the roses so my allergies didn't flare up too badly, but close enough that I could appreciate their beauty.

Not that I was paying much attention to the flowers. My mind reeled. The familiarity. The way we finally started falling back into our easy pattern of that summer. It lulled me into a false sense of security.

And now every cell in my body wanted to be as close to Ashton as possible. God, this was so frustrating. This up and down and back and forth. No wonder I was so wound up, as if any touch could set me off. I took a sip of water to calm the heat building inside me. This was the perfect setting to pick up where we'd left off that steamy summer.

But I needed to be stronger than that.

I took another drink of water.

Ashton nudged my foot with his. Dark-brown Top-Sider boots bumping into my black Converse hikers. "Hey."

I sat up straight. Waited.

His eyes softened. "I still can't believe it. After all this time, you're sitting in my *garden*. I never thought I'd see you again."

"Yeah. About that."

"About that," he repeated, then rubbed the back of his neck. Then he stared at his shoes for what felt like ages.

"Ashton. Just tell me."

"It's complicated."

"I think I can keep up."

He nodded. Then he let out a world-weary sigh. "So, my family. There's this history. We've got these bloodlines.... My mother goes on and on about how we need to stay within our circles"—his voice lowered to nearly inaudible, and he cringed— "and with our kind."

Silence. Then, "Your parents didn't like me?"

"Mother did like you." The color in his cheeks deepened as he ran his fingers through his hair. "My parents. They're old-fashioned and conservative. Said you were nice enough, but not suitable for our family."

My jaw clenched. "I wasn't white enough, you mean?"

He sucked in a breath, his face on fire. "My mother thought I was experimenting. Said she expected me to. But I brought you to the beach house. Multiple times. That's when it sank in that you weren't a fling. That's when the bullshit started."

My breath thinned. "Experimenting? What does that even mean?"

He gave me a pained look. "Do you really want me to say it? Because I don't want to say it. I don't want to think it."

And then I got it. *Experimenting*. Tasting the naughty, forbidden fruit before settling with the socially acceptable WASP princess for a lifetime of snobby, white-bread bliss.

I wish I could say I was surprised, but I knew better. You don't attend an exclusive private school with an endowment without learning about the politics of old money. Generations of wealth. Legacies that had built entire towns and industries. And schools.

My legacy wasn't power and money and control. It was camping trips where we snuggled together in a tiny tent, Dad telling ghost stories that weren't scary at all. Eating pasta until we had to crawl from the kitchen table. A mom who could sell a million-dollar mansion but would never own one. Whose quiet pride and strength enveloped my entire family. A dad who was addicted to Nestlé Crunch bars and watched *Riverdance* and tried to imitate the steps when he thought no one was looking. Who worked his butt off so I could focus on my studies instead of working an after-school job. Parents who would never make me choose politics over someone I loved.

Stuff like that didn't matter in Ashton's world. Seemed like all they cared about were appearances. Having pure blood. Well, I seriously doubted I had any blue blood in my veins. My father: 100 percent Irish. My mother: 100 percent Black. Me? Apparently not good enough for Ashton's family.

I wasn't surprised, but it still stung like hell.

"I'm not proud of it," Ashton said. "Any of it. And I made it worse. Instead of standing up to them, I ran."

"Why?"

"My father is the ultimate authority. When he talks, you listen, you do what he says, and you get the fuck out of his way." Ashton's expression grew stony. "He terrifies me, Devon, so that's what I did. Instead of standing up for you, instead of *being up-front* with you, I ran."

"Yeah. You did."

He didn't turn away. If anything, he became more focused. More intense. "There are no words for how sorry I am, not that you want to hear them anyway."

"I mean, I kinda do want to hear them," I admitted.

A small smile, then he grew serious. "You made that summer so *good* for me, and I repaid you in the shittiest way possible."

"I waited for you," I said quietly. "I sat there for hours."

"Oh." Another deep breath. "I suck. *God*, I suck. Devon, I don't even know how to begin making this up to you."

"You can start by letting me kick your ass."

He raised an eyebrow. "You want to kick my ass?"

"I want to hurt you like you hurt me."

He winced. "I deserve that."

I was hurting all over again. Not so much because of the race stuff. Eighteen years of microaggressions coming at me every day had made me good and numb to that. But his mother's lying. Her phoniness. Smiling in my face while thinking God knows what about me, my family, my heritage. *That* was bullshit. And I didn't know if I could forgive her for that.

I couldn't even make sense of the emotions rushing through me now. It was too much. And also not enough.

"Why did you bring me here?" I asked. "Was it to show me what I'm not good enough for?"

"No! Devon!"

"I'm sitting here in this gorgeous garden and looking at your beautiful house, and all I know is that people live there who think I'm not good enough because I wasn't born the right color and I don't have the right size bank account. Do you know how shitty that feels?"

"My parents suck," he spat out. "I'm ashamed to share their so-called bloodline."

"They're your family."

His cheeks darkened again. "I'm not like them."

"Sorry not sorry I don't exactly believe you right now."

He groaned and rubbed his face. "I don't blame you." Then he was looking at me again, full-on. Completely open. "I missed you every single day. I dreamed about you every single night."

I raised my eyebrow.

"Well, sometimes I had dreams about zombie Easter Bunnies or giant beanstalks, but that's beside the point."

I stared at him. Was he joking? Now? But, no. There was no crinkle around his eyes.

"I'd wake up thinking you were there," he continued. "I wanted to touch you so much. Make sure you were real. But you never were."

"I'm here now," I said, my voice shaky.

"Wearing the necklace I gave you." He reached toward my pendant, then pulled his hand back slightly. "I still want to touch you."

There was no mistaking the longing in his eyes. It was the same look he'd given me before he kissed me for the first time. Like he thought I'd hung the very stars I loved so much. The same look that could slowly melt all my anger and tamp down my frustration and make me forget everything except right here and right now.

"What's stopping you?" I asked.

A long pause. Then, a new look on his face. It was heart-breaking, but not as much as what came out of his mouth. "I have a girlfriend."

Hell. No. My hands shot out to shove him, but he caught my wrists, restraining me.

"Let me go."

"Devon."

My fists clenched. Focusing on that kept my eyes from stinging. "Let. Me. *Go!*"

Because *of course* he had a girlfriend. Of course he did. I wanted to throw something. I wanted to throw *him*.

"I left," he said. "And even if I'd found you again, why would you want me after that?"

I yanked my wrists away. "You didn't even try to find me!"

He froze. "That's not true."

"Again, sorry not sorry for not believing you."

"You're the one who's not on social media."

This boy had one more time to try me before I went *off*. "Don't you dare try to blame this on me. You had my phone number. You had my email."

"Devon, my parents took my phone and my computer. They made me delete my email account. I eventually got new ones, but I couldn't get any of the old info back."

I stared at him so hard he started to squirm. "Were you with her when we were together?"

And now he had the nerve to look offended. "You really think I'd do that to you?"

"I don't know what to think. I feel like I never knew you!"

His face crumpled. "You were the *only* person who knew me."

"You have a girlfriend."

"And you don't have a boyfriend?"

Inhale...two...three...four.

Exhale...two...three...four.

Don't punch him in the face.

"Number one: not your business. Number two: What does it matter now?"

He jumped up and began to pace. "When I saw you the first day of school, I was shocked. Knocked clear on my ass.

But I figured I'd apologize and we'd go our separate ways. Then I saw the necklace. The key to my heart." He stopped in front of me. "You still wear it."

I stroked the chain. "So?"

He stared at me, the expression on his face tortured. Then his meaning crystallized.

I drew in a gasp. "Oh."

His eyes locked on mine. Then, the slightest of nods. "I never stopped, Dev."

For a second I was wildly happy. Then my heart sank with a pang. "But what about her?"

He collapsed onto the bench again and buried his face in his hands. "Rochelle."

Rochelle. She had a name. That made her real. And I'd bet anything she was beautiful and rich and the perfect shade of ivory. His parents probably didn't have any problem with *Rochelle.*

My lips wouldn't stop trembling.

Fuck. No. I wasn't going to cry. I refused.

Ashton rubbed his forehead. "Hooking up with her...it made sense at the time. I've known her forever, since we were kids."

And that was that. How could I ever compete? They had history. All I had was a summer.

We sat in silence. Bees moved from the daisies to the roses. A light breeze lifted my hair and tickled my nose. But I was still too aware of him beside me.

I took several deep breaths. This was so unfair. Why did

it have to be this way? Why couldn't I have him? Or at least *hate* him? I closed my eyes and tried to fight all the love washing over me. I tried to grab my anger and hold it close, bury it in my heart so I wouldn't do something irrational. My head pounded with the effort. My emotions were spinning out of orbit, and I was terrified of crashing.

"You are a bastard," I said, my voice shaking. "I can't be around you." My voice had steel in it now. No way was I going to show him I was falling apart.

His eyes pierced mine. "I'm going to make things right. I promise."

"How? By telling Rochelle that your old flame from two summers ago waltzed back into your life?"

"That's exactly what I'm going to do."

I couldn't listen to this. "Take me home. Please."

We didn't talk except when I murmured directions to my house. It was dusk by the time we got there, the brightest stars already popping out. Those damned stars. Since when did any wish on them come true? Why did they have to bring him back? And why hadn't I been more specific? *Next time, bring back the boy without the crappy parents and the girlfriend, thanks.* The girlfriend. Did he twirl her hair in his fingers when he kissed her? Did she know he had a mole at the top of his right thigh? Did she kiss him there like I used to?

When we pulled into the driveway, the front curtain parted slightly and the outline of my mom's Afro appeared in the light. Then the porch lamp snapped on.

I unlocked the door. Then I paused. "Are you sleeping with her?"

He stared at the steering wheel, chewing his bottom lip.

"Okay." I got out of the car and slammed the door.

It was not okay.

I was not okay.

Chapter 11

EVEN THOUGH I'D BEEN STARING AT THE NIGHT SKY FOR YEARS, I still found something new every time. That was the thing about the universe. I'd never be able to explore it all. Most of the time, I was okay with that, because no matter what, I could always find my center here. This was my heart and my soul and my world.

Every time I stargazed, I focused on something new. Let it consume me. Like now, lying on a sleeping bag in my backyard, looking for the Orion Nebula.

Really trying to distract my mind from Ashton, and from tonight. Trying to stop the heartache and concentrate on my future. The stars. But the memories were relentless, sneaking in every time my mind went blank.

So I let my eyes slide out of focus, blurring the sky like a van Gogh painting, and gave in....

"Hey." Poke. "Hey." Poke poke.

I grabbed his finger. "What are you doing?"

He pointed up to the sky. "What star is that?"

I squinted at him. "Is this how you get your kicks? By giving me astronomy quizzes?"

"As opposed to . . ."

"Kissing me?"

He grinned. "I mean, I should at least pretend I'm not just hanging out with you 'cause you're hot."

I shoved him so hard he fell over into the sand. Laughing, he pulled me so I tumbled down next to him.

"You didn't answer my question," he said.

"It's Deneb. The brightest star in the Cygnus constellation. Part of the Summer Triangle."

"Does this mean you can't see it in the winter?"

"Yes."

He frowned. "That sucks. Can you believe summer is over?"

"I know. Feels like I just got here."

"Best two and a half months ever. Not looking forward to going back to my regular life."

"I kind of am," I said. "Astronomy isn't going to learn itself, you know."

"Okay, first of all, that makes no sense. Second of all, you are weird. But I'm not even surprised. How else are you going to get that doctorate?" He smiled. "Devon Kearney, PhD. I will always love the way that sounds."

I swallowed. "Do you think we'll still know each other then?"

He went quiet, staring out at the sea. "I hope so. Already seems like I've known you forever."

"I feel the same. Is that weird?"

He kissed my forehead. "Maybe. But I don't care. That first time I saw you, I knew you were going to be important to me. And you are."

I glanced over at him. "Do you believe in soul mates or twin flames?"

"I don't even know what a twin flame is."

"Ashton." I poked his shoulder. "What do you know?"

He grabbed my finger and kissed the tip. "I know that you come here every year. You love sushi and sub sandwiches, but you hate the sound of people chewing. You got the money for your first telescope by doing odd jobs for your neighbors. I know you love the stars and would take them home if you could."

"But that's a bunch of stuff I told you. What do you know?" I put my hand on his chest. "In here."

And then he looked at me as if he'd rather do nothing else in the world but look at me. "I know the thought of not seeing you every day just feels wrong, because when I'm around you, everything actually makes sense. I know you make me excited about the future. This summer has been so perfect. It scares me how perfect. And it scares me how much . . . how much I love you."

Heart pounding. Breath shallow. "What?"

"I'm falling in love with you."

Oh wow. I hadn't expected this. Why, I didn't know. Because I felt it. Every time I looked at him, my stomach fluttered like someone with her first crush. Every time he touched me, my body tingled so much it was a miracle the vibrations didn't shock him. I could spend hours with him and still get thrilled when he called or texted not even ten minutes after saying good night. When we were together, we were the only two people in the world. No one else needed. No one else allowed.

My breath caught as I stroked his face with trembling fingers. Traced his lips with my thumb. Then said, "I'm falling for you, too."

"Yeah?" He grinned. "I love you. I love you. I'll never get tired of saying that." He grew solemn. "I love you, Devon."

"I love you, too."

And then we were kissing as if the whole world had disappeared. All that existed was his skin against mine. His soft breathing. His intoxicating sweet, salty taste.

"I don't want this to end," he murmured, "just because the summer does."

Summer romances were supposed to be fun, intense flings that got filed away into warm, glowing memories. I didn't know anyone who tried to make it more than that. But with Ashton...I wanted it to be more.

I drew a heart on his chest. "Tomorrow's our last day together."

"I think we should try to make it work," he said.

"Is that realistic?"

"I want to try. I know after tomorrow we have to separate, but I'm going to make sure it's only for a little while."

"Tomorrow's going to suck."

"No. We're going to make our last day together awesome. The whole day, the whole night, just me and you. And then, it's going to be me and you forever."

I gripped his shoulders. "Don't say it if you don't mean it."

He fixed steady eyes on mine. "I want you forever, Devon. And I absolutely mean it."

But he hadn't, had he?

Because now he had a girlfriend.

He had a girlfriend.

I ripped up a clump of grass.

Whatever. I'd been doing fine all this time. I would certainly be fine again. I didn't need him. I didn't need him. I did not need him.

I stared at the Orion Nebula, observing what looked peaceful but was really a swirling, evolving phenomenon, a stellar nursery churning out new stars by the hundreds. It reminded me of myself. A tower of control on the outside, a wild, unpredictable spiral on the inside.

I needed to resolve the things causing my heart to race and my breath to catch...and I needed to resolve them now. Nothing could stand between me and my dream. No boys. No heartbreak. No pain. From now on, it was going to be hard work, dedication, and focus.

I had this.

Chapter 12

THREE AND A HALF WEEKS INTO THE SCHOOL YEAR, THE Yearbook Club was still fighting over the theme. "It's got to be impactful, but comforting. Universal, but unique. And truly representative of our class."

My head hurt from Auden's posturing. Why couldn't anything ever be simple with her?

"You're thinking about this *way* too hard," Colton said.

"Someone has to!"

"Okay, yeah, because in a year, people will care. Get a grip, Auden." Tyrell tossed his pencil and caught it. "It's not that serious."

"It is to me. What about you, Devon?"

I mean, it was, but . . . "Don't bring me into this."

Professor Wilcox yawned. "You folks need to come up with

something *today*. Even if we have to come back after school and stay here all night."

Oh hell no.

"How about *A Splash of Class*?" Auden asked.

"Absolutely not," Tyrell said. "Way too cute."

"I *like* cute."

"That's because you *are* cute," Colton said with a wink.

Auden flushed with pleasure, but crossed her theme off the list. "Fine. What do you have in mind?"

"A Year to Remember."

"That's basic as hell," Tyrell protested.

"I don't see you coming up with anything, Jenkins."

"That's because brilliance takes time."

Colton put Tyrell in a headlock, which Auden and I ignored. Because this happened at every single meeting.

I didn't talk much at the meetings, which was silly, considering I was supposed to be one of the people in charge. It's just that Colton and Tyrell had such big personalities, and Auden was so freaking bossy, it was easier to sit back and let things unfold. I spent most of the time calculating sales and billing advertisers anyway.

Everyone in school eventually bought a yearbook; it was just a matter of how soon we could make the sales. The sooner we got funds, the more cool stuff we could add to the book. This year, Colton's charm had the things flying off figurative shelves.

"You need to get serious," Wilcox said. "I can't even think of working out a color palette until the theme is locked."

"How about *These Are Our Moments*?" I asked.

Silence. And then: "Let the crowd say amen!" Tyrell pumped his fist, his voice ringing out like a gospel preacher's. "She hast spoketh, and brilliance hast poureth forth."

Wilcox beamed. "That's it, Miss Kearney. That's the theme. Anyone have any objection to Devon's idea?"

We all looked at one another, then at Wilcox, whose smile grew. "Great. Now on to the next. Who's covering the Harvest Ball this weekend?"

"I'm on it," Auden said. "I've got my fancy camera ready to go."

"Perfect," Wilcox said. "Let's do this thing."

Chapter 13

I KNEW THE HARVEST BALL WASN'T GOING TO BE AN ORDI-
nary dance, but this was beyond anything I could have
imagined.

The President's Club, located down the street from Preston
Academy, was another staple in the ritziest neighborhood in
town. The stone building glowed under golden spotlights as
limo after limo dropped off beautifully dressed students.

The ballroom took my breath away. Gauzy material and
twinkling white lights stretched across the walls, giving the
room a dreamlike ambience. Crystal chandeliers threw rain-
bows against gleaming platinum pillars. Huge orange lilies
decorated every table. A DJ spun lush remixes of the popular
songs that everyone claimed to hate but still danced to.

"This is ... wow."

Blair looked around, her eyes shining. "I'm so happy with it. With everything."

"You should be. You poured your heart and soul into this thing."

"I did, didn't I?" She grinned. "Let's party!"

I'd never seen so many pretty dresses outside of red-carpet specials on TV. My classmates looked like movie stars, but no one came close to outshining Blair in her long, slinky red dress.

My dress was a golden A-line with a sweetheart neckline. Tonight, I felt like a movie star, too.

"Smile!" Auden held the official school camera up. "Wait, where are your dates?"

"Devon's my date," Blair said, throwing her arm around me and kissing my cheek.

Auden's eyes gleamed. "I knew it!"

"Knew what?"

"You guys are totally lesbians! Oh my God, this is so cool." And then she snapped about one hundred pictures.

After dinner, the dancing really started. The floor filled with sweaty bodies and teachers trying to keep the dry humping to a minimum.

Guys pulled Blair onto the dance floor left and right. I danced with my share of guys as well, but I was most surprised when Auden took my hand, twirled me around, and then spun away.

I seriously did not understand her sometimes.

"What's up, Devon!" Tyrell bounced up to me, looking like a snack. Good enough to eat. I just wished he would consider asking Blair out. But there was that whole anti-dating-outside-his-race thing, which sucked for my best friend.

"Are you seriously wearing sunglasses?" I asked, laughing.

"Am I pulling it off?"

"You kinda are."

"Nice." He looked around appreciatively. "This party is off the hook. Blair organized all this?"

"She did."

"Yeah...this is her style."

Hmm. Curious. I tilted my head and raised my eyebrow. "And how would you know her *style*?"

He gave me a look like I was the densest person alive.

I looked at him like he'd lost his ever-loving mind. Tyrell was never one to be nervous about a girl. Dude was as cocky as they came. Then realization dawned. "Oh my God. Wait. You like her?"

"She's all right."

"Tyrell."

"I know. But I'm trying this new thing called 'keeping an open mind.'"

I smirked. "That's because you like her."

Tyrell's jaw twitched. "She scares me."

"And I don't?"

"You scare me on a different level, Devon. But not like Blair does."

My smirk turned into a grin. "You should ask her to dance."

He glanced over at her and smiled. I knew that expression—the dopey look guys got when they saw the girl of their dreams doing something they thought was absolutely adorable. Blair had her eyes closed, her hands waving in the air, while spinning in a circle. She looked ridiculous and totally blissed out, and therefore, breathtakingly beautiful.

I nudged him. "It's one dance."

He nodded, a thoughtful expression on his face. "You're right. I will."

After the song ended, I made my way over to the refreshments table. I watched Tyrell tap Blair on her shoulder. She spun around, and the look on her face lit up the entire room. They started swaying, looking absolutely stunning together. Seeing all the couples twirling around the floor made me achingly sad, but I found enough room in my lonely heart to be thrilled for Blair. She looked so happy, and I loved to see my friend glowing like that.

"I need another dance with my best friend forever." Grinning, Blair pulled me back out to the dance floor.

"Let's do this!" We threw our hands in the air and yelled *woo* and shook our hair and shimmied and it was awesome.

Blair shone like a star, brilliant and radiant. Her party was a major success, and people kept coming up to her to compliment her handiwork. I'd bet good money this was the best Harvest Ball ever.

Laughing, Blair and I held hands and whirled around and around. When the song ended, we collapsed against each other, still laughing, my head spinning with exhilaration.

And then I spotted Ashton.

He glanced around, taking in the scene, his expression one of deep appreciation.

I couldn't look away.

He was like the sun, blinding and painful. His dark suit did nothing to dim the glow emanating from his entire being.

"Oh," I sighed.

"What?" Blair shouted over the music.

I turned away from him and focused on her. "Nothing."

She glanced over and her eyes shone with mischief. "You gonna ask him to dance?"

"No."

"He's looking over here."

"I don't care."

"Bullshit," she sang. "You totally care."

"I really don't."

"He's coming over," Blair said.

Breathe, breathe, breathe.

I turned toward the guy nearest to me. Tall, curly dark-brown hair, ivory-colored skin, shining green eyes. Jeremy something or other. Played basketball. Happy to dance with me.

I could see Ashton, though. Frozen in place, the expression on his face dark as he watched Jeremy and me dance to hip-hop that spat out rapid-fire rhymes.

Ashton would not stop staring.

Even when the song changed and I grabbed Colton Myers. And good Lord—the boy danced like a stripper. Downright obscene. His blue eyes sparkled while he gyrated to the DJ's dubstep remix of the latest and greatest by everyone's favorite pop diva.

Ashton was still there. On the sidelines. Unwavering.

Then there were four of us: Blair, Jeremy, Colton, and me. R & B. Hip-hop. Fast, sweaty, exhilarating. I tried to get lost in the dancing, but I could feel Ashton's eyes burning into me, calling to me, tempting me. But I refused to turn around. I refused to give in.

"Last dance," the DJ murmured into the mic as the beats faded away and the slow song filled the air.

I glanced at Blair, but she was back in Tyrell's arms. Jeremy and Colton had disappeared. I swallowed and turned to go grab a soda . . . and came face-to-face with Ashton.

He traced a light fingertip down my arm. *Oh God.* Breathing, thinking, reasoning became a distant memory as my skin flooded with sensation. I stood there, shaking. Trying to resist . . . and giving up as he pulled me close. I melted right into him. Gave in to the passionate look in his eyes and his hands on my body. The way the music moved us. The shrinking distance between us.

I tried not to inhale too deeply, lest I become intoxicated by the scent of his skin. I tried not to tremble as he trailed his fingers down my back. I tried not to lose myself in the feel of his arms around me, his warm breath against my neck, his heartbeat next to mine.

I completely and utterly failed.

We were so close right now. My fingers tickling the back of his neck. Our lips brushing. My mouth aching to be pressed against his. I could almost taste the mint on his breath.

I wanted to taste it. *Him.* I wanted to taste him.

Then the song ended. The lights rose and the voices around us grew louder. The world slowly came back into focus but I couldn't—wouldn't—look away from him.

"What are we doing?" I whispered.

"Longing," he answered in a low voice, his eyes still locked on mine.

"What now?" I asked.

But I knew exactly what he wanted. It made me shiver to see him smoldering with such blatant desire.

"Give in," he said thickly.

I wanted to. So much. But what did that say about him? About me?

"Come home with me," he said, his gaze intense.

My fingers curled, crushing his shirt. "Why?"

"You know why," he said. "You know exactly what I want to do with you. All night. Every night."

Yeah, I knew. And I wanted him to do everything he wanted. Again and again and again.

"Dev..." His voice trembled.

And that did it. Unbearable heat shot through me and I was desperate to do something about it. Was this the best course of action? Hell no. But I'd long left the Land of Rational Thought and was straight-up cruising toward Yes Please Even if Only for Tonight Town.

"Are you still with Rochelle?" I managed to get out.

Abruptly, he let go.

That answered my question.

Chills ran down my body like a bucket of water dumped over my head. Then exhaustion. I was tired of his intense desire. I was tired of being frustrated and lonely. I was tired of the back and forth and the up and down and all of it. I was just done.

The solution was obvious. But I couldn't be the one to point it out to him, and I wasn't about to be one of those girls who thought she could run someone else's life. I could take control of mine, though.

"Stay away from me."

Chapter 14

I DIDN'T GO INSIDE AFTER THE LIMO DROPPED ME OFF. INSTEAD, I slumped on the stoop and searched the skies for Aquila, the Flying Eagle. In Greek mythology, Aquila belonged to Zeus and carried his thunderbolts across the sky. He also kidnapped the son of the king of Troy—Aquarius, another of my favorite constellations. I liked that they were up there, playing out their story night after night. But right now, clouds ran across their stage, obscuring my sight. I wouldn't find comfort in the stars tonight.

I heard the door open and shuffling behind me. "Pumpkin?"

"Hey, Dad."

"When did you get home?"

"About an hour ago."

"Feel like company?" he asked as he sat beside me, so I guess I was getting company no matter how I felt. "I never see you anymore."

"You work too hard."

He bumped my knee with his. "So does my daughter."

I looked up. "I have big dreams."

"I know you do. It's *why* I work so hard." He paused. "So. Mom and I have been talking. About your college."

I studied his face. Dad had bags under his eyes and lines on his forehead that hadn't been there before the summer. His chestnut hair was a hot mess, tousled every which way and even sticking straight up in some places. "Oh?"

"I know you have your heart set on McCafferty. I don't know anyone who deserves to go there more than you do."

I straightened. "But?"

"McCafferty is very expensive."

I sighed. "I know, Daddy."

"You know I'd give you the whole world if I could. I just don't know how much Mom and I can give you for McCafferty."

I shook my head. "No, I get it." We were in this weird no-man's-land where my parents made too much for me to qualify for aid, but not enough to pay for school outright. "I filled out a billion scholarship applications. I'll take out loans. I'll do whatever it takes. I never expected you and Mom to foot the bill for my education."

"Well, maybe it won't be quite so bad," Dad said. "We *do* have a college fund set aside for you. There's no way it's going to completely cover your tuition, but it will help make a dent. And the Preston endowment will open up some scholarship doors."

"I'm counting on that."

"Have you considered living at home for your first two years, then getting an apartment for the last two?" Dad asked. "I know you want the dorm experience, but that's going to tack on an extra twenty grand a year."

I hadn't considered that at all. In my mind, college meant living in a too-small room with a roommate, sleeping on a bunk bed, and eating cereal, popcorn, and ramen noodles every day. Mom had showed me this music video from the nineties that had three Black girls living in a college dorm. The feeling of *belonging* I got while watching it—it stuck with me. If dorm life was anywhere near that cool for real, I wanted to be a part of it.

"Think about it," he said. "As I told you, we have a chunk put aside, but we don't have the three hundred grand to cover everything."

I shook my head again. "I'll figure out a way to make it work."

"*We'll* figure out a way to make it work," he corrected.

I wrapped my arms around him and breathed in his dad smell. Mint and Irish Spring soap and chocolate. "You've been snacking again, haven't you?"

He smiled and ruffled my hair. "Don't tell Mom."

"Your secret is safe with me." I held out my hand. "For a price."

He fished a mini Nestlé Crunch bar out of his pocket and dropped it into my cupped palm. "How was the dance?"

I groaned. I'd almost forgotten about the dance. And Ashton. "It was great. Up until the end."

"What happened?"

My face warmed. "Forget it. It's nothing."

"*That* I refuse to believe, when you're squirming like a spider crawled up your leg."

"Daddy, I would not be sitting here if that happened. I'd be running all over the yard screaming like I was on fire."

Dad started laughing. "Do you remember—?"

The screech of car tires startled me so much, I dropped my candy.

Dad shot up. "Who in the hot green hell?"

Holy crap, holy crap, holy crap. I knew that car, and I knew the person driving it. I was standing, Dad's hand heavy on my shoulder, when Ashton popped out and ran up to me.

"I'm going to break up with Rochelle," he blurted out.

Stunned, I couldn't do anything but stare at him. Then Dad cleared his throat.

"Dad, can we have a minute?"

"Everything okay?"

I waved him away. "It's fine."

"What I did at the dance was uncool," Ashton continued once the porch door closed. "I never should have been so close to you tonight."

"You're right," I said. Then I sighed. "But it's not like you were dancing by yourself."

"Doesn't matter. I'm the one with a girlfriend." He shook his head. "I was being extremely unfair to both of you. I've been unfair for a long time. Too long."

I wasn't about to argue with that.

"Rochelle's in France. For school." He held out his phone. "I just bought a plane ticket."

I stared at the boarding pass. "Ashton..."

"I have to do the right thing, in person." He also stared at his phone. "I don't want to be the jerk who left a girl hanging again."

"Okay."

He lifted his eyes to meet mine. "I'll be back soon."

"Okay."

"Dev." He pulled me close and I relaxed into him, reveling in the feel of his arms around me. His fingers in my hair. His heart beating against me.

I wanted to hold on forever.

"I have to go," he whispered. "I can't miss this flight."

SHINE

Chapter 15

"You're awfully quiet," Blair said at my locker Monday morning. She'd slicked back her hair with a plaid headband, so her eyes looked enormous. And all the more penetrating. "Anything you need to tell me?"

Two could play at that game. "I could say the same about you. I tried calling yesterday. Where were you?"

Her cheeks turned pink. "Ty and I went to the zoo."

My mouth dropped. "And you didn't text me?"

"I forgot to charge my phone."

This was suspect. Blair was never without a fully charged phone and a battery pack to keep it that way.

I studied her face. "Are you keeping secrets from me?"

"Of course not." Her eyes shifted from side to side. "I'm telling you now, aren't I?"

All kinds of shady.

"So, what's going on?" I asked.

"He bought me blue cotton candy and a stuffed giraffe. I named her April."

"Cute." Then it dawned on me. *"Ty?"*

She huffed out a breath. "It's not a big deal."

"Not a big deal? That's a nickname. Nicknames are special." My suspicions grew. "What else happened?"

Her cheeks turned crimson.

I gasped. "Did he kiss you?"

She nodded, her cheeks flaming.

I grinned and rubbed my hands together. "What else?"

"That's all. Pervert."

"Whatever. You're totally a freak."

She smirked. "I'm saving my freak side for our second date, I'll have you know."

I raised my eyebrows. *"Second* date? Hey now!"

"We're going to the aquarium. Should be a nerdtastic time."

"Blair, that's awesome. I'm so happy for you."

"Don't book the temple yet. Speaking of, I hope you went to church or something yesterday, because that dance Saturday night was downright sinful!" She fanned herself. "Have you recovered?"

"Well, get this..." I told her about Ashton's plans.

"I'll be damned. It almost justifies you giving him another chance."

I looked down.

With a gentle smile, she shook her head. "You're totally giving him another chance."

"Is that bad?" I asked in a small voice.

"Well, to give him credit, it's romantic as hell that he's doing this because he wants you that much. I just don't want you to get hurt again."

"That summer was like a dream. I have to see if it was real."

"Before Saturday night," she said, "I would have been a real hard-ass on you. But since this thing with Tyrell? I get it. I don't understand it, but I get it." She shrugged. "Love just kinda happens."

I regarded her flushed cheeks. Her sparkling eyes. The smile that she tried to tamp down. "You said *love*."

She rolled her eyes. "You know what I mean."

Yeah, I knew. But that didn't stop me from thinking she might be actually falling for this guy.

Chapter 16

Thursday evening, I settled in to study the wonders of the electromagnetic spectrum. The doorbell rang, but I ignored it. It was probably a solicitor anyway. Which would make Dad happy. He loved arguing with them.

Then Mom sent me a text:

> Sum1's @ the door 4 u.

Why couldn't she text like a normal person? She and Dad were the only people I knew who used shorthand like that.

I texted back:

> **Who?**

Mom:

> **A q.t. pie**

A jolt zinged through me. Because no effing way. There had been no trace of Ashton since Saturday after the dance. Why was he here now?

Mom:

> **Want me 2 send him away?**

Me:

> **Be right there**

I pulled on my zip-front hoodie and brushed my face with powder, then headed to the living room.

The jolt turned to a rush of adrenaline when I saw Ashton *standing in my house*, looking rumpled and travel-worn in a pullover hoodie and jeans. His hair stood up all over his head, like he'd been running his fingers through it over and over.

I wanted to run to him. I wanted to freeze in place. I wanted to throw myself into his arms, and I wanted to hide away.

"Can we go somewhere and talk?" he asked. "Please?"

I was rigid with tension. Then I took a deep breath and nodded. "Okay."

Dad, who had probably been gearing up for a fight with a salesman or whatever, cleared his throat. "Don't be too late."

"We'll be back before ten."

"Where are we going?" I asked Ashton once we were in his car.

"It's a surprise," he said. Then he switched on the radio. Heart pounding, I settled back and listened to the DJ wax poetic about "no money down, six months same as cash" furniture.

"How was your trip?"

"Let's put it this way," he said. "I'm glad it's over."

"That bad?"

"Truth? All I wanted was to be back here with you."

He knew the right things to say, that's for sure. My guard slowly slipped away. "Did you come straight from the airport?"

He nodded. "I'm exhausted."

"You didn't sleep on the plane?"

"Couldn't."

We drove for an hour, the sun setting in a swirl of fiery cotton clouds as we raced along the highway. "My second favorite time of day," I said.

"I know," he said. "Sunset girl."

I let the nostalgia wash over me. "You used to call me that."

"I know," he said again.

I didn't say anything else the rest of the ride. Just watched the sky put on one of its spectacular autumn shows before the night took center stage.

"You probably figured out where we were going by the signs," he said as we pulled into a parking lot.

"The planetarium? Yeah, I did. Why are we here?"

"I had a feeling you'd love it here."

"I do," I said quietly.

So now my palms were sweating...as he made his way around the car and opened my door. As he reached out his hand and helped me out, giving me the most heartbreakingly beautiful smile.

"What's going on?" I asked in a shaky voice.

"Do you trust me?"

"To be honest? Not really."

His face softened as he looked into my eyes. "Can you trust me for the next five minutes?"

I wanted to. "I'll give it a shot."

"Ah, Mr. Edwards! Welcome!" A tall, wavy-haired, pale-skinned guy bounced from behind his desk to shake Ashton's hand. "Everything's ready! Right this way."

"Ben. Dude." Ashton shook his head as we walked. "Too much."

"I'm being professional," Ben said, then he winked at me.

Ashton turned to me. "This dork is my best friend, Ben."

I raised my eyebrow. "Your best friend works at the planetarium?"

"Indeed, he does," Ben said, his dimple deepening as he grinned. "He's also a lifeguard and a barista."

"And he talks about himself in third person way too much," Ashton said.

"You work three jobs?"

"Acting lessons don't pay for themselves," Ben said. "You must be Devon. I've heard a lot about you."

"Oh no."

"Good things. I promise. Anyway," he said, making a gesturing motion, "the Star Theater. It's all yours for the next hour."

Ashton tried to slip Ben some cash, but Ben pushed it away. "You know where I am if you need anything."

"Thanks, man." Ashton took my hand and led me into the dark theater.

I'd been here many times. Of course I had. But tonight was different. No parents. No strangers. No classmates and no astronomy professor. Only the domed ceiling, the reclining seats...and us. Ashton and me.

The lights turned down and the stars turned up.

"What is this?" I asked, my voice trembling.

"It's the sky from the night we met," Ashton said.

I whipped my head around to stare at him. "What?"

"That night, Devon. I'd never met anyone like you, and I don't think I ever will. My life changed. Did yours?"

I swallowed. "It did."

"All I can think about is what we had, how perfect it was, and how I messed it up." He looked up. "I watched the stars every night because they reminded me of you."

"The whole time we were apart?"

"The entire time."

We stood quietly, staring at the ceiling, my mind reeling.

"France was a shitshow," he said. "I mean, it absolutely sucked. But it was also the easiest thing I've ever done, because I knew you were here."

"Even though we're not a sure thing."

He nodded. "I had to do the right thing. It was never fair to Rochelle, because I couldn't let you go. I never let you go."

"So now what?" I asked softly.

With shaking hands, Ashton took mine in his. "I want to be with you. I can't think of anything I want more than that."

My first emotion: numbness. Or maybe denial. I'd been waiting for this for so long that I didn't even know how or what to feel right now. Could I trust him? Was I willing to try?

Second emotion: fear. Because letting him in right now meant the chance of more heartbreak. I wanted to believe I was strong. But I had a feeling he was going to test that strength, and I wasn't sure if I was ready.

Third emotion: relief. It was done. No turning back from that. It was done and he was here and he was right now. And I loved him. No turning back from that, either.

"I'm so scared you're going to hurt me," I admitted.

He nodded, catching his lower lip between his teeth. "I did a lot of things wrong. I know this. You have every right not to trust me, and I wouldn't blame you one bit. But I know this, too: I don't want to be away from you anymore."

He wasn't lying, not with the desperate hope I saw in his eyes.

"I want you to be happy," he said. "I think I can make you happy. If you'd just give me another chance."

It would be so easy right now to let go of the past and let him in again, 100 percent, no-holds-barred, full-on relationship. And I wanted to.

But something told me to guard my heart a little longer. "I'll think about it."

The expression on his face...This look of trying to be strong but barely holding on. It almost broke me.

He nodded quickly. "That's more than fair." Then he brushed a curl behind my ear. "Is it okay if I hold you?"

I took a step toward him. "Yes."

He slid his arms around my waist and pulled me close. We stood there, the two of us clinging to each other, bathed in a sea of stars. Heartbeats in sync. Breathing in sync.

Our eyes locked. Long, torturous seconds passed while we stared at each other. He reached up to caress my cheek, looking at me like he couldn't look long enough. Like he could never look long enough. Then my hands were clutching his hoodie, pulling him closer, closer, closer. My eyes fluttering shut.

Our lips came together in a collision of breath and salt and skin. Stars and galaxies and entire universes. And I was falling into him. His passion and his hunger and his heat, consuming me and mirroring my own. We were a supernova, expelling all our layers, clinging to the core of us.

"Devon." Again and again, he said my name. A mantra between breaths. "Devon."

I ran my fingers over his flushed cheeks, over his trembling mouth. He closed his eyes and planted small kisses in the hollow of my neck. A moan escaped my lips, and his arms tightened around me. *Closer, closer, closer.* Breathless, he leaned his forehead against mine and we stood together, gasping. Shaking. Wanting.

"Ashton," I whispered. My own prayer.

He let out a shuddering breath and buried his fingers in my hair. "God, I missed this. I missed you."

"Then don't leave again."

"I'm not going anywhere," he whispered against my lips. "Promise."

I put my hand on his chest. "I still don't trust you."

"I know."

"And I still don't forgive you."

He twirled one of my curls around his finger. "I wish more than anything I didn't mess up that summer, but I'm excited to spend time with you again." His voice lowered. "Kiss you again."

Just don't hurt me again.

Chapter 17

Ashton was waiting at my locker the next morning. "Happy Friday! I got you tea. Or should I say 'syrup'?" He grinned. "Three sugars, three drops of honey?"

A goofy smile spread across my face, then I took a sip. "It's perfect. Thank you. I can't believe you remember how I like my tea."

"I remember everything about you."

"Oh no." Blair's groan came from behind me. "Don't tell me you're going to be one of those super-sickening mushy couples."

Now Ashton's eyebrows were raised. Then he smiled and turned to Blair. "I would love it if Devon and I became one of those ooey-gooey whatever-you-said couples."

We stopped outside homeroom. "This is me," I said.

Blair stepped close to Ashton. "Listen up. The second you turn my best friend's smile upside down, I will knock your ass back to the beach where she met you."

Ashton stared blankly at her. "Okay."

"I mean it. You hurt her again, you answer to me. And you won't like what I have to say."

"Oh my God. Come on." I yanked her into the classroom. "See you later," I said to Ashton.

He kissed his fingertips and pointed them toward me, then headed down the hall.

"I can't believe you threatened him," I said to Blair after we'd gotten settled.

"Do you even know who I am? Of course I threatened him. It's because I love you."

I squeezed her hand. "And I appreciate it. But you might have scared the crap out of him."

"If that scares him then he's not worth the floor you walk on, Devvy."

"I know."

She pulled out her compact. "You're happy now. I like that. For all our sakes, I hope you stay that way."

"Blair is a piece of work," Ashton said in his kitchen that afternoon.

"She's my best friend."

"No one's ever talked to me that way before."

I watched him closely. "Does it bother you?"

He shook his head, his expression thoughtful. "It did at first. But it's not like I don't deserve it."

"Well, I'm not going to argue with you there."

He grabbed an orange from the fruit bowl and rolled it back and forth across the counter. "Thanks for coming over."

"Thanks for inviting me." I looked around. "I still feel weird here. Your parents—"

He tossed me the orange. "It's my home, too, and you're my guest. Okay?"

"Okay."

"So." He ran his fingers through his hair. "We probably have a lot to talk about."

I raised my eyebrow. "Probably?"

"Definitely."

"Good afternoon." Ashton's mother entered the kitchen, her navy suit perfectly pressed, her ivory skin silk smooth, her blue eyes like glass. "I didn't realize we were having company."

"Mother." Ashton stood up straight, and his hand clasped mine. "You remember Devon."

Her lips curved into a polished, political smile, but the way she clutched her pearls betrayed her. "Of course I do. How are you, dear?"

"I'm well, thank you."

Ashton didn't seem to mind the buckets of sweat pouring from my palm, so I let out a breath and tried to relax.

"That's wonderful to hear." She turned to Ashton. "I need to speak with you. In private."

He stood like a wall. Immovable. "You can't say what you need to right here?"

"It's quite sensitive." She turned that political smile on me. "I'm sure we wouldn't want to bore Devon with it."

With an apologetic look, Ashton squeezed my hand and then joined his mother outside the kitchen. I could hear a few whispered snatches—it did not sound like a fun conversation. Nor was I having fun, standing there feeling all awkward and gawky.

I returned the orange to the fruit bowl. My appetite was gone, anyway.

By the time they came back, I'd managed to compose my face into (I hoped) its own political smile.

"Make yourself at home," Mrs. Edwards said to me. To Ashton, she threw a look that clearly said, *This isn't over.*

Ashton stiffened, then grabbed my hand again. "Let's go upstairs."

"Is everything okay?"

"Is it ever?"

Ashton's room was more like a suite. There were two sections—a sitting area with a squishy love seat, a leather recliner, and a huge TV, and a sleeping area with a cozy-looking bed.

A sleek silver laptop sat closed on his desk, next to a mug full of pens and a bowl filled with M&M's. His room was so tidy, almost sterile. No knickknacks. No toppling mountain of laundry, no shoes scattered all over. But there were photos everywhere. Beaches and landscapes and sunsets. Pictures of his horse and those mean swans from his garden. The only thing missing from the photos was people.

I picked up a photo of a towering mountain. "You took this?"

"I took all of them."

I looked around again. "They're stunning."

He shrugged. "They're okay."

"No, this is more than okay." I turned to look at him. "I knew you took photos. But, Ashton, you're super talented."

"I have fun."

"This kind of fun could make you rich." I paused. "Oh wait."

"Ha ha," he said with a smirk, which then slid away. "I can't really pursue it, anyway."

"Why not?"

He pointed to himself. "Family business. It's all on me someday."

Oh right. Of course. A lot of people at school had to deal with that. No matter what they wanted, their futures were already mapped out and tied up with family expectations and reputations. At least I had the freedom to make my own choices, as long as I was willing to work for them.

Ashton dropped his book bag and sank into the recliner. Then he looked up at me. "What?"

"Are you going to get in trouble?"

He shrugged. "It doesn't matter."

"Except it kind of does. Should I be here?"

"Of course you should be here. You're my guest. You're my *girlfriend*."

I held up my hand. "Whoa."

"Eventually," he corrected. "I hope."

"But I don't want to be ripping your family apart."

"You won't. Once they see how important you are to me, they'll come around."

"Do you really believe that?"

A long pause. "I'd *like* to."

I studied another photo. "What did you do when we were apart? Besides the girlfriend thing?"

"Mostly scrambled around trying to get my shit together, failing, and then giving up. Over and over and over."

I looked over at him. "Elaborate."

"Not much to tell, really. Spent a lot of time playing catch-up at school. I'm not that keen on going to class."

So I'd noticed.

He shrugged out of his blazer and tossed it onto his desk. "I struggle a lot with my grades. It's one of the many reasons my father wants to send me to military school. Preston is the last resort. If I embarrass him there, I'm done."

Here's what I couldn't understand: If Preston was his last resort, why did he keep skipping school? Why didn't he seem to take it seriously?

Ashton picked up one of the photos. "The one good thing about boarding school was that we took a lot of trips. Something about broadening our horizons or something. I saw some seriously impressive things. I met cool people, ate awesome desserts. Took a lot of pictures." He handed me the photo. "This was my favorite."

A distinct temple. Tall trees. A stunning sunrise. "Your school took you to Angkor Wat?"

"Oh my God, Dev. I've never seen anything like it. It was incredible."

"It looks like it." I set down the picture. "You know what's even more incredible? How much I need your bathroom right now."

"Right through the closet."

"Thank you."

Ashton's closet was twice the size of my bedroom and perfectly organized. Preston blazers, all in a row. Suits arranged by color. Shoes arranged by style and season. And then the bathroom. Double sinks. Huge soaking tub. One of those rain showers with the big flat heads. And there was his cologne. Ashton's scent, right there in a bottle. I picked it up and inhaled. Fresh, like rushing river rapids. Like grass waving in the wind.

Like him.

It was while I was drying my hands that I noticed the medicine cabinet was ajar. I shouldn't have been snooping, but I couldn't help glancing inside before I closed it.

So. Many. Pills.

One. Two. Three. Four bottles. I nudged the cabinet open farther and studied the labels. They were all his. I didn't recognize the names of the drugs, but they all had multiple refills. What could he need so much medicine for? Was he okay? Then I stepped back, ashamed. I shouldn't be prying. He'd tell me in his own time. *If* he told me at all.

"Hey, Dev, did you fall in?" Ashton called.

I jumped and barely stopped myself from slamming the cabinet shut. Then I burst out of the bathroom.

"I hope you sprayed some air freshener," he said, smirking.

My cheeks grew hot. "I did not go number two!"

Laughing, he grabbed my hand and tugged me so I tumbled into his lap. When our lips met, my body came alive with tingles that made my heart pound.

Pills completely forgotten.

I slid my hand under his shirt and rested it on his warm, smooth skin. He planted gentle kisses in the hollow of my neck, making me shiver. I moaned as our lips met again. And again. And I was lost. Lost in the thrill of this deep, passionate kiss. Lost in the way his fingers slid under my blouse, stroking my waist and tracing my belly button. Lost in the way he expertly explored underneath my bra.

Amazing that a kiss could erase all doubts and trepidation from my mind, at least for a moment. Amazing that my body responded completely opposite to what my brain would suggest...if it were working.

Amazing how a kiss could completely stop my brain from working.

For at least an hour we made out, touching each other, breathing each other. Thrilling each other. I didn't want it to end. I wanted to stay forever in this recliner, in his arms, in this universe we'd created. So much could happen, and I kind of wanted it to.

No.

Not yet.

"Wait." I pulled away and put my hands on his chest. "It's too fast."

He wrapped his fingers around mine. "Sorry."

Breathless, I leaned my forehead against his. "We really should take our time. But sometimes—"

"I know. I just want everything to be okay with us. I'll do anything to make it okay."

"You can start by being completely open with me."

"Okay."

"And I'll be honest with you." I nibbled my thumbnail. "I looked in your medicine cabinet."

He flushed. "So you saw my pills."

"I'm sorry. The door was open and I—"

"It's fine. Maybe it's better you saw them."

"Will you tell me about them?"

He hesitated, looking down, then met my eyes. "Remember when I told you I was dealing with stuff?"

I nodded.

"The medicine helps me deal."

"Elaborate," I said for the second time.

He sighed and trailed his fingers lightly down my back. "I don't want to scare you away."

"You won't. Unless you're a serial killer or a rapist or a pedophile. Are you any of those things?"

"What the fuck, Devon? Of course not."

"Okay then. Tell me."

He did one of his slight nods—as if he'd made a choice. His final answer. "Sometimes I get depressed."

"Like, really sad?"

"It's more than that." His eyebrows furrowed. "It's like having this big black weight constantly pushing down on every part of you. Everything is dull and dark and scary. And you feel helpless because you can't stop it. Outside, you're pretending you're okay, but inside you're screaming." He sat for a while, that faraway look on his face again. "No one hears because you're too ashamed to say it out loud. Because saying it out loud makes it real." He stared at me then, his expression solemn. "And you don't want that to be real."

I'd been hurt. I'd been sad. But I couldn't fathom the depth of feeling pain like that. And I hated that it happened to him. "I'm so sorry."

"I hate it, which is why I take the medicine, even though I hate that, too."

"How long have you been taking it?"

"It feels like forever. I don't like needing it."

"But why? If it helps you, that's a good thing, right?"

"Not everyone thinks so. They think people like me are unstable. Irrevocably fucked up."

I tried to catch his eye. But his eyes darted back and forth, looking everywhere but at me.

"I'll never think that," I said. "What about you?"

He was quiet for a long time. Then: "I hope you don't run away, now that I've dumped all that on you." His tone was light, but there was a strain around his mouth that hinted he wasn't joking at all.

"You didn't dump. I asked. And even if you weren't okay, *I'm* not going anywhere. Are you?"

"What do you mean?"

"Are you going to let this come between us? Because if so, then I should know now. I'm not waiting around to be dumped again."

"I told you, Dev. I'm not leaving. Not again."

"Okay."

He stared at me. "You don't believe me."

"No. I won't for a while. But I'm here. Does that count?"

He nodded. "It does. And that's all I want right now."

After dinner, I sat at my desk.

Depression.

I typed the term into Google, and the results came up instantly. The first four sites were ads. I clicked on the fifth: National Institute of Mental Health. The site listed five different types. I scrolled down to the SIGNS AND SYMPTOMS for clinical depression.

> Fatigue
>
> Feelings of worthlessness or guilt
>
> Diminished interest or pleasure for almost all
>   activities
>
> Suicidal thoughts

I tapped my desk, thinking. A few things came to mind.

Especially the first time Ashton and I had gone to his family's beach house. His parents weren't supposed to be there...but they were. Which meant awkward introductions and trying to cover up that Ashton and I had been looking for a place to be alone so we could make out...and maybe more.

Eleanor Edwards was tall and had a presence that demanded respect. Tristan Edwards was broad and imposing, with tan skin that suggested loads of business deals done on golf outings. They were handsome, in a severe, old-money kind of way.

They scared the crap out of me.

But what was worse was how much Ashton changed around them.

My playful, passionate boyfriend turned into an uncomfortable, formal young man with ramrod straight posture and a mouth that couldn't smile. His father seemed to go out of his way to put Ashton on the spot—warning him about straying away from his set path, almost threatening him if he even *thought* otherwise. His mother studied both of us, her eyes narrowed over the rim of her wineglass. Still, her voice was pleasant enough when she asked me about the things I was interested in. She seemed charmed by how Ashton and I met. She seemed to even like me a little.

But Ashton seemed a shell of himself. He answered questions mechanically—until he talked about me. He lit up in a way that made his mother's eyes narrow even more.

I thought he'd go back to normal when we were alone again, but instead he stayed pensive. "Can you believe it's always like that?" he'd asked.

And then he said something that should have scared me at the time, but I'd been too caught up in our romance to notice:

"I can't imagine living the rest of my life like this."

God. How did I not see it?

I didn't know much about depression. I didn't know if it came on suddenly or if it was a gradual thing. Was it different for everyone? How come some people seemed to function okay with it, but it brought others to the brink of death? Or beyond? And where was Ashton on that scale?

I didn't know what to think. Was I getting in over my head? What did this mean for me and our relationship? Did it mean anything? Did it matter? Because God knows I was falling for him again.

I sat on the floor and took deep, calming breaths. Things were different this time. They were new and wonderful. Everything would be fine.

Chapter 18

"HORSEBACK RIDING," ASHTON ANNOUNCED AFTER I CLIMBED into his car Saturday morning. "I can tell you've been stressed. I think this will relax you. Plus, I want to show you what I do when we're not together."

What I saw at Bishop Stables made me feel out of my element, with my minimal riding skills.

Expert riders sitting astride marching, shining horses, some hunched over and racing around a track. Other riders straight and proud, jumping with their horses over what looked like hurdles or fences. One body, one motion. Spellbinding.

"Equestrian." Ashton pointed out the jumpers. "And dressage over there."

I blinked. "Those horses are dancing. Why would someone teach a horse to dance?"

"It's how horses were trained for the military a long time ago."

"Have you ever done dressage?"

He laughed. "Not really my thing. Give me a trail and nice weather and I'm good."

I looked down at my jeans, white blouse, and black Converse. "Should I have worn boots?"

"I'll grab you some before we start riding." We stopped at a stall inside the whitewashed stable. "First, I want to introduce you to Leander."

A chocolate-colored horse with a white muzzle regarded me with big brown eyes before gently nudging Ashton's hand. Ashton opened his palm, revealing a large sugar cube that vanished between Leander's enormous jaws.

"He's gorgeous," I said. "Can I pet him?"

"He'll love it."

I stroked Leander's silky face. "He's got a sweet tooth, like you."

Leander blinked and bumped me with his nose.

"He's a gentle guy, but you have to let him know you're the boss," Ashton said quietly. "Don't let him push you around."

"Okay." I planted my feet and refused to sway when Leander bumped me again.

"Good," Ashton said, his voice full of affection. "I really want you to like each other. He's my best friend in the world."

"Should I be jealous that I'm number two in your life?"

"Number three. You forgot about Ben," he said with a wink.

"Smart-ass."

He flicked my hair. "I arranged to have Maisie saddled up for you. She's smaller and extremely gentle. Great for beginners."

I'd taken the mandatory class at Preston when I was a freshman, but that had been so long ago. I didn't mind having the mare at all.

"That's her right there."

I gasped at the sun-dappled horse grazing in the pasture. "She's all white! Ashton, she's stunning!"

"Let me get you a helmet and some boots," he said, smiling. "I'll be right back. Then we'll go on the trails."

It was a stunning fall day, a last hurrah before the cold set in. The leaves burst off the trees in fiery reds and oranges. The bright-blue sky stretched on for days, the breeze a warm caress. I inhaled deeply, taking in the friendly scent of fresh air and horse.

Maisie chewed some hay and looked bored, but Leander watched me with big brown eyes. I kept petting his nose, then I leaned my head against his, letting out a sigh. I could see why Ashton loved this horse so much. Leander's very presence was relaxing.

Ashton handed me a hot-pink helmet. "You two are getting along really well."

"I like him. But Maisie won't have anything to do with me."

"She's just shy. Come here, baby girl," he said to her, clucking his tongue. She walked right over to him and gently nudged him. "Would you like to meet Devon? She's the girl I've been telling you about. She's going to take you on the trail today."

This time Maisie nudged *me*.

"See?" he asked. "Told you she likes you."

"I like her, too," I said, smiling. "And I like *you*."

He kissed me then, his lips as gentle as that warm breeze. Sweet and lingering...and interrupted by an impatient head bump from Leander.

"I guess it's time to hit the trail," Ashton said, laughing. "Ready?"

I pulled on the tall black boots. "Ready."

"Then let's ride." He put his hand on my back. "I'll help you up."

Yikes. I'd forgotten how high I'd be sitting. The ground seemed miles away, and my head spun. I had to take a few deep breaths when I settled into the saddle.

"You okay?" he asked me once he was on Leander.

I held tight to the reins. "I will be."

Once we were on the trail, I relaxed. Golden leaves floated from skinny trees as we wound our way through the woods, Maisie and Leander clip-clopping slowly on the paved roads. The scent of nature put me at ease and the gentle rocking of the horse calmed my racing heart.

"This is nice," I said. "I can see why you spend so much time with him."

"It's peaceful," he agreed. "I come here to get away from my parents. They've been fighting."

"Oh no."

He sighed. "Basically, the only way they communicate is by fighting, unless they're both pissed at me. Then they get along great. But it's been worse lately."

"Do you know why?"

"My father wants to stop paying for counseling. He thinks I just want attention. I mean, yeah, I'd like my fucking father to talk to me without ordering me around all the time, but I don't fake being depressed for him to do it. My mother thinks he should just pay the bills and get off my case."

"And what do you think?"

"I think if they stop my counseling, it'll get really bad for me. And I get scared my father is going to win that fight. He can be really loud and persuasive."

"When you say really bad, what do you mean?"

He grew quiet. Then: "My therapy helps keep me from falling apart."

A monarch butterfly landed on Maisie's mane, flapped its wings once, then flew off again. "Do you feel like you're falling apart, Ashton?"

He looked down and waved his hand, like he was throwing the subject away. "What scares you?"

"I get scared you're going to hurt yourself," I admitted.

"Dev. I'm fine. Really." He tugged at his collar. "Tell me something about you."

I stared down at Maisie's mane. White as snow, glowing

brilliantly against the gold that surrounded us. "I'm afraid of failing. I have all these goals, and I worry that all my hard work is for nothing...because what if I don't make it?"

"It blows my mind that you, of all people, worry about this stuff," he said.

"What do you mean, 'of all people'?"

"You're smart, and you work so hard. Not like me. I get to go to McCafferty because that's how it's been done in my family for generations. And then you come along, working your ass off to get what you want, while it's all been handed to me. It's not right."

Jealousy burned bitter in my throat. "You've been accepted? To McCafferty?"

He fidgeted, and his voice lowered. "As good as. Legacy, you know?"

"Is that how it is?" Dismay descended over me like a shadow. "All the spots get taken up by people like you?"

"Not all. Enough, though."

I slumped. "Is there any point in me trying?"

"Every point. They need you."

"I hope you're right," I said. "The hundred and twenty dollar application fee would scare me off if I didn't want it so bad."

He stared at me in disbelief. "A hundred and twenty dollars? To apply?"

"I guess they want to make sure they only get serious applicants." Or wealthy people who'd have no issues paying their tuition. McCafferty was the only school on my list that didn't accept fee waivers.

"Well, that's definitely you," Ashton said. "I can't think of anyone who deserves it more. And for what it's worth, I'm one hundred percent sure I'll see you on campus next year."

"We'll see, I guess. Maybe we can take some classes together."

He grinned. "That would be awesome."

We rode for another half hour, then stopped to let the horses drink from the stream and to have a snack of our own. By now the sun burned overhead, making the golden leaves glow all around us. As if we were in the middle of the sun itself.

"This is so relaxing," I said. "You come here a lot?"

"Almost every day."

"It's your sanctuary."

He spread peanut butter and Nutella on an apple slice and handed it to me. "It really is."

"Thank you for sharing it with me."

He slid his arm around me and squeezed. "You're my sanctuary, too."

"Yeah?"

"I love being around you. Makes me happy."

"Ashton, that's so sweet."

"It's the truth." He gazed at me with that tender look. "Even the first time I saw you. Remember how we met at that party? I saw you that morning, when Todd and I first arrived. You were wearing this shiny blue bikini and trying to get up the courage to get in the water. It took you forever."

I smiled. "The water is always freezing there."

He looked off into the distance. "First, you kept dipping your toes in and jumping back and squealing. Then you went for it, letting out this adorable scream when you finally got in. You were laughing so hard. Your laugh. It's like music, Dev. I swear I fell in love with you right then."

"And then you met me that night."

"I almost lost my shit when you walked up to us." He nibbled his lip. "I told my cousin I was going to marry you someday."

I handed him a Nutella-covered strawberry. "Marry me, huh? What did he say?"

"He told me to quit being a pussy."

I snorted. "Figures."

He paused, then looked at me. "I still think that, you know."

"That you were being a pussy?"

"No. Dork." He grew serious, his cheeks slightly pink. "I still think about marrying you someday."

It took a moment for the words to truly sink in. "But... Ash. I'm still figuring out what we even are right now."

He didn't even try to hide the hurt. "You're still not sure?"

"Sometimes I'm okay. Really okay. But then I remember. You said you loved me, but you left. And we're only eighteen."

"I know we're too young. But I think about it a lot. Don't you?"

I dipped another strawberry into the Nutella. "Here's the thing. I can't imagine my life without you. But marriage is so far off my radar."

"I get it."

"Did you and Rochelle ever talk about getting married?"

"No way." He shook his head. "My parents talked about it, though. It was all planned."

"You're kidding."

He grabbed the knife and started slicing another apple. "They want to get the family lineage thing squared away as soon as possible. Mother wasn't happy when I told her I broke up with Rochelle. Said I was ruining all their plans."

"Plans? Like an arranged marriage?"

"Not quite. But, yeah, in a way."

"Could they make things worse for you if you don't go back to her?"

With rapid slashes, he finished slicing the apple. "Every move my parents make has nothing to do with my happiness and everything to do with their image and growing our empire."

"But isn't growing the empire going to help you down the road?"

He handed me another peanut butter–covered apple slice. "You're determined to give them the benefit of the doubt."

"I don't want you to hate me for breaking up your family."

He rolled his eyes. "They say things like, 'What do you have to be depressed about? You're a descendent of the most powerful family in the county. You will never want for anything if you do what's expected of you.' Which means fall in line and marry *her*, and everything will be peachy keen. Except it won't."

He grabbed another apple and started slicing. "Sometimes I wish I were one of those ruthless motherfuckers who did whatever he wanted, no matter the consequences. But I'm not, so I guess that makes me a failure."

I frowned. "Do you really wish you were that kind of person?"

"It should be enough that I'm taking over the business. They shouldn't get to choose who I marry."

I absolutely agreed with that. "Why do they want you with her so much, anyway?"

"Her family is powerful. My family is powerful. A merger like that?" He let out a long, low whistle. "We'd be unstoppable."

"What *is* your empire, anyway?"

He screwed up his face, thinking. "The newspaper, the museum, the library, some of the housing developments, Preston Academy, of course, and the bank."

"All of that's coming to you?"

"Not all. I have cousins."

"Do you want *any* of it?"

He shrugged. "Here's the thing. I still want my parents to be proud of me. Even if I don't agree with ninety-nine percent of the shit they preach. Isn't that pathetic?"

"No. Of course it's not. I mean, despite everything, you love them, right?"

He went still. "I don't know."

Oh.

Wow.

Had he ever admitted this out loud? I didn't think so. Not with the hauntingly sad look washing over his face. *Good going, Devon.*

"I'm sorry. I shouldn't—"

"No. It's fine." He shook his head. "Things are complicated with my parents. I'm an only child, so all this pressure is on me. But I'm not great at school, I'm not dating the girl they want. I'm doing everything all wrong, and they don't know how to relate to me because I'm not acting how they think I should act. I can't be who they want me to be. And sometimes? I hate it. I hate *me*."

"But of course they don't hate you?"

He shrugged again. "Mother is protective of me, but I don't know if it's because of the family name, or if it's because I'm her kid, you know?"

I didn't know, either. So I didn't say anything. I squeezed his hand instead.

"And my father," he said. "His father was hard on him. I think it's the only way he knows how to be."

"Even with your grandmother?"

"I think she didn't start speaking up more in the family until my grandfather was gone. I don't remember him much. He died when I was a baby."

"God, Ashton. I'm so sorry."

He swatted at a fly. "It is what it is."

"But they're your parents."

"It is what it is," he said again. Case closed.

Since I was already tossing out the heavy hitters, I swallowed and forced out the next question. "Would you have married Rochelle?"

The sun cowered behind a thick bank of clouds. "Maybe."

His answer punched me in the gut and made my skin burn. "Did you love her?"

He fixed troubled eyes on me. "Does it matter, Devon?"

"It shouldn't. But it does."

"She and I have a lot of history. But I don't love her like I love you. I'll never love anyone like I love you."

I looked down. "That's not an answer."

"Dev, Rochelle's my oldest friend. I love her in that way. *Only* that way."

"I feel like if anyone could take you away from me, it's her."

"No. You've got me. All of me." He sat quietly for a moment, then asked, "Do I have you?"

I caressed his cheek. With a sigh, he closed his eyes and kissed my palm. And that's when I knew my answer. I'd known for a long time.

I touched my trembling lips to his. Let myself fill up on his taste, his scent, his sweet, salty essence. Whereas our kiss in the planetarium had been explosive and dramatic, this one was tender, slow, and soft. Binding and emotional and true. I felt it through every part of me, through my soul and beyond.

"Dev?"

"Yes," I whispered.

"Yes?"

"You have me. I'm yours."

He put his hands on my cheeks. "I won't let you down again."

"No. Don't do that. Don't make a bunch of promises. Not today. Just be with me."

He opened his arms so I could lean into him. "I can do that."

Chapter 19

I COULD NOT SLEEP.

Saturday night. Halloween. Most of my classmates were probably out, or just getting home. Blair was at her grandmother's for the weekend. Ashton was probably in bed. He was like me, one of those people who turned in impossibly early, even on the weekends, and woke up bright-eyed before the sun rose. Except tonight. It was almost midnight, but I was wired. I lay in bed and stared at my ceiling. The glow-in-the-dark stars had faded hours ago. My eyes were gritty, and I couldn't stop yawning, but my mind would not turn off.

I threw off the covers and grabbed my laptop. The bright monitor temporarily blinded me, but my eyes adjusted quickly. My fingers flew across the keyboard as I typed in the McCafferty web address. Then I logged in and stared at my profile.

There was another reason I lay here wide awake. It wasn't just any Saturday night. Tomorrow was November 1: The deadline to turn in my early action application.

My application, my essay, and my scholarship paperwork sat neatly in my account. My letters of recommendation, transcripts, and test scores had already been forwarded to the admissions office. Everything was ready. Everything except me.

I hadn't been able to bring myself to click the SUBMIT button. Even though everything had been vetted by Professor Trask. He'd said it was "go for launch." Yet, I was still so nervous. What if everything wasn't perfect? It *had* to be perfect.

My essay needed to be written from the heart, but not show weakness or begging. Did I outline my accomplishments without bragging? I'd agonized over every single word. I had to strike the right balance. They had to think they needed me, not the other way around.

I gave up on sleeping, grabbed my phone, and shot a text to Ashton. Unlikely he'd be up, but I needed to blow off some steam. I'd feel better, and he'd get the message in the morning.

I lay back and stared at my ceiling. Again.

The phone buzzed and I jumped, knocking my stuffed bunny to the floor. I clutched my chest as I answered. "You're up."

"I'll be there in fifteen."

"You don't have to—"

"I want to. Besides, I have something to show you."

I was so glad to hear from him. "See you soon."

I pulled on yoga pants and a hoodie, and when my phone

beeped, I padded into the living room. My parents were snuggling on the couch.

"We're watching a documentary," Dad announced. "Conspiracy theories. Project Monarch and all that."

"Why?"

"It's fascinating," Mom said. "Want to join us?"

"No, thanks. I'm going out for a bit."

Mom sat up. "So late?"

I slipped on my tennis shoes. "It's not a school night."

She studied me carefully, eyebrows raised, then nodded. "Be safe."

"I think you're in more danger than I am, watching that weird stuff."

"Don't be out too long," Dad called.

I pulled on my sneakers and headed outside, where Ashton sat in his car, his fingers dancing across his phone in that playing-a-game sort of way.

A grin spread across his face when I opened the door. "Hey, you." He shoved his phone into his pocket, then leaned over to give me a quick kiss. "I'm so glad you texted."

"I'm surprised you were up."

"Couldn't sleep."

I paused. "Everything okay?"

The grin evaporated as he rolled his eyes. "Is it ever? But this isn't about me. It's about you."

"Ashton, if you need to talk about anything—"

"I don't." He put the car in gear. "I want to show you something. It's a surprise."

I stared at him, but his face was impassive, his profile brightening and darkening as we passed the lights on the street.

"Ashton—"

He reached over and took my hand. "No. It's really okay." His shoulders relaxed. "I'm sorry for snapping."

I looked out the car window and tried to decipher where we were heading. We passed the old-fashioned soda fountain and ice-cream shop. The flower shop run by cranky Mrs. Armstrong, who thought teenagers were "hoodlums," except when it came time to buy all her corsages. The locally owned coffee shop that had a line out the door, and the Starbucks that didn't.

"We're here," he said after about thirty minutes.

A park. One outside of town. I sometimes ran here, but tonight, it was deserted. Peaceful. We walked until we got to the playground. He stopped me with a gentle touch on my shoulder. "Look up."

And wow. Above me was the Milky Way, swirling in its majestic glory, all purples and blues and hazy white clouds. Vast and sweeping, broad and infinite. Stunningly gorgeous. I drew in a breath and let the awe wash over me. This would never, ever get old.

Ashton stepped behind me and slid his arms around my waist. "I discovered this a few weeks ago when I needed to get the hell out of my head. Came here to think, and then I looked up. I knew right away I had to see this with you."

"I'm glad you brought me. I haven't seen it like this since I was a kid." Observatories, yes. Google images, definitely. But not with my boyfriend, who I was falling harder for every day. Not when his waterfall scent, mixed with the night air, helped empty my mind. Filled it instead with magic.

The sky was so clear. Only a half hour away from my house, but the park didn't have orange streetlights and trees blocking this glorious view. How did I not know about this?

He rested his chin on my shoulder. "Tell me about your first time."

I smiled. "Yellowstone. My parents took me camping. I stayed up so late staring at the sky, watching the stars move. When I got home a few nights later, I googled 'why do the stars move.' I fell down a rabbit hole and learned it was actually us moving. That's when I figured out I wanted to study astrophysics."

"Do you keep falling down these rabbit holes?"

"All the time. Did you know there are hundreds of billions of planets in the Milky Way?"

"I had no idea," he said, looking at me in wonder.

"And maybe even a trillion stars. All kinds. Lots of supernovae." I shook my head. "God, it's so beautiful."

"Do you think there are others out there? I mean, we can't be the only ones, right?"

I nodded. "And I want to find them."

"Dev, you're going to get into McCafferty. They need someone who loves this like you do."

I stiffened, then turned to face him. "If I send the application."

His forehead furrowed with wrinkles of confusion. "What do you mean *if*?"

"This is my one shot, and I'm terrified I'm going to blow it."

"Dev. You are young, scrappy, and hungry. You're not throwin' away your shot." Then he sang the last two words. "Rise up!"

I let out a small laugh. "Are you singing *Hamilton*?"

"I'm singing a variation of 'My Shot' from *Hamilton*." Serious again, he put his hands on the sides of my face and stared into my eyes. "Devon. Promise me you'll send that application."

I nibbled my thumbnail. "I'm scared."

"Why?"

"What if they don't let me in?"

"Devon, if you don't send it, the answer is already no."

"That's what Professor Trask said."

"Professor Trask is a very wise man." Ashton gently pulled my thumb away from my mouth. "Devon, do you promise?"

I let out a trembling breath, steamy in the cool air. Then I nodded. "I promise."

"Good." He brought my thumb to his lips and kissed it gently. Then he leaned close and pressed his mouth to mine, making me forget everything except him and me and the twirling stars above us.

Chapter 20

"Let's go to my house," he whispered later.

"Why?"

"I wanna make out."

"What about your parents?"

"Out of town."

I smiled and let him take my hand.

"I feel so naughty, sneaking around like this," I said once we got to his room. It was mostly dark, the only light coming from a small lamp on his bedside table.

He edged me closer to the bed. "You *are* naughty."

Our clothing rumpled. Our hair grew wild. But the kissing

was nonstop. Warm, slightly salty, all him. Deeper than a sugar rush, sweeter than candy. The best kind of intoxicating drug.

Since getting back together, we'd only made out with our clothes on, wandering fingers exploring heated skin under our shirts. Tonight, something reckless came over me, and I pulled off my hoodie and T-shirt. Then we kissed again.

"I want to see you," I said against his lips. "It's been so long since I've seen you."

Ashton sat up, his chest rising and falling with his breath. Then, with his dark eyes locked on mine, he slowly pulled off his T-shirt. I let my gaze skim over his golden body. He was thin but toned, with slight definition in his arms and abs. I ran my hand over his warm, smooth skin, then smiled.

"What?"

"You're so skinny."

He raised an eyebrow. "So?"

"You've changed. Since that summer." I traced a heart onto his arm. "I like that you're not a beefcake."

He burst out laughing. "Beefcake? Who talks like that? And you've changed, too. Your boobs are bigger."

I stared down at my chest. Leave it to him to point it out.

He drew in a breath as his eyes swept over me. "God, Devon. You're flawless."

My face grew warmer. "No way."

"Every way."

We were kissing again, his hands moving along my back, unhooking the clasp on my bra. Then his fingertips slid down my bare shoulders, taking the dainty straps with them. His lips followed, planting delicate kisses along my collarbone and shoulders, sending electricity everywhere they lingered. Then his eyes met mine again, silently asking if it'd be okay if he slid the straps all the way off.

It was okay.

We lay back down together, our kisses growing in passion and urgency. Flesh against flesh, heartbeat against heartbeat. My body aching as those kisses traveled all over my face, my neck, then back to my lips again.

"I want to touch you," he murmured. "Everywhere."

"I want you to," I admitted, then trembled.

Another deep kiss, then his fingers were dipping below my waist. He hadn't forgotten what I liked. His fingers brushing just the right spot, making my heart beat faster. Intense sensations that made my toes curl. He still remembered how to make the feelings spiral out until I was lost in a state of breathless bliss. God, *he still remembered*.

"Good?" he asked.

"Mmm."

"Like before?"

"Better."

"Good," he said again, his eyelids lowered, his smile lazy and content.

I kissed him again, then trailed light fingertips down his abs. "Now it's your turn."

"I'm finally getting sleepy," I said with a yawn later, then reached for my hoodie. "I should probably get home."

"I want you to do something first," he said. Then he led me to his desk and flipped open his computer. "Send it, Dev."

And just like that, my palms were sweating and my knees were trembling. The warm contentment from earlier was gone, replaced with stark fear.

"I get that you're nervous." He stroked my wrist. "But you'll regret it big-time if you never send it."

Why was this so hard? All I had to do was type in *McCaffertyUniversity.edu.*

Enter my username and password.

Hit SUBMIT.

But instead I froze, staring at the screen.

"I'm right here," Ashton whispered, his breath warm and comforting on my neck.

"Maybe you can do it for me," I joked, but not really.

"This is your dream," he said gently. "It has to be you."

The screen burned in front of me. "No pressure or anything."

"You shouldn't do it if you're not truly ready." Now he was stroking my arm. "But I think you are."

"Then why can't I do it?"

"Because it's a big deal, Devon. And once you hit that button, it's out of your hands. That's scary as hell."

I ran my fingertips over the slick black keys. "Event horizon."

"What's that?"

"Like you're at the edge of a black hole, and once the gravity catches you, that's it. No turning back. Have you ever felt like that?"

He nodded. "When I got on that plane to France. I knew I was going to piss off my family, and Rochelle would not be happy. But once I was in the air, it felt right. And so will this."

"Do you regret it?"

"Not one bit, Dev. I can't think of anywhere else I'd rather be right now."

I wrapped my arms around myself. Why the hell was I shaking? It was a college application. Not a big deal. Seriously.

Not. A. Big. Deal.

So why couldn't I hit SUBMIT?

"Dev, you've wanted McCafferty forever. If you don't do this, you're already doomed. Then what?"

"I'll beat myself up."

"And neither of us wants that."

He was right. I needed to get a grip. This was my dream. Time to get my head on straight and do this thing. Now.

I pulled out the leather chair and sat. Then I clicked through the uploaded documents one last time. Application. Essay. Scholarship applications. Everything was still there. I typed in Dad's Visa information—memorized by this point. Closed my eyes and said a tiny prayer. Took three long, deep breaths, and finally hit that SUBMIT button.

A white screen, a twirling gray circle, then:

Thank you for applying to McCafferty University!

And I felt...nothing. No relief. Not a drop of impending fear. Just ordinary. As if this was how it was supposed to be all along. My palms stopped sweating. My knees stopped shaking. And everything was okay.

I was okay.

Ashton squeezed my shoulder. "Now I can take you home."

Chapter 21

I HATED WHEN IT SNOWED BEFORE THANKSGIVING. THREE weeks ago, we'd been horseback riding. Now Ashton's car was slipping and sliding as he pulled up to my house after school.

I let go of the bar above the window. "I think you should stay for dinner."

Ashton swallowed. "Tonight?"

I nodded. "Mom just texted. They want you to."

His hands trembled on the steering wheel. "What if they don't like me?"

"They already love you." I brought his hand to my lips and kissed his wrist. That's when I noticed the scar. Silvery white, almost faded. Easy to miss if you didn't look too closely. I traced it lightly, then turned to him, asking the question with my eyes.

He was looking at the scar, too, his nostrils flaring with his breath. Then he shook his head. *Not now*, his expression said. His voice said, "Okay. I'll have dinner with your parents. But if I don't make it out alive, I'm blaming you."

"Come on."

Ashton looked, well . . . *ashen* as we stepped onto the porch.

I touched his cheek. "It'll be okay. I promise."

His expression indicated he believed the exact opposite of that.

"Take that, you rat soup–eatin' lowlife son of a bitch!"

Ashton froze, his hand gripping mine. "Was that your *mom?*" he asked in an urgent whisper.

"And if you attack her again, I will annihilate you and your cow!" Dad this time.

I rolled my eyes. "They're playing video games."

A look of comprehension dawned. "Makes perfect sense."

I dragged him into the living room.

Mom and Dad threw their headsets aside and smiled big ole Kool-Aid smiles. No one would ever guess they'd probably been making twelve-year-olds cry thirty seconds ago.

Mom sat there in all her hippie glory, wearing a tube top and a long flowing skirt. Dad had on a Hawaiian shirt (a Hawaiian shirt!) and cargo shorts. Because somehow, neither of them had gotten the memo that it was snowing outside.

"Well. Look who we have here," Mom said, a mischievous glint in her eyes. "The person who's been making my daughter glow like a glowing thing that glows!"

"Thank you for inviting me in, Mr. and Ms. Kearney."

Then he gave me a look like *Am I doing okay?* Of course he was. His political self was on, the epitome of perfect manners and charm.

"So." My dad cleared his throat and rubbed his hands together. "What are your intentions with my daughter?"

Mom closed her eyes and shook her head. My mouth dropped. "Dad."

But Ashton didn't seem shocked at all. "I like hanging out with Devon and getting to know her." Then he gazed at me with his soft look. "I hope we stay close for a long time."

"You're staying for dinner, right?" Mom asked. "We're having spaghetti. Unless you have a food allergy? Or restrictions? Because if you do, I can rustle up something else. Or we could order out. We're especially fond of sushi."

Ashton's mouth formed an O. "You have no idea how perfect that sounds, Ms. Kearney. I haven't had spaghetti in forever."

"Lori," she said. "I insist. And welcome to our home. We're glad you're here."

With that, Ashton's shoulders relaxed. "Thank you."

"Let me give you the grand tour." I squeezed his hand.

I tried to see my home through Ashton's eyes. It wasn't a grand, stately mansion with a million rooms. It didn't reek of old wealth, and it wasn't full of museum pieces. But it was warm and comfortable. Rich with history, like my growth marks on the bathroom wall. Like dried spaghetti noodles on the kitchen ceiling from Mom's al dente tests. And like the glitter in the carpet from last spring's BananaCon costume.

Mom's bohemian signature echoed throughout every room. Fairy lights strung along the walls, the scent of Nag Champa incense permeating the hall. Beaded curtains adorning the windows, wild green plants reaching for the ceiling, and books tumbling onto scuffed wooden floors.

Ashton's face took on a faraway, serious look as we poked our heads into the family room, the kitchen, the formal living room that we never used except for holidays or family parties.

I bumped my shoulder with his. "You okay?"

"There's so much love here. It's palpable. Like, yeah, *this* is a home."

I slid my arm around his waist. "And now you're part of it."

He fixed those mesmerizing eyes on mine. "Do you mean it?"

"Yes," I whispered, and kissed him. His lips were trembling. I touched his cheek with my thumb.

He slowed down to study my "hall of fame": school pictures from every year since preschool. "You were a very cute kid."

"Thank you. I wonder what happened?"

"You grew up to be a knockout, that's what happened." He picked up a beaded frame from a side table. "Are you wearing a Cinderella dress?"

"I was at Disney World! Of course it's a Cinderella dress."

He gave a slight smile. "Damn, that's adorable." Then his expression became solemn again. "I've never been there. To Disney World."

I squeezed him. "I'll take you someday."

He set down the frame and nodded slowly. Then he wrapped his arms around me and rested his chin on my shoulder. "I'm kinda jealous of your childhood. And by 'kinda jealous,' I mean really jealous." He pulled away slightly and picked up the picture again. "Look how your dad is looking at you. He still looks at you like that, Devon. You are literally his little princess. My parents—they never look at me like that." His mouth turned down. "They never look at me at all."

"Ashton—"

"No." And as quickly as it had appeared, his somber mood was gone. He was bright again, like a fire that burned too hot. He broke our embrace and glanced down the hall. "Show me your room."

I pushed open the door and led him inside. Then I watched as he ran shaking fingers across my desk, over and over and over. "Ashton? You sure you're okay?"

He jerked his head. "I'm fine."

He wasn't fine. The way he wouldn't look me in the eye, the way his mouth turned down at the edges, made that clear. But he was sure putting a lot of effort into trying to convince me, and probably himself.

"Wow," he said, looking around my room, his smile forced. As if the gleam of his white teeth could scare off whatever was trying to take him over. "Exactly how I pictured it. Yoga mat on the floor. Desk with a huge stack of books. Telescope. What kind of bed is that? It looks like it really wants to be a couch. I like the canopy, though."

"It's a daybed. Couch by day, bed by night. Ashton—"

"And who's this?" He picked up my stuffed bunny and nuzzled her nonexistent nose. "She looks very loved."

I sighed. "That's Honey. I've had her since I was a baby."

"She's sweet. Like you are." And then he set her down oh so carefully and gave her a gentle pat on her head.

"I wish you'd tell me if something's wrong."

"I told you. I'm fine." He pulled me close again. "Why's it smell so good in here?"

With reluctance, I let it go. He changed the subject every time, and it was starting to frustrate me. But no point in forcing him to talk when he didn't want to.

"I burn incense constantly," I said. "In fact, I'm going to light some now."

He tossed his blazer onto my bed, then walked over to the window. "Is this the telescope you saved up to buy?"

"I can't believe you remember that. I told you that forever ago."

"One of these days you're going to believe me when I tell you I remember everything you said that summer." He bent and peered through the eyepiece. "Do you use your telescope to stargaze or to spy on your neighbors?"

I laughed. "Have you seen my neighbors? Trust me, no one wants to spy on that."

"I wonder if any of them are spying on *you*." He looked up and waggled his eyebrows. "I know I would be."

"Ew."

"I'm kidding."

"I really use it to stargaze, for your information. It's a basic refractor, so I can see some cool stuff. But I really want a reflector. Or a catadioptric."

He stretched, making his shirt pop out of his pants. "What's the difference between this one and that...whatever you said?"

I pointed. "Well, with this one, I can see planets and stars, but with a reflector or a catadioptric, I could see deep space. Galaxies and nebulas and things."

"I don't even know what a nebula is, but it sounds cool." He slid his arms around my waist. "You're going to be the best scientist."

"I hope so."

"I know so. No one as passionate as you could be bad at it." Ashton was completely relaxed now, his agitation from earlier vanished. Or maybe well hidden. He moved forward, pressing me against the wall. "Now if you don't mind, I'd really like to kiss you right now."

"Only if you promise to never spy on me."

"I promise to never spy on you, stalk you, or do any other creepy things to you," he said solemnly. "My hot scientist girlfriend."

His soft lips worked their magic as the kiss grew deeper and more urgent. Wandering fingers eased under my shirt to stroke my skin and shoot bolts clear to my toes. I could taste his hunger and his passion, and it made me think reckless things.

Sexy things.

"Ahem!" Mom cleared her throat.

Ashton and I jumped apart so fast he knocked two books off my desk.

Mom threw me a knowing look. "I was coming to see if Ashton wanted something to drink, but—"

The tips of his ears flamed. "I'm fine, Ms., er...Lori."

She smirked at him. "I'm sure you are. Maybe you two should join us out here."

Faces burning, Ashton and I followed Mom to the family room.

"Sorry," he muttered.

Dad stalked in behind us and thrust a video game at Ashton. "You play?"

Ashton stared at the game, his mouth wide open. "This is *Tidal Destruction III*. But it's not even out for another month. How—?"

"That, I'm afraid, is classified."

"No, that's cool...but...wow." Ashton was all but drooling. I'd never seen him look so undignified. It was both adorable and unnerving.

"Wanna play?" my dad asked.

Ashton didn't hesitate. "Yes. Yes, I do."

"We'll leave you boys to it," Mom said, then she and I went into the kitchen. "So, your boyfriend." She gave me an appreciative look. "Dang, girl."

My face warmed. Okay, it was one thing for girls my age to fall all over Ashton. It was quite another for my *mom* to do it.

"I ain't mad at *you-ooo*," she sang, filling a pot with water.

Now I was hot all over. I could barely focus on chopping the lettuce, I was so embarrassed. "Can you not?"

"Hey, I might be off the market, but that doesn't mean I can't enjoy the selection."

"MOM!"

She was laughing. "You have got to stop embarrassing so easily. Your boyfriend is very handsome. Enjoy it."

"Believe me, I do," I said without thinking. And now I was officially on fire.

She stared at me in wonder. "You're in love with him."

I relaxed and smiled. "Madly."

She raised her eyebrows. "Do we need to talk birth control?"

"I think so. We haven't needed it yet, but ... "

She finished breaking the spaghetti, and put her arm around me. "But it's getting close?"

I was having a hard time keeping my clothes on whenever Ashton and I were alone these days. To be honest, it's not like I tried that hard. Or at all. There was something about opening up emotionally with him that made me want to open up physically. The more we shared, the closer I wanted to be to him. I was addicted to the sensation of his flesh against mine, and I wanted to feel all of him. *Getting* close? We were practically there.

A slow nod. "Yeah."

"I figured," she said. "I can tell by the way you two look at each other. And the way you two were all over each other when I walked in on you."

200

Now I was burning up again. "Sorry about that."

She squeezed me, then went to stir the noodles. "Hey, like I said. Enjoy it. Enjoy him."

"You don't think we're moving too fast?" I asked in a small voice.

"I'm your mother. You can be married with three kids and I'll think you're moving too fast. Do *you* think it's too soon?"

I started tossing the salad. "Not at all." *Not soon enough* is what I wanted to say.

"Well, if you feel ready, and you're responsible enough to handle it, I say 'your body, your rules.'"

"Does this mean I can get his name tattooed across my chest?"

She turned and stared at me, the look on her face worth every embarrassing moment I'd just suffered in this kitchen.

"Mom, you know I'm kidding, right?"

"God." She fanned herself. "You almost gave me a heart attack. Please never get anyone's name tattooed on you."

"But you said my body, my rules."

She sighed. "I'd *prefer* it if you wouldn't get someone's name tattooed on you."

"I know Mom. I love you."

Later that night, I sat at the same desk Ashton had run his fingers over.

Depression.

I'd been typing the term into Google every day since Ashton told me his diagnosis. The results were always the same:

Fatigue

Feelings of worthlessness or guilt

Diminished interest or pleasure for almost all activities

Suicidal thoughts

My hand froze. The scar on Ashton's wrist. The desperate look in his eyes when I'd noticed it. As if he wanted to disappear. As if he wanted the car to swallow him whole.

What if he'd tried the unthinkable?

I closed my eyes and took deep breaths. Then I did another search. Found a link to a site on supporting a loved one with depression. Bookmarked it.

Just in case.

Two knocks, then Mom walked in holding a little paper bag. I closed my laptop and leaned back in my chair, crossing my legs lotus-style. "What's that?"

"What we talked about earlier," she said, closing the door.

Oh right.

Mom had given me "the talk" years ago, so I knew the mechanics of sexual intercourse. What I didn't know were the other things: How did it feel? Was it scary, being so close and so vulnerable with someone?

Would it hurt?

"Condoms," she said. "Brochures. A list of websites for the things you're too embarrassed to ask me about. And if you decide to go on the pill, here's the name of my gynecologist.

You can go by yourself if you want, but I'll be happy to take you, too."

"Did you have this stuff waiting for me?"

"As soon as you started spending all that time in the driveway with him. Don't think I didn't notice those foggy car windows."

"Um…"

"And, Bun? Talk to him. If you can't sit down and have a frank discussion about sex, you shouldn't be having sex with him."

"What do we talk about?"

"What *don't* you talk about?" she countered. "Talk about everything. Birth control, your history, testing for STDs. And don't forget the logistics, like when and where, what you both like and don't like, and how much you're willing to explore together. Talk about it *all*."

That made perfect sense. "I will."

She pointed to the bag. "Look through that, and if you have questions, come to me. Okay?"

"Okay." I sifted through the bag, then I looked up at her. "It's all very serious, isn't it?"

"Damn right it's serious. I've tried to be sex-positive and open-minded with you, but I have to give it to you straight. It's a big deal when you let someone get so close to you for the first time. If you take that step, he's going to make you feel things you've never felt before. That can do a number on your head and your emotions. There are a lot of risks, and I'm not only talking about getting pregnant or STDs."

I nodded. "I know, Mom. I'm not taking this lightly. I love him. Deeply."

"I know. But it wasn't that long ago you were crying over him. I like him, but I don't quite trust him yet." She kissed my forehead. "However, I do trust you. And I hope he's worth it. You only get one first time. I want yours to be special."

Chapter 22

"MY TEACHERS HAVE LOST EVERY OUNCE OF SENSE," BLAIR groaned the Wednesday after Thanksgiving. She didn't look panicked this time. Just annoyed. "I have to come up with a budget for Home Management—like I know anything about budgeting? That's what we have accountants for. And it's not like I can slack off. The Fashion & Design Institute will be checking my grades until I graduate, so I have to do *everything*." She faded out, muttering under her breath and cursing various Preston instructors. When she got like that, it was time to step back and let the steam work itself out of her ears.

My planner didn't look so great, either. The homework would not stop coming. I spent a lot of time in the library, digging around the stacks, trying to find that certain thing that would give my projects an edge. My laptop went everywhere with me, and I was constantly making charts and spreadsheets, typing papers, even editing videos. Then there were the exams themselves. In addition to statewide testing, there were Preston's own stringent exams to pass. No, not just pass. *Ace.*

When I wasn't working on school projects, there was Yearbook. Hours sorting pictures, coming up with clever captions, laying out pages. Keeping track of orders and balancing the ledgers. It was slowly beginning to resemble an actual yearbook instead of endless blank ladders—diagrams outlining what was going in the yearbook—that looked insurmountable.

This was my legacy. It had to be perfect.

Hard.

Core.

Pressure.

And then there was Ashton. I had so much work, but let's be real. It was hard to concentrate when all I wanted to do was rip his clothes off.

I craved him. Constantly. Closing my eyes and losing myself in the scent of him, the feel of him. His deep, deep kisses. That delicious thrill when he unbuttoned my shirt, then trailed tiny kisses all over my chest and down my belly. His skin against mine after I slid off his shirt and tossed it to the floor. The questioning look in his eyes as his fingers stroked beneath my skirt, wordlessly asking if it was okay for him to explore more. And, finally, I craved the shiver that came after I told him yes.

"Earth to Devon." Blair waved her hand in front of me.

"Did you want to come over after school today? Model some dresses for my portfolio?"

"Oh man. I'd love to, but I already have plans with Ashton."

"Sexy plans?"

My face got hot. "Maybe."

She shook her head. "You have it bad."

She had no idea.

After school, Ashton and I rushed up to his bedroom, as we often did. Lay in his bed and kissed until our lips were swollen. Let our fingers start to wander to those secret places. But this time, I stopped him before we got carried away. "We should talk," I said breathlessly.

Talking was the last thing I wanted to do.

"This sounds ominous," he said against my mouth, his eyes half-closed. "Is everything okay?"

"Actually." I touched his bottom lip. "I don't know."

His eyebrows drew together. "What's going on?"

I flipped his hand so the silvery line on his wrist showed. "I need to know. Did you...?" The words caught in my throat.

He didn't say anything for a long time. And then... a slight nod.

I squeezed his hand. Hard.

"It happened that summer," he said quietly. "Our summer. I used a razor blade. My mother found me."

Our summer...

"My parents took me away. Stuck me in a hospital." He stared at his lap and lowered his voice. "That's the real reason I didn't get to tell you good-bye."

I swallowed, then brought his wrist to my lips. Tried to stop from shaking. I loved being right as much as the next person, but I hadn't wanted to be right about this. Never this.

"Why did you do it?"

"I don't even know how to explain it, Dev."

"I just... I want to know. I want to know *you*."

He rubbed his face while he found the words. "I call it the Dark. It's always there, sleeping right under my skin. Most of the time I can live with it. I don't like it, but I deal. But then something happens to wake it up. And when it's awake, I want to rip my skin off." He gripped a handful of his hair and yanked. "That night? I was already upset the summer was ending and I wouldn't get to see you all the time. Then my parents forbade me to see you at all. Like, ever. So by now, the Dark was roaring. Asking me why I couldn't ever do anything right. Telling me I was the worst person ever, since my parents were always pissed at me."

"Oh my God, Ashton." I put my hand on his cheek.

"It just keeps going, telling me how I'm a loser. Making me wonder why the fuck I'm even wasting space here." He squirmed. "That night, I knew that no matter what choice I made, someone was going to be upset. I knew it would make you cry. I couldn't bear it. So..." He drew in a breath. "I decided I was a shitty person. And shitty people don't deserve to live."

"You're not shitty, Ashton. Not even a little bit."

He shook his head. "The Dark doesn't care about that stuff. And I was desperate. I slit my wrists to get it out so it would finally leave me alone. Even if it meant I had to die."

He'd talked about the darkness inside him before. And I'd seen hints of it. Him going inside himself. His mouth a straight line as the thoughts took over. But then he'd turn to me and smile brightly enough to convince me everything was okay.

But his darkness was bigger than I'd imagined. He thought of it as an actual *entity*, something that could consume him. Completely.

"Do you still think about…doing that?" I couldn't bring myself to say the words. Saying it would make it real, and it felt real enough already. "Does the…is the Dark still trying to consume you?"

"Dev…" He buried his face in my neck.

"Is it?"

He nodded slowly. "Yeah."

"Ashton." I wrapped my arms around him. Closed my eyes and tried to swallow the fear.

"My counselor calls it 'suicidal ideation,'" he said. "I think so much about death, and how much better off everyone would be if I were gone, that it feels like a part of me. It's like a reflex. I don't even know I'm doing it half the time."

I squeezed him tighter. "How serious are these thoughts? I mean, I know they're serious, but…"

"I don't have plans to go through with it. Not anymore."

Not anymore.

"Do you promise?" I bit my lip to stop it from trembling. "I don't want to lose you."

"I promise."

I studied his face for hints that he was lying. But he looked normal. Whatever *normal* meant.

I wasn't so sure anymore.

"I messed up on so many levels that summer," he said, his fingers drumming the bed. Moving so quickly they blurred. "But leaving you like that? I'll never forgive myself."

"Ashton. We've worked through that already."

"I should've tried harder to find you."

I grabbed his hand. Intertwined his fingers with mine until they stopped jerking. "You were in the hospital."

"There was no excuse. I went with what was easy instead of what was right, and that whole time, I never stopped loving you. I never stopped thinking about you, missing you, wanting you. Not even once." He sat for a bit, clenching and unclenching his free fist. Then his expression turned thoughtful. "I need to show you something."

He hopped up and went to his desk. Dug through a drawer, then handed me a book.

A photo album. "Wow, this is so old-school," I said lightly. But then my throat caught. The album had fallen open to that photo of us I loved so much. Sitting in the sand, his arm lightly around my waist. My hand on his chest. Our curved lips close, as if we shared a secret. Our secret. And then page after page of photos from that summer. Pictures of me and him, our feelings obvious in the way we filled each other's space. Pictures from the day we went to that driftwood beach and he took a billion photos of me. There were photos of the sand, the sun, the moon, the water, but most of the album was about us.

I was so in love with him then. And I was so in love with him now.

"I don't expect you to believe me," he said, "but not a day went by that I didn't wonder where you were. What you were doing. If you still loved me." He stroked my cheek with trembling fingers.

"Even when you were with Rochelle?"

"She's not you, Dev."

I kissed him. Deeply, passionately. Desperately. We kissed like the world would end if we stopped. We kept kissing until we were breathless and our hearts were beating fast. And then we kissed some more.

We pulled away slightly to catch our breath, but we stayed close, our noses touching. Our eyes locked. There was turbulence in his. And now these afternoons of making out and touching weren't enough. I wanted to take things further. I wanted to share all of me with him.

"Dev..." He undid the top two buttons of my blouse, then planted kisses against my collarbone.

"I want you," I murmured.

His head popped up, his eyes wide. Then he swallowed. "Right—right now?"

"Soon."

"You look terrified."

"I kinda am. I've never done it. Had sex, I mean."

"That's okay. We'll figure it out together. Just warning you, though—it'll probably be messy and awkward." He gave me the most adorable sheepish look.

"Messy and awkward?"

He pulled me close so I could settle into his chest. "*Mmm-hmm.* Sex is a strange thing, Devon. You sure you want to do it with me?"

"Positive."

"Good. Because it can also be an amazing thing, and I really want to share that with you." He stroked my thumb. "I've wanted to for a long time."

"Same," I said softly. "But I don't want to make bad choices because we're so caught up in the moment."

"I'll make sure we do everything right."

"*We'll* make sure," I corrected.

"Even better."

Chapter 23

"I CAN'T BELIEVE I LET YOU TALK ME INTO THIS." BLAIR pursed her lips at the SATYA YOGA sign. "We should be heading to the nail salon for our Friday ritual, and instead you're making me do this. You know my delicate skin can't handle exercise."

"But your 'delicate skin' can handle anal bleaching?"

"That was one time," she grumbled.

I pulled open the door. A small reception desk covered in plants sat off to the left, a coatrack to the right. Photos of yogis in various poses graced the walls. Sunlight streamed through windows while girls with ponytails padded across shiny wooden floors. The scent of white sage permeated the air. I inhaled deeply. So did Blair.

"Smells like someone's smoking up in here," she muttered.

I poked her shoulder. "It does not."

"Says the girl who's never smoked up."

"Devon?"

Oh God. Not her. Not in my happy place. "Hi, Auden."

Auden came out from behind the desk, bringing with her the strawberry scent of her hair. "I didn't know you took yoga."

"And I didn't know you worked here."

"Sort of work here," she said. "It's part of my seva."

"What's seva?" Blair asked.

"Selfless service. A way of giving back to the yoga community." Her smug smile. "I'm doing it as part of my teacher training."

Blair stared at Auden, a skeptical expression on her face. "You're going to be a yoga teacher?"

Auden's grin turned up to toothpaste-commercial bright. "Alongside physical therapy. School for PT is intense, so I'm getting my teaching certification now. Are you guys taking the five o'clock class?"

"I'm considering it," Blair said, her suspicious expression intensifying.

Auden beamed. "Oh, you totally should! I'm apprenticing, so I can teach you a pose." She glanced inside the studio. "I need to go set up. See you in there!" And with a toss of her ponytail, she was gone.

"Auden Cooper. A yoga teacher. Who'd have thought it?" Blair mused.

"No kidding." As we made our way into the studio, I tried to squash down a flicker of resentment. Maybe this had nothing to do with me, but my heart wasn't about to listen to reason. Auden had her shit together. I wanted to have *my* shit together.

But yoga is about being present, so I needed to try to do that. I inhaled the sage scent. I enjoyed the warmth of the sun-warmed studio. I focused on the altar, with its green cloth covering and its candles, with its statues of Hindu gods such as Shiva, the god of creation and destruction, and Ganesh, the remover of obstacles. I certainly could think of a few things I'd like removed. Such as all the stress I was currently under.

I settled on my mat and rolled my shoulders. Yoga. Mani-pedis later, and sushi for dinner. All with my best friend. Today would be good for me. It had to be.

"This seva stuff sounds like a scam, but that's just me." Blair glanced around and frowned. "I'm having second thoughts."

"Why?"

"It's weird." She pointed to the altar. "What's up with all those statues and things? And what if they make us chant or something?"

"They won't make you chant."

"Wait, you're saying there *will* be chanting? Devon?"

"Hi, everyone. I'm Serena," the instructor said in a dreamy voice. "Welcome to yoga level one. I'm so glad you're here today. Make your way into a comfortable seated position, and we will begin our practice by bringing awareness to the breath."

This was good! This was fine! I could always get behind connecting with my breath.

"Inhale deeply, allowing your stomach to expand with the

breath. Exhale smoothly, allowing your stomach to become soft."

Inhale...two...three...four.

Exhale...two...three...four.

"Envision a white light at your heart center. As you inhale, imagine that light expanding, filling your entire chest. As you exhale, imagine that light spreading out, surrounding you, like an egg."

And that's when I checked out.

The worries of the past few weeks bum-rushed my brain like a runaway train.

I'd turned in my application to McCafferty over a month ago. Had they gotten to it yet?

I'd turned in all my scholarship applications, but no word from them, either.

Auden. Sitting on a bolster next to Serena, looking confident and secure in her future. Already doing something tangible to reach her goals, while all I had was a legacy of hard work and a head full of dreams. Would it even mean anything if I couldn't get the money to fund those dreams?

Ashton. His depression. How far he went to try getting away from it.

Our love. Making love.

I didn't want to be here. I wanted to be where he was. But I needed to focus and be present, like a good yogi. Except the worry kept rushing through me so intensely I could barely lie still on my mat.

"If you find your mind wandering, allow the thoughts to

come, but don't dwell on them. Simply watch them float by, like clouds in the sky."

Too late.

Later, in the nail spa, I sank into the soft leather chair and tried again to relax.

"You know," Blair said, "I always thought meditation was a bunch of woo-woo hippie bullshit, but it really helped me today. I feel a lot better about Tyrell."

Instantly my guard was up. "Do I need to smack a bitch?"

She laughed. "No. He's just struggling with his beliefs about interracial dating while dating me. He talks in circles a lot. Like, a *lot*. And I decided that I'm going to let him figure it out on his own instead of trying to 'fix' him or whatever."

"And you're okay with that?"

"I am now! Seriously, meditation is the best thing ever." She tilted her head. "In fact, I think it could help me stop smoking."

"That would be great. I'd love it if my best friend didn't die of lung cancer."

The salon was playing Mozart. Sonata no. 11 in A Major. Rapid, bouncy piano, which usually made me hyper and totally did not match with this conversation.

"Anyway. What's got you all agitated?" A look of realization dawned. "*Ohhhh*. Auden. Of course."

I watched the nail technician smooth citrus-scented scrub on my calves. "She's got all her shit together. Meanwhile, I'm supposed to hear from McCafferty this week, and I'm freaking out. What if…?" I shook my head. I couldn't even think it.

"I know what I think should happen, but the universe doesn't always have the decency to listen to me. I wish I could tell you everything is going to work out how you want. But I can't, Devvy."

"And then there's everything with Ashton."

Her shoulders tensed. "He's fucking up already? Because I might be happy from meditation, but I can still cuss out a Rat Bastard."

"No! It's not that." I spilled everything. It felt good to get it out of my head, but now I was darn near hyperventilating.

"Look. I'm going to ask you something, and you might not like it," she said. "You have so much going on, do you really need to add Ashton's stuff to the mix?"

"I love him. And you don't give up on someone you love."

"But at what cost?"

"There's no price."

The look she gave me—a mixture of sadness, pity, and understanding. "But this is heavy stuff. I'm scared you're going to lose yourself."

I swallowed as the technician colored my toenails a soft green. Maybe I was a bit scared, too.

Chapter 24

DEFERRED.

First, there was shock. Cold blood. Icy fingers. Then there was shame. All-encompassing, consuming, burning shame. It licked through my veins, taking away all the cold and filling me with fury. All I'd talked about was going to McCafferty. Everything I'd done was to ensure my admission to my dream school, and now I was reading an email that told me I didn't get to live my dream just because I'd dreamed it.

I stalked into the living room and thrust my computer at my parents, who were playing some game where they built forts and killed people. I don't know. They stared at me with furrowed foreheads, then at the laptop screen. Mom's face fell. Dad's did, too.

"Oh, Bun," Mom said in her soothing, rich voice. "I'm so sorry."

I didn't say anything. Just stood there, fighting to keep the pooling tears from falling.

She pulled me down to sit next to her. "It's not the end of the world. There's still a chance you'll get to go to McCafferty."

It hurt to force the words past my throat. "And if not?"

"Then, frankly, it's their loss," my father said. "I can't imagine what the hell they're thinking!"

"I know, right?" I took the computer back and stared at the email.

We are writing to inform you that your application is being deferred for further review.

I slammed my computer shut. Because fuck this. Seriously.

"Didn't you apply to five other schools?" Mom asked.

I gritted my teeth. "Yes."

"And they have excellent science programs, right?"

I shrugged. "I guess."

"So you won't be selling yourself short if you go to one of those schools instead."

"But I won't get the assistantship and the specialized astrophysics curriculum. I want McCafferty." I pouted.

"And you should have McCafferty," Dad said.

"James, you are not helping."

"I feel like such a trash human being right now." I was being overdramatic, but I did not care. My dreams had just been shattered to pieces. Surely I was entitled to one temper tantrum?

"Listen." Mom held me at arm's length, her eyes fixed on mine. "I'm going to say something, and you won't like it."

Why did everyone keep telling me things I wasn't going to like?

"Sometimes what we think we want is not always what we need," she said.

I fought to keep from rolling my eyes. "I love you, Mom, but I can*not* with the hippie stuff right now."

"Devon." Dad's voice held a warning note. "I'm upset, too. But your mom is a fountain of wisdom. Maybe give her a listen."

Unfazed, she continued. "Maybe you're being pointed in a different direction. You've been so single-mindedly focused on this one school that you're oblivious to what else is out there. Maybe there's a better fit for you."

I wasn't trying to hear any of that. I'd applied to the safety schools because I had to have alternate plans. It just never occurred to me that I'd need to use them.

How arrogant of me.

The thought of rearranging the next several years made my heart ache. But the thought of going nowhere hurt even more. So now what?

I stared at Professor Trask's desk as he searched through his file cabinet. His Mickey Mouse collection had grown since the last time I'd been in here. Even his office accessories were Disney-fied. "New mouse?"

He grinned. "You like?"

221

"It's shaped like Mickey's glove. What's not to like?"

"You have great taste. Have I ever told you that?"

Professor Trask sat and handed me a pamphlet that read *Deferrals and Waitlists: Now What?* The cover featured a girl staring at a piece of paper in disbelief. Probably with the same expression I'd had.

"So, Devon. I know you're disappointed, but the first thing you need to do is realize that you're still a strong candidate. They would have flat-out denied you if you weren't."

That's what all the websites had said, but so what? "All I can think is that if I was so strong, why didn't I already get accepted?"

"Could be a number of reasons, but what's done is done and it's not going to do you any good to dwell on it."

"You're right," I said quietly. Tough love. Professor Trask was an expert at doling it out.

"McCafferty likes for its deferred students to make a case, so now you need to follow up," he said. "Write a letter to the admissions counselor spelling out your commitment to McCafferty. Talk about the professors you've researched and desire to study with, and be sure to outline the opportunities they offer that aren't offered anywhere else. Be specific about what draws you to McCafferty."

"That'll be easy."

"You're in the regular admissions pool now, which could be advantageous for you, Devon. Follow all their directions, keep studying and working hard, and most important, don't give up hope."

I stuck out my lower lip. "That part's not so easy."

"Even if so, it's time to focus on the future."

I nodded. "Onward and upward and all that."

He tapped his desk. "Get that letter written, and give it to me to look over. We're going to do what we can to get you on that campus next year. But know this: Even if McCafferty doesn't work out, you have some great options. You'll be fine no matter what."

Chapter 25

"LET'S GO STRAIGHT TO MY PLACE TODAY." ASHTON STARTED the car and pushed the button to turn on the heated seats. "The weather's supposed to get cray-cray."

I laughed. "Cray-cray?"

He grinned and switched on the *Hamilton* cast album he loved so much.

"Will your parents be around?"

"Nope. They're upstate at a fund-raiser or something, and I'm so glad they didn't drag me with them."

"Me too." Last weekend, Ashton's parents had carted him off to some boring political event downstate. He'd texted me the entire mind-numbing play-by-play of the speeches, fake conversations, and power plays.

"Would definitely rather spend my Saturdays with you," he said now, taking my hand.

"How was Happy Paws this morning?" I asked.

"Busy. Lots of people wanting to adopt." He screwed up his face. "I had to sneak time with Buddy. I really want to bring him home, but my parents would be furious."

"My parents never let me have a pet, either. Not even a goldfish."

"I don't get that. Well, I kinda do in my case. I was away at school." He frowned thoughtfully. "Just seems like all kids should have a dog or a cat or something."

"I wanted a bunny."

He looked over at me. "Bunnies are cute. Like you."

I squeezed his hand. "At least you have Leander. He's pretty awesome."

"I do love that horse. But it's not like having a dog in the house, you know? Someone who's always happy to see you no matter what. Buddy was so thrilled when I came in this morning. Especially when I gave him a new bone to chew on."

"I'm glad today was good for you. But Ash, you need a shower."

He grinned again. "What, you don't like Eau de Puppy?"

I wrinkled my nose. "Not really."

"Meh. You just don't appreciate my fine essence."

"Dude, have you smelled yourself? You are *ripe*. Did you even bother to shower before you went to the shelter today?"

He shrugged. "No."

At his house, he hung our coats in the coat closet and then we went to his room. I watched as he pulled off his clothes and tossed them into the hamper. I loved that stripping down in front of each other wasn't a big deal.

"Wanna take a whiff before I wash it all away?"

I wrinkled my nose. "No, thank you."

He made a motion as if he were going to smash my nose into his armpit. "You sure?"

"Get away from me!"

"I'll be out soon," he said, laughing.

I didn't really mind his natural scent. It was undeniably him, comforting and arousing. But no shower plus dog hair and slobber? Not so sexy.

While he showered, singing "The Story of Tonight" at the top of his lungs, I looked more closely at the photographs displayed around his room. There were new ones now. One of Buddy demolishing a ball. One of a golden full moon. And one of me from the day we went horseback riding, the sun's rays streaming through my hair and illuminating my skin. I looked ethereal, glowing. Is this how he saw me? No wonder he called me his sunset girl.

The weekend after Thanksgiving, Ashton and I had gone to the art museum. He'd pointed out a photo essay by some famous photographer whose name I didn't remember. "I want to take pictures like this," he said. "See how they tell stories?"

"I think your photos tell stories," I said, but he shook his head.

"No, mine are okay. Some of them might be good, I don't

know." He shrugged. "I want to move people, even if my picture is just a sunset or a mountain."

He was selling himself short. I could guess exactly what mood he was in when he snapped each shot. Even the ones from that summer. The early ones were bright and cheerful. Lots of sun and colors. But by the end, they were jagged glass and dark driftwood, all sharp points and edges. His newer photos were colorful again, but more muted. And that photo of me? I could hardly believe it *was* me. But it was obvious the photographer was deeply in love with his subject.

Photo tour done, I settled into the recliner with my astronomy book.

Ashton and astronomy. Both so large in my life right now. Both competing for the same spot in my brain. My body in perpetual adrenaline overload. *This isn't sustainable* constantly thrummed in the back of my mind. Maybe some spreadsheet calculating was in order. Just to make sure my priorities were in the right place.

Ashton burst out of the bathroom in a cloud of billowing steam and the waterfall scent of his cologne. His jeans fit just right and a T-shirt clung to his damp chest. His hair was dripping and dark and oh my God, yes.

"Is this better?" he asked.

"Much. Get over here." I yanked him toward me and kissed him deeply. We sank into the chair together and let ourselves get carried away. We kissed and kissed…until my stomach let out its trademark monstrous growl. We pulled apart and cracked up.

"Jesus, Devon," he said between snorts. "Let's go eat."

After lunch, we headed to the entertainment room. Ashton had a retro video gaming system, so we played old games and laughed at the cheesy graphics. "Her boobs are literally triangles," I said. "Look at that!"

"Hey, they did the best they could with what they had."

"There is nothing good about triangle boobs. Ever."

Sadly, it didn't matter that the games were old. I still sucked.

After old-school Lara Croft fell off another cliff with a bloodcurdling scream, I gave the controller to Ashton. "You do it. And you know what? I think you're so good because you own the system. You have home team advantage."

He shook his head. "Nope. You're just the worst."

"I'm not *that* bad."

He looked at me as if I were the cutest thing ever. "Yeah, you are."

"Keep on with the trash-talking!"

He threw the controller aside and tickled me until I was shrieking in delight. "Admit it," he said. "I'm the video game champion!"

"Never!"

"Then I'll never stop tickling you!"

"No!" I wiggled out of his grasp and darted for one of the luxury theater seats. He caught me, but his phone buzzed as he was moving in for more torment.

He glanced at the screen and frowned. "It's my mother. I should take this." He jumped up, already starting to pace.

After a moment, he hung up and ran to the window. "Holy shit," he muttered. "Come look at this."

I joined Ashton and had to blink several times. So much snow whipped through the air, I couldn't even see the tree right outside the window. Complete whiteout.

"You should call your parents," he said. "Tell them you won't be coming home."

"It's supposed to do this all night?"

He nodded. "My parents are staying upstate." He glanced out the window again. "I really don't want to drive in that."

I was already pulling out my phone. "On it."

"Stay exactly where you are, Bun," Mom said a few minutes later. "I don't need you risking your life out there."

"I've never seen anything like it."

"We're supposed to get at least two feet," Mom added.

"Well, we're in for the night."

"You've got food and bottled water? Blankets? Flashlights in case the power goes out?"

I looked at Ashton. He nodded.

"We have everything," I said to Mom.

"Condoms?"

"Mom."

"Do you have condoms?" she asked firmly.

"Yes!"

"Okay, then. Have a good night. Be careful," she said.

I didn't think she was talking about the snowstorm.

The atmosphere got super charged when I hung up. Ashton gazed steadily at me, his expression making my heart pound.

"Um, we should probably gather up the emergency stuff. In case the power *does* go out," I said. "Flashlights, blankets, bottled water—"

"Devon, we don't need to gather up all that stuff. We have a generator, so if we lose power, we have backup."

"I'll feel better if we have something close by. It's the Girl Scout in me."

He blinked rapidly. "You were a Girl Scout?"

"Once upon a time. Then we had to sell cookies. My troop took things way too seriously. I couldn't deal with the pressure."

He took my hand. "Let's go get all the stuff. Everything's in the mudroom. Except the blankets. Those are upstairs."

Upstairs.

"Okay."

I didn't understand why I was suddenly so nervous, but he picked up on it right away and put his hand on my arm. "It's only a blizzard. It's supposed to be gone by morning."

He had to know good and well that I wasn't shaking because of the weather. He *had* to. We were alone. In his house. Would be all night long. And he was looking so good and smelling so yummy....

Our conversation about having sex seemed like it had happened eons ago, and I was so ready to be with him. But the situation never seemed right. Too much homework. Too much parents being around. Not enough time.

But things were falling into place right now.

I hadn't woken up planning to have sex with Ashton today.

But now that the opportunity was here, I had every intention of it.

He fixed his eyes on mine and we stood there, gazing at each other. Could he tell what I was thinking? Did he have any idea that right now, my mind was filling with images of him and me, as close as we could possibly get?

He brushed a curl from my forehead. "Come on. Let's gather everything, then we can relax."

We dumped everything on the floor in the game room. Extra blankets, extra bottles of water, extra snacks. Of course snacks. I ran my finger along the edge of a pool table that was probably worth more than my mother's car. "Your house seems even emptier when it's cold outside."

"This house," Ashton said, looking around. "It used to give me nightmares. I thought it was going to swallow me." His mouth turned down slightly. "It still makes me feel so small. Like I'll never live up to what it expects from me."

"Can I ask you something?"

"Of course."

"Does depression run in your family?"

"If it does, I don't know a thing about it." He went into an imitation of his mother's clipped voice. "Such things aren't discussed."

"What do you think?"

He picked up a pen and flipped it through his fingers. "I don't know if anyone has it like I do, but I'm pretty sure it's there."

I slid my arms around his waist. Hugged him close. "Did you know that I think you're amazing?"

He squeezed me back. "No. You are."

I gave him a small smile. "There's so much you don't know."

"I know. I want to learn, though. Everything."

"Like what?"

"Does your family have any scandals I should know about?" Now he was twirling the pen like a baton.

"Well...did you know that I'm half *Black*?" I asked in an exaggerated whisper.

The laughter exploded out of him. "You are such a dork!"

"My mom's side of the family looks like a Benetton ad."

He tapped my nose with the pen. "What's a Benetton?"

"Dad told me about it. It was this fashion campaign a long time ago that showed people of all races together. Didn't see much of that back then, I guess, so it stood out."

"What about your dad's side?"

"From what I know, they're all alike. Same chestnut hair. Same blue eyes and pale skin. I haven't had much to do with them, though. I relate more to Mom's side of the family. They never make me feel like I'm less than, or that I don't belong because I'm not full Black."

"You and your mom have such a cool relationship."

"She's the best. Fiercely loyal. She never let me feel ashamed of myself when white people said I was dirty and teased me about how big my hair was, or when Black people were calling me Oreo and zebra."

The color drained from his face. "People called you dirty?"

I nodded. "Yep."

"Fuckers. Let me get my hands on them."

"I get it from both sides. The good and the bad."

He raised his eyebrows. "Your father's family?"

"Most of them flat-out stopped talking to him when he married Mom. It didn't matter that she'd been around since forever. Marrying her crossed some kind of line, I guess."

Ashton frowned. "That's terrible." He paused, then a look of sadness came over his face. "And it explains why my parents didn't surprise you."

I swallowed. "Have you ever wished I was white?"

The sadness turned to confusion. "Why would I wish that?"

"To avoid all of this"—I waved my hand around—"stuff. With your parents. Everyone. You know people have to be talking."

He fixed his eyes on me, steady. Intent. "Do you ever wish you were white?"

I thought about his question for a long moment. There were some things I didn't like about being who I was. Like wondering what people were thinking when they stared at me a little too long with downturned mouths and wrinkles in their foreheads. I didn't like being hyperaware that I was different...or being reminded of it whenever I managed to forget for a few minutes.

But there was so much good that came with being me. My awesome mom and dad. Blair. School. And there were always the stars. So wanting to be someone else? Some*thing* else? I shook my head. "I never wish that."

"Good. Because who you are? Is perfect. I hope you never forget that."

"And you're willing to put up with people's attitudes about...our kind of relationship?"

"Devon, if I have to cuss some motherfuckers out, even if I have to kick the shit out of somebody, I'll do it. I'm not going to let anyone come between us. So to answer your question: No, I don't wish you were white. I don't want you to be anything other than who you are. Because that's who I love. I love every part of your heritage and your history and your *now*."

My knees shook at the way his fingers trailed up and down my arms. The way he pressed against me. "I love you, Dev."

I kissed him then. Slow. Tender. Intense. I couldn't hold him tightly enough. I couldn't get enough of the taste of him. Slightly salty. Slightly sweet. All him. All mine.

"Dev," he said quietly, "wanna go upstairs?"

I knew what he was really asking.

"Yes."

Chapter 26

Ashton and I were kissing not even five seconds after he closed the door behind us. Ten seconds after that, my sweater hit the floor. Then my bra. His T-shirt. He pulled me close and we kissed again. The feeling of his skin against mine, his strong heartbeat, his breath—I loved it all so much. I loved *him* so much. I let my fingers slide down his chest. His abs. Then I reached down to unbutton his jeans.

He sucked in a breath and covered my hands with his. "Are you sure?"

I drowned in his deep, dark eyes. "Yes."

He led me to his bed. Over and over our lips met, possessing each other, consuming each other, overcoming each other, and it still wasn't enough. Would never be enough. I wanted . . . needed more of him. All of him.

With trembling hands, we finished undressing each other. I shivered as he looked at all of me.

"God, your skin," he said, his voice shaking. "A real, live sunset. I need to touch you, Devon."

"Do it," I breathed. "I want you all over me."

He moved his fingers lightly over my skin, sending jolts everywhere, making my breath come in short gasps. He trailed kisses down my body, taking me to the edge and withdrawing just in time, leaving me wanting. By the time he made his way back to my lips, I was aching for him.

"Now," I gasped. "Please."

He stroked my cheek with his thumb. "I'm going to go slow. I don't want to hurt you."

I nodded and watched as he put on the condom, his hands shaking.

"You're nervous," I whispered.

His eyes met mine as he moved close to me again. "Yeah."

"But you've done this before."

He put his hands on both sides of my face. "Not like this. Not when it matters so much."

His skin warm against mine. His heart pounding against my chest. His breath tickling my lips.

My body tingling all over.

"Devon," he murmured. "I love you."

"I love you, too. So, so much."

Slow and passionate, tender and warm. Sweaty flesh against flesh, sensation heightened beyond reason. His waterfall scent, his weight, his sweet, salty taste filled my senses, and there was so much of him right now...but it was still not enough. Would never be enough.

Our eyes locked as my body blossomed, little by little, to let him in more and then more. I took deep breaths, getting used to this new sensation. Getting used to moving with him. This was me and this was Ashton and this was *us*. There were no words, but I could feel him. I could feel him in a way that was beyond the physical, beyond cosmic, beyond anything I could understand or had ever experienced. And I could see him. All of him. Raw, vulnerable, naked. *Mine.*

After, we lay tangled up together, trembling and breathing hard. I didn't want to say anything and break the spell we were under, and he seemed to sense that. He traced circles on my arms, and I buried my fingers in his hair. I floated in some sort of in-between place—a land of light dreams. Still aware that his arms were around me, but also on another plane. He held me until my heartbeat slowed and the sweat on my forehead cooled. Then we lay there, looking at each other, his expression tender, tranquil. Haunting.

"Dev? How are you feeling? Are you okay?"

I trailed a finger down his cheek. "More than."

"A little freaked out?"

A small smile. "Yeah. Are you?"

"I never knew it could be so..."

"I know."

"Yeah," he said with a sigh. "It's overwhelming, how much I feel right now."

"Fragile," I said. As if the slightest movement would shatter me.

"Was it really okay for you? I saw you screw up your face when I . . . when we were first together. Did it hurt?"

"A little. At first."

"I'm sorry. I tried to be gentle."

"And you were. Really. I'm fine." I traced his lips with my thumb. "What about you? How was it for you?"

He didn't answer for a long time. I checked to see if he'd fallen asleep, but he was wide awake, chewing on his lip. "Do you ever worry that things are going so good, something's bound to come along and fuck everything up?"

I stared at him. "What? No."

"I do," he said. "Like right now. I'm too happy. It feels wrong to be this happy."

"You think we're wrong?"

"No! We're perfect. And that's why I'm so scared. The last time I felt this happy was that summer. And you know what happened then."

I traced the scar on his wrist. "Ashton, I want you to be honest with me. Are you thinking about hurting yourself?"

"I just wish the *wrong* part would go away."

"What if you focus on the best parts? About us? About tonight?"

"Okay." He intertwined his fingers with mine. Now I couldn't reach his scars. "Well," he said after a pause, "there was the part where we kissed forever. And the part where you let me take off all your clothes and touch you everywhere. But my favorite part was you being so close to me."

"Can we do it again? Soon?"

"Are you kidding me? We're going to do it again and again and again. I have so much I want to show you." His voice lowered. "So many things I want to do with you."

"And it'll always be messy and awkward? And then...wow."

He raised his eyebrow. "You thought it was awkward?"

"At first, when we were...when you were...Hey, you said it'd be awkward!"

He kissed my forehead. "This is ours, Dev. Awkwardness and all. Is that okay?"

"It's perfect."

Chapter 27

"SOMETHING'S DIFFERENT ABOUT YOU," BLAIR SAID MONDAY morning.

I shook snow off my coat and hung it in my locker. "I don't know what you're talking about."

She tilted her head back and forth, studying my face. Then she nodded. "You slept with him."

"Keep your voice down!" I glanced over at Ashton's locker, but there was nothing to worry about. He wasn't there to overhear anything, anyway.

Which sucked.

Yesterday morning, I got to be with him again, and I'd loved every minute of it. After, we'd had breakfast, then he took me home once the roads were clear. We talked on the phone last night. But I hadn't seen him since... well, since *Then*.

I was desperate to see him.

Blair squeezed my arm. "My little Devvy is growing up."

"You're being creepy."

She waggled her eyebrows. "What was it like? Was it like in the romance books? Did you see stars? Did he rock your world?"

"Oh my God, I'm not talking about this here!"

"Talking about what?" Tyrell appeared behind Blair and slid his arm around her shoulders.

"Our periods," Blair said.

He nodded. "Cool."

Blair gave him the kind of soppy look I never thought I'd see cross her face.

"Good morning, you lovely people!"

I held back a sigh. The sudden scent of strawberry shampoo and lip gloss could only mean one person. "Yes, Auden?"

She gestured to Tyrell. "So, like, you're okay with him being all up on your girl?"

"We're not lesbians, Auden," Blair said.

"Wait, what?" Tyrell sputtered. "You thought Blair was into girls?"

Auden rolled her eyes. "I'm teasing. God. But to be honest, it would be nice to have some *family* at this school." Then she turned slightly pink. "Pretend you didn't hear that."

I looked at Blair. Blair looked at me. Tyrell looked at Blair. Then we all looked at Auden.

Auden looked at me. "I really came over to talk to you."

I shouldered my bag. "What's up?"

"Calculus. Rumor has it that Professor McJunkin's planning a pop quiz."

What the heck? Girlfriend was never one to give away any intel that could take away her advantage. "Why are you telling me this?"

She grinned her smug grin. "My New Year's resolution is to be nicer to my rivals. But I figured, why wait until some arbitrary date to start? So this is my kind deed to you, my dear rival, Devon."

I blinked. "*Okayyyy*. Thanks, I guess?"

"See ya at Yearbook!" And then she was gone.

"This is such a weird day," Blair said. "So many revelations. I need coffee."

"Then let's get you some coffee," Tyrell said. "Catch ya later, Devon."

Blair pointed to me. "We are definitely having a talk later, young lady."

Young lady. Okay, Blair. I waved them off. Glanced at Ashton's locker again.

He'd never shown.

Chapter 28

THE VIBRATING OF MY PHONE JOLTED ME FROM A SOUND sleep. I rubbed my eyes and focused on the display. Four in the morning. Christmas Day. A text from Ashton telling me he was on my front porch.

What the hell? I jumped out of bed, yanked on my yoga pants, and tiptoed to the front door so my parents wouldn't hear me. "What are you doing here?"

"Can I come in?" he asked, his voice a fervent whisper. "It's kind of cold."

I pulled him inside. "You're not supposed to be here until ten."

He dropped the bag he was carrying and wrapped his arms around me. Buried his face in my neck.

"Hey." I stroked his back. "What's going on?"

He pulled away and stared at me. "I had to see you."

"Everything okay?"

He didn't answer. Instead he looked around, taking in the stockings hanging on the fireplace, the Christmas village on top of the entertainment center, the twinkling lights on the tree. Then he inhaled deeply. "Is that a real tree?"

I regarded the soft, fragrant needles. "We cut one down every year."

"It smells so good." He inhaled again. "This place is a Christmas wonderland."

My dad grew up Catholic, but my family was not religious at all. Mom and Dad were spiritual and believed that every spiritual leader, and therefore every holiday, was important.

But Christmas was their favorite.

They were like little kids, tearing a ring off the countdown chain every day. Shaking presents under the tree and baking dozens of cookies. Watching *A Christmas Story* again and again while sucking on candy canes and snuggling in front of the fireplace.

"My parents go kind of overboard," I said.

"It's perfect, Devon." He nibbled his bottom lip, eyes darting all around.

"Ashton?"

A shrug. "It's all manufactured at my house. Decorators and catered food. But here, it feels real. Like on TV." His forehead wrinkled. "Wait, that makes no sense."

I slipped off his beanie. It was damp from melting snowflakes. "I'm glad you're here."

Finally, he met my eye again, his expression soft. "I swear, just looking at you makes me feel like everything might be okay again."

"Is everything not okay?"

"No. But I'm here."

"Want to talk about it?"

"No. I want to kiss you."

I squeezed his hands and planted a kiss on his lips. His skin was frozen, but he warmed up fast.

"*Mmm*, you're all tousled and sleepy-like. Sexy," he murmured.

His mood swing made me nervous. How he could go from dark to light. But before I could think too much about it, his lips brushed right below my ear, sending delicious tingles all the way through me. "We could get in so much trouble right now."

"You got a stocking," I said, trying to distract him. And myself.

He raised his eyebrows and slid his hands down my body. "We should go to your room."

"Ashton." I caught his hands and intertwined our fingers. "If we go there, we have to behave. I'd feel weird doing *that* with my parents right next door."

He nodded. "Okay."

"I mean it."

"I'll be good. I promise."

Being good meant long, tender kisses and gentle caresses. Holding each other close until he fell asleep in my arms. I did not mean to be that girl watching her boyfriend sleep, but I was totally that girl watching her boyfriend sleep.

I told Ashton I loved him at least twice every day. But in this quiet moment, the love overwhelmed me. What in his dreams made his lips curve like that? I wanted to know that like I knew his breathing. His scent. His passion. His pain. His life.

I buried my face in his hair while he slept on. At some point I dozed off, dreaming of fresh waterfalls and warm breezes. The dream changed. A supermassive black hole, sucking away everyone I loved. Blair, gone in a swirl of cigarette smoke. My parents, whirling around and around like water spinning down a drain. Then Ashton, desperately reaching for me. Calling for me, his face chalky white. But I couldn't save him. My hands, slippery with sweat, lost their grip on his fingertips.

And he was gone.

Bright sunlight yanked me back into the real world. No, not sunlight. Ashton was staring at me, his eyes wide with concern. It was his voice I'd heard in the dream, only it had been real.

I shot up and stuck my thumbnail in my mouth. Started to chomp.

"Devon." Ashton's voice was quiet. His fingertips gentle on my cheeks. "You had a bad dream." He pulled me close and stroked my hair. "You were crying. I wanted to jump in and snatch the nightmare away."

"I wish you could've. It was awful."

"Do you want to tell me about it?"

I shook my head. "I want to forget about it."

"What can I do?"

"Hold me."

"Okay." He tightened his arms around me and rested his chin on the top of my head. Eventually the nightmare faded, and it was just us.

"I'm so glad you're here," I said.

"Can you imagine?" he asked, his lips against my temple. "Waking up like this every day?"

"Is that something you want?"

"Not the nightmares."

I puffed out a snort. "Yeah."

"But the waking-up-beside-you part? I do want that. Very much." His voice grew quiet. "You make me excited about the future, Dev."

I looked up at him. His expression was faraway.

"Gives me something to focus on when things get hard," he added.

"I know they're hard now. Do they get hard a lot?"

"Most of the time, thinking about the next hour is overwhelming. So I think: *If I can survive the next five minutes, it'll be okay.* And then another five. And then another. Some days, that's all I can do."

"Even on the good days?"

"Sometimes the good days are even worse. I'm constantly waiting for everything to fall apart. And what's messed up is I don't even know what that looks like. I just know it's bad."

"The Dark?"

"I'm scared it's going to wake up again. And I won't be able to stop it."

I brushed some hair from his forehead. "You know you can always talk to me, right? You don't have to give in. I'm here."

He nodded slowly. Then he gave me a bright smile. He was like a Ping-Pong ball. Back and forth and back again. "Will you please tell me about Christmas dinner? What can I expect tonight?"

I watched him closely, but he looked fine. "Turkey and Honey Baked Ham."

"I don't think I've ever had Honey Baked Ham," Ashton said thoughtfully.

"You're kidding."

"Nope. Judging from your expression, I've been missing out. What other foods will you make that I've never had?"

"Greens. I doubt you've had those."

"Greens? You mean like kale?"

I snorted. "Uh, no. Hell no. Mustard and turnip. We cook them with smoked ham hocks or turkey necks."

"Turkey necks?"

"For flavor. You're going to try them, right?"

He raised his eyebrows. "The turkey necks or the greens?"

I gently shoved him. "The greens."

"I'm going to try everything. I'm already hungry thinking about it. Please tell me sweet potato pie is involved, because I had some a long time ago and it was the bomb dot com."

"The bomb dot com? How old are you? That's the kind of thing my parents would say."

"I actually did hear your dad say it. What other things will we have?"

My stomach grumbled. "Mashed potatoes. Macaroni and cheese. Dressing."

"Dressing?"

I tapped his chest. "You white folk call it 'stuffing.' Only we don't actually put it in the bird. And we use cornbread to make it. But Mom makes stuffing, too. Dad and Stephanie's family insists on it. You remember Stephanie, right?"

He nodded.

"And you'll get to meet my grandmother Mama Lee, and my uncle Ricky."

He squeezed me. "I can't wait."

"I think you'll like them. And I think they'll like you."

He grinned. "I haven't been this excited about a holiday in forever."

"Is that why you showed up so early?"

His grin faded. "Truth?"

"Tell me."

"Last night, my mind went to a billion dark places. I didn't want to be alone."

"You never have to be again."

He nodded thoughtfully. "Thank you."

"You don't have to thank me."

He kissed my temple. "Did you know you're my favorite person?"

I sent him a mischievous smirk. "I had a feeling, but you can keep telling me if you want. I don't mind."

He poked my shoulder. "You. Are. A. Dork."

"You love me."

"I do." Another temple kiss. "More than anything. I'm so lucky to have you."

"Yes, you are. Never forget it."

He let out a soft laugh, then gave me a quick kiss. "I won't. Promise."

We lay together a while longer, then he headed to the living room while I snuck in a short yoga practice, showered, and dressed. When I joined him, he was grinning at his phone.

"What are you doing?"

"Talking to my grandma on FaceTime." He'd already pointed the phone toward me. "Come say hi."

There she was, wearing an ugly Christmas sweater and big bauble earrings, her smile wide and her eyes twinkling. "Devon!" She clapped her hands. "I'm delighted to finally meet you. You're even lovelier than your photos."

Her voice sounded like pink cotton candy, soft and sweet. I liked her immediately. "It's nice to meet you, too. Ashton's told me a lot about you."

"Everything scandalous, I hope?"

"She knows all your dirty secrets, Grandma," Ashton said, wrapping his arms around me.

"You didn't tell her I stack the deck when we play cards, did you? Because that's really you, and you know it."

Eyes shining, Ashton let out a joyful laugh. "Busted!"

I rarely saw this side of him. Completely relaxed, guard let all the way down, easy and wide smile. I loved it.

"I hate to cut this so short," his grandmother said, "but my ride is here. I'm off to lunch with some close friends. We're all wearing our ugly Christmas sweaters."

"Nothing could ever look ugly on you," Ashton said.

"Such a charmer." She beamed. "I'm so glad I got to talk to you both. I hope to see you soon, Devon."

"Same."

"Don't get in too much trouble, Grandma," Ashton said.

"Who, me?" She winked, then disappeared. Ashton's home screen—a picture of me—came back up.

"Okay, she's awesome. I can't wait to meet her in person someday."

"Well. It just so happens that my family is hosting a New Year's Eve party. I'd love for you to be my date."

"Your grandmother's gonna be there?"

He nodded. "Normally, I'd be visiting her in Monaco, but I wanted to stay here with you. She's flying over on the twenty-seventh."

The thought of ringing in the New Year with Ashton's parents filled me with trepidation, but I really wanted to meet the family member he loved the most. "In that case, I'd love to be your date."

The corners of his eyes crinkled as he grinned. "Awesome. Keep smiling like that." He pointed his phone at me again and snapped a photo. "Perfect."

I gestured toward his phone. "Can I see?"

He handed me the phone, then turned to the fireplace. "Can I open my stocking now?"

"Go for it."

While Ashton dug into the velvety-red stocking, I scrolled through his camera roll. All the pictures were artistic. Deliberately framed or meticulously staged. Evergreen trees coated with snow. A frozen pond, the smooth surface sparkling in the sunlight. Even the candid pictures looked beyond. None of the stuff that filled up most people's camera rolls, like Blair's endless selfies or pictures of her various lipsticks. Or selfies of her *wearing* the various lipsticks. Or my pathetic attempts at astrophotography that usually ended up a blurry mess. "Ashton. These are so good."

"Hmm?" He'd shoved half a sugar cookie covered in M&M's into his mouth.

"Oh my God. Do you have any self-control?"

He swallowed. "I lose my mind when M&M's are involved."

I handed him his phone. "Your photos. They're gorgeous."

His cheeks turned pink. "Thanks."

"I think you could do this professionally."

"I love it too much for that. I want to keep it fun." Then he pointed the phone at me again. "Smile!"

By the time my parents joined us, Ashton had eaten half his cookies, and a snack-size bag of M&M's, and was sucking on the end of a candy cane. Mom's eagle eye went straight to him, then a side-eye to me. "Hello, Ashton!" she said. "We weren't expecting you until later."

"I couldn't sleep," he said.

She gave us both a knowing smirk. "Excited for Santa?"

He and I glanced at each other. "You could say that," he said, the tips of his ears turning pink.

Dad turned from the fireplace, where he'd just lit a crackling blaze. "When can I open my new watch?"

Mom stared at him, her hand on her hip. "Who said you're getting a watch?"

"I have a feeling."

"Or you listened to all of the packages until you found one that ticked," I said.

He put his hand on his chest and had the nerve to look offended. "Well, I never."

"*Suuuuurrreeee.*"

Mom handed Ashton a small gift bag. "This is for you."

Ashton froze in place, a wrinkle between his eyebrows. "What? You didn't have to—"

She shook her head. "Open it."

Face flushed, Ashton pushed aside sparkly green tissue paper and pulled out a game controller ornament inscribed with his name and the year. His mouth opened slightly, and the pink in his cheeks deepened. "Oh wow."

"We want you to hang it," Mom said.

"Are you sure?"

"Pick your spot." Dad gestured toward the tree.

The grin that covered Ashton's face warmed the room even more than the blaze in the fireplace.

My parents squeezed each other's hands as Ashton searched for the perfect spot to place his ornament. Then he turned to us, his cheeks still pink, but this time, with pleasure. "Thank you."

"Come sit with me," I said, pulling him onto the couch. "There's more where that came from."

Ashton grew quiet after we passed around the gifts. He stared ahead, his eyes muted. He was suddenly so pensive, so...still. Something in his expression frightened me, and I glanced away, focusing on the fireplace. The flames danced and retreated, wrestling with the wood as if it were their destiny.

I turned back to Ashton and glimpsed that same struggle in his eyes. What was *he* wrestling with? I gingerly touched his arm, and he turned to me, his face breaking into a smile. The angst melted like a snowflake on hot asphalt. Gone. Just like that.

He must have sensed my concern, because he leaned close and whispered, "I'm fine. Really."

I didn't believe him, not with that guarded look in his eyes.

Mom was organizing the opened boxes under the tree when Ashton nudged my foot with his, a clean white sock bumping against a candy cane–patterned novelty holiday sock. I glanced up to find him holding another box out to me.

"What's this?"

"Open it." Was it my imagination, or did he look nervous?

"It's heavy." I ripped the wrapping paper and my heart stopped. "Are you kidding me right now?"

He stared at me. Hard. "Do you like it?"

"Ashton." My eyes were prickling. I was getting light-headed. Because there was no way, no absolute way he'd done this for me.

"Wow, that looks expensive," my father, Captain Obvious, said.

"This is...it's a Celestron NexStar...." I managed to choke out. "Oh my God. I can't even believe you got me this. I mean, I can't...I've wanted one for so long."

"What is that, exactly?" Dad asked.

I started nibbling my thumbnail. "It's a catadioptric telescope."

Dad stared at me, a blank expression on his face. "Should I know what that means?"

"I'll be able to see Cassini Division and the Great Red Spot and galaxies and nebulas...."

"Yeah, I'm lost."

I took three breaths and turned to Ashton. "How did you know which one?"

"I talked to Professor Trask."

"But, Ashton..." The enormity of what he'd done was sinking in, making me dizzy. I'd gotten him his own copy of *Tidal Destruction III* and a DLC card to go with it, but that was nothing compared to this. My mouth opened and closed, opened and closed. Speechless.

"Don't you dare say you can't accept it," he warned. "This is too important to you. To both of us."

I threw my arms around him. "Then I'll tell you 'thank you.' So much. I love it. And I love you. So, so, *so* much."

He buried his face in my hair. "I love you, too, Dev."

Dad coughed, pulling Ashton and me out of our bubble. "Enough with the mush already. I need to wash my eyes out with some of that *Tidal Destruction*." He turned to Ashton. "You in?"

With reluctance, Ashton pulled away. "Okay?"

"Yeah."

Ashton grabbed a headset and sent Dad a thumbs-up. "Then I'm in."

"Come on, Bun. Let's make breakfast," Mom said.

In the kitchen, she pulled a carton of eggs and a packet of bacon out of the refrigerator. "Take the strips of bacon and lay them in the glass baking dish. Set the oven to three fifty."

"We're baking the bacon?"

"Why do you think they call it 'bacon'?"

"Um, I don't think—"

"We need to talk about you and Mr. Ashton."

Oh. "What do you mean?"

She pulled on her apron and threw me a look that said *You know damn well what I mean.* "I know he's loaded, but he bought you a very expensive gift. Devon, that's not normal high school romance stuff. Your dad gave me candy bars and bought me chocolate milkshakes."

"Yes, but high school for you was a thousand years ago."

I ducked as she swatted me with a dish towel. "I am not that old, and I look even younger."

This was true.

"You guys are moving extremely fast," she said. "He's buying you expensive science equipment and looking at you like you hung the moon. How long have you been dating?"

I concentrated on separating the bacon strips. "Six months, if you count that summer."

"I'm not sure I do." She stared at me, her eyes narrowed in

thought. "The thing is, I don't want you to get so wrapped up in him that you don't even realize who else might be out there for you." Then she smiled. "But when I see how you two are around each other, it reminds me of your father and me when we were your age. I'm happy for you, but I can't help but worry. No matter what happens, he's going to be okay. His family's wealth will make sure of that. But you can't afford to get distracted. I don't want this romance to derail any of your plans."

"Mom, school is my number one priority. That will never change."

She gave me a long look. As if she couldn't decide whether to believe me or not. "Okay. But make sure you come to me with everything and anything. I'm always here for you."

"I know. And I appreciate it. I really do."

She hugged me, then got down to business. "I really am starving, so we need to get cooking. What should it be? French toast or waffles?"

"French toast," I said. "The cinnamon kind."

I watched as she cracked eggs into a bowl. Added milk and vanilla. Whisked it all together. "What was it like with you and Dad? Did you always know? Did you ever doubt?"

"Of course I had doubts, Bun. But they weren't coming from me. I was so busy worrying what everyone thought about me falling in love and getting married so young that I forgot to listen to my own heart. Once I did that, it was easy." She dipped the bread into the eggs, coating both sides. "Are you listening to your heart? When you envision your future, do you see him there? And are you happy about it?"

I nodded and smiled. "He belongs there."

She wiped her hands on her apron and hugged me again. Then she held me at arm's length, studying me. "I hope he keeps making you as happy as you look right now."

My grin spread. "Me too."

"And for the record, yes, I did always know with your dad. When we were five, I told him I was going to marry him. He threw a worm at me and ran away." Her expression became dreamy. "That's when I knew it was meant to be."

"You're kidding."

"Not one bit." She gave me a wink. "I've always liked worms."

Chapter 29

"I CAN'T EVEN BELIEVE YOU'RE ABANDONING ME TO HANG out with your boyfriend." Blair smoothed moisturizer onto my cheeks. "I mean, I know it's New Year's Eve, the night when that all-important kiss sets the tone for the whole year, but jeez, Devon. Whatever happened to hos before bros?"

"I think you have that backward," I said. "And it's not like you aren't going out with your own bro."

Things were *seriously* progressing with her and Tyrell. She'd run into him while skiing in Aspen over winter break, and they'd spent a lot of time "keeping each other warm."

"Now I get why you look so happy-silly all the time," she'd said when she'd arrived earlier today.

"How do you pull *it* off with your family hovering?"

She had smiled mysteriously, her eyes twinkling. "Where there's a will, there's a way. And believe me, I have the will."

I believed her, all right. Especially because she gave me a detailed play-by-play of the Event. It was something I'd have been better off not knowing.

I wasn't going to be able to look at a jar of Nutella the same way ever again.

"When is Tyrell picking you up?" I asked.

"Ten," she said, then shook her head at me. "You are hopeless with makeup."

"I can't help it that I'm a natural beauty," I said. The actual truth was that I didn't see any need for makeup. After my mom spent a hundred dollars on makeup to make it look like she wasn't wearing any, I figured I'd skip the whole thing and not wear any at all.

Besides, I had a hard time finding colors that went well with my complexion and eye color. But Blair didn't seem to have that problem. She studied my face, the gears in her brain turning, then went into her makeup kit and pulled out colors that complemented me perfectly.

She bopped me on the head. "It's not about making an ugly girl pretty. It's about taking all this beauty and making it pop."

"Remind me where you and Tyrell are headed," I said.

"The President's Club." She grabbed a water bottle.

"*Ooh,* swanky!"

Her brows furrowed. "A cocktail party and dinner at the Founder's Mansion is pretty swanky, too."

"I know. A ton of important people are supposed to be

there, and Ashton said he would introduce me to all of them. But you'll get the real VIPs. The President's Club is big-time. They televise the local countdown from there." A thought occurred to me. "Maybe you'll be on TV!"

"Ha. I wonder how my father would react if he saw me dancing with Tyrell on TV."

"His innocent, precious daughter out on a date? With a *boy*? I can only imagine," I said.

Blair spit out her water. *"Innocent. Okaaaaay."*

"Just sayin'."

"Yeah, *stop sayin'*. I need to do your lips."

"Knock knock." Mom popped her head in, then came over and ran her fingers through my hair. "I'm here to do your bun, Bun."

I groaned. "Mom."

Her strong fingers massaged coconut oil into my scalp before she started gathering and twisting the springy strands.

"Doesn't Devon look pretty, Mrs. K?"

"She always looks pretty," Mom said, ever so loyally. "But you did an incredible job on her makeup."

"And her dress, too," Blair said. "I'm especially proud of it."

"I still can't believe you designed this for me." Dark-green, sparkly on top with a sweetheart neckline, flowy chiffon bottom. "My first-ever couture piece. It's stunning."

"I'm glad you like it." Her cheeks flushed with pleasure.

"Like it? I'm obsessed!"

At precisely nine, the doorbell rang.

"Your date is here," Dad called.

I swallowed down the panic rising in my throat. "I'm nervous."

"You're going to blow them all away," Blair said.

I squeezed her hands. "Thank you. For everything."

She hugged me and pushed me ahead of her.

And there was Ashton, his gray suit fitting him perfectly, his smile radiant.

"How do I look?" I asked, modeling my dress.

"You're beautiful," Ashton said, his eyes filled with longing. The way he looked at me always affected me all the way to my core.

He took my hand and heat shot through me. "Ready to go?"

I nodded.

"Pictures first," Mom called.

"Mom, it's not prom."

"Humor me," she said. "You're both dazzling. I want to document it."

After the paparazzi session ended, Ashton took my hand again. "Come on, gorgeous. Let's go ring in the new year."

"Have fun, be safe, yada yada," Mom called.

"Don't wait up," I said.

"Wasn't planning on it."

I grabbed my peacoat and tiny purse, and we went out into the crisp air. Then I stopped dead at the sleek maroon vehicle. "Are you serious?"

He grinned. "I thought you'd like it."

"Your father let you take the Maserati?"

Ashton opened the door for me. "I'm allowed to drive any of the cars, Devon."

I sank into the buttery leather seat and inhaled deeply. *Mmm.* "I can't believe I get to ride in this thing."

He climbed in, pulled on a pair of driving gloves, and started the car. "If you're good, I'll let you drive it home tonight."

"Don't even tease me."

"I'm not. You can drive home tonight."

"The Maserati?"

He waggled his eyebrows. "*This* Maserati."

The growl of that engine. The power in that rev. Chills. Everywhere. "You are the best boyfriend ever."

He gave me a smile that made every part of me smolder. "Can I tell you that you look really, really hot tonight?"

"You can always tell me that."

"You look so hot," he said. "And as soon as I get you alone, I'm going to kiss you until your knees buckle."

I shivered. "Tell me more."

"I'm going to get you out of that cute little dress," he murmured. "Then I'm going to taste every inch of your body and touch you until you can't breathe."

"Then what?" I asked softly.

He looked at me meaningfully. "What do *you* think should happen next?"

"I think we should make love," I whispered. "All night long."

"Yes, yes, a million times yes. I wish we could skip dinner

and go straight to bed. Wouldn't that be a way to ring in the new year?"

"The best."

We rode in silence for the rest of the trip, our eyes meeting from time to time.

"Come here," he whispered after we parked. "I need to kiss you. Now."

I ripped off my seat belt. "I'm always good with that."

Our lips came together in a fevered rush. Ugh. Who put this console and wheel in the way? I wanted to be on his lap, straddling him. Claiming him. Loving him with all of me. We kissed for a good ten minutes. At least, it felt like ten minutes. Losing track of time while kissing him was a regular thing, though, so who knows how long we were out there?

"We're making out in a Maserati," I said with a small grin.

"Damn right we are," he said, then kissed me again. Hands everywhere.

"We're going to be late," I murmured after another indeterminable amount of time.

"I don't care," he said breathlessly, his eyelids lowered with desire.

"We're going to get in trouble."

His lips tickled mine. "Worth it."

"Ashton."

Another long kiss. Then he pulled away and let out a deep breath. "I have to tell you something."

"Why does this sound ominous?"

"Rochelle's here. I didn't even think about it until my mother said something to me today."

Of course. The universe decided to thrust Rochelle right in my face. Nice. "So, basically, it's going to be awkward."

He winced and nodded. "Basically, yeah."

"Great." I grinned so much my face stretched. "Fantastic."

"I guess we'd better get inside and face the music." He shook his head. "But don't smile like that."

"Hold on, you have lipstick all over your face."

"Whoops." He pulled out a handkerchief and fixed himself up. "Better?"

"Much. How do I look?"

"Like you've been making out forever and thoroughly enjoying it."

"I mean, I have been, so…" I pulled out my compact and fixed my own mouth.

"Ready to head in?" he asked when I was done.

I took a fortifying breath and nodded. I could do this.

"Hello, Mother."

Mrs. Edwards wore a sleek, long black dress and a diamond choker that shot bolts of lightning right into my eyes. *Her* eyes swept over my own dress, and finding no fault there, she leaned in to kiss my cheek lightly. The scent of her Chanel No. 5 filled my nostrils and tickled my throat.

I could do this.

"Hello, Ashton. Devon, you look lovely as ever."

I had to do this.

"Thank you. So do you."

She chuckled and ran her hands over her hips. "You're too kind. Ashton, dear, will you take Devon's coat?"

He gave her a stiff smile. "Of course."

Mrs. Edwards hooked her arm through mine. "I'm delighted you're here. I must show you the new piece of art we got yesterday. I know you liked to look at the paintings at the beach house."

This woman had some nerve, I had to give her that. Referencing that summer as if it were yesterday. As if there hadn't been more than a year of pain and betrayal between then and now. Phony people truly amazed me.

I wasn't really into art. I liked pretty pieces, but an aficionado I was not. I couldn't tell you if the artists used acrylics or oil or watercolor paints, or even if they used paint at all. Looking at the artwork at the beach house had been something to do while waiting for Ashton's parents to go to bed.

"Here is a piece by Liudmila Kondakova," Mrs. Edwards said. *The Magic Hour.*"

I took in the whimsical pinks and purples, the fluffball trees. The depth of the painting as the rooftops accentuated the focal point: the Eiffel Tower. "It's really pretty."

"Of course, it's Paris, your favorite, no?"

How did she know this?

"Everyone should spend some time outside the US, in my

opinion," Mrs. Edwards said. "Get a better perspective of the world. Have you ever been to a foreign country?"

"Not yet." The Paris Observatory continued to call my name. Not as loudly as McCafferty did, but the whispers were always there.

She trailed a finger around the rim of her wineglass. "I'm sure you know that Ashton brought you here tonight with the intention of formally introducing you to our circle. It seems that you and he are getting very serious."

"I love him," I said, my voice soft.

"I know," she said. "And it's evident that he loves you. But I have some concerns. Today, I overheard Ashton asking his grandmother about rings."

I froze. "Engagement rings?"

She made me nervous, the way her eyes bore into mine, as if she were trying to unravel my every secret. "You seem nonplussed. He hasn't talked to you about this?"

"Only in passing, Mrs. Edwards. A someday-maybe type of thing."

She kept those eyes on me. "But he's thinking about it enough to ask. Which raises some serious alarms with me."

With me, too. Why hadn't he mentioned this to me? And why wasn't he a part of this dialogue right now?

"First of all, you're moving very quickly," she said. "Too quickly. To talk about marrying a girl he's only dated a couple of months—well, that's downright foolish."

I had to admit that I partially shared that concern. Just

like that summer, my relationship with Ashton had become intense very fast. And I was okay with it. Most days I was able to push aside the niggling worry that he could turn on me again. Walk away, like he did before. But it was there: I loved him very much, but did I trust him? I wasn't sure.

I stood there, letting that sink in.

After all this time, even after sleeping with him, I still didn't completely trust Ashton to not hurt me again. And if I couldn't trust him, I had no business entertaining, even in a fantastical way, the idea of marrying him. Not that I was, anyway. So Mrs. Edwards needed to calm the hell down.

"Second, you're so young," she continued, pulling me out of my trance. "You may not be the same person in three months, let alone in three years. But if you marry him, it's for the rest of your life. The Edwards family does not divorce."

She made it sound so final. Like a death sentence or imprisonment. That's not what marriage represented to me. My mom and dad were each other's favorite person—it was obvious in so many tiny ways, and so many big ways. How her face lit up as soon as he walked in the door after work. The way they danced together when one of their songs (and believe me, they had a lot) popped up on a playlist. When he brought her tea every night, exactly the way she liked it.

But Ashton said his parents fought constantly. They wanted him to marry a girl who could make him even richer, instead of the girl he loved. Maybe that's what happened to his mother. So maybe marriage *was* a prison sentence for her?

"Most important, my husband's family is very powerful.

We have an image that we need to uphold, not to mention the responsibilities of being a part of the Preston-Edwards empire. If we were to allow this marriage to happen, there would be things expected of you that I'm not sure you're equipped for."

Allow?

Like a betrothal? Blessings and courting and calling cards? He'd said his parents were old-fashioned, but this was beyond what I ever pictured.

She smiled and shook her head. "You make my son happy. He lights up when he talks about you. But I'm not sure that's enough, with your backgrounds being so different."

"How *do* you know so much about my background?" I asked cautiously.

"We researched you to the hilt that summer, Devon. The first time he brought you to the beach house, I knew you looked familiar. You're in the running for valedictorian at Preston Academy, which you're attending on a full scholarship. I was one of five adjudicators who made the decision to accept you."

Wait, what?

No, seriously.

What?

She went on, oblivious to my shock. "Those of us who endow Preston get letters every year outlining the progress of its recipients."

I should not have been shocked. His family *founded the freaking school*, so of course they had a say in who got accepted into the academy and who got the money. Then something dawned on me. "Once you realized who I was, you pushed for Ashton to break up with me."

"You have to understand where I was coming from," she said. "Here was my only son, ready to risk it all for a girl he'd only known for a few weeks. At age sixteen. Don't get me wrong—I was thrilled to see him so happy. But there were far-reaching consequences he wasn't even considering. Someone had to set his head straight."

"But it was only a summer romance."

"You and I both know it was more than that," she said. "And if you were to marry Ashton, you'd be set beyond your wildest dreams."

The implication kicked me in the gut. "You think I'm a gold digger."

"Maybe you didn't start off that way, but it would give you a reason to hold on, wouldn't it?"

I fought to keep from clenching my fists. Here's the thing: Mrs. Edwards knew everything about my family's financial situation; we'd had to disclose so much information to be in contention for scholarship funds, even the merit-based ones.

"That's not fair," I said. "First, I had no idea that he was part of this massive empire when we were together that summer. Second, you know so much about me, so you should know how hard I work."

"But marrying into this family would make things so much easier for you. My son is going to inherit a legacy beyond comprehension. Our money and connections would open so many doors for you. Including a spot at McCafferty."

My heart nearly skidded to a halt. I'd practically give up my firstborn to secure a spot at McCafferty. But she couldn't know that. No one could know that, because to broadcast it would be to broadcast weakness. I could not afford to be weak right now.

"I can't say I've been sitting around thinking about it," I said, struggling to keep my voice steady. "I just want to be with Ashton."

"In addition, we've never had people who are—diverse, for lack of a better term—in our family," she continued. "Ashton marrying you would introduce a whole new dynamic, and the senior members of the family will push hard against you, knowing that you're not like us."

Not like us. Did she even hear the words coming out of her mouth? How could she be so composed, standing there sipping her wine, when I was about to burst into cold flame?

"I'm the same as you are," I said in a small voice. "How could you say I'm not?"

She sighed. "I like you. And I like what you do for Ashton. But I'm afraid it's not so simple." She regarded me then, her expression thoughtful. "Your family is important to you, right?"

I nodded. My family meant everything to me.

"And you'd do anything for them."

"Yes."

"So you should see where I'm coming from. I have a legacy to protect. *His* legacy. *My* family. You'd do anything to keep your family from harm. That's what I'm doing."

"I don't want to harm your family," I said quietly. "I just want to love your son."

"And I want to believe you," she said sadly. "I truly do. But too much is at stake. If you want to become a part of this family, you need to prove you deserve it."

We stared at each other for what felt like an eternity. Then a soft bell tinkled.

"Dinner is soon. Let's go join the others." Ashton's mother squeezed my arm and went into the dining room.

Chapter 30

WHAT. THE. HELL. WHO PICKS A PARTY TO HAVE A CONversation like that? Especially one she was supposed to be hosting? I dug my fingernails into my palms. How dare she?

Prove you deserve it. Except most of the people chattering in the next room had been born into this. Why should I have to prove myself when I had the same right to be here—the same right to *exist*—as they did?

Prove you deserve it. Anger flooded my veins. I trembled so hard my bones rattled. I was so done with people shaming me, my family, our values, our life. The desire to walk out the door and let this family rip itself apart over power plays and politics grew with each breath. But that's exactly what she wanted, and there was no way in hell I was giving it to her. Even with the amount of scrutiny I'd been under and would be under as long as I was with Ashton.

Ashton. Always Ashton. With his gentle support and fiery touch and all-consuming love. Ashton, who I discovered in the dining room chatting with a stunning girl. Flawless dark-brown curls. Even, smooth complexion. Curves that made me look like a twelve-year-old boy. And she wasn't wearing tiny high heels like I was. She had on stilettos, because of course someone like her would be wearing grown-up shoes.

Rochelle.

She embodied everything about this world: fancy cars, expensive champagne, designer clothing, and sparkling diamonds. The opposite of me: wild hair, clothes from the mall, and grades that I had to work my ass off to earn. She looked as if life was effortless for her. And it probably was.

What was I doing here? There was no way I could compete with Rochelle. With any of these people.

I was crumbling. I was not okay. I rushed to the bathroom to compose myself and caught my reflection in the mirror. Flushed cheeks. Silvery eyes shining with unshed tears. Trembling lips. Whirling nausea.

Inhale . . . two . . . three . . . four.

Exhale . . . two . . . three . . . four.

I refused to fall apart. Because if I couldn't keep it together tonight, how in the hell could I expect to do so when his family started really putting the pressure on me?

I could do this.

I *would* do this.

But the bigger question: Was Ashton worth all this?

All I wanted was to love him. Go to McCafferty. Study the stars.

Mrs. Edwards said it wasn't so simple, but why couldn't it be?

I could stay in here all night, sitting on the cozy settee, sniffing the pretty soaps and perfumes. Hiding from the pretty people milling around, waiting for their pretty dinner.

But I was better than this. *So get out there, Devon.*

Now.

I splashed my face with cold water. Wiped my eyes. Redid my lipstick. Then forced myself to leave the powder room.

And there they were.

She leaned close to him and whispered something that made him laugh. God, they looked like a perfume ad. I wanted to chuck something at them.

Instead, I swallowed hard and made myself walk over to them.

I tickled Ashton's hand lightly. He turned to me and smiled, his entire face lighting up. Even with his gorgeous ex-girlfriend standing right there, he still managed to make me feel like the prettiest girl in the room.

Feeling bolder now, I turned to Rochelle. Her gaze swept over me, making me feel like a little kid playing dress-up. The urge to run and hide came again, but I clamped it down. I refused to leave him again with this girl who was the perfect fit for his perfect life. The girl he'd have married, if I hadn't come back into the picture.

Breathe.

"You must be Devon." She was smiling, dimples flashing, but there was something behind her eyes that I couldn't quite read. "I'm Rochelle," she added.

"Hello." Her handshake was firm, which disappointed me. But I shouldn't have expected someone who looked like a Victoria's Secret model to have a wimpy handshake.

Ashton's mother beckoned to him, and with an apologetic look at me, he went to meet her across the room. Leaving me with Rochelle. The ex-girlfriend. Oh my God. Why.

"So you're Ashton's sunset girl," she said. Her eyes swept over me again, then she nodded. "I can see it."

A sudden rush of love—and possessiveness—for Ashton almost knocked me over. I looked over at him. Whatever his mother was saying to him was pissing him off, making his jaw twitch like mad.

"He told me about you a long time ago," Rochelle said. I forced my eyes away from the mother-son exchange and turned to pay attention to her. "The look on his face when he talked about you . . . the way he said your name, even. I knew if he ever saw you again, I'd be history. Never thought it'd actually happen."

Again, what was I supposed to say to that?

She glanced over at him again. "He's kinda fragile, but he's special. Don't break his heart, okay?"

I snorted. "He's more likely to break mine." Whoa. What was wrong with me, trading intel with the ex? *Abort, Devon. ABORT.*

"He does kind of have a track record in that department," she said. "What he did to you was shitty."

"You know about that?"

She fluffed her hair. "I had to drag it out of him. He was miserable over it for a long time."

"So was I."

"Understandably so." She sighed. "Listen, take care of him. Unless he hurts you. Then you should kick his ass. I'll help."

Huh. I liked her. In another life, we probably could've even been friends. "Is that his grandmother who just joined them?"

Now Rochelle offered me a full, dazzling smile. "His favorite person ever. I'm going to leave so he can introduce you without it being all weird." She gave my arm a reassuring pat and sauntered away.

Ashton's grandmother was tall, with impeccable posture, a severe bun, and an air of quiet authority. She wore a long, elegant gray dress accented with a diamond brooch. She glanced over and saw me staring. Her face lit up with delight, and she leaned over to whisper to Ashton.

Ashton's face softened as his grandmother spoke to him. As they walked over, his posture relaxed and the wrinkles on his forehead smoothed out. But the fists at his sides and the way he kept cutting his eyes at his mother showed me he was barely holding it together.

Up close, Ashton's grandmother's eyes twinkled. A small smile played around her mouth, suggesting a secret mischievousness. My heart pounded as if I were in the presence of a celebrity.

Ashton slipped his arm around my shoulders. "Devon, I'd like you to officially meet Harriet Edwards, my grandmother," he said. "Grandmother, this is Devon Kearney, my girlfriend."

She clasped my hands in both of hers. Warmth and acceptance poured out of her like fine wine. "Devon. It's wonderful to officially meet you."

All my tension faded away. "Likewise."

The dinner bell rang a second time.

Ashton looped one arm through his grandmother's and the other arm through mine, and led us to the dining room. After everyone settled at the table, he threw his mother a hard look. Then he leaned over to me, his face pinched, his mouth a straight line. "You were upset earlier. What did my mother say to you?"

I shook my head. "I'll tell you later."

He nodded. "Later, then."

During dinner, I watched Ashton and his grandmother. Their easy conversations, their inside jokes. The way his face was smooth around her, happiness radiating off him. He included me in their conversation as much as he could, but I kept fading out, content to watch as they interacted.

After dinner, the adults headed to the sitting room. A four-piece jazz band played bouncy tunes while a steady stream of people took advantage of the open bar. Some of the older couples whirled around the dance floor to classics like the fox-trot. Most of the younger people gathered in a corner. Ashton had explained that they were his peers: people he hung out with because their parents were all Very Important People who hung out together. Played golf together. Hosted charity fund-raisers together. Did business together.

More guests arrived in a whirlwind of fur coats, expensive perfume, and flashing jewelry. Ashton spent time greeting these new arrivals, then spent the next hour making nice with everyone who had come to the party.

"This is my girlfriend, Devon Kearney," he said proudly to the press, to his friends and family, to anyone who would listen. Ashton's arm stayed around me the entire time. Almost defiantly, as if he was daring someone to say something out of line.

"Smile," photographers from society publications called as shutters clicked and the flashes popped.

Once the articles were printed, Ashton explained, it would be official. I'd be a part of society. The funny thing was, these people weren't so very different from those in my world. They simply had bigger bank accounts, wore fancier clothes, and drove expensive cars. But those things were important in his world, and for now, I had to play the part.

Watching Ashton play the part was both fascinating and unnerving. The perfect blend of formal and charming, he knew exactly how to flatter, and they ate it right up like lions feasting on gazelles. He stood tall and proud, embodying his family's power in a way that impressed and intimidated me.

This was nothing like the passionate, vulnerable boy he was when we were alone. Were all wealthy people like this, able to shed one skin for another when it suited them? Conflicting feelings about his family's legacy caused him constant angst, but you wouldn't know it tonight. It troubled me in a way, seeing him slip into this act so easily. How much of it even was an act? I didn't know. But I did know this: Ashton fit into this world in a way I never would.

A gentle hand on my shoulder made me nearly spill my sparkling cider. "You're doing well for your debut," Ashton's grandmother said.

"Oh, hi." I put my hand on my chest.

"Oops. Didn't mean to startle you. Although I should have noticed how hard you were staring at my grandson."

My face warmed. "I'm glad you came to talk to me, Mrs. Edwards."

"Please call me Harriet," she said, looking around. "I know this must be a lot. All these people staring at you, asking you questions, taking pictures."

"It's a little overwhelming, yes."

"But you'll get used to it. I know you will."

My hands trembled, making the cider slosh. "You think I'll be around long enough for all this to matter?"

"Ashton looks at you like you're his whole world. Even if no one else believes it, he does. And for the record, I do, too."

I let out a long breath. "Thank you."

"Listen. I know his mother is kind of a"—she leaned down to whisper—"hard-ass."

I bit back a snort.

"She takes things like class and lineage very seriously."

"Believe me, I know."

"I used to be the same way. But I've learned there are things more important than how blue your blood is or how much wealth your ancestors have accumulated. Love. That's what's important. And if you have one person you truly love and who truly loves you, then that's all the wealth you need."

Beautiful sentiment, but she was filthy rich, so I wasn't sure I completely bought it.

Still. It was a nice thought.

"What about his father?"

We watched as Mr. Edwards beamed and gave Ashton a hard pat on the back. He *acted* proud of Ashton, but honestly, it didn't seem as if they liked each other one bit. Ashton was smiling, but there was a subtle strain there. Only someone who knew him well would be able to tell that he was uncomfortable.

The sides of Harriet's mouth turned down slightly. "Tristan is very conservative. He thinks things should stay a certain way, and nothing should ever deviate from it."

"So, his son dating a middle-class biracial girl—"

"Is definitely deviating from what's normal. For him. My influence only goes so far. His father was hard on him, and, unfortunately, I didn't stand up to him much. Big mistake on my part, I realize that now. Naturally he doesn't think I have a right to tell him how to run his life. But when I try to point out the same thing about Ashton—"

"He gets loud."

She gave me a sideways glance.

"So I've heard," I added.

"Sometimes I feel like Tristan resents that I give Ashton

the attention I should've given him as a child. I don't want to believe that of my son, but that's the way he treats him. All the restrictions and the demands, then making Eleanor do all the dirty work. It hurts my heart. I imagine it hurts Ashton's, too." Regret etched itself into the lines on her face.

"So, what do I do?"

"Love Ashton. Be by his side. Fight for him. I'll do what I can, but it's ultimately up to you two."

"How are you holding up?" Ashton asked once the cameras were turned off, the recorders put away.

"Hanging in there."

"I'm glad you're here."

I caressed his cheek. "I'm glad I'm with you."

Thirty minutes before midnight, the party kicked way up. Loud laughter, free-flowing champagne, and *oh my God* some of the dancing the parents were doing. And this, after living with *my* parents, poster children for PDA.

During the countdown, Ashton pulled me aside and gave me a long, gentle kiss. His lips felt so good against mine that I didn't want to let him go.

Maybe I didn't fit in his world, but he and I did fit together.

While everyone sang "Auld Lang Syne," Ashton and I slipped out of the sitting room. He studied my face, then brushed a curl from my forehead.

"Something's bothering you," he said. "Talk to me."

"I love your grandmother," I said. "She believes we have a

future together. But your mom doesn't." I froze. "I shouldn't have said that."

His expression turned stony. "No. Keep going."

At first I held back. This wasn't the time or place. But he'd asked, so I let him have it. When I got to the part about his mother calling me a gold digger, he froze, stone-cold anger hardening his features. By the time I got to the diversity stuff, he was clenching and unclenching his fists and his jaw. Then he exploded.

"I find the one thing, the one damn thing that makes me happy, and she wants to snatch it away? To hell with her."

I shook my head. "No, I mean, I get it. There's a lot at stake." And now I sounded like his mother.

He shook his head, his jaw set. "No, there isn't. We have a whole royal family with a biracial duchess existing in this world. That's real. The crap Mother's saying to you? It's bullshit." His forehead furrowed. "Did she threaten you?"

"Not exactly, but—"

"Come on."

He pulled me into the sitting room. Right to his mother and Rochelle...and another woman, who had to be Rochelle's mother. She had that same thick curly hair, those same deep dimples. The same effortless glamour.

They were all holding half-empty champagne glasses and laughing together. Carefree. Privileged. Shiny-perfect.

"Oh, look, it's Ashton." Mrs. Edwards squeezed his shoulder. "And his little friend Devon."

"My *girlfriend* Devon," he corrected, his voice ice-cold.

Rochelle's mother whipped around to stare at her daughter, sculpted eyebrows nearly jumping off her forehead. "Girlfriend?"

Rochelle rolled her eyes. "We've talked about this. God. Devon, this is Janelle Ryan, my mother."

"Pleasure to meet you, Ms. Ryan." I held out my hand, but she didn't extend hers. Instead, she clutched her glass more tightly.

Okay then.

"This is the girlfriend?" Ms. Ryan said. "He picked *her* over you?" Then her expression changed. "Oh, I get it."

"Do you have a problem?" Ashton asked quietly.

"Ashton!" Mrs. Edwards grabbed his shoulder, but he was unmovable.

Ms. Ryan gave him a wan smile. A knowing smile. "Not at all."

Whatever. I could tell by her sideways smirk, the way her eyes swept over me and skipped away, that she figured I wasn't any sort of threat. As if I wouldn't be around long. Then things could get back to the status quo.

Rochelle's face was a mask of utter exasperation mixed with horror. But she didn't say anything. So did that make her just as bad?

"Mother, I need to speak with you," Ashton said.

"Ashton, this is really not the time or place—"

But Ashton had already turned and was dragging me away. I heard Mrs. Edwards murmur an apology, then the click of her heels behind us. "Ashton Edwards. How dare you embarrass me in front of my guests?"

He snorted. "Oh please. Janelle is so blitzed it'll be a miracle if she remembers anything ten minutes from now."

Mrs. Edwards sighed and pursed her lips. "What is this about?"

"How could you say those things to Devon?"

Mrs. Edwards flashed those icy blue eyes at me. "I'm looking out for our family. You, more than anyone, should know that."

"Mother—"

She slashed the air with her ring-laden hand, the diamonds painfully brilliant. "We will discuss this when it's appropriate."

Ashton stood tall, face-to-face with his mother. "Devon's my girlfriend. I love her, and I'm not letting anything come between us again." His voice was a deadly calm that made my hands tremble. "Not even family."

Mrs. Edwards's smooth skin turned blotchy. "You'll see the choices you have to make when you become a parent." She glared at me again. "I need to get back to my guests." She spun on her heels and left Ashton and me in the foyer.

He stood stock-still, fury flashing in his eyes. "Like later is ever going to come," he muttered. "This family is a joke." Then his shoulders slumped. "I shouldn't be dragging you into this mess. I don't even know why *I* stick around."

"Because it's your blood. Because you have a legacy."

"Yeah, well, maybe we should start our own legacy."

I stared at the floor. "I don't know. Sometimes I feel like I don't belong anywhere."

His face softened, the sternness—and maybe a touch of hurt—melting away. "Dev..."

I wrapped my arms around myself. "Most of the time I can push it aside. But then your mother said all that stuff, and those bad feelings came rushing back."

He gripped my shoulders and held tight. "Listen to me. You belong here. More than anyone. And you sure as hell belong with me."

"You asked about engagement rings," I blurted.

"Because I'm seriously imagining a future with you. I know you don't need me to take care of you, but I want to. I think about it all the time, Dev. But...I shouldn't have done it. Not without talking to you first."

"You could be with Rochelle and avoid all this drama. She's perfect, and your mother obviously loves her." I glanced into the sitting room, where Mrs. Edwards and Rochelle were laughing together again. "I can't compete."

Ashton moved close to me and buried his fingers in my hair. My bun came loose and curls tumbled around my shoulders. "There is no competition. There never was. I broke up with her because I wanted to be with you. Because I *needed* to be with you." He fixed those eyes on mine, searing me with his intensity. His urgency. "I need you."

I shivered as his lips covered mine. Now I was messing up *his* hair, but I didn't care. Not one bit. I leaned against the wall as we kissed again, deeply and passionately. The whole length of his body pressed against me, showing me his need more than anything he could say. I shivered again, aching for him in the most carnal way.

"Come upstairs with me," he whispered against my lips.

"Leaving your own party?"

"I have to be alone with you. Right now."

This was Ashton. My beautiful, complicated boy. The boy I loved more than anything. Was he worth it? Yes, and then some. To hell with everything and everyone else.

"Let's go."

Chapter 31

JANUARY 25. BLUE MONDAY. SOME SAID IT WAS THE MOST depressing day of the year. The holidays over, the reality of the long cold winter ahead. The Christmas bills rolling in. The failed New Year's resolutions.

But for me, it was the day my boyfriend's world shattered.

The chef had prepared minestrone soup, and Ashton and I were about to tear into it when the vibration in the kitchen changed. I glanced at the doorway, and there was Ashton's father, his expression grave.

"Do you want sparkling or still water?" Ashton asked, his voice muffled by the thick refrigerator doors.

"Ash." I nudged him gently.

"Hmm?"

I didn't say anything, which made him pop out of the

fridge. "What…?" Then he saw his father. Immediately went stiff. "Father."

"Ashton and I need a moment," Mr. Edwards said.

"Of course," I answered, my voice quiet.

Ashton touched my arm, his fingers tightening just a little bit. "I'll be right back."

I nodded, and they disappeared, leaving me alone.

An eternity passed before Ashton came back and gripped my hand. I could tell he wanted to say something, but the words would not come. It was the way he kept opening and closing his mouth. The shallow, hitching breaths. The look of devastation on his face.

"Ash…?"

"It's Grandma," he blurted out. "She's gone."

In the movies, funerals always happen on rainy days. People dressed in black and holding black umbrellas, standing around a coffin while a preacher says prayers. People throwing dirt on the coffin before walking away from the gravesite, their expressions solemn.

This day was not rainy. It was bitterly cold, and I nearly froze in my black dress and tights. I'd almost slipped on the ice twice in my heels, but I didn't even care.

My boyfriend was grieving, and it was breaking my heart.

I met him at his house that morning. The atmosphere was gravely quiet except for the ticking of the grandfather clock. Mrs. Edwards's eyes bore into me, but my eyes were only for

Ashton. He didn't talk, even when I straightened his tie, which didn't really need fixing. He just stared at me, almost as though he was trying to draw strength from looking into my soul.

"It's time," his mother said, pulling on her coat.

"Ready?" I asked him. He shook his head, but then took a deep breath and slipped his hand into mine.

The service was stiflingly formal. Sadness was prominent here at Holy Name Lutheran Church, of which, according to the obituary, Ashton's grandmother had been a part since she'd been a little girl. She'd kept in touch with the parish after she'd moved to Monaco, making generous donations and visiting whenever she made her way stateside. A home base, so to speak, in our small town. So many people had come to pay their last respects, dabbing at their eyes with silky handkerchiefs. And the flowers. Beautiful greenhouse ones that made my eyes water and my throat itch.

Pancreatic cancer took Harriet Edwards's life. She'd refused chemotherapy and radiation, as the disease had been too advanced by the time she was diagnosed. She hadn't shared the details of her diagnosis with any of her family, instead choosing to live her life as fully as she could, until the end.

She was eighty-two years old.

I wish I'd gotten the chance to talk to her again, but my sadness was nothing compared to what my boyfriend was feeling. The storm brewed in his eyes, showing me the barely contained grief, the hopelessness.

I sat with Ashton and his parents. He squeezed my hand

so tightly I was afraid my circulation would get cut off. But I didn't let go.

Ashton wouldn't let himself cry. He also wouldn't eat. He barely acknowledged the people who had come to pay their respects. Even his best friend knew to steer clear. And when the after-service talk at his house went from somber to jovial as they started to share memories, Ashton dragged me to his room. "I couldn't take the laughing," he said. "I couldn't take any of it."

"Even if they're sharing good things?"

"It's all an act, Devon. Wait until the will is read." His face crumpled. "We'll see if they're laughing then."

The threads holding Ashton together were snapping right before my eyes. He sank onto the floor and buried his face in his hands. I pulled him close as he shook with silent sobs.

I stroked his hair and kissed his forehead. I brushed the wetness from his cheeks. I let him take as long as he needed, until he looked up at me, his eyes red and swollen.

"I wanted to take you to Monte Carlo with me," he said in a choked whisper. "For spring break. The stargazing there— it's supposed to be unreal."

I had no idea what to say.

"A few weeks after…that summer, she was the only one who didn't treat me like I should have been ashamed to screw up like that. She was the only one who understood how desperate

I was to get away from the Dark. And she told me…she said as long as she lived, she would protect me from it. I knew she really couldn't, but it was a nice thought. Except now she's gone."

He let out a hitching breath and leaned his head on my shoulder. "Who's going to protect me now?"

The pungent cloud of Chanel No. 5 reached us even before the click of heels made us jump apart. Guilty conscience, even though we weren't doing anything wrong.

"Why aren't you downstairs with the family?" Ashton's mother asked him, her voice sharp enough to cut glass.

"I needed some time. Alone."

"Except you're here with your girlfriend, which is highly inappropriate." Her eyes cut to me. "As you both know."

Her son was a wreck, and she could only focus on propriety?

"We were talking." Ashton stood and pulled me with him. "Since when is that a crime?"

She pressed her lips together. "You're dishonoring your grandmother's memory. Couldn't you have braved it out for one more hour? People are leaving now."

"I. Couldn't. Stand. The. Bullshit."

"Language."

Ashton grabbed his hair and yanked. "We just buried the only person in this family who gives—*gave*—a damn about me. I don't—" He stopped and rubbed his forehead. Then he took a deep breath, stood up straighter, and looked Mrs. Edwards in the eye. Like magic, the flush in his cheeks and the tremor in his hands disappeared. The emotional breakdown had somehow been diffused, and now he was as polished as a politician.

How the hell did he do that?

"You're right," he said, the passion in his voice gone. "I'm sorry. We both are."

Wait, what? I had nothing to be sorry for, so why was he saying this stuff?

"Apology accepted. I understand that you're upset. Don't let it happen again," she said briskly. "Either of you."

"I'm taking Devon home." He swept past her, pulling me with him.

"Ashton," she called.

"Yes?"

"She's not the only one."

He stiffened.

"Your grandmother. She wasn't—she's not the only one in this family who cares about you."

My parents were out. I took Ashton to my room and switched on the Christmas lights. He watched as I yanked off the stiff dressy clothes and got comfy in my yoga uniform. Then I plopped on the bed and let out a long sigh.

"Better?" he asked with a small smile.

"Much." I reached out my hands. "Join me."

He climbed in beside me and played with my fingers.

"What was that all about? At your house?" I asked. "It was like Dr. Jekyll and Mr. Hyde."

He laughed then, bitterly. "Sometimes it's easier to let her believe she's right than to fight it."

"You totally could have won, though. She had guests to save face in front of."

He let out a snort. "She said she cares about me. She's sure got a fucked-up way of showing it."

"I'm sorry. I wish I could fix it all for you."

He shook his head. "Whatever. I'm done talking about it."

He wasn't done thinking about it. His pinched forehead showed me that. I ran my fingers across the wrinkles until they smoothed out. Until he let out a sigh and lay on his back. "Come closer. Please."

I snuggled up to him and buried my face in his neck. Inhaled his scent. Let the events of the day fade away.

He squeezed my shoulder. "I love your ceiling. Are the stars arranged by actual constellations?"

"They are. I put them up when I was eleven. I was a colossal brat about it because I wanted it to be perfect. My parents were so done with me."

He chuckled. "I can't see you acting that way."

"Ask Dad. He'll be happy to tell you all about it." I stroked Ashton's cheek so he'd turn to look at me. "Do you want to stay with me tonight?"

He rubbed his nose against mine. "I don't want you to get in trouble."

"I don't care about that right now. I only care about you."

"I do want to stay. Today sucked. I want to forget all about it."

I fiddled with his tie. "Maybe I can help you take your mind off things. If that's . . . if it's okay."

He sucked in a breath. "Yeah, I think that'll be okay." His voice shook and his hand trembled as he reached up to touch my face.

I kissed his fingertips. "I love that you still react like this."

"It'll never not be special, Devon," he said. "Twenty years from now, I'm still going to react this way. Every single time."

"I like when you talk about our future," I said. "I worry about you."

"Don't worry right now, okay?" he said, closing his eyes. "Let's just love each other."

I kissed him then, and we didn't speak for a long time.

Chapter 32

"You wanted to see me, Professor Trask?"

He nodded, eyes grave. "Please sit."

I knew why I was here. I'd nibbled my fingernails down to the quick, waiting for this moment. Or one much worse.

Winter had descended full force. Every day we got pounded with freezing winds, blowing snow, and frigid temperatures. The weather was definitely getting me down.

So was Ashton's sudden distance from me.

We'd had the best Valentine's Day ever, holed up in his house watching movies and eating junk food. I wore the heart-shaped Tiffany earrings he'd given me every day since. But it had been a month since then, and these days, he was quiet. Withdrawn. Mysterious, but not in a good way.

I'd texted him three times today with no answer. And he'd skipped school again.

"Some of your professors are concerned about you," Professor Trask said. "You're missing homework assignments, and you didn't score as highly as usual on your last few quizzes. Is there anything you want to talk about?"

Yes, Professor Trask. Where should I start?

1. My boyfriend's depression was taking over and he was shutting me out.

It was the first time I'd admitted it to myself. But the signs were there. The withdrawal. The exhaustion that bruised the skin under his eyes. The eerie silence that was nothing like our usual comfortable quiet. Instead, he was engaged in some private war within himself. Even on our good days, he'd been distant. His mind, a million places, but not with me. And now he wasn't talking to me at all.

2. I still had a month until I got a final answer from McCafferty. Knowing the date probably should've calmed me down, but it only made me more anxious.

3. Therefore, school didn't seem quite as important as keeping my boyfriend from doing something desperate. Except he wasn't talking to me.

4. The complete lack of control I felt about *everything* in my life right now.

I didn't want to flunk out of school. But I was exhausted from caring so much about so many things that there was no room in my brain for calculations and research and hardcore studying. And this was how I knew something was terribly wrong.

Since when did I not have time for the stars?

"Devon?"

"I'm fine," I blurted.

Of course Professor Trask didn't believe me. *I* barely believed me.

"Devon, you're our top student, but if you keep performing like this—"

"I know."

He shook his head. "I don't think you do. You're obviously having a hard time, but I can't help you if you won't let me. You have too much to lose here, so please, think about what you're allowing to happen. And please get help, even if it's not from me."

I stared at my lap.

"You still have time to get back on track," Professor Trask said gently. "It's up to you how you're going to proceed."

"I'll do better," I said, my voice raspy. Husky.

"Don't tell me. Tell yourself. Then actually do the work."

Chapter 33

THE WEEK RACED BY IN A FLURRY OF PROJECTS, REPORTS, and assignments. I was on autopilot. The only thing that pulled me out of my stupor was getting a D on an Astronomy pop quiz. A *D*. In *Astronomy*, of all things.

I stared at the paper, the words swimming, the red D blurring into a bloody smear on my academic career. And at that moment, I hated everything. I hated Professor Trask's look of concern and disappointment. I hated Ashton for making me worry so much. And I hated myself for giving in and screwing up my grades. My *life*.

Voices rattled around my head constantly. Professor Trask, the disappointment evident as I was late with yet another homework assignment. Auden, "touching base" with me for the millionth time about the invoicing for the yearbook. Blair,

her forehead wrinkled as she asked a million leading questions, trying to make the dam burst.

I had to stop staring at Ashton's empty seat during lunch. I
had to stop checking my phone every ten seconds. I had to stop
jeopardizing my future for a boy who refused to let me in.

Time to make a new plan.

What do you want? I mentally screamed at myself.

I wanted, no, *needed* my drive and ambition back so I could
go back to kicking Auden's butt.

What's standing in your way?

Worrying so much about Ashton.

So what's the solution?

Eliminate the worry, regroup, and refocus.

But for now, I balled up the quiz and sat blankly through
Professor Trask's lecture.

Chapter 34

I LOVED THE STARS. THERE WAS NO DENYING THAT.

But sometimes I needed a break from them.

I loved Ashton. There was no denying that, either.

But I needed a break from him, too.

(It wasn't like he was answering my texts, anyway.)

Friday night. Not out and about, but home, where it was warm and quiet. Green tea incense cleared my mind as I pulled up the yearbook-builder website on my laptop. Logged in. And clicked through.

Analyzing hundreds of photos probably shouldn't have been as satisfying as it was, but there was something meditative about finding that perfect shot, then tweaking it so it was sharper, more colorful, more alive.

As I flipped through, I had to laugh at how Colton managed

to photobomb every club's group photo. Like his steak-loving self would be caught dead as an actual member of the Vegan Club. But there he was, standing in the back and grinning like a maniac. I marveled at Tyrell's talent to tell stories with the way he laid out the pages. I even had to begrudgingly nod at Auden's foreword, and how it managed to capture perfectly the theme of the book, and of our school.

There were photos of our dinner out—a special treat from Professor Wilcox for managing to sell all the yearbooks before spring.

She'd probably regretted taking us out in public. Auden and Tyrell snapping at each other like they always did. Colton sneaking bites from everyone's plates. Me picking at my food because my mind was in a million places at once.

And now my face was wet. Seeing these photos—batches from every grade—brought back a boatload of memories. Blair taking me under her wing my first day of school, when I was scared and lost. Auden's smug smile on my second day, declaring our Unofficial Official Competition. Professor Trask with his warm belly laugh, further encouraging my obsession with all things cosmos.

Afternoon teas, thrown by Dr. Steelwood to help new freshmen get more easily acclimated to the school. Sophomore year finishing classes, where we learned how to hold our forks and properly eat bread at a formal dinner. Junior year standardized testing prep. Stress magnified.

And now senior year was flying by. Preston was full of so many personalities, and even though I didn't spend a lot of time outside my little circle, it still hurt that soon we'd all be separated. I would miss them all.

Even Auden.

With my time at Preston Academy nearing its end, with Ashton being so distant, with my future studies uncertain, I felt like a broken butterfly, being tossed here and there by the wind. Everything that held me together was unraveling, and I wasn't sure what was next. For the first time, I wasn't ready for the future.

I was terrified of it.

Chapter 35

SATURDAY MORNING, I CALLED ASHTON FIRST THING. "DAD lent me his car. I need to go to Happy Paws. Do you want to come with me?"

"I think I'm going to stay home." His voice was dull, flat.

"But our brunch date?"

A long pause, then, "That's today?"

"We were going to try the new waffle place. Remember?"

Another pause. "Can I take a rain check?"

"Ash, we don't have to go out. I can come over when I'm done at the shelter."

"No, Dev. You should enjoy your Saturday. Don't worry about me."

"I'll always worry about you," I said quietly.

"Well, don't. Okay? I'll talk to you later."

He hung up. Stung, I sat frozen on my bed. Heartbreaking scenarios raced through my head. What if it wasn't his depression at all? What if he didn't love me anymore? What if we were over? God, I hated this limbo. I needed to get answers out of him, but how could I do that when he wouldn't talk to me?

No. Sitting here feeling sorry for myself wasn't an option. I had too much to do. I swallowed the lump in my throat, grabbed the car keys, and got the hell out of the house.

I hadn't been to Happy Paws since I finished my volunteer hours in September. I probably would have never come back, except they'd needed me to fill out one more piece of paperwork so my hours would actually count. The bright lobby was warm and welcoming, a stark contrast to the bitter cold outside.

"Hi! Devon, right?" There was Angelica, as chipper as the first time I'd met her. This time, her hair was dyed to mimic a rainbow.

I tried to make my smile radiate like her curls. "That's right."

"Great. I'll have your form in a bit. In the meantime, do you want to say hi to Buddy? He's our official mascot now."

"He's still here?" I frowned. "That makes me so sad."

"He's pretty sad, too. His friend hasn't been by in a while."

I froze in alarm. "Ashton?"

She nodded. "It's been at least four weeks."

What the hell. Ashton loved that dog. But then, he said he loved me, too, and look where we were.

I sent him a text, asking what was up. No answer. Seriously, *what the hell*, Ashton?

Buddy had been moved to a smaller room that housed older dogs who lay curled up and watching me with sleepy eyes. I sat on the floor, and Buddy padded over and laid his head in my lap. I scratched behind his ears and he let out a content sigh. How could so many people come through this shelter every day and pass up this awesome creature? How could Ashton abandon him? I sat with Buddy and pulled out my phone.

Depression: Supporting a Family Member or Friend.

Symptoms:

Irritability?

Check.

Loss of interest in hobbies?

I looked sadly at Buddy. Check.

Forgetfulness?

Yup.

I knew them well by now. What I needed to know was how to help him. If I could help him. Except the site was no help, either. *Talk to the person.* Okay, right. Not useful when the person wouldn't talk to *me*. Frustrated, I shoved my phone into my bag and buried my face in Buddy's fur.

After I filled out my form, I drove around town, trying to decide what to do. Ashton had said for me to enjoy my day, but how could I when my brain kept playing the worst scenarios over and over? And yet, I wanted to respect his boundaries. Give him space if that's what he wanted. Except I didn't know if that's what he actually wanted, or if the Dark was telling him that being alone was what he deserved.

I parked at the grocery store and leaned my head against the steering wheel. I hated everything about this. I hated depression. I hated its lies and its darkness and its all-consuming power. I hated how powerless it made me feel. And if *I* felt powerless, how was Ashton feeling?

My fists clenched. Screw this.

I put the car in gear.

Chapter 36

I DROVE TO THE GATE AND PUNCHED IN THE CODE. CIRCLED the fountain and parked right in front of the main door. Marched directly upstairs and burst into Ashton's room.

He was sprawled on the floor, holding a video game controller and staring at his TV. He looked like a hot mess, and didn't seem surprised to see me when he gazed up at me with dull eyes. Pajama pants. Shiny face. Greasy hair. Junk food wrappers everywhere.

"Hey," I said. "Can I sit with you?"

He didn't say anything. Just handed me the other controller.

The quest was to retrieve a chest of gold before the ogre woke up. But there were traps and timers and tricks, and they got me every time. We played until I lost all our lives.

"Sorry," I said.

He dropped the controller and offered me a tiny smile. That little sign of life filled me with relief, albeit short-lived.

I dropped my controller, too, and wrapped my arms around him. He closed his eyes and nestled close to me, burying his face in my neck. And we sat like that, so still, so quiet, for what felt like hours.

"Ash," I said against his temple, "are we okay?"

He stared right into my eyes. Then he nodded.

"Are *you* okay?"

No answer this time. Just his arms, tightening around me.

"How can I help?" I was asking this even though I felt as helpless as he looked.

He let out a long, trembling sigh. "I don't know if you can."

"I can try. I don't pretend to know what you're going through, but I'm here. I'll always be here. I love you."

He squared his shoulders and gave me a bright smile. One that didn't quite reach his eyes. One that crackled, its intensity was so high. "Don't worry, Dev. I'll get through this. I'll be okay."

Who was he trying to convince? Himself or me?

And why couldn't I believe him?

Chapter 37

CELESTIAL COORDINATES: THE POSITIONS OF STARS, PLANETS, and galaxies. There were five different celestial coordinate systems to determine these positions, and I had to learn them all. This should have been right up my alley. It amazed me that these complicated calculations could tell me so much about something so far away.

Except I couldn't bring myself to care about any of them right now. I stared hopelessly at my Astronomy textbook, watching letters and numbers and symbols spiral into an indecipherable mess.

I'd wanted to glue myself to Ashton's side last night. But my phone had started blowing up with messages from Mom.

Where u at?

> I'm starving! U ok? Been here 10 mins.

> If I don't hear from u by the time I count 2 thirty I'm calling police.

> & eating ur bacon.

Ashton had practically shoved me out the door, telling me I should enjoy my Mom-Daughter time and not worry about him. Why did he always say that? He had to know that I was going to check my phone over and over. That Mom would snatch it away so I could be present and enjoy our breakfast for dinner at the old-fashioned diner.

"Bun, you aren't eating," Mom had said last night. Dark-brown eyes scrutinized every bite I pushed around the plate. "You've barely touched your blueberry French toast."

"Not that hungry."

"But you love breakfast for dinner. Is everything okay?"

I twirled my fork, mangling my toast and ripping it to shreds. "Everything's fine."

"How are you feeling?"

Like a jumbled-up, mixed-up mess. But I swallowed those emotions and forced a bite. The French toast really was delicious. "Just tired."

There was no way she believed me. I could tell by the way her eyes narrowed, the way her lips pursed. But as I said, Mom always knew when to give me space, even when she really didn't want to. Even when I wasn't sure I wanted her to.

"Then you should hit the sack early tonight," she said. "You can't afford to get sick now."

No, not with second semester midterms coming up.

Which was why I was studying right now. Trying to, anyway. Ashton had some serious stuff going on, and despite my best efforts—which, let's be honest, weren't that great these days—it was still affecting my grades. Professor Trask's warning had simply floated away, like those thought clouds yoga teachers were so fond of talking about during meditation. Every day I sat in class, nibbling my nails, anticipating a call to the office where Dr. Steelwood would tell me I'd been kicked out. My concentration was festering in hell, and instead of formulas and solutions, I saw Ashton's face. The desperate look in his eyes. The strain around his mouth.

I pushed my book aside and flipped to a new page in my notebook. Then I pulled up the calculator on my phone. Because I needed to concentrate, but I also needed to obsess over Ashton. It made no logical sense, but I knew I wouldn't be able to study until I got him out of my system, at least for tonight.

Calculations, calculations. I loved calculating. But no matter how I rearranged the figures, no matter how many charts I drew, I could not work out a good balance. And this was a problem.

I slammed the notebook shut and marched over to the mirror. This is what stared back at me: frizzy golden spirals, pale cheeks, and dark circles under my eyes. No more stars.

But my voice was strong.

"Devon Kearney, you are better than this. This is your future. Yours. No one else's. Get yourself together and do it *now*."

I needed to be more forceful.

"This is serious. This is your life. Your dream. Now act like you have some sense, and get your priorities straight!"

My reflection stared back, her mouth set in defiance. I had to get out the big guns.

Deep breath.

And go.

"If you don't straighten up, then you'll need to choose. School or him." I swallowed. Hard. "Do you want to give up Ashton? Because you'll have to if you don't get it together. And that's not an option."

I gripped the dresser. Even saying it made my head spin. I was so scared of losing him. I absolutely did not want to give him up. But I had to stop this foolishness.

My eyes hardened. Who cared about those silly calculations? I had this. I could keep up with school, and I could keep him, too. It wouldn't be easy, but nothing worth doing ever was.

Bring it.

I picked up my phone and shot him one last text:

> I'm here whenever you're ready.

Then I forced myself back to my textbook and my notes.

I'd just finished an equatorial-to-ecliptic conversion when the doorbell rang. I dropped my pencil and ran to the door, and there was Ashton, standing in the cold. "Hey, you!" I threw open the door and pulled him inside. Then I noticed his expression. Helpless. Hurting. Devastated. "What happened?"

"We have really awful fights all the time, you know?" His voice was low and thick. "My father and me. But he's never gotten physical."

"What?!"

"He grabbed me. Threw me. I fell and knocked over his drink cart. He—" Ashton let out a shuddering breath. "I can't talk about it anymore. I can't even believe it happened."

I clenched my fists and closed my eyes.

Inhale...two...three...four.

Exhale...two...three...four.

"Why?" I choked out.

He collapsed onto the couch and buried his face in his hands. "He was drunk. Said awful things. He drinks all the time now. And when he starts drinking, I have to get out of the way. And ever since Grandma died...it's a fucking nightmare."

I grabbed his hands. "Oh my God."

He continued as if he hadn't heard me. "He said I was worthless. Called me a waste." His hands started shaking. "I'm not a waste. I'm not a fucking waste." Then he looked at me, his vulnerable expression breaking my heart. "Devon, am I a waste?"

"You're not a waste." I squeezed his hands. "You are not a waste."

He was still for a few moments, gathering himself. Then he sat up a bit straighter. "They read the will yesterday."

"Were you there?"

"I tuned out halfway through, but the gist of it is that everyone's pissed at my father. And me."

"But what in the world did you do?"

He let out a bitter laugh. "Be her favorite."

I could only imagine what that meant.

"Now my father, his brothers and sisters—they're all fighting. He came home last night and got wasted. He stayed home today and got drunk again. I was in the wrong place at the wrong time."

"Holy shit, Ashton." I traced his face, looking for bruises or cuts. "Does your mother know?"

He snorted. "She's no better. All she does is go on about me being with you. On and on about how 'being with Rochelle is more aligned with our family goals.' How she's more equipped to deal with the pressures of being in a powerful family. How she's more suitable. Doesn't matter if I don't love Rochelle, Mother says. Because apparently the Edwards family marries for power, not"—he went into a snooty imitation of his mother—"fleeting, silly things like puppy love."

"Great."

"Here's the kicker: Rochelle's seeing some titled dude in Europe now. I thought telling them that would get them off my back, but no. They still don't want me with you because apparently you're a distraction from me finding the 'right' person."

"The 'right' person," I repeated bitterly.

"Father threatened to cut me off if I didn't break up with you."

I covered my mouth with my hand.

Something in his grandma's will must have triggered this. Therefore, I needed to be dismissed as soon as possible.

Dismissed. My stomach lurched. "Is that why you're here? To break up with me?"

He glanced at me out of the corner of his eye. "If I was cut off, would you stay with me?"

Oh hell no. Family drama or not, this was some bullshit. "I can't believe you would even ask me that. What the hell?"

"No. Dev." He shook his head. "That's not what I meant. It's because of me. Why would you be with someone whose parents don't even like him?"

I was so tired. "Ashton, I'm not dating your parents."

"I know, but—"

I gestured between us. "They have nothing to do with what's going on right here."

He swallowed. "You're right."

"But to be honest, I don't think you'd stay with me."

His face colored. "What the fuck? Why would you say that?"

"Listen. You getting cut off wouldn't be a big deal to me, but you grew up with all that. That's all you know. Can you live like a regular person? Do you even know how?"

He sighed, defeated. "All I know is that I love you and I'll do anything to keep you in my life. What you and I have? It's the best thing in my life, and I'm not about to throw us away. Not for my parents. Not for anything."

"Even your family's money?"

"Especially that."

I could make it easy. I could break up with him. He could keep his money. He'd eventually find some WASP princess to settle down with. There would be harmony in his family, and I wouldn't have to deal with their drama, politics, and scrutiny.

But the thought of doing that made bile rise in my throat. Regardless of what happened in the future, he was my right now and I loved him so much. And call me selfish, but he was mine, and I wasn't about to hand him over. Besides, no matter what choice I made, I would come out looking like the gold digger his parents thought I was. So why break his heart when whatever I did wouldn't make a difference, anyway?

At least this way I'd get to keep him.

"I told my father to go fuck himself," Ashton said. "That's why he hit me."

I couldn't even blame Ashton. I had my own choice words for Tristan Carter Preston Edwards right now. But I kept quiet. The man was still Ashton's father, and I wasn't about to disrespect him.

Not that he *deserved* any respect from me. But still.

"Do you know what it's like to have your father look at you like he's disappointed in you all the time?" Ashton glanced at me. "No, of course you don't know. I'm glad you don't know. Because it's awful. I wish I didn't care. But I do, and I hate it."

"Of course you care, and of course you hate it. And that's okay."

He jumped up and started pacing. "I don't know if I can live like a regular person. But I'm willing to try. I would love to take my place in the family business and show them—show *him*—that I can make it bigger and better than before." He stopped and ran his hands through his hair. "But I have to get the hell away from him, even if it means leaving all of it behind."

"But if they cut you off—" I broke off.

One thing I'd learned about wealthy people is that they made sure they were taken care of, no matter what happened. But I didn't know how it all worked. Could his parents seize all that? Would they leave him destitute? It didn't make sense to me, but maybe there were rules in his world I'd never understand.

I nibbled my thumbnail. Everything was so complicated now. That summer, things had been so simple. Ashton and me: two people in love. Now it felt political. Then adding his depression, plus my own pressures with school…the weariness climbed into my bones and settled heavily there.

"Devon, we'll be okay," he said. "Right?"

I slid my arms around his waist and closed my eyes. "I hope so."

Chapter 38

My parents were the ultimate hippies, and Mom sometimes took mysticism to a whole other plane. Because of my obsession with the stars, I was more pragmatic. Didn't really get into the whole psychic-connection-ESP thing.

Except I couldn't ignore the pang in my gut that told me Ashton was in danger.

He'd skipped school today. Said he was going home. Running right back to the very place he hated so much.

And I wanted to be right there, holding him and distracting him from the darkness taking him over. Convincing him not to do what I was so afraid he was planning to do. I wanted to climb into bed with him and relive last night, after we'd stopped talking about his parents and fell silent, eyes locked. When the need to be close to each other took over, and our lips met as if it were our first and last kiss. When we were naked in each other's arms, immersed in our own world. A world with no pain, no drama, and no demons to torment him. Just me and Ashton, connecting in our ultimate way. Close and raw and passionate and real.

Last night, after he'd pulled on his coat, I'd traced his face and given him a gentle, lingering kiss. Then I rested my thumb on his bottom lip. "I love you, you know."

"I love you, too. So much." Then he'd given me a look that filled me with alarm. It was like he was soaking me in, saving me up for when I wasn't there. As if he was never going to see me again.

And there was no text from him when I woke up.

Now, with every class, every ring of the bell, the foreboding feeling ballooned until it completely consumed me. Auden scribbled away on our Calculus pop quiz, that annoying smug smile on her face. But for me, the questions swam on the paper until they were nothing but piles of black gibberish.

My phone buzzed.

Two texts from Ashton that shot terror clear through me.

Oh.

God.

I had to get to him.

Wait. Failing this test would ruin my GPA and knock me out of the top spot, obliterating any chance of me getting into McCafferty. Leaving school unexcused could get me a demerit, which would jeopardize my scholarship.

Him or my future? What was it going to be?

Blair met me by my locker. "I'll drive you."

We rushed straight to his house. Straight to his room.

"Ashton." I sank to the floor next to him, aware of nothing except the sick boy hunched over, sweating and shaking, in front of me. I yanked his head up so we were nose to nose. "What did you do?"

But I knew what he'd done. Of course I knew. Why else would I have rushed here?

He raised desperate eyes to meet mine. "I'm so scared," he said, his voice faint, his words slurred.

I swallowed a sob. "Ash..."

"I wanted everything to stop. The fighting, the yelling. I wanted the Dark to go away." His eyelids fluttered. "I thought I wanted to die, but I don't." The look in his eyes turned wild, feral. "I don't wanna die."

"Then you've got to stay awake," I said, my voice firm. The exact opposite of what I was feeling: a meteoric explosion of fear.

"I'm calling 911," Blair said. "I'll take the pill bottles with me."

Pill bottles. There were pill bottles. How had I missed them? "Ashton," I said firmly, "I need you to stay with me."

"I'm sorry," he said, closing his eyes again. And that's when I stopped trying to hold back. It was too hard to stay strong.

"Please don't leave me." Hot tears blazed down my cheeks. "I can't lose you again. Please."

He opened his eyes. Unfocused. Glazed. "Dev. When did you get here?"

I didn't try to fight the sob this time. "Ashton Edwards, you cannot go to sleep, do you understand me?"

His voice hitched. "I'm so scared."

I wiped his forehead. Cold, clammy, and sweaty. "Then don't go. Not now. Not today. Stay with me. Please, please stay with me."

His face crumpled. "I'm going to be sick."

I grabbed the trash can and thrust it in front of him, then rubbed his back as he was violently ill. He was pale and trembling by the time he was done.

"What did you take?" Anything to keep him talking.

"I don't know. Vicodin. Oxy-something." His voice started to fade again. "Some other stuff."

"Where did you get them?"

"Bought 'em."

Which meant that he'd been planning this. How long had he been planning this?

"Stay with me," I pleaded again. "Please."

He was still, except for his lips. Trembling. His fists. Clenching and unclenching.

Fighting.

Yes, Ashton. Please keep fighting.

"You have to make it," I said desperately, because I needed him to believe it, and I needed to believe it. "You're going to survive this. You are."

He focused on me then, and his face softened into that tender look.

"Devon," he whispered. "I love you. And I'm so sorry."

"Ashton, stay awake. Please." I was losing him, and there wasn't a thing I could do but watch him give up his life. All the cracks in me from holding it together for him were splintering. Pieces of me were falling to the floor and shattering. And Ashton's eyes were closed.

I shook him. "Wake up. Please, wake up!"

He was unresponsive. But he was still breathing. Short, shallow breaths. He was here now... but for how long? I buried my face in his hair and sobbed. Where was the ambulance? They needed to get here soon. Oh God, let them hurry.

"They're in here." Blair's voice sounded like it was underwater.

Two paramedics rushed over to Ashton. They checked his pulse. Shoved an oxygen mask over his face and strapped him to a gurney, shouting urgent instructions to each other the whole time. I followed the paramedics downstairs and into the chilly air outside. I didn't want Ashton out of my sight.

The paramedics wouldn't let me ride with him. Blair's strong arms kept me from scratching their eyes out. Anger and desperation rose in me as I struggled against her. Ashton needed me. Why couldn't anyone see that?

I couldn't see a thing; I was crying so hard my head spun. Tiny, frightened, and shaking. My Ashton, my love. Was he leaving me?

The flashing lights. The disembodied voices coming through the radios. The rattling diesel of the engine. How was this happening? How was this real?

"Wake him up," I sobbed. "Make him wake up!"

"Devon, they're going to take care of him," Blair said.

I wanted to believe her. I did. But I watched him give up. I saw him close his eyes, and I heard him say good-bye. *Please, God, don't let this be good-bye.*

I smelled her familiar coconut scent before I saw her. Before she wrapped her arms around me.

"Mom?" I choked out. When had she gotten here? Where was I? What was happening?

"Thanks for coming, Mrs. K," Blair said. "She's in shock, and I'm scared."

"I'm taking her to the hospital," Mom said. "Do you want to come with us?"

My best friend had paled to the point of translucency. "Yeah," she said, her voice wobbly.

"Let's go."

Ashton's parents were in the waiting room when we arrived. His mother screamed abuse at the receptionist while his father paced, his eyes wide and empty. I glared at him, wanting to blame someone, because Ashton was back there having God knows what done to him, and I had to sit here with tears getting in my hair.

I couldn't stop crying.

"Let's sit down," Mom said. Blair sat on the other side of me and held my hand. I couldn't tell which of us was shaking more.

Days passed. Or maybe it was hours. It could have been

minutes. Someone wrapped me in a blanket. Blair, Mom, and I huddled together, waiting to hear something. Anything.

Ashton's mother ended her tirade and joined her husband in pacing. Around and around and around. Hypnotizing, watching them circumvent each other. Watching them treading so carefully. But I could see her. I could see the cold fury flashing in her eyes every time she glared at her husband, and I could see the shame in his.

The doctor came out and took his parents aside. He spoke to them in low murmurs. I was desperate to go over, but it wasn't my place. I loved Ashton more than anything in the world, but I was only his high school girlfriend. Someone who might not even be around in a few months, as far as they were concerned.

Ashton's parents went through the double doors. What did that mean? My heart beat faster and my palms grew damp. Mom held me tighter while I buried my face in her shoulder and tried to keep from imagining the worst.

Another eternity passed, and finally, Ashton's mother emerged from the back and came over to me. I pulled away from my mom slightly as Mrs. Edwards took my hand.

"He's stabilized for now," she said. "They're moving him to intensive care."

"Is he awake?"

She closed her eyes and kept them closed for a long time. Then, slowly opening them, she said, "He's still unconscious."

"I need to see him," I said, my voice raspy.

"You should go home. Get some rest."

"I won't be able to sleep." I shook my head. "Not until I see him."

She nodded and sighed. "I thought you might say that. But they're not letting anyone back there other than family."

"Is he going to make it?"

She swallowed and looked down. "We don't know."

I covered my mouth with my hand.

"He took a lot of pills. They had to pump his stomach. It's a good thing you showed up when you did. My husband and I weren't supposed to be back for hours. I don't know what would have happened if—" She broke off.

"I have to see him." My voice cracked. "Please."

"Devon," Mrs. Edwards said, "I'll be here. And I promise I'll get in touch with you if things change."

If.

"Come on, Bun," Mom said. "It's late. You can come back tomorrow."

NEBULA

Chapter 39

BLAIR CAME HOME WITH ME. WE DIDN'T WATCH MOVIES OR experiment with makeup. We sat stone-still, shocked and quiet. At some point, I climbed into bed, but sleep didn't come. I lay awake. Wide-eyed. Empty.

I closed my eyes, but sleep still wouldn't come. Tears did, though. So many tears. So much fear and so much worry. What could I have done to prevent this? I should have helped him more. Why didn't I help him more?

His texts had burned into my memory:

Dev, I did something.

I'm scared.

The fear turned my stomach over and over. The images wouldn't go away. Those terrifying texts. The flashing ambulance lights. His pale face and clammy skin.

I gave up on sleep and stared at the ceiling. Watched my glow-in-the-dark stars fade as the room lightened with the dawn of a new day. Would Ashton ever see a new day?

I squeezed my stuffed bunny and prayed.

When the alarm went off, Blair jumped a clear two feet. Then, without a word, she hopped up, shook her head, then trudged into the bathroom.

My eyes were gritty with fatigue and my head hurt, but I dragged myself out of bed anyway. Skipped yoga. Skipped breakfast. Would have skipped my shower, but Blair drew the line at that.

Mom gave me permission to stay home from school, but I wanted the distraction. I wanted the work and the bells and Auden's obnoxious smile. I wanted the lectures and the slamming lockers and my turkey sandwich for lunch.

But nothing helped.

Weak with worry, I kept my eyes lowered and focused on organizing yearbook orders. Taking notes that might or might not make sense later. Barely hearing any lectures. But the effort only made my head hurt worse. Blair hardly left my side. She stayed quiet during lunch—a miracle for her. I could sense her watching me, even while she tried to pretend to be immersed in whatever was on her phone.

My phone stayed silent. I nibbled my nails, desperate to hear anything. No, not anything. I wanted good news. I *needed* good news.

"I'm sorry, but I can't let you back," the nurse said. "You're not family."

My fists clenched. "Your policy says significant others count as family. I'm his girlfriend."

"The rules are different for intensive care. I'm sorry."

Shaking with rage, I made my way back to the waiting room. I'd rushed here right after school—hadn't even bothered to change—and I wasn't about to turn around and leave. Maybe they could stop me from going back there, but damn if I would leave this hospital without hearing something from someone. I collapsed into one of the orange vinyl chairs and tried to breathe.

Inhale goodness, exhale badness.

My eyes stung.

Inhale goodness, exhale badness.

A sob escaped. And yet, I kept inhaling…*two…three…four.* Exhaling…*two…three…four.*

"Devon?"

My head snapped up. Mrs. Edwards stood outside the waiting room, gazing at me curiously.

Her usual polished look was gone. Still wearing her business suit from yesterday, she had runny makeup and messy hair. This woman I'd been so resentful of was a shell of herself, mirroring my worry and my grief and my love for the sick boy down the hall.

"How is he?" I asked.

"He still hasn't woken up."

"They won't let me see him."

"You were going to just sit here?"

"I need to be close to him."

She gave me a strange look. "You really do love him."

"He's my everything," I said quietly.

She nodded and swallowed. Made her way across the lobby and collapsed into the chair next to me. We sat for what felt like hours, the drone of the news in the background. I jumped when she started talking.

"I was raised in a household where we didn't show a lot of affection," she said in a trembly voice. "It just wasn't done. So that's how I raised Ashton. I let the nanny pick him up when he was crying. She raised him until my husband sent him to a boarding school. But Ashton, bless his heart, craves love." A bitter laugh. "If I hadn't been so concerned with doing things the 'right' way... if I'd learned from the first time he tried this, maybe we wouldn't be here again."

Without even thinking, I reached my hands across the cold metal armrest to clasp with hers. I had a feeling she craved love as well.

"I sent him to his grandmother every chance I could because she was different from the rest of us. I pushed him away, then I wonder why he's distant." She shook her head. "Stupid."

I didn't know what to say. Maybe I didn't need to say anything at all.

"My husband hit him and I froze. I didn't do a thing to stop it. I failed my son. Again." She shook her head. "That changes today. That changes right now. If he makes it." Her eyes squeezed shut. "Please let him make it."

The sleepless night was catching up to me. My head began to nod. But it snapped right to attention when the man in blue scrubs came over to us and uttered the two most gorgeous words in the English language.

"He's awake."

"Oh, thank God. Thank God, thank God, thank God." Mrs. Edwards sagged with relief, but then seemed to remember herself. Back was the smooth face, the collected composure. "Take me to him."

"Certainly," the doctor said.

Mrs. Edwards squeezed my hand, and said to me with genuine warmth, "Let's go see Ashton."

She and I followed the doctor through the double doors. I barely noticed the antiseptic scent stinging my nostrils. The nurses in scrubs holding IV bags and rushing into rooms. The blazing fluorescent lights.

A big contrast to the dim lights and gentle beeping of the heart monitor in Ashton's room.

He was collapsed against his raised bed, tubes and wires snaking around him. His skin matched the stark white of the sheets, and there were dark circles under his eyes. He could have been sleeping, the peaceful way his chest rose and fell. But there was nothing peaceful about my boyfriend lying in the hospital because he'd tried to die.

My brain went to war. I wanted to run to him, but I

stayed rooted in place, watching as Mrs. Edwards went to her son. Brushed his hair from his forehead. Let her tears flow.

His eyes blinked open. Then he stared at her, his expression unreadable.

"I'm so sorry," she said to him. Then she buried her head in his chest while he sat, unblinking.

I shouldn't have been seeing this. My instincts screamed for me to step into the hall, let them have their moment. But then she gestured for me to come closer.

"I'll give you some privacy." She squeezed Ashton's hand before leaving and sliding the door shut.

I took his hands into both of mine. He moved over, making room for me in the hospital bed. I climbed in and pulled him into my arms.

"I was so scared," I whispered.

He let out a shaky breath. "I know. Me too. I—I'm going to get help."

"Promise? Because I don't ever want to pick out clothes and flowers for your funeral." I let out a shaky laugh. "I'm sorry. That was morbid."

He gave me a weak smile. "I get it."

"I'd much rather do that for our wedding someday. You know that, don't you?"

That soft look came over his face. "You still want to be with me? Even after all this?"

I smoothed his hair back. Ran my hands down his cheeks.

Over and over and over. He was warm. And breathing. Not cold and stiff. Not dead. "Yes."

He closed his eyes and leaned against me, his fingers curling into my blazer.

We didn't talk anymore. We clung to each other like life preservers. And in a way, in that moment, I think we were.

Chapter 40

Two days after his attempt, Ashton got switched from the ICU to the psychiatric ward. While he was there, I visited him every day after school. He didn't talk much, but he always moved over and made room for me in the hospital bed. He wrapped himself around me while I did my homework, and I kissed his forehead and played with his silky hair in between subjects. He was always so still, so quiet. What was he thinking about? He never said. Instead, he listened. He listened to me when I babbled on and on about school. He laughed when I told him about Blair's shenanigans, and grew indignant when I told him about Auden's latest obnoxious attempts to unsettle me with all her smack talking. And I brought him junk food, which he devoured.

A week later, he transferred to Lucerne Institution and Rehab Center, right outside town. They cut him off from the world so that he could focus intensely on treatment. I counted the days until I'd get to see him again.

April 16. Decision Day. I sat on the couch between my parents and refreshed my email over and over. Mom flipped through a magazine on one side of me and Dad screamed into his headset on the other, and neither of their activities did a thing to calm my jumping, jittering nerves.

I took deep breaths, trying to mentally prepare myself for the denial from McCafferty. Because, frankly, the chances of me getting in regular decision after being denied early action were very slim. The stats were dismal: less than 3 percent. Not even worth hoping for, really.

So I spent a lot of time psyching myself up to send my offer acceptance to DeKinsey, one of my backup schools. DeKinsey had a good science program. Not a specific astrophysics one like McCafferty, but enough core courses to prepare me for graduate studies at a school that did. Also:

1. DeKinsey cost way less than McCafferty, which meant less student loan debt.

2. They'd also offered me a scholarship, which was always a good thing.

3. I'd also gotten a bunch of private scholarships, and one corporate scholarship. My grades were making their way back to pre-Ashton-meltdown levels, and if I kept it up, the Preston senior scholarship was in the bag.

4. Campus was ninety minutes from home, too far to commute but close enough to come home and do laundry on the weekends.

It would be better to go there for so many reasons. So what if Auden was prancing around with her acceptance to *her* dream school? DeKinsey had a big, beautiful campus with another clock tower for me to fall in love with. Decent food in the cafeteria. Skilled professors. Most important, they wanted me. Things were going to be fine. They were.

No matter what happened.

No matter what happened.

My inbox dinged and

There.

It.

Was.

I grabbed Mom's arm. She dropped her magazine. "Well?"

I froze. "I can't do it."

"I can't, either."

We looked at each other.

"So now what?" I asked.

She reached across me and poked Dad. "James."

"One second . . . YES. Got you, you mouth turd!"

Mom thrust the laptop at Dad, who stared at her in confusion. "What?"

"It's Devon's letter from McCafferty."

"Oh. *Ohhhhhhh!*"

He clicked. "It says I need to log in."

"Just click the link. My password should be saved."

Dad clicked twice, then, his face giving nothing away, turned the screen toward me.

Dear Miss Kearney,

Congratulations! On behalf of the staff and faculty at
McCafferty University, it is with great pleasure . . .

"I'm in." I sat stock-still while I waited for it to sink in. "Oh my God, I'm in!"

Mom screamed and threw her arms around me. Dad did two quick fist pumps and yelled out the biggest "YES" I'd ever heard. That broke the tension and we all collapsed in laughter. We laughed and laughed. It felt so good to feel joy again.

"Honey, this is wonderful," Mom cried. "Cancel all your plans—we're going to celebrate! Call Blair! Tell her to come with us."

"I'm so proud of you," Dad said, squeezing me. "Frankly, I'm not even surprised, but that doesn't make this moment less special. How are you feeling?"

"I'm in shock," I said.

They laughed again. But I wasn't kidding. Was this really happening?

The proof was right there. I couldn't see the stars right now—it was still daytime—but I knew they were out there. And now I was going to be able to catch them.

I turned to the sky and silently said *Thank you* to the universe.

Meanwhile, Dad was already crunching the numbers. "With your scholarships and what we have put away for you, we won't need to take out too much in loans to cover the rest of your undergraduate career."

"And I can always work."

Dad's forehead wrinkled. "Mom and I would rather you focus on your studies."

"In that case, I qualified for some student loans," I said quietly. "I filled out a FAFSA when I did my Common App."

Stunned, Mom and Dad looked at each other, then at me.

"Sorry not sorry, but your TurboTax password was super easy to crack." I pulled up a file, then turned the screen to Dad.

With a slight frown, he nodded and punched more numbers into the calculator on his phone. Then he and Mom looked at each other again. She gave him a slight nod.

"So, here's the deal, Pumpkin," Dad said. "Mom and I talked a lot since our chat in the fall, and we've already decided we're going to take out a loan for you. We've qualified for a private one with a great rate."

"You don't have to—"

"Save your direct loans for graduate school. Let us take care of you for now."

My breath caught. "So, this is real."

"This is real, Bun."

"McCafferty is a go?"

"McCafferty is a go," Dad confirmed. "Send in that acceptance and make us all proud."

Chapter 41

LATE APRIL, ASHTON FINALLY REPLIED TO THE THOUSAND letters I'd sent him. My eyes welled up when I saw the letter in the mailbox at the end of a craptastic Monday. I couldn't get to my room fast enough to read it.

Dear Devon,

How are you doing? I hope okay. I miss you all the time.

Thank you for writing so many letters. Now I have something good to read every night before I go to sleep.

You asked about my days. They wake us up every morning at six, even on the weekends. I get a ten-minute shower, and I have to use an electric

shaver because they don't trust me with blades.
Breakfast is okay on cereal days. Group therapy
freaks me out. I sit with a bunch of other kids
who are as fucked up as I am, and the leader
picks on one of us every day. I had my worst day
Thursday. I ended up in the quiet room, where
they send us to freak out. For some reason, that
moved me up a level, and that's why they finally
gave me your letters.

I have a private therapy session every day. The
therapist asks a bunch of really hard questions,
and I think he gets off on making me cry. Every
time I have a session I think was bad, he tells me
to keep up the good work.

I can have visitors on Wednesdays and
Sundays. I hope I'll see you soon.

I love you always,
Ash

Lucerne was a colonial-style brick building with fancy land-scaping and lots of trees. The lobby tried to give off a semblance of comfort, with its big green chairs and dozens of plants, but I could taste the unease in the air. My hand shook when I signed in at the front desk. The receptionist led me to the common area where the patients visited with family members or friends. I tapped my foot while I waited for Ashton to appear.

I'd researched how to support someone after a suicide attempt, so I was ready. I was ready to be positive for him. Encourage him. Make plans with him. I was ready to be an ear whenever he needed me. Every single time he needed me.

When Ashton finally appeared, escorted by who I guessed was a social worker, I had to draw in a breath. He looked younger in his polo shirt and jeans. The lines were gone from around his mouth and eyes, and his hair was shaggy.

"Dev!" His face lit up, and I launched myself into his arms. There was no familiar waterfall scent this time, but he smelled clean, like a bar of pure white soap. I held tight because I couldn't believe I was touching him again, feeling his heart beating against me.

"You're here," he murmured into my hair.

"I got your letter Monday. I wanted to come that night."

"I'm so glad to see you." Already his fingers were twirling my curls. "Come on, let's sit over here."

He took my hand and led me to a quiet corner. We sat together on a squashy green love seat. For a few minutes, we regarded each other. Soaked each other in. It felt so perfect to have his eyes on me.

"You look good," I said.

He ruffled his soft waves. "I need a haircut."

"I kinda like the shagginess. Makes you look less intense."

He frowned thoughtfully. "I didn't realize my look was intense."

"Sometimes you didn't look quite so wound up. Mostly when you were sleeping. You actually look your age today."

"What, you're saying I looked old?" He smirked, so I knew he was teasing.

"Well, not exactly old. More like stressed out. Now you remind me of how you looked that summer." Except maybe more tired. Sadder.

He took a deep breath. "I hate that you saw what happened that day."

"Ashton, it's okay."

"It's not, really." He looked down. "I was really sick. I still am."

"But you're in here. Getting better."

"Trying to."

I wrapped my arms around his waist and snuggled against him. He rested his chin on my head and twirled my curls around and around his fingers.

"I miss you," I murmured, closing my eyes and sighing. I loved when he played with my hair. When he threaded his fingers through the spirals. Massaged my scalp. He never seemed to mind getting coconut oil all over his fingers if it meant getting to touch me that way.

I glanced around, taking in the families playing card games, the patients eating junk food, the counselors keeping a discreet watch over the whole scene.

"Tell me about some of these people," I said.

Ashton nodded in the direction of a stocky redhead with glasses. "That guy over there? That's my roommate, Luke. We don't talk much, and he's in a separate group from me, so I have no idea what he's in for."

"But you know about the people in your group?"

"What they share. We don't really get to talk outside of group."

"Why not?"

"Not allowed. Not allowed to be alone, either, really, especially if you're a suicide risk."

Suicide risk. He said it as if it were no big deal. As if it were the flu or something.

"My first week in here, they watched me all the time," he said. "I couldn't even go to the bathroom without an escort. I still can't have floss or mouthwash."

"You must hate that. Why?"

"I could hurt myself with the floss. And mouthwash has alcohol."

I sat back, astonished. "People get that desperate?"

"You'd be surprised." He gestured toward one of the attendants watching the room—a pale, college-aged, brown-haired guy wearing scrubs. "That's Brett. He was my escort. He's an intern."

"He looks nice."

Ashton grabbed a marker and started flipping it around. "I hate not having my freedom, and I hate being watched all the time. But I'm used to the routine now. It's good, in a way. They keep us so busy, I don't have time to think too much."

"Have your parents come to see you?"

"My mother came this morning. She ate lunch with me and brought me a bag of snacks." He sighed, his expression tired and sad. "She's trying."

"That's a good thing, right?"

"Yeah. I mean, it's going to take more than Cheetos and M&M's for us to be okay. But it's a start. As for my father ... we're in group therapy. It's going as well as you'd expect." His face darkened. "I wish she would divorce him. But she's so worried about her image, and all that other WASP bullshit."

"But your family doesn't do the divorce thing, remember?"

He frowned, tapping his lips with the marker. "My mother can be the first, then. A trailblazer. Shaking things up."

We were quiet for a while. The chill from the air-conditioning blew right on me, and I wrapped my arms around myself.

"I got into McCafferty," I said.

He dropped the marker. "What? Holy shit, Dev! That's awesome." He sounded excited, but the light didn't reach his eyes.

"So I guess we'll see each other on campus next year?"

He shifted. "Maybe."

"What do you mean 'maybe'?"

"Dev," he said with his wry smile, "I'm a mess. Like, truly a mess."

I brushed his hair from his forehead. "A beautiful mess."

"Nothing beautiful about this. It's not romantic at all, Devon." He shook his head. "You shouldn't have to put up with it."

"I'm not *putting up* with it," I said, my voice quiet. "I'm here because I love you. This is part of loving you."

His expression turned serious. "Devon, you're heading to your dream school. Your life is about to become epic, and you should be focusing on that, not worrying about if I'm going to hurt myself." He chewed his lip. "A lot of times I feel guilty about dragging you back into my life."

"But you didn't drag me. I wanted you like you wanted me. I still do."

"And you're the best thing that's ever happened to me. God, I love you so much."

"So why does it feel like you're pushing me away?" I asked in a small voice.

Ashton picked his nails—since when did he do that?—then ran his hands through his hair. "I'm going to be in here a long time. My counselor thinks I can get better with a lot of work. He thinks we can make the Dark go away, but I don't know. I'm on a ton of medication right now, and I'll be on medication for the rest of my life. I'll probably have to go to therapy for the rest of my life, too."

"Okay."

"I don't want to force that on you," he said. "And I don't want to make you wait for me."

"You're not making me do anything."

"Aren't I, though?"

I looked him in the eye. "Sometimes I'm scared that I'm not strong enough to deal with"—I waved my hand around—"this. I don't know what it's like to want to take my life. I have no idea how to relate to you in that way. I worry that I'm going to do or say the wrong thing."

"No! God, no." He put his hand on my cheek. "You could never."

"After that day in the ER, I kept wondering how I could've kept you from taking all those pills."

He wiped away the tear racing down my face. "None of this was your fault, okay? It's my brain. I get so deep inside my head that I don't remember what's real. See, this is what I mean. This isn't the life you're meant for. I'm not worth it."

"Don't ever say that," I said fiercely. "You're everything to me."

He took a deep breath. His hands shook. Something strained came over his face, and the tension was suddenly rope thick. I could barely breathe.

"What if I let you go?" he asked. "You can go to college, date other people. Meet someone who's not messed up like me. You deserve that, Dev."

I grabbed his wrists. "There are two of us in this relationship, Ashton. I want to stay with you."

"But is that the best thing?"

"You can't go through what we did and throw it away."

"But that's just it," he said, his voice scarily calm. Steady. "You shouldn't have had to go through it."

"Yeah, but it happened, and we're here—"

"Devon, I want you to live a normal life."

My throat was stinging. "Well, stop it. I want to live *our* life. Together."

He shook his head and turned away.

"Don't," I said. "Do not shut me out. Don't you dare."

He turned back to me, his face flushed. "I look at you sitting here, and all I can think is that you can do so much better.

You're beautiful and incredible. There's a world out there waiting for you to conquer it, and I'm holding you back."

"Stop! I know things suck for you right now, but I'm here. I'm *right here*, Ashton."

"I just need some time. Okay? We both do."

I tried to control my breathing but the air got stuck in my throat, choking me. Burning me. "I can't believe you're doing this. You promised you weren't going to leave again."

He leaned his forehead against mine. "I love you with all my heart, Devon. But you gotta let me go."

I grabbed his wrists again. "No, dammit. I already told you *no*."

He kissed the top of my head. Then he stood and walked away.

Chapter 42

STUNNED.

Absolutely, positively stunned. There was no way he'd just broken up with me.

Somehow, I made my way out to my mother's car. I sat frozen in the driver's seat, not seeing anything. Not feeling anything.

Numb.

I had to stay numb. I couldn't let this destroy me. I couldn't let *him* destroy me. Not when I'd promised myself I would be stronger. Not when I'd promised myself I would be better.

Pain.

I pinched my thigh hard so I would stop focusing on my heart, which I thought was going to jump right out of my chest. I was shaking so much I couldn't get my seat belt to buckle. It would not go in. A sob caught in my throat, but I swallowed it back down. Because I wasn't going to do this. Not again. Never again.

Somehow, I got home. Mom sat in the living room, legs crossed, eyes closed. Meditating. Her calm face a complete contrast to the meteor storm inside me. I focused on her orange tank top. On her big gold hoop earrings. Her flawless brown skin. Anything to keep my mind off what had happened at Lucerne.

Her eyes fluttered open. "Hey, Bun. How'd it go?"

"Fine," I said with false brightness. "Great."

Her smile faded and was replaced with concern. She was gearing up for a big old heart-to-heart, but I could not do that right now. I needed to do something physical. Hard. Intense. Yoga wasn't going to be enough. I needed to run.

Ten minutes later, I was flying down my street. The trees were soft with their rosy pinks and cottony whites. Flowers were shyly poking colorful heads through the soil. Everything was coming to life around me.

But I was dying inside.

Sometimes, looking at stars didn't make me feel excited. Sometimes, stargazing made me feel small and insignificant. As if nothing I did or said on this Earth mattered in the long run because I was nothing but a tiny speck in the midst of billions of red giants and pulsars and galaxies and planets.

And I know it was clichéd to feel like that. But how could I not?

That night, I dragged my telescope out to the backyard and strained to see the stars through my tears. The technology was top-notch. Ashton had chosen well. But what did it matter when I couldn't stop shaking enough to even focus on the Big Dipper? So I gave up. I let myself feel small and insignificant, because this way, at least I had a real reason to be sad, instead of being pathetic and feeling sorry for myself. That night, I raged at the sky, at these stars that had let me down. Wishes didn't really come true, and the thing was that I'd always known better.

"What the King Kong fuck?" Blair exploded. "I'm going to fucking kill him if I see him."

"Don't do that," I said flatly. "Your going to prison isn't going to help anyone."

"He doesn't get to do this to you again, Devon," she said. "Not after everything you've done for him. You saved his life! And you were in that hospital every damned day. I was rooting for him, and he pulls this shit? I swear, I'm going to Lucerne to kick his ass for hurting you again."

"He asked his grandma about rings, Blair." My voice broke then.

She gave me a fierce hug. "I'm so sorry. You've been through so much with him. I really hoped you two would make it."

That didn't help, either. I clenched my fists and sobbed into my best friend's shoulder.

I had gone back to Lucerne the next visiting day, Sunday. When the attendant told me that Ashton wasn't able to see me, I'd nodded and walked out, my throat tight.

Okay. Fine. Whatever. I didn't need him. But if it had to be like that, I wanted the last word. After I got home, I pulled out stationery and chewed on my pen.

What I wanted to write:

You probably think I miss you. Well, I don't. I don't miss you at all.

I'm starving for you. I'm longing for you with every part of me, and it's tearing me apart that you're not here. Do you think about me half as much as I think about you? Wait, don't answer that. It would break my heart if you said no. Because I can't stop thinking about you.

I can't stand that you ended it. Ended us. We were amazing together. But right now, I hate you.

What I wrote instead:

> I shouldn't even be writing, but once upon a time, I told you everything. It's a hard habit to break. You were such a big part of my life, and now you aren't. You didn't give me a chance to say good-bye—again—so I guess I'm doing it now.
>
> So...this is it. Please take care of yourself.
>
> Love,
> Your Sunset Girl

I debated all evening whether to mail it. Finally, Monday morning at school, I put the letter in the mail drop. Now it was up to him to make the next move, and up to me not to obsess about it.

Time to move on.

Again.

Chapter 43

THE WEEKS PASSED BY IN A BLUR OF PROJECTS AND EXAMS and senior activities. College acceptances or not, the teachers continued to squeeze every drop of work out of us before we left this place for good. I was grateful for the demanding assignments because they distracted me so thoroughly. Graduation loomed, but I couldn't bring myself to get excited.

I was so over *everything*.

"Hey, I heard about Ashton," Auden said to me right after Mother's Day. She tugged one of my curls. "Is he all right?"

Leave it to her to be doubly annoying right now. Today had been long and exhausting, and I just wanted Calculus—and this day—to be over with. "Did you just touch my hair?"

"It's so silky," she said. "I didn't expect it to be that silky."

What. The. Hell.

"He's getting better," I said through clenched teeth. "And if you touch my hair again, I'll bite you."

She grinned. "I'm glad to hear he's better. You've been totally out of it, and it's no fun antagonizing you when you just sit there and take it."

I rolled my eyes. "Whatever. I beat you on yesterday's pop quiz, and you are still salty."

"Ha, listen to you, being all ghetto."

Whoa whoa whoa. Hold the phone. "What the hell, Auden?"

She poked my shoulder. "Don't tell me you're mad. It's not like you're really ghetto."

I took a deep breath to keep from smacking her, but I didn't erase the threat from my voice. "I'm not mad. I'm tired. I'm done."

She switched on her tablet. "Lighten up, Devon. You're being too sensitive. It was a joke."

A joke, my ass.

"Auden, why is that word even in your mouth? Is it because I'm Black?"

"Of course not! There are ghetto white people."

Inhale two . . . three . . . four.

Exhale two . . . three . . . four.

I could not make a scene right now. Because I was in a rich, white private school on a scholarship and going off on Auden, who was really very clueless and also really very wealthy, would not be good at all. Thank God the teacher started droning on about derivatives. Derivatives made sense. Derivatives had order. Just like me, on the outside. I could go on pretending that everything was fine, just fine.

During the days, I faked it pretty well. I smiled when I was supposed to smile, laughed at all the right jokes, participated in all the senior activities, and posed for a billion photos. I had everyone fooled. I was rocking this. Everything was great. Fan-fucking-tastic.

Night? Not so much. I literally ached, longing to hold Ashton again. Kiss him again. I wanted to hear his voice, stroke his hair, breathe in his waterfall scent. I hated that he was in that institution all alone and that I wasn't there to hold his hand when things got hard. I hated that he didn't want me there. But mostly, I hated that I missed him so much. I hated how weak it made me feel. And I hated that I couldn't control my feelings. Turn them off like a faucet. Then destroy the sink so they wouldn't come dripping out again.

Then there were the nightmares. Dream after dream of those texts of his flashing ominously, like strobe lights. Of me rushing to his room that day, only for it to be too late, only for him to be gone forever. I lost count of how often I jerked awake at the sound of my sobbing. Then stayed awake, soaking my pillow once I remembered that he was indeed alive, but still lost to me forever.

Because as the weeks went by, it became evident that he wasn't going to write me back. And one day it sank in. It was really and truly over. I hadn't even realized I'd been holding out for a change of heart. So this sucked.

Dad found me crying in bed that night. I tried to dry my face with the pillowcase, but he wasn't fooled. Not at all.

"Whatever it is, I can make it better," he said, hugging me tightly.

"No, Daddy. Not this," I choked out.

Mom sat on the other side of me and stroked my hair. My parents stayed with me for hours, comforting me with their quiet strength. And when the words came tumbling out, they listened, without judgment—only with love.

After Memorial Day, Mom and Dad sent me to therapy.

"I don't need a therapist. I'm fine," I told them. And I really was! I had finally stopped crying myself to sleep every night, and my appetite was halfway back to normal. I still missed Ashton, but I really was getting better.

"You've been through a lot," Dad said. "Ashton's suicide attempt was a serious situation, Pumpkin. And the breakup on top of that. You need to talk about stuff. Process it. Mom and I aren't equipped. We want you to see a professional."

They made me see the counselor for other reasons, too. "You need to find your way back to yourself," Mom said. "I know you think you're okay. But, Bun, you're not. You haven't been for a long time."

I hated Dr. Braun. I hated her bland office with its ugly tan rug and dull beige couch and blocky brown bookcases. I hated her clipboard and clicky pen, her sensible shoes, her boring khaki pants and white blouse. I hated her wavy brown hair and milk-white skin and mauve lipstick. I hated how she was always calm no matter how much I yelled. But mostly, I hated how she dug and dug and dug until I was sobbing in her office. She made me feel so weak, so pathetic because I loved Ashton so much. Because I apparently didn't love myself enough to realize that my relationship with him had become "codependent" and "unhealthy."

"Were you with him because you truly loved him, or because you felt like you needed to be with him so he wouldn't hurt himself?" she challenged, her beady eyes burning holes into mine.

"I loved him," I told her, my fists clenched. "I loved him before I knew about this stuff, and I love him now."

"You constantly redefined your boundaries for him. You were worried and stressed all the time over him. Do you think being codependent equals love? A good relationship?"

"What does that even mean?"

"Devon, on more than one occasion, you rearranged your life for him."

"But that's what people in relationships do. They make room so the other person can fit."

"Might you have been making an excessive amount of room, especially near the end?"

"I worried about him," I said in a low voice. "I still do."

"I know," she said gently. "And while it's normal to be concerned about your loved ones, this isn't healthy. Have you considered that it's better for you to not be with him? At least while he's healing?"

True, it was easier knowing he was at Lucerne, where he couldn't hurt himself. Knowing that professionals were looking after him, so I didn't have to feel responsible for making sure he was okay. But was it better? I didn't think so. I still thought about him constantly, and no matter what, I couldn't make myself stop loving him. I couldn't stop wishing he and I were back together.

"Do you ever feel like he's holding you back?" she asked, her voice even more gentle.

"I'm getting awesome grades. I'm going to college. I got scholarships. I'm okay."

"Are you sure?"

Why couldn't she understand? I hadn't been looking for love, but it came steamrolling in, and it changed me. But I was still the same Devon at the core. *Wasn't I?*

I crossed my arms. "I'm sure."

She studied me with her irritating calmness. As if she could see what I tried to hide, even from myself—especially from myself. Except I *wasn't* hiding anything, so why did she have to keep picking—*tearing*—into my soul?

"Stop!" I yelled. "Please stop it!"

"You're angry."

"I—" I started to protest, but then I clamped my mouth shut, clenching my jaw until it ached. She had it wrong. I wasn't angry. I was furious.

"Who are you angry at?"

361

"Him. Me. Everyone."

She watched me with that annoying thoughtful expression. "Why are you angry at yourself?"

I picked at the fringe on my gray T-shirt. "I should have known better than to fall in love with him again when he hurt me before."

She sighed and leaned back. "I wish you wouldn't beat yourself up over falling for him. In many ways, he sounds like a good person. And even if he wasn't—again, love plays by its own rules. *It's okay that you love him.*"

"Even when it hurts so much?"

She nodded. "Even then."

"Oh."

"You said you're angry at him. Tell me why."

"I don't know if I can." My throat hurt. It was hard to talk.

"Can you try?"

I nibbled my thumbnail. "I don't like being angry at him. He's sick."

She set her clipboard on her desk. "What do you want to say to him?"

I closed my eyes and let the anger settle into my bones. I let the hurt and rage I'd been trying to resist overcome me until the words flew out. "I don't know what I want to say, but I know I want to make him cry, like he made me cry." I dug my fingers into my jeans. "Sometimes I hate him. I hate him for hurting me; I hate him for not wanting to live for what we had, because it was beautiful. And I hate him because he won't let me be there for him. And those feelings are horrible, so I feel guilty on top of everything, and I hate him for making me feel *that*, too."

She held up her hand. "Hang on. This is not the time to be so judgmental of yourself, Devon. Earlier you told me that he made promises to you, that he was even making plans for your future together. Your feeling of betrayal is completely normal."

"But he's sick! I'm a terrible person for thinking these things."

"Feelings aren't good or bad," she said. "They just are. But how you handle them is what makes you a terrible person or not."

I managed to let out a small snort. "Thankfully, my brain is still working even though my emotions are a hot mess."

She glanced down at her clipboard. "You said you were angry at him for not wanting to live for what you and he had. Do you think he was selfish?"

I wrapped my arms around myself. "I think I could've helped him more."

"There's nothing you could have done to fix this. You said it yourself. He's sick. Only proper treatment—whatever that entails for him—can help him cope with his depression and suicidal ideation. You have to stop blaming yourself, especially when you did an amazing thing. By checking on him that day, you saved his life."

She crossed her legs, then tapped her clipboard. "Devon, I don't know Ashton other than from what you've told me, but I do know something about depression. You said you were deeply in love. In the meantime, he was fighting a constant war with himself and what his brain was telling him. I'm going to wager that he felt he didn't deserve what the two of you had together. That he didn't deserve you."

"Sometimes I wish he was normal," I blurted. "But I know I don't mean it, because I don't even know what *normal* is. His depression is a part of him. And I love *all* of him."

"You wish things could be easier."

"Yeah." I nibbled my fingernail. "Is that bad?"

"He needs a lot of help, way more than you're capable of giving him. That doesn't mean you can't be there for him, but I'd hate to see you neglecting your own life trying to save his."

"I worry about him. All the time. I don't think that's ever going away. I'd be okay with that if it meant I could have the rest of him, too. But now, all I have is the worry, and I'm pissed off that he made it like this. If I'm going to have all these feelings, I want everything else that comes with it."

"Except he took that choice away from you."

I nodded. "That's another reason I'm mad."

"And as I said, that's okay. But, Devon, try not to let the anger consume you. It won't bring him back, and it'll only hurt you."

I let out a long sigh. "So what should I do?"

"Focus on you. Whenever you start to think about him, turn it back to you. You can do that by journaling. Talking with your best friend, your parents. Don't keep your feelings bottled up. You have to process them so you can heal."

"Will I ever stop loving him so much?" I asked in a small voice.

She gave me a tissue and a sad smile. "He was your first love. He'll always have a special place in your heart. But one day you'll be able to move on. I promise."

"But what if I don't *want* to move on?" My voice, smaller still.

"Ultimately, only you can decide what's right for you. I do urge you to take care of yourself. Loving a person who has a severe mental illness is challenging at best. Devastating at worst, with every high and low in between." Her phone let out a tiny ding. "That's our time for today, but I'd like to see you next week. Will you come back?"

I nodded and gathered up my stuff. "Thank you, Dr. Braun."

"You're going to be all right. You know that, don't you?"

I paused, then nodded. "Yes."

Chapter 44

GRADUATION DAY. SO BITTERSWEET. ON ONE HAND, I WAS super excited to walk that stage and hold that diploma in my hand. The stars were waiting for me, and I was so close to catching them! But on the other hand, how could I say goodbye to a place that had been my second home for so long?

I stared in the mirror, putting the finishing touches on my hair. A million bobby pins to keep my graduation cap from tumbling to the ground. A few golden curls to frame my face. Then I slipped on a pair of sparkly earrings and smoothed my white sundress. Perfect.

Sugary breakfast scents wafted into my room, making my stomach grumble, so I headed to the kitchen.

Dad looked up from frying eggs and making cinnamon

toast. "There she is! The woman of the hour! Ready for your big day?"

"Totally."

"I'm so proud of you." Mom squeezed me. "You're graduating at the top of your class. Dream college sewn up, scholarships in place. You really are incredible, you know that?"

My cheeks grew warm with pleasure. "I guess I'm all right."

When we got to school, my parents took their seats in the courtyard while I met Blair in the staging area next to Campbell Hall. The scent of freshly cut grass tickled my nose, and a light breeze took the edge off an already boiling sun.

Blair grabbed my hands. "I still can't believe today is our last day of high school," she said. "Finally!"

I glanced up at Bishop Hall towering over me in all its glory. Any minute now, the bells would ring to signal the start of the ceremony. "I'm going to miss this place."

"Ugh. You would. I thought we'd never get through it. I'm so looking forward to summer. No homework. No rushing from class to class. Just long, lazy days with my best friend forever."

"Damn straight!" I grinned at her, but she was looking over my shoulder, her expression suddenly hard.

"What in the—?" I turned around and found myself looking right at Ashton. "Oh."

I hadn't seen him since that Ugly Day in April. His graduation gown flowed in the wind, but the cap sat on top of his head like a perch. He leaned against a tree, a thoughtful frown on his face. I wasn't prepared for the ache that rushed me as our gazes locked and held.

His lips parted as he gave me a slight nod, and I managed to nod back before turning to Blair. I needed to keep it together. I was the valedictorian, and I had a speech to give.

But ugh, really? Not so long ago, he and I had been naked in each other's arms, connected in the most intimate way possible. And today, I get a nod from across the courtyard?

"Want me to smack him?" Blair asked, her face pink and tight with irritation.

"Your violent tendencies are really starting to concern me."

"What can I say?" She shrugged. "He inspires rage. The Rat Bastard."

"Hey, Devon." Auden popped up and held her hand out to me. "It was iffy for a while there, but you earned that top spot fair and square. Congrats."

Leave it to her to bring up a time I'd rather forget. Thank God for makeup tests, extra credit, and the willpower to study until my eyeballs were raw. I didn't lose my straight-A status, although I came very close.

"Listen, I'm sorry about the 'ghetto' thing," she said. "I messed up. But I'm learning to be better."

I'd almost forgotten about that. But this was big of her. Auden never apologized for anything. "We're good. But keep learning."

"You got it. Sign my yearbook?" She thrust our final creation at me. They'd come out beautifully. Hunter green and gray, every page told of our legacy. From the Harvest Ball, to pop quizzes, to exams and meetings, to lifelong friends and people who changed us forever.

These Are Our Moments.

Damn right they were. Good and bad, painful and joyous. They were ours. They were mine.

I handed my yearbook to Auden and chewed on my pen as I thought of what to write in hers. What did one say to someone so annoying?

"Ahem." Dr. Steelwood cleared her throat. "Everyone please line up."

I shivered all over when the music blared. Elgar. "Pomp and Circumstance March in D Major, Op. 39, no. 1." We marched in to the slow, hopeful rhythm of the violins, filing into row after row of white wooden chairs. My face heated when I spotted my parents. They were shameless: Mom dancing in the aisle and snapping a billion pictures, Dad yelling *woooooo* like a frat boy. And I loved them for it.

The crowd roared as the top ten students marched across the stage. The brilliant sunshine kept my mind off my sweaty palms. I barely paid attention as we sang the school song, and I totally zoned out when the speeches began. I almost missed them calling my name, but I managed to make it up to the podium without incident and deliver my farewell speech without one flaw. The cheers that rose from the audience sent my heart soaring. The rest of the ceremony sped by in a blur, and then I had my diploma in my hands. We tossed our caps in the air and screamed. And just like that: High school was over. A chapter closed, and now I was waiting for the next one to open.

After the ceremony, we gathered in the field. Some people snapped photos, others signed yearbooks. My parents handed me a dozen pink roses—which would wreak havoc on my allergies, but I didn't care because I loved them so much—then captured a million photos of me.

Blair bounced over, hand in hand with Tyrell, her blue eyes twinkling. "We need pictures with our diplomas!"

I set my roses on the ground, and then Blair and I struck silly poses, grinning as the cameras clicked.

"Wait, one for Instagram!" Blair yelled, handing her phone to Tyrell, who snapped a million more pictures.

"Okay. I have to get going—my parents want to take me and Tyrell to a fancy lunch," Blair said, hugging me tightly. "I'll see you later at your party?"

"You'd better."

"We should get to the house," Mom said. "People are arriving for your party in an hour, and we've still got to pick up the cake."

"Okay." I started to walk with them, but then I remembered my flowers. "I need to get my roses."

"We'll meet you at the car," Dad called.

Preston Academy's courtyard was quiet now. The noon sun beat down on me, making me sweat. But I didn't mind. I'd take this over the dead of winter any day.

"Devon."

I froze. I knew that voice, except it wasn't icy. Not anymore. "Hello, Mrs. Edwards."

"Eleanor," she said. "Please call me Eleanor. And, Devon, I'd like to apologize to you."

It was all I could do to keep my mouth from dropping open. "Okay."

"I made many unfair judgments about you, and I was wrong for that. You're a kind person with a good heart, which is the only thing that should have ever mattered as far as I was concerned. Ashton is lucky to have you."

Is. Have. Present tense. Had he not told her he broke up with me? I had to admit that as much as I still missed him, it had been nice not having to deal with Edwards Family Drama.

I nodded stiffly. Because if she expected me to tell her she was forgiven, she had another think coming. Still, it must have taken a lot for her to admit this. I did give her credit for that.

"Congratulations on McCafferty," she said. "I know you will succeed there."

"How did—?"

"Endowment report. Remember?"

"Oh. Right." I gave her a small smile. "Thank you."

She squeezed my shoulder. "See you around."

Mind reeling, I headed back across the courtyard. White chairs were strewn haphazardly all over the lawn, along with crushed graduation programs and crumpled coffee cups. But no flowers. They weren't where I'd left them. I twirled around to look for them and crashed into something hard. No, not some*thing*. Some*one*.

"Whoa, sorry," Ashton said. He handed me the bouquet. "You all right?"

"Yeah," I choked out. "Fine."

I wasn't fine. My head was spinning because he was right

here and gazing at me with his intense look that made me lose all reason.

No, Devon, do not lose even a little bit of your reason.

"They sprung you, huh?" I tried to keep my voice light, but my heart was practically pirouetting out of my chest.

"Two weeks ago."

I gave in to looking at him. Drinking in his skin, which looked clear and healthy. His eyes, which were bright and deep. His hair, which was short and neat and thick. The dark shadows were gone, the lines faded. He was still skinny, though. He'd probably be a rail his entire life.

And he still took my breath away.

Would I ever stop having this reaction to him? Would I ever be able to look at him and feel nothing?

"You didn't come back to school," I said.

He shook his head. "I needed to take care of some stuff."

"How did you—" I gestured toward his diploma.

"Tutoring. Lots and *lots* of it. Basically, once I was well enough, all I did was study."

"Cool."

A crumpled program skittered across my feet.

"Can we talk?" he asked.

"You never wrote me back," I said.

He looked at the grass. "I did write you. I just never sent them." His voice lowered. "Didn't feel I had a right to."

More silence. God. How were we back to this awkwardness again?

My phone buzzed. A text from Mom:

> Where r u?

"I need to meet my parents—"

"It won't take long."

I almost said okay, but then I remembered what Dr. Braun had said about me redefining my boundaries for him. My parents were waiting for me, and I needed to respect that. "I really have to go. But come to my house later. We're having my graduation party."

"You sure?"

I touched his hand. "I want you to."

I need you to. It's not fair how much I still need you when you were the one who said good-bye, but right now I don't care. I just want to be close to you.

He gave my hand a gentle squeeze. "I'll stop by."

By the time the sun set, the party had died down except for my parents and a few stragglers, mainly my grandmother Mama Lee and my uncle Ricky (who had closed down every family party I could remember) hanging out on the back deck. Deep down, I had been nervous about Ashton showing up or not showing up, but I put on a brave face to entertain my guests. So many people had come to celebrate with me. It was overwhelming to be showered with so much love and support, but loneliness crept in when they all started to trickle home.

I curled up on our new porch swing, swatting mosquitoes and wiping beads of sweat from my forehead. I was sticky all over—from the heat, from the chocolate cake my parents had gotten custom-made for me, from all the line dancing with my family. "Electric Boogie." "Trans-Europe Express." Even "Boot Scootin' Boogie." It was one of those steamy nights where the air was so thick I may as well have been breathing in soup. I loved it.

When Ashton's car pulled up to the curb, I had to remind myself to breathe. By the time he stepped onto the porch, I was trembling all over. We looked at each other for a long time.

Then he pulled me close, and we stood there, clinging to each other as if the world would end if we let go. I buried my face in his shirt, but I refused to cry. He was never going to see a tear from me again.

NOW

"I CAN'T BELIEVE YOU BROUGHT YOUR TELESCOPE TO THE beach." Blair's voice came from behind me, the familiar lilt of affection rising and cresting with the waves. "You really are a nerd."

"This is the first time I've had one small enough to haul with me." I peered through the eyepiece again. "The sky is breathtaking out here."

"I'll take your word for it," she said. "Here, have some water."

I grabbed the bottle and drank deeply. "*Mmm*. I hadn't realized I was so thirsty."

She plopped down and dug red-painted toenails, which matched her skimpy red bikini, into the sand. "Sit with me. I want to talk to you."

With reluctance, I put the cover on the telescope lens and settled next to Blair. Buried my own (light-blue) toenails in the sand. Let the surf tickle my feet as it washed the sand away. "I've always loved this beach."

"It's really gorgeous here," Blair said. "And your cousin is awesome. So optimistic and happy. She's a complete gem."

"Well, it runs in the family. The gem part, I mean."

She poked my shoulder. "And you're a diamond, except when it comes to volleyball."

I buried my face in my hands. "Oh God."

She laughed, long, low, and rich. "What's up with you running away every time the ball comes toward you?"

"That bump thing hurts my forearms."

"You're such a wimp," she teased.

I shrugged. "I don't like balls flying at me."

She snorted. "You said *balls*."

"Oh my God. Why are you twelve inside?"

"You thought it was funny. Admit it."

"Okay, yeah, it was kinda funny."

"I'm going to miss this so much," she said. "Even though I'm excited to go to the Fashion & Design Institute."

"You're going to blow them away. I cannot wait to see what you come up with while you're there. And which free outfits you're going to design for me."

"Yes," she deadpanned. "Once you're a rich and famous astrophysicist, you can wear my clothes and everyone will want them. Free advertising for me!"

"Sounds like a win-win." I looked around with a content

sigh. "Summer in the Hamptons last year was awesome, but this place has my heart. Can't believe I almost let you-know-who ruin it for me."

Blair glanced at me, her eyebrow raised. "You needed time to heal. Nothing wrong with that."

"Maybe." I wrapped my arms around my knees. "What did you want to talk about?"

She pulled a bag of Doritos out of her tote. "We're talking about it now."

"Ashton?"

She offered the Doritos to me. "Do you miss him?"

"Of course." I grabbed a couple and started munching.

"I can tell. It's in your eyes."

"You've been gazing into my eyes? How romantic."

She poked me again. "I'm being serious."

I dragged my fingers through the wet sand. "I'm having a great summer, but I'm not going to lie. We made memories all over this place." My voice lowered. "I just want the real thing, too."

Blair pulled a joint out of her bag and lit it. Then she took a long drag, holding the smoke in longer than I thought was humanly possible. She blew out a series of smoke rings, coughed, and sipped her water. Her shoulders relaxed as it took hold.

"Better?" I asked, smirking.

"Oh yeah." She closed her eyes and smiled. Then she turned to me, blinking lazily. "So. Remember last week when I went to see Tyrell?"

"I kinda wish I didn't. You went into way too much detail about your reunion."

Her lips curved into the kind of smile that told stories and held secrets. Secrets involving whipped cream and...oh God, brain, stop.

She pulled an envelope out of her bag and tapped it. "I wasn't going to tell you, but I feel bad keeping things from you."

"What things?"

"I ran into Ashton."

I froze, my hand stuck in the sand.

"Do you want the lowdown?"

"I don't know. Do I?"

She rolled her eyes. "He wasn't with a girl, if that's what you're wondering."

"I wasn't—okay, I was." I couldn't even pretend with her. And my relief must have shown front and center on my face. "So? What's new?"

"He had a dog with him. Said his name was Buddy."

This meant a couple of things to me. First: Ashton must have been doing better if he took Buddy in. Second: Maybe he would stick around for a while. People who were planning to die by suicide didn't adopt pets, did they?

"Do you want a hit of this?" she asked.

I shook my head. "I'm good."

I wasn't good. Because now a million questions rushed through my head: Did he miss me? Did he think about me? Had he kissed another girl while I was spending the summer here? And what about those nights when the longing for more than kissing got to be too much? I went running on the beach. What did he do? Who did he turn to?

No. I refused to fall down that spiral. It wasn't my business, anyway.

"Does he seem happy?"

She tilted her head. "I mean, he doesn't seem *not* happy, but he looks better. If that makes sense."

"It makes perfect sense."

"How long's it been since you've seen him?" Blair asked.

I picked at the label on my water bottle. "Graduation night."

She stared at me. "Did you have sex with him?"

I nodded slowly. "Yeah. I thought I could handle it. I was wrong. So I told him I needed time off to think. Haven't talked to him since. But I'm still confused. And scared of how much I still love him."

Blair touched my shoulder. "You've been holding this in all this time? Why didn't you tell me?"

I breathed out a small laugh. "I was embarrassed. He hurt me *again*, and then I turned around and slept with him. Who does that?"

"A girl who's in love would do that. Devvy, you never have to be embarrassed with me."

I nodded and looked out at the rolling waves.

"Do you ever think about clearing the air?" Blair asked.

"Every single day. I just don't do it. I don't know what I want. Wait, that's not true. I still want him. But since I'm still so confused, I should just...*not* with him."

More smoke rings. "I get that, and I approve."

"School starts in two and a half weeks."

She rolled her eyes. "I know. You won't stop talking about how you're going to live in the dorms and join the Honor Society and study all the astronomy and physics and math forever and ever amen."

"I think he's going to be there."

She sighed. "It's a big campus, though, isn't it?"

"Not that big. Maybe we can have a fresh start."

She stared at me again, blinking those ridiculously long eyelashes. "You guys have way too much baggage for a fresh start."

I nodded again. "You're right."

Blair regarded me then, her dark hair blowing all around her face. Then she handed me the envelope. "He asked me to give this to you. I wasn't going to, just so you know."

I stroked the smooth, stiff envelope. "What changed your mind? I thought you hated him."

"I never hated him. I hated that he hurt you." She pointed to the envelope. "Are you going to open it?"

I slid my fingers under the flap and pulled out a photo. "Arcturus." In all his orangey-red glory. Standing out against his fellow Boötes constellation friends, a grand disk glowing among shimmery dots.

I let out a trembling breath, then stared out at the crashing waves. My eyes were blurring and I knew it wasn't from the sea spray. Or Blair's "herbal" refreshment.

"Told me he went out every night for two weeks, trying to get the perfect shot," she said. "He *begged* me to give it to you."

I studied the photo again. Perfect composition. Crystal

clear. He'd printed it on matte paper, which he'd once said was more professional than glossy. Eight by ten, the perfect size to frame and hang in my dorm room.

"I see the longing on your face when you're thinking about him." Blair's voice tugged me out of my thoughts. "It's like how I feel when I see a rare steak."

My head jerked up. "I don't want to *eat* him. God."

She stared at her joint, which barely had a single hit left. "I'm still not sure giving you that picture was the right choice. But I really want to believe you're stronger now."

Two summers ago, I'd sat in this same surf. The tide had carried the sand from under my toes. I'd had no idea that I was going to meet a boy who would change me in so many ways. I'd had no idea that I was going to fall deeply and relentlessly in love. I'd had no idea that my life would never be the same.

I'd never love anyone like I loved him. This I knew for sure. Maybe there was still a future for us, but it would take a lot of hard work to get there. That was okay. I wasn't afraid of hard work. I couldn't be, not with what McCafferty had in store for me.

But I was ready for McCafferty and its rigorous curriculum. Anything to push me toward my dream? I welcomed it with open arms. But was I ready and willing to do the hard work of being with Ashton? I knew I could handle it. Except there was this: I didn't want to be waiting around, wondering if and when he was going to break my heart again.

No matter how much I loved him.

I gazed at the sky, then at my photo of Arcturus. My red giant. I let myself fill with the star's strength one last time. Because now I needed to do things on my own. Make good choices. Be strong and smart and *ready* . . . for what was coming. For my dreams. For my life.

I was *so* ready.

I pulled out my phone. Scrolled to Ashton's name. The contact picture was the two of us on Christmas Day. Happy, radiant, excited. I smiled at the photo. Let out a long breath. Stroked the key pendant on my chain and relaxed. I didn't have to make a choice now. Because here was the thing: With or without him, no matter what happened, I was going to have an epic life.

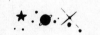

AUTHOR'S NOTE

I WAS DIAGNOSED WITH DEPRESSION IN 2004. AFTER YEARS of wondering why my mood tended toward darkness, it was a relief to have a reason why. The diagnosis filled me with shame nonetheless. I struggled for years with taking my medication properly, with internalizing certain negative attitudes, with feeling as if I should be able fix it all myself.

Spoiler: I couldn't.

These days, with medication and therapy, I'm doing better. But even now, depression can sneak up on me and yank me back down into a hole I've been climbing out of for months or even years.

Sometimes it comes out of nowhere, taking over and making me so tired it's easier to give in than to fight it. Sometimes it's triggered by certain events. But all I care about is that it's here. Again. Pressing down on me like weights on my chest. Filling my brain until all I see is fog.

It lies and makes me think no one cares. That I have to do this all on my own. It tells me that I'm powerless. And the worst thing depression does is tell me that I'm unlovable.

I wanted to show my depressed character, Ashton, being loved—deeply.

Depression takes many forms for many people, but for me, the main constant is the lack of control I feel when it's taken over.

I wanted to write a book where my characters are taking control. Maybe they don't always get it right, but they try.

It's okay to keep trying. It's okay to keep learning. It's okay to get help.

We don't have to do this alone. There are resources out there. And it's always okay to turn to them.

Suicide Prevention

National Suicide Prevention Lifeline: suicidepreventionlifeline.org

In a crisis, call their free and 24/7 US hotline: 1-800-273-TALK (8255)

National Hopeline Network: 1-800-442-HOPE (4673)

American Association of Suicidology: suicidology.org

American Foundation for Suicide Prevention: afsp.org

Suicide Awareness Voices of Education: save.org

Suicide Prevention Resource Center: sprc.org

For Suicide Loss Survivors

Alliance of Hope for Suicide Loss Survivors: allianceofhope.org

American Association of Suicidology survivors page: suicidology.org/
suicide-survivors/suicide-loss-survivors

Friends for Survival: friendsforsurvival.org

National Suicide Prevention Lifeline survivors page:
suicidepreventionlifeline.org/help-yourself/loss-survivors

Understanding Mental Illness

Mental Health America: <u>mentalhealthamerica.net</u>

National Alliance on Mental Illness: <u>nami.org</u>

National Institute of Mental Health: <u>nimh.nih.gov</u>

ACKNOWLEDGMENTS

THE ROAD TO PUBLICATION IS LONG, AND FILLED WITH A LOT of ups and downs. Lots of feelings. Lots of hard work. Lots of *people*.

People like my agent, Caitie Flum, who told me she *dreamed about my characters*. I'd already known she was the right person—sensitive and fierce—to represent Devon's story, but that solidified it. Her vision for my book perfectly aligned with mine. Caitie, I must say we make a great team.

People like Kheryn Callender, who believed in me and in Devon's story, and who pushed for it to be out there. So grateful you took a chance on me.

People like my amazing editor, Nikki Garcia. She is a true rock star and a fierce editor, loyal and understanding, who knows just how much to push to get me to take risks and try new things. Nikki, every day, I'm happy and honored to work with you.

Thank goodness for organizations like We Need Diverse Books and POC in Pub, who continue to help pave the way for new stories and voices. You all laid the path, and I'm so happy I get to step onto it. I look forward to bringing others along with me.

Little, Brown Books for Young Readers has been my dream

publisher for years. They lived up to my expectations and more. My everlasting thanks to the editorial team for their hard work and thoughtful notes; the Novl team for their enthusiasm, incredible hugs, and excellent Instagram stories; my publicist, Katharine McAnarney, who is so chill and masterful; Lindsay Walter-Greaney, whose timeline work is worship-worthy; and the designer, Marcie Lawrence, who gave me the most perfect cover. I couldn't have dreamed up a better one!

I tried to give up writing many times. I am so glad I had an army of people behind me who refused to let me go through with it. Thank you to my critique partners: Rachel Foster—who refused to let me get away with anything; S. F. Henson—who was my cheerleader; and Regan McDonnell—whose notes always terrified me but were always spot on. Kody Keplinger, you saw a pretty early version of the manuscript and set me on the path to shaping it into an actual book. Thank you.

Thank goodness for #ChiYA—Samira Ahmed, Gloria Chao, Kat Cho, Lizzie Cook, and Anna Waggener. Yummy brunches, carpools, and delicious ice cream. Love you all.

Thank you to all the groups and group chats that have offered me support and love over the years: Black Fiction Squad, #SuperBlackGirlMagic, Kidlit Alliance, Novel19s, and Kidlit Authors of Color. You were there when I needed you, and for that I am grateful.

Dear Writing Weasels 2016, in a cold (to me) mansion in Scotland, you let me read my query and first chapter aloud. You encouraged me to keep going. Marieke Nijkamp, you have the best style, and I love how you move through the world. Fox

Benwell, you are perfect and I miss your restful nature. Dawn Kurtagich, you are as lovely as you are talented (Hint: That's a *lot*), and Cecilia Vinesse, I'll never be as cool as you are.

Rachel Strolle, you lovely, amazing person you! Your love for our books, and your tireless work to get them into the hands of people who want and need them, is not unappreciated or unnoticed. Thank you, thank you, thank you.

Jen aka The Book Avid, your voice is more important than you could ever know, and I'm so glad to know you.

#TeamCaitie! I feel like I found a group of sisters and brothers but we all write, too, and it's awesome!

Kendare Blake, you took a look at this book in its very, very, very early stages, and gave me feedback that made me want to keep going, keep improving, to get this out there. You're a true cheerleader, my friend.

Dearest Ivy Decker, you were one of my very first-ever online friends and my very first critique partner. You were one of the first people who took my writing seriously, who encouraged me to follow this dream. You've taught me so much over the years, not just about writing, but about life.

Mandy Hubbard...you've believed in me for fourteen years. You were with me from my very first baby steps into this industry, and I'm so glad you're with me now. Those hours-long AIM critique sessions finally paid off! Thank you for your incredible instincts and honest feedback. They helped mold me into the writer I am today.

Thank you to Chris Davis, for your encouragement when I tried this publishing thing the first time around.

Sarah Lisenbee...thank you for helping me stay sane on this journey, for keeping me grounded, and for your gentle encouragement. I'm so glad we have our Mondays.

Andy Green, you have been there for me so much for so many years. You are a true treasure, honestly. I mean, you believed in me so much that you once bought me a laptop! Finally, finally, I get to say, "Here is your book!"

Thank you to Wanda Lotus, for your support, for your love, and for inspiring me with your own creativity. Most important, thank you for *all* the attention!

Thank you to Adib Khorram, for always knowing. Just knowing. Your friendship is one of the best things that has come out of this book journey.

Thank you to my buttercup Jennifer Niven for your bright light. You are the Helen to my Gladys, my soul sister, my bestie. Here's to more European tours, plates of carpaccio, and quality time in the ABBA museum.

Rena Barron, you are my brainstorming partner, my rock, my safe space, my best friend. Words can't express how much you mean to me and how much I look up to you. Clown-face emojis forever!

Thank you, Lenora Kita, for never denying me the joy of reading and writing. For never making me turn out the light when I was reading under the covers (except that one Christmas Eve). For letting me dream. You're the best mommy a girl could ask for.

Thank you to Adam Selzer for putting up with me and my quirks, for indulging my Disney World obsession, and for building me my little writing nook, which is one of my favorite places in Chicago. This *is* the Good Place!

Thank you to Aidan Davis, for being the actual best son a mother could ever ask for. You're everything I wish I could be, but better. I still don't know how I got so lucky.

And finally...thank you, Dear Reader, for taking a chance on me, and on my words. I hope they've touched your heart, and I sincerely hope you come back for more.